EAST HAMPTON
A TOWN AND ITS PEOPLE
1648-1994

By
Nancy Hyden Woodward

First Edition
ISBN 0-89824-221-5

Printed in the United States of America

•

Fireplace Press 19 Railroad Avenue, Suite 407
East Hampton, NY 11937

ACKNOWLEDGMENTS

Grateful acknowledgement is made to Art News, The East Hampton Independent, The East Hampton Star, Esquire and The New York Times for permission to reprint previously published material.

I also am indebted to Vida Diederichson, Sherrill Foster, Nancy Nagle Kelley, Dr. Jean Lane, Jeanne Marriner, Patti Osborne and Stuart Vorpahl, Jr. for making documents available to me, to Peter Matthiessen for the quote from "Men's Lives," and to Helen Rattray, for allowing liberal quotes of past issues of The East Hampton Star.

My appreciation also goes to Dorothy Barnes, Clarence Barnes, John Behan, Tony Bullock, Larry Cantwell, Robert Cooper, Cile Downs, Anthony Biddle Duke, William Durham, Don Eames, Averill Dayton Geus, Ed Gorman, Karl Grossman, Rosalie Gwathmey, Robert Hefner, Gene Chipps Henderson, Dan King, Ernestine Lassaw, Arnold Leo, Cathy Lester, Richard Lia, Josephine Little, Milton Miller Sr., Carol Morrison, Charlotte Park, Nancy Scheerer, Sony Schotland, Carolyn Lester Snyder of Round Swamp Farm and Enez Whipple for sharing their recollections; to Carleton Kelsey, for always answering "one more" question, and to May Okon, for reviewing the manuscript in progress.

Without the wealth of material that reposits in the *Long Island Collection* of the East Hampton Library, the format of this book would have been nigh impossible. In the nearly four years that it took to research and write this book, many hours were spent in the *Collections*'s rooms. And, without the help of Dorothy King, the *Collection*'s steward, agonizing moments that invaded my research would have been more "mind-splitting" than they were.

Some readers will wonder why *this* or *that* is not within these pages. It was impossible to include every piece of news.

NHW   February 1995

ALSO BY AUTHOR:

If your child is drinking…
The World of Tea
Vacation!
The Food Catalog
The Mariner's Cookbook

for
Dorothy King
of *The Long Island Collection*
East Hampton Library

•

East Hampton's baymen and surfmen

•

my sister, Susan

•

and, in memory of
Cri
(Christina Paolozzi Bellin)

CONTENTS

Introduction

Seen from the vantage of a ship's deck, fish-shaped Long Island is flat. One hundred and eighteen miles in length, the country's fourth largest island barely reaches four hundred feet at its highest point. Wide sandy beaches backed by dunes form its Atlantic coast, while deeply-indented bays and moderate cliffs define its shoreline on Long Island Sound.

At its east end, the island divides into two elongated flukes. Separated by a bay, the strips of land are known as the North and South Forks. The latter fluke is of special interest to a variety of people. For historians, the South Fork - through Gardiner's Island in the Town of East Hampton - is the site of New York State's first English settlement.

For politicians, the South Fork is a valued source of campaign revenue garnered, for the most part, at high-priced summer fund raisers. For preservationists and developers, both flukes hold riches of another kind. Until the stock market plunge of 1987, competition was fierce for the island's last large tracts of open land.

The South Fork also is renowned for its resident artists, a loosely-strung colony of painters, sculptors, photographers, and printmakers, whose collective imprint on the art world reached its zenith during the second half of the twentieth century. To the world in general and, to people watchers in particular, the South Fork is *the Hamptons.* A catch-all label, it conjures up images of excitement and excess, of glittering summers and gala soirées lavished upon persons of wealth, fame and notoriety. But, the Hamptons is more than a mecca for endless rounds of parties, benefits, openings, and sun-filled days at the beach.

Behind the curve of the road, under the soil, in the vaults and repositories of private collections, and across the very land itself, lie the roots and the legacies of Long Island's first English settlements. Three and a half centuries have elapsed since their harsh beginnings were carved out of an island's wilderness. Three hundred-plus years. Time filled with legends and heroes, storms and wars, scandals and mysteries, people of consequence and persons with quirks. Time marked by changing styles and mores, tales remembered, and ccuriosities all but forgotten. History and heritage.

i

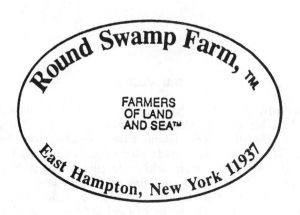

Round Swamp Farm,™

FARMERS
OF LAND
AND SEA™

East Hampton, New York 11937

Round Swamp Farm, also known as the Lester Farm by friends and customers, is located at the eastern end of Long Island. For nine generations, it has been the family's good fortune to enjoy living on and working this special farm which is so rich in the rewards of the land.

When Carolyn Lester Snyder was a little girl, she helped her parents, Albert and Barbara Lester, sell fresh-picked cucumbers and tomatoes from the roadside. Today, Carolyn, her husband, Harold, their daughters, Lisa Niggles and Shelley Snyder, and close to a dozen famly members continue to build on this tradition, as they operate the market.

What was once a small roadside stand has blossomed into a gourmet marketplace. It offers fresh seafood caught by the family, a salad counter that uses fresh produce and seafood in an array of ways, and, with the arrival of autumn and cooler weather, a variety of homemade soups.

The market's shelves are laden with homecooking fare, from Lisa's blueberry muffins (twice as many berries as usual), brownies, and rich, moist traditional chocolate fudge cake, to the banana bread, sour cream coffee cake, and carrot cake that isn't just about carrots, made by Carolyn's sister, Claire Lester Olszewski.

People who are looking for a few items to take home after a week-end visit in East Hampton can try some of the homemade jams, pepper relishes, or pickles. All of them are made from scratch, following favorite family recipes. Or, they might try the beach plum chutney made by Carolyn's other sister, Dianna Lester Catozzi. The plums are native to this area,

A 20-acre farm spreads out behind the market. From there, come many of the items that are found in the large, attractively-displayed produce section.

Prologue

When, on summer Friday evenings, traffic out of Manhattan is bumper to bumper on the Long Island Expressway; when, on summer week-ends, it takes forty minutes to travel the twelve miles that separate the villages of Southampton and East Hampton, it is difficult to imagine a time when all of Long Island was lifeless, the only movement across it that of a cold, cold wind.

When surrounded by pop art and abstracts at a retrospective exhibit at Guild Hall, it boggles the mind to overhear a conversation in which the word *modern* is being applied to something that occured millions of years ago.

Through the time frame of geologists, modern life on Long Island began with the end of the latest Pleistocene glaciation, and with the melting northwards of the ice from the Wisconsin Advance. On the island, only hard-part remains of organisms survived the brutal freeze which had covered much of the globe. With the gradual change to a warmer climate, stark Long Island was ready to receive life and new growth. In the beginning, that growth was the simplest of plants.

About five thousand years ago, Indians began crossing the river, to hunt the island's woods and take from its waters. Migrating with the seasons, they eventually colonized. Always sparse in number, the settlements comprised various tribes of the woodland Algonquins. Gentle, proud, innately peace loving, these natives were as one in their fear of the mighty Iroquois, to whom they paid annual tribute. A warring nation, the Iroquois lived up the river, and roamed far and wide in their conquest of lesser tribes. As the seventeenth century opened, thirteen tribes frequented the island.

During the first years of the new century, England was in the throes of great change and discomfort. Tyranny, persecution and plunder stamped the times and ruptured lives. Religious intolerance and the use of royal courts, outside the bounds of common law, smothered freedom of thought and belief.

Restrictions of another kind weighed on the tenant farmer. Reaching its peak during this century, the *inclosure* system enabled landowners to fence in waste land by whatever

iii

method they chose. A proviso required that they make this land available to their tenants. Too often, however, that access was denied and the farmer found himself unable to pasture his cattle, sow his crops, feed his family. Those who could, fled to the Netherlands. From there, some of them gambled on a new life in a new world.

The Dutch, at this time, were a progressive and free people. In contrast to their neighbors across the channel, they led Europe in trade, scholarship and the fine arts. Their ships sailed the seven seas, returning time and again with luxuries and spices from the Far East.

England coveted this trade and, in 1600, Queen Elizabeth chartered the British East India Company, with one purpose in mind: break the Dutch monopoly half-way around the world. Twenty-three years later, however, England found it prudent to abandon this objective and set its sights on developing a lucrative trade with India.

Not content with their successes to date, the Dutch longed to expand their trade and attain closer ties with their Asian colonies. To this end, the government chartered the Dutch East India Company in 1602. In time, the Company's phenomenal success and its search for a quicker route to the Far East would bear directly on Long Island and, on that part of the island which includes *the Hamptons*.

The Seventeenth Century

1609

March 25. Henry Hudson, an English explorer in the employ of the Dutch East India Company, and a crew of twenty well-traveled men sail from Amsterdam aboard the "Half Moon." Their mission: find the northeast passage to China. (Twice before, Hudson failed to locate it for the English.)

. Somewhere north of Norway, ice and freezing weather block his ship's passage. Ignoring orders that were given before he set sail, Hudson changes course and heads west. Now, his hope is to find the elusive passage through the New World, which he visited the previous year.

September 4/12. Part way down America's coast, Hudson tacked his ship and ran it north. On the 4th, the "Half Moon" anchors in waters which Hudson names Gravesend Bay.

. Crewman Robert Juet recounts the events of the 5th in his journal: "...as soon as the day was light, we found it was a very good harbor. Our boat went with net to fish. The people of the Country came aboard of us, seeming very glad of our coming, and brought green tobacco and gave us of it for knives and beads. They go in Deerskin, loose, well dressed. They have yellow copper. They desire clothes and are very civil."

. Hudson writes in his journal that the natives wear "mantles of feathers," while others are "in divers sorts of good furs."

Some of the crew go ashore. In so doing, they become the first white men to set foot on this land. Hudson notes that the sailors found it "pleasant with grass, and flowers, and goodly trees as ever they had seen, and very sweet smells..."

. Over the next eight days, Hudson sails up a river that he believes will lead him to China, makes friends with the Iroquois who live along its upper banks, and, reaching non-navigatable waters, realizes this is not the route, and turns back.

1614/1617

. Dutch traders receive a three year monopoly on trade in the New World. Under the banner of The United New Netherland Company, they build a trading post on *Manhattoes*, across the water from where the "Half Moon" anchored, and hire Adriaen Block to retrace Hudson's river travels.

After Block spends the winter far up Hudson's river, he discovers that Manhattoes is on an island, and that the land to its east is an island, too. He names that one Lange Eylandt, and gives his name to a smaller island, near by.

1620

. On behalf of a consortium of English merchants, Thomas Weston offers Pilgrims in Dutch exile a patent obtained earlier from the London Company of Virginia. It grants its holders the right to start a colony anywhere in Virginia. Weston tells the Pilgrims that, after working for the merchants seven years, the company's assets will be divided between them and the merchants, on a pro rata basis.

Septembe 16. The former wineship "Mayflower" sets sail from England with fifty Pilgrims and fifty-two "Strangers" on board. Though they remain faithful to the church, Weston was able to recruit the "Strangers" to fill the ship, by offering them the chance to own land in the new country.

November 3. King James I grants the Plymouth Company a new charter. (The Company has been inactive since its three failed attempts, between 1606-1608, to colonize America.)

Now called the Council for New England, the Company obtains exclusive right to "planting, ruling, and governing" all the land in the New World between forty and forty-eight degrees north latitude, extending from one sea to the other." Lange Eylandt, which the Dutch already have claimed, lies within this latitude.

November 11. The "Mayflower" drops anchor, four hundred-plus miles north of its destination. Her passengers find themselves in a wilderness, where their patent is without meaning, and they are without any plans for survival.

November 21. Before anybody leaves the ship, forty-one Pilgrims and Strangers draw up, and sign, a social contract. The first of its kind, the non-political *Mayflower Compact* provides for a temporary government among them. Rule will be by majority vote, with just and equal laws for all.[1]

December 26. After nearly a month of exploring, the Pilgrims decide to settle on the mainland side of the bay. On their map of the New World, this area has been named Plymouth.

1621/1624

. In 1621, the Dutch States General expands its horizons with a charter to the Great West India Company. Organized two years later, the Company is given exclusive license to all Dutch trade and navigation along the west African and New World coasts, and near limitless power within its jurisdiction. Lacking only authority to declare war, the company is directed to "advance the peopling of those fruitful and unsettled parts" and to build "fortresses, fortifications, and settlements."

The company sends ships up Hudson's river, enters into successful trading with the Iroquois, and builds two forts. One is near the river's source, the other is on Manhattoes. The Dutch name their territory New Netherland, appoint Cornelius Jacobsen May its first Director-General, start to build on Manhattoes, and issue licenses to merchants who will trade with the Indians.

Reminded by England of its prior claim to the territory, the Dutch reply that they do not plan to colonize. (England bases its ownership on John Cabot's royal patent, granted March 5, 1496 by Henry VII, and on Cabot's subsequent landing on North America - albeit, much further north. Under English common law and the divine right of kings, conquered or discovered lands are held by the crown, for the ruling regent to hold or grant as he/she wills.)

Promises notwithstanding, the first permanent Dutch colonials arrive on Manhattoes in 1624. Some of them settle at the foot of the island and name their community New Amsterdam. Others cross the river to Lange Eylandt, or venture up Hudson's river, to Fort Nassau. New Amsterdam is made the capital of New Netherland, and Peter Minuit is appointed its governor.

1626
. Peter Minuit buys Manhattoes from the Indians for twenty-four dollars worth of trinkets.

1631
. Members of the Plymouth Company found Windsor, on the mainland of the New World.

1635
. The Dutch settle Queens on the western end of Lange Eylandt.
April 22. The Council for New England responds to an order from King Charles I to divide its New World territories among its members.

William Alexander, Earl of Stirling is given the area from Pemaquid to the St. Croix River. But, because France has usurped English trade east of Pemaquid, the Council equalizes Stirling's share by issuing a patent to his eldest son. It is for "All that Island or Island heretofore commonly callled by the several name or names of *matowack* or Long Island and hereafter to be called by the name of the Isle of Starlinge scituate lying and beinge to the Westward of Cape Cod or the Narohigansets within the latitude of ffortie or ffortie one or thereabouts ..."

(The Earl of Stirling is a poet, former tutor of Prince James of Scotland, and the King's Secretary for Scotland. Unlike his son, he never has been to America).

August 18. Lion Gardiner English army officer and crack military engineer, and his wife, Mary, sail from London aboard the bark "Bachelor." His mission is to supervise building the fort at the mouth of the Connecticut River.

November 28. John Winthrop, Governor of the Massachusetts Bay Colony, records Gardiner's arrival: "Here arrived a small Norsey bark of twenty-five tons, sent by Lords Say, &c. with one Gardiner, expert engineer for work base, and provisions of all sorts, to begin a fort at the mouth of Connecticut. She came through many great tempests, yet through the Lord's great providence her passengers, twelve men and two women and goods, all safe."

1636

April 26. Lord Alexander appoints James Farrett to represent his American holdings. He instructs Farrett to dispose of the land, as he sees fit, and to select a portion of it for himself.

(Farrett claims for himself two islands close to each other. One he calls Robbins Island. For three years, the other one is known as "Mr. Farrett's Island.")[2]

1637

May 3. Lion Gardiner buys an island from Poggaticut, sachem of the Manhassets, and his wife, Aswaw. Purchase price for Manchonake is ten cloth coats.

The island lies within Alexander's patent, between the two flukes of Paumanacke (the Indian name for Lange Eylandt). Gardiner names his land Isle of Wight. Nine miles long and less than three miles wide, it is blessed with 3000 acres of wooded hills, wild life, sandy shore, coves, and inlets.

Mid-summer. Gardiner moves to Isle of Wight with his wife and children, who were born at Fort Saybrook.

1638

November 1. Six months after Lord Alexander's death, an augmentation to his patent gives his holdings to his father.

1639

. The government of the New Haven colony is formed.

June 12. Farrett signs over "all Rights, Titles, Claims, and demands of and from all Patent Right, of all those lands lying and being bounded between Peaconeck and the easternmost point of Long Island with the whole breadth of the said island from sea to sea with all lands and premises contained within the said limits, excepting those lands already unto any person by me ... unto Edward Howell, Daniel Howe, Job Sayer, and their associates heirs and successors both now and forever."

August 20. In London, Lord Stirling ratifies Farrett's disposal of his lands "according to the custom of New England."

1640

March 10. In Lynn, Mass., Howell, Howe, Sayer, Edward Farrington, and four other men who hope to fare better on Paumanacke, draw up articles of agreement. Called *The Disposall of the Vessell,* the document covers the manner, settling, and governing of the plantation that they will found on Long Island. The vessell is the sloop which the men have bought and consigned to Howe. In exchange, Howe agrees to take them to Long Island and to return to Lynn three times, each of the next two years, to fetch goods for the plantation.

. This same day, the Earl of Stirling issues Gardiner a grant for his island.

April 7. Farrett formalizes his agreement with the eight Puritans. They may establish a colony of *eight miles square* (not eight square miles) anywhere on Paumanacke. Payment for this right has been set by Connecticut's Governor, John Winthrop, Jr., who is anxious to see an English settlement on the island. The Puritans are to pay Farrett four bushels of ripe Indian corn. Winthrop confirms the price on the back of the signed contract.

May. Early this month, the eight men from Lynn, accompanied by a woman and child, land on Dutch-held property in the western part of Lange Eylandt. There, they take the first steps towards establishing a settlement.

May 13/19. In Fort Amsterdam, Dutch Director-General Willem Kieft and the Council ponder the news that foreigners at Schout's Bay have begun "to build houses, cut trees...had there thrown down their High Mightinesses' arms...and on the tree to which they were nailed, was a fool's face carved..."

On the 15th, Kieft orders Secretary Cornelia van Tienhoven to set out with soldiers, arriving "unexpectedly...best, in our opinion, at the break of day...and...prevent the English have recourse to any force; and you shall forthwith inquire who hath thrown down the arms, and who gave them commission to do so, and oblige them to come here and defend themselves...

"if it happens that so many additional English have come (which we do not anticipate)...you shall make a strong protest against such proceedings, have it served and come back, taking care above all things, to avoid all bloodshed."

Van Tienhoven returns to Manhattoes with six of the "strangers." On the 16th, they are interrogated in Kieft's home. They are asked to give their names and ages, and tell from whence they came, and why they left their previous place. Satisfied that they did not desecrate the "arms of the Lords States," Kieft frees the men "on condition that they do promise to depart forthwith from our territory, and never to return to it, without the Director's express consent."

May 27. The Puritans sail into a bay and through an inlet to a land-locked harbor on eastern Lange Eylandt. They name the inlet North Sea, and call the land on which they first set foot, *Conscience Point.*

June 12. Farrett issues the Puritans their deed for "all those lands lying and being bounded by Peaconeck and the whole easternmost point of the island with the whole breadth of the said island from sea to sea."

They name their plantation Southampton and, following the text of the *Disposall of the Vessell*, form a government, determine responsibilities, and set aside times for Town meetings and military trainings. Majority vote is to prevail at all times, on all matters. Division and ownership of land rests with the original "undertakers," those who signed the contract.

December 13. The Shinnecock Indians deed a portion of their land to the settlers. For this, they receive sixteen coats, already in hand, guaranteed delivery of sixty bushels of corn September next, and their neighbors' promise to defend them against any unlawful or unjust attack by other Indians.

. Lord Stirling dies, leaving his estate holdings to his grandson.

1641
September 14. Lion and Mary Gardiner's daughter, Elizabeth, is born on the Isle of Wight.

1643
September 8. After meeting in Boston in May, to draw up a series of resolves that will bind them together, as equals, the colonies of Connecticut, Massachusetts Bay, New Haven, and Plymouth become the United Colonies of New England.

Covering the northeast coast and rivers of America, from Long Island to New Hampshire - Rhode Island and Maine excepted - the union was forged to enable worship free of interference, promote cooperation, and provide sufficient defense.

1648

April 29. Interested in expanding English settlement on Long Island, the colonial governors of Connecticut (at Hartford) and New Haven negotiate with the Montauketts for 30,720 acres of land, east of Southampton.

This day, the blood-brother sachems of the Montauk, Shinnecock, Corchake, and Monhansuck-Ahaquazuwamuck tribes convey to "Theophilus Eaton Esq., Governour of the Colony of New Haven, and the worshipful Edward Hopkins, Governour of the colony of Connecticut and their assocyates... the Land lyinge from the bounds of the inhabitants of Southampton unto the East side of Napeak, next unto Meauntacut high Land, with the whole breadth from Sea to Sea, not Intrenching upon any in length or breadth, which the Inhabitants of Southampton, have and do possess...for and in consideration of 20 coats, 24 Looking Glasses, 24 hoes, 24 hatchets, 24 knives, and one hundred mucxs, already received by us...and reserve unto ourselves free Liberty to fish in any and all the cricks & ponds, and hunt up and down in the Woods and without molestation...giving the English Inhabitants noe just offence: likewise are to have the fynns & tails of all whales cast up, and desire they may be friendly dealt with in the other part alsoe to fish for shells to make Wampum of...."

(For the Indians, the whales' "fynns & tails" are the most sacred offering that they can roast for their God.)

1648/1649

. The nine men who settle east of Southampton name their plantation Maidstone, after the English town from or, near to which some of them came. (Within months, *Maidstone* and *Easthampton* alternate in the record books).

Their first spring east of Southampton, the settlers sow their fields of crops and prepare for the winter. Shelter that first year is no more than a shored hole in the earth. The following year, livestock and families start to arrive. Maidstone's founders are Joshua Barnes, Robert Bond, John Hand, Sr., Daniel Howe, John Mulford, Robert Rose, John Stretton, Sr., Thomas Talmage, Jr., and Thomas Thomson.

Others follow: Thomas Baker Charles Barnes, William Barnes, Samuel Belknap, Nathaniel Bishop, Richard Brookes, Thomas Chatfield, Ananias Conklin, Fulke Davis, Ralph Dayton, William Fithian, Lion Gardiner, Joshua Garlicke Stephen Hand, William Hedges, Jeremiah Meacham, John Miller, John Osborn, Thomas Osborn, Thomas Osborn Jr., Samuel Parsons, Richard Shaw, William Simonds, and Jeremiah Veale.

Laid out east and west of the first road to be cut, the original lands allocated in Maidstone range in size from eight to twelve acres. Their measure depends on the amount its owner invested in Maidstone's founding.

The first above-ground dwellings face a swamp of cedar trees. The houses are made of daub and wattle and covered with thatch. The earliest chimneys are of wood, later, of brick fired from clay at Fresh Pond. A brick oven next to the fireplace or, in the cellar as part of the chimney, is used on Saturdays to make the family's week-long supply of baked goods.

The swamp is cleared and drained to make a watering pond for the cattle. The cemetery is established on a rise just east of it. The thatched-roof church/meeting house is built next to the burial ground. The cattle-driven mill is built a few yards north. Roads are cart wheel ruts across the commons and through the woods. Pasture land (known as "wind mill lane," "calf pasture lane," etc.) is leased each spring to individuals.

The undivided lands are owned by the paying founders, in proportion to their initial investments, their heirs, and their assignes. Referring to themselves as "the town," they allocate the tracts of undeveloped land and decide when woods are to be cleared and pathways are to be cut.

A General Court (General Meeting, Town Meeting) and a Special Court make up the government. Comprised of the Town's freemen and led by the clerk, the General Court enacts all laws, regulates Town affairs, determines who will be allowed to live in Maidstone, who will be asked to leave it, where to build a church, who will be its minister, how much property each resident may have, and to whom a man may sell his land. Election of officers is annual. During the early years, they are chosen from among the original founders.

Meeting "at eight o'clock in the morning on the 2nd day of the 1st week in every month," the Special Court of three - later, four - members oversees minor controversies. General Court hears Appeals. Serious cases are tried in Connecticut. Punishment for offenses is not severe. Great care is taken not to duplicate the harsh, sometimes fatal, sentences handed down in England - and even in the Connecticut Colony. The most serious misdeeds net the convicted time in the stocks or, a series of whip lashes. A jury of seven men judges criminal suits and actions that involve more than forty shillings. A constable carries out the Court's decisions.

At different times, during the town's formative period, invitations to settle in Maidstone are extended to persons who can supply a trade that the town lacks. A carpenter from

Weathersfield, Conn., a blacksmith from Huntington and a weaver from Southold accept such offers. For moving to Maidstone, each man is given a home lot, acreage for farming and pasturing, some money, and exemption from paying taxes.

Far removed from the route of travel between the mainland colonies, and the influences of outside intrusion, the fledgling plantation runs itself well, and with fairness. Each citizen takes his turn protecting it. Two men stand guard at night, one is on watch during the day. Everyone is expected to attend the town meetings and to vote on all decisions. Absent and non-voters are fined. To the extent that all landowners had an equal vote, it could be said that the early governments of Maidstone and Southampton were close to democracy at its purest. It will be eight years before the outside world intrudes on the East End.

1649

April. After Indians scalp Thomas Halsey's wife, Phoebe, in the herb garden of her Southampton home, the Southampton Court sends for Wyandanch, who lives many miles east of the English settlement.

The Court wants the Montaukett sachem, who is chief sachem of all of Long Island's Indians, to find and identify her killers. Fearing that he will be killed in retaliation, Wyandanch's advisors urge him not to go. But a visiting friend encourages him to heed the request. Lion Gardiner says that he will remain as hostage of the Montauketts, to ensure his return.

Near the end of his ride, Wyandanch happens upon two Shinnecock Indians, whom he does not recognize. He takes them to Southampton, where they are found to be Pequots from Connecticut. Phoebe Halsey's killers had disguised themselves, in order to bring trouble to the Shinnecocks.

. Lion Gardiner and his family move into East Hampton.

1650

January 23. Thomas Baker, Robert Bond, and John Mulford agree with Southampton representatives on their common border. A "firm peace" is to be kept "at all times and from time to time...noe parson or parsons whatsoever shall drive or place any hogs or other Cattell within half a mile of the line or bounds that is at the partinge of the plantations....unlese such party or partyes doe Dayly attend upon such Cattell...

"If any trespassing occurs, and there is damage to the cornfields or orchards, the livestock owners are liable to fines."

April 27. Lion Gardiner writes Gov. Winthrop, asking him to be on watch for a suitable pastor in East Hampton:

"At present we are willing to give this man your writ of 20£ a year, with such diet as I myself eat, till we see what the Lord will do with us; and being he is but a young man, happily he hath not many books, therefore let him know what I have. First, the Three Books of Martyrs, Erasmus, most of Perkins, Wilson's Dictionary, a large Concordance, Mayor on the New Testament; some of these, with other that I have, may be useful to him. I pray you, for the Lord's sake, do what you can to get him hither, and as I am engaged to you already, so shall I be more...

"p.s. I pray you send me word speedily about the cows or else I must dispose of them some other way."

(Gardiner has been selling cows to Winthrop, who has been sending him free hayseed from Connecticut.)

October 3. The first Tuesday of the month, the Court chooses four men and a constable "for ye ordering of ye affairs of ye Towne...these 5 men shall have power to try any case under ye sum of ffortie shillings but if anie case or action to be tryed yt is above, then it is to be tryed by a jurie of 7 men."

Among the laws passed this day are:

"whomsoever shall take up a lot in Towne shall live upon it himselfe..."

" any man shall have libertie to purchase a Cort for ye tryall of any action or sute he paying forthwith to everie man yt shalbe therein imployed one shilling sixpence and for entering an action 2s."

"...if any man shal refuse or neglect to come to any Towne meeting...he shall...pay a fine..."

"...if any whales be cast up within our bounds that every householder shall do his part of ye worke about cutting of them out according as his turn shall cum the towne being for this worke devided into two parts ye one halfe to goe at one time & the other at an other, and everie one upon warning given is to take his turne to look out to find them and whosoever shall be found to be a delinquent in doing his part in cutting or looking out when his turn shal pay a fine to ye value of 5s."

"if Any Indean find a whale and do forthwith tiding of it he shall have 5s for his pains..."

. In Hartford, the United English Colonies commissioners resolve: "...Connecticut hath liberty to take Easthampton, upon Long Island, under their government, if they submitt." Easthampton would not lose its independence. The resolution would bring the town under Connecticut's protection.

1651

March 7. The General Court orders: "Ralph Dayton to go to Keneticut for to procure the Evidence of our Lands, and for an acquittance for the payment of our lands, and for a bodie of laws."

"Any man have libertie to set guns for to kill wolves, but not within a mile of the town...no man shall set any gun, but he shall look to it while the stars appear, and take the gun up by the sun rising...

"Any man who owns a bitch that goeth to Dog shall kepe upp their bitches Duringe the time that they go to Dog uppon the penaltie of paying 20s...

"Every man shall fence the land that he doth enjoy that is ... his Land on the plaine."

April 16. Easthampton receives written "evidence for its lands" from Connecticut:

"Whereas, by direction from Theophilus Eaton, Esq., and me Edward Hopkins, a purchase was made by Thomas Stanton and others, of a part of the Eastern Part of Long Island, of the Indian Sachems, the true proprietors thereof, in the name of Theophilus Eaton, Esq., aforesaid, and myself, with our associates, as by the said agreement, dated the 29th of April, 1648, may more fully appear, which said purchase was paid by me, Edward Hopkins, and amounted to the sum of 30£ 4 shillings eightpence, as may appear by a Note of Particulars, under the hand of Thomas Stanton, to whom the said sum was paid, now delivered to Robert Bond of Easthampton.

"This writinge witnesseth that I have received the forementioned sum of 30£ four shillings eight pence, of the inhabitants of Easthampton, and have delivered unto them the writings of the said purchase, and all the interest that thereby was purchased. in witness whereof, I have hereunto subscribed, the 16th of April 1651."

May 14. The Town orders: "every man shall have A certain quantitie of land Joyninge to the Reare end of their house lotts ... that every man may goe from his house lott uppon his other Devision without trespassinge uppon any other." On the long, fenced-in acreage behind their homes, the settlers now will grow their crops __and__ pasture their goats, cattle, horses and sheep, when they are not on the common land. (In addition, each landowner also owns a portion of woodland.)

May 19. Majority vote orders: "whatever great cattell shall break through or leap over any sufficient fence and hurt been Done the ptie yt owneth those sttell shall forthwith put a piece of wod vppon the horns of the beast."

August 23. The Town agrees to pay its first minister, young Reverend Thomas James, 45£ per annum, lands (including woodland, from which to cut wood) free of tax, and the first grain that will be ground at the mill each Monday.

October 7. General Court orders three men to oversee the Town's orders the coming year, instructs Daniel Turner "within the space ffortnite eythe sojourne in some ffamily or bee a servant to some man or else Depart the Towne," and warns every home owner to have on his property, within six weeks, a ladder that will reach the top of his thatched roof.

November 6. The Town appoints Goodman Mulford to "call out ye Town by succession to look out for whale." (The watch for whales that drift ashore is kept from a "stage," a tree trunk or wooden structure stuck into the sand, on the eastern part of Napeague.)

The Town votes that every man who can bear arms is to be provided with "a good gunne powder shott sword worme and scourer shotbagg rest bolt and a fitt thinge to carrie powder in." Starting in March, General Training is to occur six times a year.

November 17. The Inhabitants agree "that there shal be a meetinge house built 26 foote longe 20 foot broade and 8 foote stoode....that the three men that are chosen for town affaires shall set out the place for the meeting house and the five men that get the thatch shall fence the same nere that place."

Until the house is up, Thomas Baker will be paid 18 pence "for evry Lords Day that the meeting shalbe at his house."

1652

May 4. The Town orders: "the Land of the East plaine shall be for the 2 Division laid out 80 pole longe and aker for aker no allowance neyther for Distance nor stubbs but only in case any man fall in the runninge rootes that are beyond the 2 mile hollow."

In response to grumblings among some of the land owners, the Court also orders "that those men Ralph Daiton Thomas Osborne senior William Edwards shal quietly enjoy their land that they now possesse without any more Questioninge."

May 8. The Town orders that "the land on the litell plaine shall be all measured that every man may have his Just Due and they that lay it out shall lay out a cart way to Wainscott where it may be most convenient except Thomas Talmages lott."

May 17. The Town orders "yt every man that hath six Cowes shall keepe a bull to goe with them" and "yt those that have bulls with the herd of cowes shall have Sixe pence ffor every cowe yt their bulls serve or others for this present yeare."

July 7. General Court orders the meadows at Accabonacc to be laid out in three divisions. "...in case the hay on the inner parte of Acabannocke cannot bee brought out without makinge a hie way that then the way shal be made by the whole towne."

The court also orders cart ways to be cut to several places in the northwest meadows, but 30 acres of those meadows are to remain untouched for now. (The salt hay harvested from around Accabonac Harbor is being used to insulate the houses, feed the livestock, and serve as bedding).

September 15. The Town orders: "every man shall set sufitient landmarkes to bound there meadowe and set there name on it... within the month... 2s. 6p fine for the defect of every lote."

October 5. General Court decrees: "if any man bee agrieved with any thinge yt is Done by the men yt are in Authoritie that then he shall have libertie to make his appeale to the next Generall court or when the ffremen are Assembled together for their publike occasions."

November 2. General Court orders: "every man shall vote by holding up his hands eyther with or against in all matters upon penalty of paying 6d the thinge beinge before Deliberately Debated."

December 3. The Town orders Thomas Talmage to "call out the towne by turnes to looke after whales this prsent yeare."

1653

January 3. General Court orders: "yt one halfe of the towne shall carry armes evry Lords Day with fower sufficient chargs of Powder and shott and whosoever is Defective herein shall pay 12d and if the Sariants see cause at a Dayes warninge to bring armes all the towne." (When not in use, each settler hangs his well polished gun, lead pouch, and powder horn over his fireplace.)

February 2. The clerk records an invitation: "It is Ordered yt there shall bee an invitation sent to Goodman Morgan of Southold if hee will come and live here and weave all the Townswork, hee shall come in free from all former charges and the Town will give him 5£ and break him up ackres of Land."

March 26. Majority vote orders "that noe man nor woman whatsoever shall sell any kind of pvisions to any Indians During the time of the neighbours plantaccon bring in this pasture upon penalty of payinge of 6d for evry pounde of bread or quart of meale."

April 26. Majority vote orders: "...noe Indian shall Come to town unless it be upon special occasion, and none to come armed because that the Dutch hath hired Indians agst the English & we not knowing Indians by face and because the Indians hath cast off their sachem, and if any of the Indians or other by night will come in to the towne in Despit of eyther watch or ward upon the third Stand to shoot him or if thay rune away to shoote him."

May 6. The clerk records: "It is ordered yt the watch shall come to take their charge as Daylit shuts in and if any shall neglect to com to take his charge the officer shall hier another and give him Dubell paye that is 2s and to keep their watch till Daylite and Defective partie is to answer his neglect, and.... it is ordered yt a firkin of powder and shott equivalent shall be sent for to Conniticutt and men shall make pay eyther in wheat butter or cheese at goodman Clarkes at the Rivers mouth at mikelmas."

May 9. Majority vote orders: "noe man shall goe forth of the towne to work or stay in other towne or place without acquainting two of the three men at the least and have liberty from them upon penalty of payinge 40s for every Days absence."

June 9. The Town orders: "there shall be a hie way on litell plaine to Georgica of 16 foote wide ... "

June 13. The Recorder enters the account of a defamation suit:

"William Edwards plt Declares It is a deepe wound that is laid upon his wife in that wch is expressed against her by Goody Price for her life lieth at stake in this Defamation...that shee is a base lieinge woman...which I take to bee a great Defamation to me and my possitiry in that hereafter it may be spoken here goe the bratts of a bse lyer and whereas formerly I would have had an end of it without trouble or Charge I now Declare that the Defamation is such as I would not have made out against my wife for a hundred pounds my wife beinge an ancient woman and the other a younge woman to whom my wife hath given no Just occasion...

"Wheras Thomas Baker affirmeth that goodwife Edwards sayd that her husband had brought her to a place where ther was neyther Magistrates nor ministers and that he brought her to live amonge a Company of heathen that the plt acknowledged and therefore there was noe more witnesses examined."

June 23. The Town votes: "there shall be a watering pond diged at the spring Eastward and the charge to be borne by the heads of cowes and to be begun the next second Day and Ralph Dayton and Thomas Baker are to oversee the worke and see

that men bring goode sufficient tooles to work with all, and all
that have cowes are to appear at the beat of the Drum."

July 5. Thirty-four allotments, ranging from two to five acres
each, are designated for the meadow at Northwest. An equal
number of allotments, one and a half to three acres each, is
recorded for the meadow at Accabonac.

August 2. The Recorder enters, "it is ordered yt the Drie heard
shall bee Driven out of Towne to wainscott evry morninge that
they Come to towne this to bee Dunn by turnes a Day for 4 and
soe pportionately and Goodman Osburne to begin and he that
Drives them one Day is to warne his next neighboure."

September 16. General Court agrees "that Goodman Davis shall
have seaven ackers and an halfe of land in some Convenient
place where the towne or thayr Comite come together with
Goodman Davis shall think fitt in lew of his first Division on the
Easterne plaine after two crops more."

November 27. The clerk records the Town's agreement with
Vinson Meigs: "...the aforesaid Vinson meigs doth Covenant
and...firmly bind himselfe and his estate unto the inhabitants...
to build and mayntayn for the use of the aforesaid Inhabitants a
sufficient serviceablle mill the same to be sufficiently keept and
mayntayned from time to time by him and his assignes for the
Doeing of the townes work without any future charge to any of
the afore sd inhabitants eyther in labor or otherwise....

"...in consideration of the afore sd...we the inhabitants ...
Covenant and firmly bind our selves unto the sd Vinson meigs
to give him the full sum of fifty £ to bee pd... in corne pork or
wampam...or else in live cattle the corne and porke to bee paid
at the price Current...and for cattell as two different men shall
value them...

"furthermore...upon his well performance of the promises
above sd...twenty ackers...laid beside the Creeke yt runs Down
into our harbor 15 ackers to be upland to ly as neere the mill as
Conveniently can bee and five ackers of meadow to bee laid out
to it as neere as Can bee the same 20 ackers to ly to the mill and
not to be sold or given from it at any time but the said land wth
the mill is to ly and remaine to the abovesd Vinson and his assignes for ever....furthermore, we...Doe pmise and Ingage our
selves...to carrie the timber for the mill and the milstones to the
place where the mill shall stand and the said Vinson Doth
Covenant to finish the mill by the 4th of June next."

December 9. The Town votes "the capitall laws, and the laws
and Orders that are noticed in the bodies of laws that came
from Connecticut shall stand in force among us."

1654

May 23. The Town decides to have the house on the Common, next to Joshua Garlicke's house, moved "to some convenient place in the midel of the towne for a prison."

June 8/June 26. On June 8 and 10, four Easthampton men are charged with masturbation.

On June 26, the clerk records: "After extended examination and serious debate and consultation with their Saybrook neighbors, the Townsmen" do not consider the act worthy of loss of life or limb. Instead, Daniel Fairfield, who has been before the magistrates (September, 1651) and who now is a servant of Fulke Davis, is put in the pillory and whipped, while John Davis and a servant of Joshua Garlicke are whipped in public. (No punishment is recorded for John Hand, Jr.. His father is one of the three Townsmen who investigated the charges.)

June 29. The clerk records today's decisions: "Having Considered the Letters That came from Connecticut, wherein men are required to assist the power of England against the Dutch we doe thinke our selves caled to assist the sd power."

October 3. Until now, East Hampton has been without a written constitution. For eight years, its inhabitants have governed by majority vote. Resolutions passed have originated from fairness, right, and the Bible. Today, the Town resolves: "...there shall be a copie of the Connecticut combination drawn forth as is convenient for us, and yt all men shall set to their hands."

October 24. Taking the Connecticut combination as their Covenant, the Townsmen add two long sentences to what becomes the Town Constitution:

"For as much as it has pleased Almighty God, by the wide dispensation of His Providence, so to order and dispose things that we the Inhabitants of East Hampton are now dwelling together, the word of God requires that to maintain the Peace and the union of such a people there should be an Orderly and Decent Government established according to God, to order and Dispose as occasion shall require. We do therefore associate and conjoin ourself to be one Town or Corporation, and Do for ourselves and successors, and such as shall be adjoined to us at any time hereafter, enter into combination and confederation together to maintain and preserve the purity of the Gospel of our Lord Jesus Christ, which we now profess;[3] as alsoe the Discipline of the Church, which according to the said Gospell is now practised among US; As also in our civil affaires to be guided & governed by such laws and orders as shall be made according to God, and which by vote of the major Part shall be of force among US & c. *Furthermore we do engage ourselves*

that in all votes for choosing officers or making orders that it be
according to conscience and our best light, And also we do
engage ourselves by this combination to stand and maintain
the authority of the several Officers of the Town in their
Determinations and actions according to their Orders and Laws
that either are or shall be, not swerving therefrom. In witness
whereof each accepted Inhabitant set to our hand."

Forty Inhabitants sign the Covenant.

November 9. The Town decides "yt Mr. Gardiner shall have
power to Call fforth men by turnes to Looke out for whales at
all seasons as he shall apoynt for this yeare...yt theare shal be a
cart way made over the swamp to the plaines...yt Every Man
shall sett the ffirst Letters of his name at Each corner of his Lott
...yt Thomas Baker shall keep the Ordinary."

1655

April 3. The Town votes: "... men shall be sent to Connecticut
to treat with them at their court in May next concerning our
coming under their Government."

(Southampton already has sought counsel and protection with
the Connecticut confederacy of Hartford, Wethersfield, and
Windsor. Southold chose to align itself with the New Haven
colony which, unlike Connecticut, denies vote to any Inhabitant
who is not a member of the church.)

. This year, school opens in Samuel Parsons' house.

May 28. The Town votes: "for prevention of abuse amongst the
Indians by selling of strong water, first that no man shall carry
any to them to sell, neither send them any, nor employ any to
sell for them; neither shall any sell any liquor in the town to
any Indian for their present drinking, above two drams at a
time; also whoever sells any liquor shall not let any Indian have
any but such as are sent by the sachem and shall bring a written
ticket from him, which shall be given him from the town; and
he shall not have above a quart at one time; and whoever goeth
contrary to this order shall be liable to pay 5s for every quart,
and so for every quantity more or less."

July 6. The Town votes: "... Mr. James shall have yt meadow on
the ffurthest side of Hooke Pond between the thickett trees &
the Beach & so along the plained side according to a row of
bushes by the meadow side....Mr. Lion Gardiner, Thomas
Chatfield, Ananias Conklin, and William Hedges shall have the
meadow at the north side of Hook Pond and at the end of it to
the Swamp they Leaving a sufficient way through it where it
shall be most convenient for the Towne."

December 3. Elected on October 3 to be Maidstone's "Townes men for the ensuing yeare," John Mulford, Thomas Baker and Lion Gardiner write to the Connecticut Governor on behalf of the plantation: "We being informed that complaint is carried to you Honr against the Town with repsect to one Arthur Chandler, who...haveing had a residence in the Town though by reason of his vicious behavior he was warned (that within a month of his being here) to be gone out of the Town, yet he hath contrary to the mind of the Town, wilfully continued in it, The Town having sufficient evidence of his being a notorious Thiefe both out of this Town & since his being amongst us, hath been the more averse to his being admitted as an Inhabitant amongst us,..

"And where its...alledged to you Honr yt ye man hath sustained dammage by reason of their causing his fabrick to be pulled down, it was but a collar & a few pallisades plucked up... & a few round sticks laid to bear up a small roofe over it, & whereas it may be further alledged that this man is left of a place to live in this winter, that is not so, for he hath had a good house over his head hitherto, & so he may have still...till hee can provide for himself elsewhere in the springe..."

1656

February 12. Town majority rules: "whosoever shall rise up in anger against his neighbor and strike him, shall forthwith pay ten shillings to ye town and stand to the censure of the Court and if in smiting he shall hurt or wound another he shall pay for the cure, and also for his time that he is thereby hindered."

And: "...whomsoever shall rise up as a false witness against any man to testifye that which is wrong, there shall be done to him as he had thought to have done unto his neighbour, whether it be to the taking away of Life, Limbe, or Goods."

February 22. The Dutch States General ratifies its 1650 agreement with the United Colonies. The Long Island boundary line between the two is "from the western part of Oyster Bay, so and in a straight and direct line to the sea."

March 19. Believing themselves to be vulnerable to England's continued colonial rivalry with the Dutch, East Hampton's freeholders order Lion Gardiner, Thomas Baker, and John Hand "to Hartford to unite East Hampton with Connecticut." . In late March, Connecticut agrees to take East Hampton under its protection. The town will remain in control of its affairs, but a Connecticut deputy is given a seat in General Court.

October 7. The Town orders: "...whosoever being chosen constabell or secretary and shall refuse to serve and not give a sufficient reason shall pay 30s; and if any that is chosen Townsmen and refuse without a sufficient reason shall pay 40s."

November 24. The Town orders: "noe man shall let any ground to any Indian for to plant on upon the penalltie of 2£ every acker it is allso ordered that no wigwams shall be sett up by any Indians whatsoever within our bounds without leave of the towne on the penallty of paying 2£ 10s...It is alsoe ordered that noe Indian shall travell upp & Down or carrie any burdens in or through our towne on the sabbath Day & whosoever bee found soe Doeing shall be liable to corporall punishment unto the nature of the offense..."

1657

February 4. The recorder enters: "it is ordered by the 7 men that noe man woman nor child shall plant any Indian corne with 8 fote of any outside fence nor set any stacks of corne or hay by any outside fencewithin the same compase above mentioned..."

April 7. The Town orders, "yt whereas formerly there was by Agreement from an Act an order made amongst us that one Generall Court should be houlden the first 3 Day of Aprill it is uppon consideracon ordered yt for time to come this Court shalbe houlden the first 3 Day of March & the other court for election to stand as formerly wch is the first 3 Day of October."

July 9. The Town clerk records: "Att a town meeting it was concluded and agreed upon that Mr. James shall have his 50 lb by the year paid him in good merchadable pay as it will passe currant to the merchant."

October 5. Robert Bond and William Mulford   inventory Annanias Conklin's Estate:

"Imprimis, one Dwelling house and one and twenty ackers of land.

"Item 2 cowes: 3 working oxen: 2 yearlings and one calfe. Item 4 goates: 7 swine. Item about 3 ackers of wheate and about 2 ackers of Indian corne and one acker of pease wheat & selfe at the whom lott... item 2 bedds & 2 boulsters & one Rugg, 2 Iron pots & one paler of pott hookes & one brasse kittle one brasse candlesticke. 2 pewter dishes, one pewter pott & one pewter salt seller one Dripping pan item 3 wooden bowles & 2 barrels one poundeing tubb one churne one lininge wheele one chest one knedinge trough. One payer of cobbirons one spit one payer of tonngs and one payer of hackes & one iron chaine & hookes for a yoke. One sithe & 2 gunes & one

fellinge axe & one paier of forke tines and one payer of woll
cardes. Item one carte & wheeles and one stone hamer. Item 6
loade and a halfe of hay."

October 7. The Town majority resolves: "It is ordered that
whosoever being chosen Constabell or Secretary and shall
refuse to serve and not give a sufficient reason shall pay 30s;
and if any that is Chosen Townsman and refuse without a
sufficient reason shall pay 40s."

November 2. General Court majority vote favors: "for The
prevention of Disorder in Courts or meetinges of the Towne by
ppounding many thinges wch may tend to confusion in yt kind
it is agree by this Court yt noe man shall ppound any matter
unto the towne himselfe but shall make knowne his case unto
one of the townsmen yt soe by them it may bee Orderly
ppounded unto the towne..."

1658

February. Early in the month, Gardiner's daughter, Elizabeth
Gardiner Howell, falls ill. For several days, she languishes in
bed with a high fever. Weaving in and out of delirium, she
curses and rails against Goodwife Garlicke (also known as
Goody Garlicke). She calls Goody a witch, accuses her of
sticking her with pins, and says, "I would tear her in pieces and
leave the birds to pick her bones."

After Elizabeth dies, the news of her accusations blankets the
plantation. On the chance that witchcraft might exist in East
Hampton, the Court decides to review the allegations.

February 19. The Court starts to hear the charges brought
against Joshua Garlicke's wife, a woman much-disliked for her
idle gossip. Under oath, Samuel Parsons states that when he
visited the Howells, Arthur Howell told him that his wife
"thought she had gotten some could with leaving off an under
waistcoate and putting on a thinner and she said her head
ached." He also tells the Court that, after Elizabeth went to bed,
he heard her cry, "A witch, a witch; now you are come to torture
me because I spoke 2 or 3 words against you." Parsons adds
that in the night, he and Howell heard a noise, but when they lit
a candle, they found no cause for it.

William Russell testifies that, on the sabbath morning, he
heard a "doleful noise on the back side of ye fire." When he
asked Howell what it was, Howell told him that it sounded like a
great stone had been hurled into a pile of other stones.

Corroborating his friend's testimony, Howell adds that, at one
point, his wife raged against the witch, "stroked" the bed, and
tried to free herself from his arms when he held her down.

Parsons, Russell, and Howell agree that when Elizabeth Howell sent for her father, she said that she didn't want her mother to know how she was "taken."

February 23. Elizabeth's husband and her father sign an agreement. Howell will have sole charge of his infant daughter and her education. He will keep the possessions that Gardiner gave Elizabeth (lot and house, across the way from the Gardiners, furnishings, and ten head of cattle), and, will take care of Elizabeth's personal effects until their daughter is fifteen years old. At that time, she will inherit them.

February 24. Goody Simons, who tended Elizabeth Howell just before she died, tells the Court that, three separate times, she heard Elizabeth say, "Send for Goody Garlicke ... " And, when she, Goody Simons, asked, "wt would you have with her?" Elizabeth answered, "I could teare her in pieces."

Goody Simons says that Elizabeth called Goody Garlicke "a duble tounged woman ... " and asked "did you not see her last night stand by the bedside readie to pull me in peeces and she prickt me with pins ..."

This same day, Elizabeth Howell's mother gives a deposition before John Mulford, John Hand, and Thomas Baker. Thomas Talmage records her words.

"The Depont Delclareth me husband he came home againe before Day &...he told me yt bettie was very badd & I said wt shall I Doe for I cannot rise & wn I rose upp I fell back againe & I lay an houre after & yn I rose upp & houldinge by Marie Stratton I went thither...& I asked bettie how she Did & she put out her hand oh mother she cried & I cried & she said mother I am bewicht and I not regarding it said you are a sleepe or a Dreamed and she tould me yt she was not asleepe and I asked her who she saw and she said Goody Garlicke in ye further corner and a black thing at ye hither corner both at feete of ye bed and then I charged her yt she should not tell her husband, nor noe living soule and I said your husband will tell."

February 27. In Court, Goody Brookes testifies that she heard Mrs. Gardiner tell someone that "her Daughter was biwicht & yt it was a woman."

Goody Burdsill reveals that Goody Davis once told her that she had just "dressed her child in cleane linnen at the Island & Goody Garlicke came in & said how pretty the child Doth loke & soe sone as she had spoken Goody Garlicke said the child is not well for it groaneth & Goody Davis said her hart did rise & Goody Davis wn she took the child from Goody garlicke she said she saw Death in the face of it & her child sickened...and never opened the eyes or cried till it Died..."

Goodman Vaile and his wife refute this story. They tell the Court that Goody Davis let her own child starve when she took in an Indian child to nurse, in exchange for some wompom.

March 11. The Clerk records Goody Burdsill's testimony:

"The Depont declareth yt when Mrs Howell lay sick on the lt Day of the weeke in the forenone yt she heard Mrs. Howell say she is a Duble tongued woman the deponant asked her who she meant but she made me noe Answere to it and then she lay still a little space of time & then she said that she had spoken but 3 words against her & now she was come to torment her I asked her againe but she gave me noe Answere to it ye Deponant farther saith that she heard Mrs. Howell say Garlick you Jeared me did you wn I came to yor house."

March 19. The Town votes "Thomas Baker and John Hand is to go unto keneticut for to bring us under their Government according unto the termes as Southampton is and alsoe to carie upp Goodwife Garlick yt she may be delivered up unto the Authoritie there for the triall of the cause of witchcraft which she is suspected for."

May 3. The union between Connecticut and East Hampton is drawn:"... whereas formerly some overtures have passed betwixt the Generall Court of Connecticut and...of East Hampton upon Long Island concerning union with one body and government, whereby the said towne might be interested in the generall combination of the united colonies; and whereas the said town of East Hampton was by the said Court entertained and accepted at a session thereof on the seavanth day of November 1649, and have after divers yeares of further consideration againe renewed their desires to bee under the said Government of Connecticut...It is concluded and agreed between the said Jurisdiction of Connecticut...and the said towne of East Hampton doe by their said Deputies for themselves and their successors associate and joyne themselves to the jurisdiction of Connecticut to bee subject to all the laws there established, according to the word of God and right reason.

"...The towne of East Hampton, by reason of their passage by sea, being under more difficulties and uncertaynties of repairing to the severall Courts held for the jurisdiction of Connecticut upon the maine land whereby they may be constrained to bee absent both at the times of election of magistrates and other occasions, which may prove prejudiciall to them; for preventing whereof it is agreed for the present untill more plantations bee settled neare the towne of East Hampton which may be helpfull each to other in publicke occasions and that by mutuall agreement betwixt the said townes and the Generall Court for the jurisdiction of Connecticut it bee otherwise ordered, there shall bee yearly chosen two magistrates inhabiting within the said towne or liberties of East Hampton who shall have the same power with the particular courts upon the river of Connecticut, though no other Magistrates of the jurisdiction bee present, for the administration of justice and other occasions which may concern the welfare of the said towne...

"It is also provided that the Freemen of the said town of East Hampton shall have liberty to vote in the Courts of Election for the jurisdiction of Connecticut (in regard of the distance of the place) by proxie...the said towne shall have Liberty to regulate themselves according as may bee most suitable to their owne comforts and conveniencies, in their own judgment; provided those orders made by them concerne themselves only..."

May 20. The Connecticut Court issues East Hampton its written opinion on Goody Garlicke: "tho there did not appeare sufficient evidence to prove her guilty yet we cannot but well approve and commend the Christian care & prudence of those in Authority with you, in searching into yt case accordinge to such just suspicion as appear. Also we think good to certify yt it is desired & expected by this court, yt you should carry neighborly & peaceably, without just offence, to Jos. Garlicke & his wife, and that they should doe the like to you..."

May 22. Wyandanch confers on East Hampton's Inhabitants the right to pasture their cattle on Montauk for seven years, and the right of first refusal to that land, should the Montauketts decide to sell it.

The document to which he puts his mark is the first direct contract made between the settlers and the Indians. It addresses lands beyond Napeague to the point named by the Indians *wampomomon*. The land is well-wooded, hilly, irrigated with fresh water ponds and springs, and contains some extensive plains. The Indians' annual rite of burning the woods and marshes in March has helped to limit underbrush growth, provide fresh vegetation for the deer, and enable them to sow corn in great quantity, with relative ease.

November 13. By his "own voluntarie motion and uppon Consideration knowne to my selfe," Wyandanch conveys to Rev. James "the one halfe of all the whales or other great fish yt shall at any tyme bee cast up uppon the Beach from Napeake Eastward to the end of the Island ... to have & to hold the same his heir & assignes forever. And the other halfe of the said whales I give to Leiftenant Gardiner my friend to be equAlly devided betwene the two: be it known yt for the first good whale they shall freely and for nothing have but the whales in future times shall bee cast uppon the beach aforesaid, they shall give to me or to my children & successors   after my Decease what they shall Judge meete..."

November 30. The Townsmen order "that the addisions on the East side of the towne shall run down to the pond or swamp..."

1659

March 2. The Town decrees: "noe man shall have libertie to sell strong waters but such as are Deputed there unto by the towne and alsoe such as are apoynted for yt end they shall kepe an exact & Just measure for to sell the same by & farther they shall not sufe younge people yt are under other mens Gouvernment to bee in their house at unseasonable times in the night contrarie unto their masters or parents knowledge or leave...." No more than half a pint is to be sold to or be drunk by four men together "but in case a stranger come in he may have libertie to have one quarter A pint if the man yt is Apoynted to sell the same doe se yt his nede doth call for it ...."

April 19. The Town recorder notes: "It is ordered that every man shall sett the two letters for his name at each end of his fence in large letters on the inside of the post above the uper raile by the 4 day next upon penalty of 2s 6d a pcell...." (Sheep, horses, and cattle must be kept on owners' land during the months when they are not grazing on Montauk and have use of the common land in East Hampton.)

July 14. Wyandanch deeds Lion Gardiner a "small tract of land" that "lieth between Huntington and Seatacut, the westerne bounds being cowharbor, easterly Arhata a munt, and southerly crosse the island to the end of the great hollow or valley ..."

   (The land is the sachem's gift to Gardiner for having fulfilled a promise he made six years earlier. In 1653, Naragansett Indians attacked the Montauketts during the ceremony uniting Wyandanch's daughter with a young Indian. The groom was slain and Heather Flower and her fourteen attendants were taken captive to the mai..land. Gardiner vowed to see that she was returned alive.)

Summer. Wyandanch dies.

1660

Spring. The Montauketts, whose numbers have been decimated the last six years by the marauding Naragansetts, flee Montauk and seek refuge in East Hampton. There, Rev. James allows them to pitch their tents on land close to the parsonage.

August 6. To underscore their gratitude for the shelter and the kindnesses which their "friends and neighbors of East Hampton" gave their people the past months, Wyandanch's widow, the sachem squa, and their son, Wyancombone, put their mark on a deed. It ratifies the earlier sale of Montauk land to the seven Proprietors, and conveys to them more of Montauk, ranging from the easternmost tip westward, to the eastern boundary of East Hampton (as defined in the 1648 purchase). Payment is to be 10£ and ten bushels of Indian corn a year for ten years.

  The Proprietors' counter bond gives the Indians and their heirs permission to live on Montauk whenever they wish. If they go on Montauk, they forfeit the annual payment of 10£ stirling, or its equal value. But, the Proprietors caution the Montauketts that they "shall still acknowledge the Land to be ours by bargaine." (Town residents, who do not own land in common with the Proprietors, pay field Rights to pasture their livestock on Montauk.)

September. The Proprietors and the Montauketts petition the commissioners of the united colonies of New Haven, Hartford, and Massachusetts for a six mile radius zone of protection from the cruelty being inflicted by the marauding Narragansetts.

September 25. The Town clerk records: "For as much as we have fully bought all Meantaquit and our purchase being approved by the commissioners and they have ordered us to record it at Hartford it is therefore ordered and agreed that no man shal sell give or lett any part or parcell of it or his commonage to any foriner whatsoever but it shall forever remain and be wholy entire to the inhabitants of this towne forever." Violators will be fined 30£.

October 1. The Connecticut Commissioners' response to the East End's petition for protection from the Naragansetts is read at a General Meeting. East Hampton, Southampton, and Southold are granted the right to resist and remove any invading Indians, providing that the "Indians on Long Island do not begin new Quarrels but behave themselves without provocation."

1661

September 2. The Town orders the owners of cattle that are going on Montauk to "pay 10£ on the whole yearly until purchase price is paid, said 10£ to be divided to every already attested inhabitant, except John Kirtland, who refused to have any share in the purchase, and attested inhabitants aforesaid are to bear their equal share in purchase."

1662

February 6. Once again the Montauketts show their appreciation for the protection they received during the latest conflict with the Pequots: "whereas of late yeaees there haueinge bene sore distress & Callamitie befalln vs by reaon of the Cruell opposition & violence of our most deadly enemye Ninnecraft Sachem of Nasriganset, whose Crulltie hath proceeded soo far as to take away the liues of many of our dear freinds & relations, soe that we were forced to flee...for shelter to our beloued freinds & neighbors of Easthampton, whom we found to be bee freindlie ub in our distress,...our dellieurers Cordiall & faithfull..." the Proprietors are given a portion of land that lies west of Fort Pond. It is called Hither wood. Like the deed of 1660, the "Deed of Gift" reaffirms their right to return to Montauk whenever they wish.

May 16. The Town recorder notes: "An agreement made betwene John Hand Stephen Hand and Isaak Hedges, and the townesmen wth the assistance of the magistrats and most of the Inhabitants thet is to say that the three men first above named shall well and faithfully keepe the drie heard at Meantaquit both great Cattell & calves for the sum of twenty shillings a weeke to be payd in wheat at 5s pr bushell or corne at 4s pr bushell half one half the other or beefe or porke at price Currant or Cattell as Indifferent men shall prise them from the day of the date here of till a month after Miheltide."

. Gov. Winthrop returns from an extended stay in England. Following the Restoration in 1660, he worried that his colony would not have legal standing. Like that of the New Haven colony, it had been operating without a charter.

To avoid any chance of legal displacement, he sailed for England to secure written confirmation. He brings back a charter that absorbs the New Haven colony into his corporate colony, and includes "islands adjacent." Deeming this to mean Long Island, Winthrop claims it for Connecticut.

October 9. Connecticut's General Assembly reaffirms "in full force & vertue all Lawes & orders of this Colony formerly made...unless any be repugnant to the Tenor of our Charter." Applying also to Long Island, the statutes include:

"Whereas Divers persons Depart from amongst us and take up their aboad with the Indians in a pfane course of life for preventinge whereof, It is ordered yt whatsoever parson or parsons that now inhabiteth or shall inhabit wth in this Jurisdiction and shall Depart from us and setell or Joyne wth the Indians that they shall Suffer three yeares imprisonment at least in the house of Correction and undergoe further sensure by fine or Corporall punishment as the perticuler Court shall Judge meet to inflict in such Cases."

November 7. The clerk records: "Upon Serious consideracon and tedious debate it is at last agreed that John Osburne & Stephen Osburne shall have eight pound for keepinge the two ould hounds a yeare...and they are to have a house built at the end of John osburnes barne and this to be borne by the whole towne except those that have pupies..."

1663

January 7. The Inhabitants agree to divide the town into three parts for the cutting out of whales "after ane more is cut by the North end,...the town shall be divided as follow into three parts: a 11 is a Company the division to be.

In addition, "it is fully agreed that Mr Jamess & Mr Gardiner shall give A quart of licker a peece to the cuters of every whale & bee free from cuttinge."

February 11. The East Hampton and Southampton Proprietors agree that Quashawam ("Heather Flower") should be chief sachem of the Montauk and Shinnecock tribes. The tribes are "to pay her all honors according to the custom of the Indians." The Montauketts agree not to "plunder" the Shinnecocks, without first consulting the Proprietors.

March 2. The Town orders the Montauketts to stay out of Town, "after sufficient notice upon penalty of paying 5s or be whipped until they be free of the small poxe." However, "they may come where they have corne on the back side."

. Lion Gardiner dies, aged 64.

1664

March 12. Charles II ignores the New World boundary agreement that was reached fourteen years ago between England and Holland. Today, the King makes a *First Grant* to his brother, James, Duke of York, his heirs, and his assignes.

The Grant sweeps across New Netherlands, from the St. Croix River to the Delaware River, and embraces Long Island. Annual payment for the Grant is forty beaver skins, if the King demands it.

(Following the deaths of Lord Stirling and his son, Charles II ordered his Prime Minister, the Earl of Clarendon, to buy - for *his* private ownership, not for the Crown's - Stirling's title to his Long Island holdings. The purchase, which did not include the adjacent islands, and did not mention the 1638 Augmentation, was made in the name of the Lord of the Manor of East Greenwich, in the County of Kent.

Through right of family inheritance that has nothing to do with his rights as Lord of the Realm, Charles is the Lord of this particular Manor. The purchase gave him personal control over Long Island. In issuing the Grant, he passes this feudal power on to the Duke, who is underlord of the Manor. Absolute authority of government extends over *all* of the land that Stirling held, not just Long Island.)

March 21. The Town and Isack Hedges agree "yt hee shall finde & maintaine a sufficient Drume and be Drumer for 40s pr annum to be paid in a town rate."

March 25. A lengthy debate ensues before the Town majority agrees "that the purchase of the Patten right should be borne by all the inhabitants accordinge to the lands evry man possesseth."

April 2. Charles II appoints Col. Richard Nicolls to be Lt. Governor of the New World holdings. Nicolls is to sail, at once.

April 26. The Clerk records today's decision: "The towne doth desire those men that doe goe to Hartford to debate together and with the neighbour Plantacons for the things of mutuall Consernement between Hartford & us for our further settlement but to conclude of nothinge, as understanding that the Governour will come over, or a committee from the Court."

August 19/29. A fleet of four British ships, with Col. Nicolls and soldiers aboard, sails into the harbor of New Amsterdam. The Dutch give little resistance. The British flag is run up at the fort, New Amsterdam is renamed New York and the Province of New Netherlands acquires the same name. Nicolls replaces Stuyvesant. Assuming the title of Deputy-Governor, he answers only to the Duke.

October 4. With Governor Nicolls present, Quashawam and East Hampton reach accord. Nicolls confirms the sachem's right to 4000 acres east of Fort Pond on Montauk. (At a recent meeting of the United English Colonies, Southampton resident and real estate dabbler, John Ogden, had accused East Hampton and Lion Gardiner of cheating the Indians of their land.)

December 1. In New York, the New York and Connecticut representatives remove Long Island from Connecticut protection and place it under the Duke of York's holdings.

. Lion Gardiner's widow, Mary, dies. Displeased with their son's frivolous spending, Gardiner had left his entire estate to his wife, with the proviso that she give David and their surviving daughter "as God shall put it into her mind what she will and to dispose of all, as she will." Mrs. Gardiner leaves the Island to David, specifying that it is to go from him to his first-born son and, from that son to his first-born son, ever more.

December 21. The Town majority votes "yt those yt come first to mill with Corne and cattell shall grind first..." and, "understanding that we are off from Connecticut, and the magistrates not willing to act further on that account, that we may not be without laws & Government, it is agreed the former laws shall stand in force till we have further order from York. It is agreed that the Constable of the Town shall be secured by the Town for not gathering the Rates."

December 25. Samuel Dayton deeds his son, Jacob, to Thomas Baker and his wife, Alice, for fourteen years. The Bakers are to feed and clothe him as if he were one of their own. Should the Bakers die during the time Jacob is with them, he becomes a free person.

(The custom of giving a child to another family is not uncommon. It lifts an economic burden on a family which has too many children, and provides more farm and house help for a small family).

1665

February 6. The Dutch Recorder enters: "On the petition of the Directors of the Incorporated West India Company of this country, it is after Consideration, resolved and concluded to authorize said Directors hereby to attack, conquer, and ruin the English everywhere, both in and out of Europe, on land and water; with whatever force, through God's blessing, the above named Company now hath under their High Mightinesses authority."

February 8. In a proclamation dispensed to Long Island's towns, Governor Nicolls asks each one to send two delegates to a meeting in Hemptstead, "the last day of the month, to adopt the *Duke's Laws*. The deputies are to be chosen by freemen... whether English or Dutch, within your several towns."

The proclamation states: "Whereas the Inhabitants of Long Island have for a long time groan'd under many grievous inconveniencies and discouragements occasioned partly from their subjection, partly from their opposition to a foreign power, in which distracted condition, few or no laws could be put in due execution, bounds and titles to lands disputed, civil liberties interrupted, and from this general confusion, private dissension and animosities have too much prevailed against neighborly love and Christian charity....

"For preventing of the future growth of the like evils, his Majesty, as a signal grace and honor to his subjects upon Long Island, hath at his own charge reduce't the foreign power to his obedience, and by patents hath invested his Royal Highness the

Duke of York with full and absolute power in and over all and every the particular tracts of land therein mentioned, which said powers by commission from his Royal Highness, the Duke of York, I am deputed to put into execution."

February 9. Thomas Talmage and Thomas Thomson are appointed to meet with Southampton and Southold deputies, to consider the best way for the towns to be represented in matters of law, since Hartford will not let them join the colony.

March 10. With Thomas Baker and John Stratton representing Easthampton, New York's first Assembly of Representatives concludes its ten-day meeting in Hempstead. ("Representatives" is too broad a stroke. The government exists only at the Duke's pleasure, and the Hudson valley area is barely represented).

Based on English law and those of New Haven and the Massachusetts Bay colonies, the *Duke's Laws* enacted in Hempstead replace the ones under which the towns had governed themselves. The towns become part of a shire, and the shires are divided into Ridings. Long Island has three, East, West, and North. The East End towns are in East Riding. Each Riding has a court of sessions, with three justices, who will meet twice a year to weigh all matters criminal, and nearly all civil.

A High Sheriff, to be appointed each year by the governor from three names submitted by each Riding, will sit with the justices of each court. (The office of sheriff, usually held by a wealthy land owner, is a carry-over from England. After the Norman Conquest, the Sheriff became the highest office in each shire, responsible for its government. In England, he answers only to the Crown. Here, it is to the governor).

In addition to formulating new laws, Nicolls has been empowered to order each town to purchase a Patent.

June 22. Nicolls sends a communique to "all officers both Civil and Military to bee Communicated to ye Inhabitants of the East Riding of Yorkshire:

"Gentlemen, I am commanded by this Nation to give you notice, that after the great Spoyles and Depredaçons done by the subjects of the states of ye United Provinces, upon his Maties good subjects in severall parts of the world, for which no Satisfacton by way of Treaty can bee obtained, his Matie for defence of his Subjects, his Crown, and his Dignity, is necessitated to enter into a Warr...you are hereby required in yor severall Qualityes and Conditions, to bee watchful in your severall Townes, to give notice to each other, of any shipps of warr, that shall appeare upon the coast, and with all Expedicon that every Towne bee Aiding and Assisting to each other; His Matie is informed that De Ruiter hath Orders to Attempt the

Recovery of this place, and commands mee to provide the best I can for the defence of it. Therefore, I require you to put yourselves into such a Posture and readynesse, that upon the first notice (which shall be sent yo) You shall immediately repaire to the fferry, over against New Yorke, as a place for a place appointed for a general meeting with your Armes, hereof you are not to ffaile, as also to make Publication hereof, in the severall Townes of your Riding as youll Answer ye Contrary at your Peril."

June 24. The Assembly addresses disposition of what it calls the Royale Fish - drift whales that come ashore, alive or dead:

"...any whale, or such like great fish cast upon the shoare of any precinct, shall be taken into the care of any of the Officers above mentioned to bee kept, or improved where it cannot be kept, and by such Officers onely, untill the Governour and Council (after notice sent) shall give further Order therein. And the Acknowledgement which shall be received for whales, or such Like great fishe cast upon the shoare of any precincts shall be the fifteenth Gallon of Oil."

September 5. The Town responds to damage, caused by neglect on the Great Plain: "Noone shall be allowed to keepe the Gin under Eighteene yeares of age and to stay till they be relieved accordinge to the former order and to pay all Damage that shall come by their neglect and noe Indian to keepe at any tyme and every man to warne his next neighbour before hee goes and he that comes not by sunn sett to relieve...shall pay 12d and soe for any that shall Depart before the tyme..."

September 11. John Kirtland transfers to Rev. James: "... all my right & interest I had in my servant Hopewell: Indyan: whom I bought of his guardyans being an orphan not one yeare ould... for the full terme of Nyneteene yeares, for a Considerable value vix 15£ in good pay; the said Hopewell being of the age six yeares this present tyme; his tyme coming forth at the age of 25 yeares according to the date hereof:

"the said Thos. James engaging himselfe heires or assignes for the good usage of this his apprentice & if hee continue with him to the aforesaid age or his heires or assignes the said Thos: doth bynd himselfe to give the said Hopewell ten pound in currant pay & a suite of Cloathes, in witnes whereof I set my hand & Seale."

Hopewell places his mark under Kirtland's signature.

October 4. Easthampton and Quashawam agree:

"1. The bounds of the town east to the Fort-pond and all the rest to the end of the island, to belong to the Indians; but not to be disposed of to any other than people of the town.

"2. The inhabitants forever to have full liberty at any time to cut grass on said lands, and for feeding of cattle, but not till the corn, planted by the Indians, shall be taken off.

"3. If cattle trespass on the Indians, by reason of not keeping up the fence, the town to make satisfaction; and if Indian dogs do damage to cattle, they to make satisfaction.

"4. Indians not to set fire to the grass before the month of March, without consent of the town. In consideration of all which, the town engages to pay, yearly, 40 shillings to said sunk-squa and Indians, their heirs and assign."

October 5. Nicolls issues David Gardiner a patent. It frees the island from being subject to any law of any town, makes it accountable only to the colonial governor or his successors, and assesses an annual quit rent of five English pounds. Payment for the Patent is to be made "at or upon the feast of St. Michaell the Archangell."

October 12. The Constable and Overseers order "from henceforth noe man shall presume to make Sale of his accomodacons or give entertainment to any Scandalous person or persons or any that may prove to be priujudiciall to the Towne without the Towne's Consent."

1666

March 13. Nicolls issues East Hampton a Patent. It ratifies land purchases already made within the set boundaries and grants the right to purchase other tracts of land within those bounds, be it from "the native Indian Proprietors, or others." The Patent also confirms that the "present habitation shall continue and retain the name of East Hampton," and it bestows on East Hampton "all the privileges belonging to a town within this government."

June 15. The Proprietors decree that no oxen may be within the "plaine fence upon the Lord's Day, unless men keep them within their particular inclosed land."

1667

January 16. The Constable and Overseers order "yt whosoever shalbe absent at any time appointed for towne meetings bing sufficiently warned 24 howers before and if any man withdraw or be absent halkfe a day 1s for not appearing when called 6d if he wt draw from the meeting 1s more, if absent ye whole day 3s."

July 19. Gov. Nicolls writes to the Constables, Overseers, and Justices of the Peace in each of the Long Island towns: "I have not given you the trouble of Alarums to interrupt yr private occasions, but the noise of warrs sounds from farr in other Plantations, and therefore it becomes necessary to direct and require you, that for the common safety in this time of danger your militia be put into the following wayes of defence and readiness to comply with these my present directions till further order:

"1. That one third of the Militia which are now in foot companies doe fitt themselves with horses, saddles & such armes as they have...to be ready at an houres warning...to answer all true Alarmes of an Enemy and my orders when I appoint them a Rendezvous.

"2. That the other two parts of the Militia remaine in or about their Plantations for the security of their Estates and families.

"3. That if any Towne be in more danger than another the Neighbouring Townes shall upon notice send releife to them.

"4. That the horsemen of each Towne hath Liberty to choose a corporall of their owne...and the whole Body shall select and make choice of their Captain, Lieutenant and Cornett."

1668

June 8. John Osborne is allotted "his division of Land laid out at wenscot which Land is to be laid out in Lew of the swampe..." His farm will be the first one settled beyond the core of the plantation.

November 3. Stephen Hand permits the Town to cut a highway "for one Cart to goe through his Lott in the woods...the highway is to be twelve foot in breadth and the length of the lott and it is only to drive carts and oxen in the yoake and to ride or lead a horse, through; and not to drive cattle through out of yoake."

November 16. Francis Lovelace, Nicolls' successor, writes to Rev. James: "...am heartily glad to see that the same hand that has influenced yr heart with a desire of advancing ye Gospell of Christ in the conversion of the Gentiles & bringing them to the knowledge of his Law has likewise bestowed on you the spirit of perseverance in so glorious a work...

"I very much approve yr composure of a catechism which as it was the primitive way of instruction so it is most practicable at this tyme for those darke souls who being not yet arrived to that degree which the Apostle speaks of being but babes in Christ...That which I shall desire from you at present is the Catechism with some few select chapters & Laudatory Psalms fairly transcribed in the Indian Language which I will send over to England & have quantities of them printed."

1669

June 28. Lovelace and the Council order: "...that a letter bee written in answer to Mr. Mulford and Mr. James, ffirst, to give them thanks for their care in engineering into the matters of ye Indians; that if they shall find ye occasion pressing, to send to all ye commissioners authorized for the carrying on ye Indyan affaires, to have a meeting and to take ye whole matter into examination, soe to send up a report of ye nature of it, and how they find it.

"That they bee very careful to shoe no apprehensions of feare, but to proceed vigorously in their acting That the Indyan called Aukeeanit bee examined and if occasion bee found, that he bee sent up hither as a prisoner...

"That Mr. James have a lycense to sell such small quantitys of powder, etc. and that he be freed from that as he desires.

"That Will ye Indyan bee ordered not to come into Easthampton or any of ye towns at ye East end of Long Island; ffor ye wch an order is to bee made..."

November 3. In a document on which they inscribe their marks, the Montauketts recognize Lovelace as their sachem:

"These may serve to informe ye Rt. Hon. ye Governor that I Ponquatton Counselor, Chekonnoo Roto, Ackompais, Keassowonk, Peniutute sachem at Montaukett, Askickotantup, Sanksquaw, do utterly disclayme any such vassalage as Ninecraft did declare to the Governor at Rhode Island & doe protest against it... & that we acknowledge ye Governour at New York as our chiefest sachem."

December 18. Reaffirming Wyandanch's agreement, the Montauketts Paunquinnacut, Wassoumann, Aukeeannitt "...doe freely graunt & confirme to ye sd Thos. James & to Jeremyah Conckling now standing up in ye rome of Lion Gardiner all the whales shall be cast up beyond ye fort pond att Meantacut, to them their heirs or assigned for ever uppon ye same tearmes as is before specified was ye graunt of ye ould sachem...."

1670

June 13. Majority vote decides that because John Osborne lives "Remote from the Towne it is granted to him...that hee shall have libertie to grinde at the Mill upon the 3 Day of every Weke from 10 a clock to 12. If any be grindinge at that time the said John osborne is to goe in next to those that come out Who ever be there in the compass of that time."

December 1. The Montauketts convey a portion of Montauk to John Mulford, Rev. James, and Jeremiah Conkling. The *Nine Score Acre Purchase* starts at Fort Pond, goes east to the woods beyond Great Pond and south to the ocean. If the three men decide to fence in their land, the Indians are to share the cost of half of the fencing.

1671

February 8. Mulford, James, and Conkling turn over to the Town all interest in the *Nine Score Acre Purchase*, their interest in the whales "excepted."

February 9. Lovelace answers John Mulford's Dec. letter:

"hope I have taken such a course (by Mr. Cooper) as may satisfy your complaint touching ye Exhorbitance of ye Indians, & truely if you reflect but on ye power I have invested you together with ye rest of your commissioners for ye Indian affaires, you will then conclude that I should rather expect to heare of ye Indians confirmitye to your orders, as to dispose them to a better temper of life than to heare any complaint of yours to ye contrary, since I have invested you with power sufficient to Exact an obedience from them but I hope all things are now to your satisfaction as to that perticular...

"I have likewise sent you my resolution concerning yours & Mr. James purchase of ye Indian land but in regard it has mett with fresh opposition from your Towne, I desire that matter may be a little suspended till I have ye opportunite (God willing) to visitt those parts & then I doubt not but to compose all affaires so as shall be to mutual satisfaction."

May 4. Rev. James and Thomas Baker are given "full power to treate and Conclude with the towne of Southampton and Southould or their Agents Concerninge procuring a Charter: and what priviledges and liberties can bee procured: either for the three Towns in generall or for this towne in perticuler or to make agreement with any persons or psons: now bound for England in order thereto."

May 11. Thomas Smith agrees to become the Town's blacksmith for six years and, to "faithfully perform his work." He will provide shoes for the horses, make the nails to hold them in place, and make nails for general use.

In return, he will have a lot, a house, and a shop that previously belonged to John Osborne ten or twelve acres of land within the eastern plaine, and "liberty to pasture six cows on the commonage."

Should Smith depart East Hampton before the end of six years, the property reverts to the Town. Should he leave after that time, the Town "is to have the forsakeing of the land they Giveing for it as much as others will Doe."

1672

March. France and England declare war against Holland.

June 24. The Town agrees "that the act of the Justices and Deputies assembled at Southold according to order from the Governour to Consider for our saftie in this time of danger and the letter that was sent by them to the Governour of their Determynation that they would Contribute to...repairing the ffort att yorke if they myht have the priveledges that other of his maties subjects in these parts have and Doe enjoy: it is well approved by this Towne and they are willing to Answer their part in the charge accordinge to their act if the priviledges may bee obtained but noe otherwaies."

("Others of his Maties' Subjects" include:

1. Rhode Island which, through a royal charter of 1663, was granted the right to representative Assembly.

2. Those who settled on a tract of land, "hereafter to be called by the name or names of New Caesares or New Jersey." It was deeded and released by the Duke of York, in 1664, to Lord John Berkeley and Sir George Carteret. Given the power to govern, the new Proprietors sought to attract newcomers to their land with an appointed council and an elected Assembly.

3. New England Colony, encompassing a dozen towns, which received royal recognition in 1662.

4. Maryland's freemen, who received right to representative assembly in 1638 from their Proprietor and Governor, the second Lord Baltimore. By 1650, these men had chosen to elect delegates to represent them in the Assembly, instead of having to meet themselves, and the Governor's advisors had formed an upper house legislature.

Meanwhile, New York Province continues under the feudal thumb of the Duke of York, as underlord of the Manor of East Greenwich, he choosing its governors.)[4]

July 3. In London, the Royall Council Clerk records:

"Upon reading this day at the Board the humble petition of His Majesty's Subjects in the villages at the East End of Long Island in America, called Easthampton, Southampton, and Southold, setting forth that they have spent much time and paines and the greatest part of their Estates in settling the trade of whale fishing in the adjacent seas, having endeavoured it above these twenty yeares, but could not bring it to any perfection till within these 2 or 3 yeares last past,

"And it being now a hopefull trade at New York in America the Governor and the Dutch there do require ye petitioners to come under their patent, and lay very heavy taxes upon them beyond any of his Majesty's subjects in New England, and will not permit the petitioners to have any deputys in Court, but being chiefe, do impose what Laws they please upon them, and insulting very much over the Petitioners threaten to cut down their timber, which is but little they have to casks for oyle,

"Although the Petitioners purchased their lands of the Lord Sterling's deputy, above 30 yeares since, and they have been till now under the Government and Patent of Mr. Winthrop, belonging to the Connecticut Patent, which lyeth far more convenient for ye Petitioners assistance in the aforesaid Trade...

"And therefore most humbly praying that they may be continued under the Government and Patent of Mr. Winthrop or else that they may be a free corporation as his Majesty's subjects for ye further encouraging them in their said Trade, otherwise they must be forced to remove, to their great undoing, and damage of sundry merchants to whom they stand indebted for their Trade...

"It was Ordered by his Majesty in councill That it be, and it is hereby referred to the Rt. Hon. his Majesty's Councill for forraine Plantations to consider of the said Petition, and report their opinion to his majesty thereupon with all convenient speed, And the said Councill is desired to give notice of this Petition to his Royal Highness the Duke of Yorke Commissioners that they may attend when ye same shall be under consideration."

July 7. Joseph Osborne marks his mother's gray colt with a star on the forehead, a crop and two slits crossways on the left ear and a slope on the hind part of the right ear. (All marks on livestock are registered with the Town).

1673

April 3. At its annual meeting, the Town resolves: "That where a professing people are planted and settled together, it is and ought to be their duty, with all care and diligence, to endeavor to the utmost for the maintenance and continuance of the Gospel of Jesus Christ amongst them, whereby their souls may be built up and edified in the ways of God."

To that end, major vote sanctions the purchase of over twelve acres on which to establish a parsonage.

. During the year, the Meeting House is enlarged.

June 13. The Court convicts John Hopping and Rebeckah Smith of fornication "by their own confession." They are fined seven pounds "for this notorious mysdemeanor." James and Hannah Bird are convicted of "incontynencie before Marriage" and fined 45 shillings.

June 24. Issack the Indian, who says that he is "Commonly known by that name among the English," acknowledges that he has hired himself to William Edwards, "Planter of East Hampton," as servant for half a year. Mr. Edwards promises to pay him 4£ for the service.

July 28/30. Confirming a report from Easthampton that a fleet of Dutch ships was sighted off the Atlantic coast, heading for Manhattoes, twelve men of war sail into Sandy Hook harbor on the 28th. Two days later, the Dutch recapture the fort.

July 31. Lovelace, who fled before the Dutch arrived at the fort, writes Gov. Winthrop: "... I am yet out of theire power & am hastening now over to Long Island to raise the Militia there ... "

August 7. The Dutch take control of their former province.

August 14. A Petition brought to Dutch officials in Jamaica by Rev. James and representatives of Southampton, Southold, Seataucok, and Huntington, is entered in government files. The Recorder writes:

"The Delegates requested an Audience and entering, delivered in their credentials with a writing in form of a Petition."

The paper memorializes their "rightfully & peacefully" union with Connecticut until 1664, when they were forced to submit to the Duke of York's agents. It also addresses the lack of intelligence received "to this day from Gov. Franc. Lovelace Esq. off what hath happened...or wt wee are to doe ..."

Then, they inform, "... since wee understand by ye post bringing the said declaration that our Gov. is peacebly & respectfully entertained into ye said ffort and citty; wee the Inhabitants off ye said East Riding or Deputies for us, att a meeting this day doe make these or request as follow...

"...if we come under ye dutch Goverrment, wee desire yt wee may retaine or Eclesiasticall Privilledges viz., to worship God according to or belieffe without anij imposition.

"That wee may enjoy ye small matters off goods wee possess, with or hands according to or Purchase of ye Natives,

"That ye oath off allegiance to bee imposed may bind us onely whyles wee are under Governmnt but yt wee shall bee bound not to act against them soe also not to take up armes ffor them against or owne Nation.

"That there may be ffree liberty granted ye 5 townes above sd for ye procuring from any of ye united Collonies (:without molestation on either side:) warpes irons or any other necessaries for ye comfortable caring of the whale designe."

The Recorder notes that the latter, or, "9th article cannot, in this conjecture of time, be allowed." (It is the only request of the ten to be denied).

. This same day, Dutch commanders Cornelius Evertsen and Jacob Bencken issue a Proclamation to the Long Island plantations: "Whereas the ffort and city on the Island Monhatons have surrendered themselves without capitulation... our said resolutions in generall unto all the English Towns upon Longe Iland & in particular upon the towne of Southampton to the end each towne should make a choice and send unto us here two Deputies with their letters of Authorization for to take oaths of allegiance, as also to bring with them the Constables staffes and colours, wee being intended instead of the same to furnish them with colours of the Prince of Orange whereuppon they shall be considered & governed without respect of nations as good and ffaithful subjects."

October 1. David Gardiner bows to the Dutchmen's wishes. He swears obedience to "their High Mightinesses" and asks that the status of both his island and his privileges remain intact. His request is granted.

October 2. On Colve's orders, Capt. William Knyf and Lt. Anthony Malipart have been visiting each Long Island town, east of Oyster Bay. They are to call Town meetings, propose that the townsmen swear allegiance "to their High Mightinesses and his Serene Highness" and promise the townsmen continued ownership of their land, freedom of expression and elections, in return for their pledge.

Today, Thomas Talmage gives the Dutch the Town's written response:

"Wee the Inhabitants of Easthampton understanding...that you desire an answer from us in particular wee being now met together doe Returne Answer that for the present our humble Request is: that there may bee noe further proceeding then hath been in former Transactions Between us and Your Selves & that for the future wee may be left to be Regulated by our fformer Lawes and that authority is resident amongst us, and this wee the more Earnstly desire from you because the severall amongst us from the first stood disaffected to any ingagement to your selves in point of government yet all of us cannot but acknowledge your Christian & Moderate dealing wth us and are as willing uppon all Occasions to retribute the like to your selves and to live peaceable Neighbours to you & doe Engage for ye future not to move in any act hostilety against you, and wee doe more Earnstly desire in that we cannot: but bee sensable of the great danger wee are in boath from those that are neere home so well as those abroad of Our owne Nation. Sr our owne Safty putting us uppon ye Suspending our further proceeding in this way wth you, soe hoping our humble desires in the premisses may find acceptance from you wee rest yours to Serve in what wee may."

October 3. Talmage writes Constable Thomas Dyment on behalf of some of the Town inhabitants: "Honord Sir - The Occasion of our writing is upon informaztion of some actings wth Respect to the answer we very lately sent by our Messengers wch wee are much troubled at wee sent a letter to you subscribed by our Recorders hand wch wee sealed, wch letter we understand was opened at Southampton before it was delivered & read to severall there wth severall Railling Expressions as wee are informed against it whereuppon our Messengers took upon them the boldnesse, to forme another our main Argument being taken out which was (that there was not the generall concurrence of the other townes with Respect to ye government as we Expected Etz) as also Etc:

"The truth is this is not the first time wee have had our letters opened & stopt at Southampton and many threatening Expressions have proceeded from severall disaffected persons there wth Respect to our submission to your government what we have yeilded unto we hope we shall never deny as some doe but shall owne & stand by what our deputy or deputies have Transacted with you but as Matters are in this confused way we know not which way to take desiring to approve our selves honest...

"...had ye Come heather to us with your commission wee should have imparted more of our minds to you & we hope to such good satisfaction to the government that they would see no Cause to lay Blame uppon us, & that the Innocent may not suffer with the Nocent we Understanding that ye were to goe on your Journey spidely & being late in the Night Could not Enlarge nor gett the Towne together but so many as could have consulted & made bold to send these few Lines as a hint how Matters are with us soe wee Remaine yours to serve."

October 22. Gov. Winthrop and the Hartford magistrates direct Samuell Willis and the governor's son, Capt. John Winthrop, (known in Connecticut as Fitz-John, to distinguish him from his father and grandfather):

"Whereas by divers Reports & Information wee are given to understand that there are some forces Expected speedily from New Yorke at the Eastern End of Long Island to force and Constrayne the People there to take the Oath of Obedience to the States Generall & prince of Orange; Wee have thought it Expedient to desire & Empower you Samuell Willis Esq. & Capt. John Winthrop or Either of you to take such necessary

attendance as you Judge meet & forwith to goe over to the said
Island or Shelter Island & treat with such forces as there you
shall meet & doe your Endeavor to divert them from using any
hostility against the said People & from Imposing uppon them
letting them know if they do proceed...it will provoke us to a
due consideration what wee are Next obliged to doe..."
October 31. After Knyf returns with a negative report on his
ride to the East End, Capt. Cornelius Evertsen sets sail for
eastern Long Island aboard the frigate *Zeehond*. With him are
the Dutch Commissioners, Councillor Cornelis Steenwyck, Capt.
Charles Epen Steyn, and Lt. Charles Quirynsen. Evertsen keeps
a daily journal.
November 6. Lying at anchor in Plumgat, the Dutch sight a
sail. Evertsen writes: "we...hoisted English colors; we supposed
him to be a west Indianman....The tide turning against him....we
lowered the English colors and hoisted those of the Prince,
whereuppon they instantly struck their colors. Commanding
them to come on board, the skipper arriving with two men,
reported that they came from New London and that Capt.
Winthrop and Mr. Willis were in his ship, being commissioned
by those of Connecticut. They said they would show us their
commission, to take a copy of it...whereuppon we showed them
our commission together with the articles penned by those of
the East End of the Island, and in consequence of it, their
nomination, and subsequent election &c.; the answer thereto
was exhibited to wit: That the 9th Article had not been
consented to, and consequently all the other articles, together
with their subsequent nomination and their actual submission to
their High Mightinesses had been rendered null & void."
November 7. Capt. Winthrop shows Evertsen their
commission and gives him a copy of a letter.
  Later, Evertsen writes down the events of the day: "...further
delivered us a copy of the Letter which was sent by the Court of
Connecticut to the Governor, Anthony Colve, and requested
that we should abandon our voyage and not proceed further in
persuading the English of Easthampton Southold Southampton
to take the oath, whereuppon we said that we were in duty
bound to execute our commission and so departed from
Sylvester's Island. In the meanwhile those of Connecticut
hoisted the King's Jack at their mainmast which was permitted
them as they were Commissioners."
. After the commissions travel to Southold, Everstsen writes,
"not one person spoke" when asked "if they would remain
faithful to their High Mightinesses...after many discussions pro

and con, we took up our commission and papers after having entered due protest and resolved to depart out of the village.

"On leaving the place, some inhabitants of Southampton were present, among the rest an John Couper, who told Mr. Steenwyck to take care and not appear with that thing at Southampton, which he more than once repeated; for the Commissioners, agreeable to their commission, had intended to go thither next morning; whereupon Mr. Steenwyck asked what he meant by that word Thing, to which said John Couper replied, The Prince's flag; then Mr. Steenwyck inquired of John Couper if he said so himself or on the authority of the inhabitants of Southampton.

"He answered, Rest satisfied that I warn you, and take care that you come not with that Flag within range of shot of our village. When taking leave of the Connecticut gentlemen they asked us to what village we intended to go first tomorrow morning, and they assured us that they should be there, as they intended to be present at every place the commissioners should visit. Entered the boat and rowed again to Shelter Island, and resolved not to visit the other two villages, as we clearly perceived that we should be unable to effect anything, and rather do more harm than good."

. In the next weeks, Dutch ships sail down Long Island Sound to Southold, threaten destruction if the inhabitants do not take the oath, attempt landings, and are surprised when their forays are repulsed by an army of men from Easthampton, Southampton, Southold - and from Connecticut.

1674

February 19. The Dutch and the English conclude the Treaty of Peace at Westminster. In exchange for the sugar-rich province of Surinam, now in possession of the Crown, the Dutch cede all of New York to England's Charles II.

June 13. The Town agrees "to Joyne with their Neighbors of Southampton and Southould to petition his Matie that they may bee Continued under the government of Kenneticut and priviledge of their Charter..."

June 27. Referring to a law in the colony which allows only those "knowne to be of an honest Conversation and accepted by the Major pat of the Towne," East Hampton's residents agree that the selectmen warn James Wright "having been here some space of time and hee not being Legally accepted of by this Towne,...to Depart this place...in their Convenient time."

October 31. In keeping with last February's Westminster treaty, the Dutch surrender their New Amsterdam territory to Sir

Edmund Andros, whom the Duke of York has appointed to be governor of his territories in America. Lange Eylandt again becomes Long Island.

. After lengthy study, English jurisprudence determines that the brief takeover by the Dutch of New York Province voided the powers of the *First Grant* to the Duke of York. So advised, Charles II issues his brother a *Second Grant.* As before, James is given absolute power over his American territory and any English person who lives within its borders.

November 18. East Hampton, Southampton, and Southold respond to a dispatch from Gov. Andros: "...being Informed by yor Honors Letter of November 5 that you much desired reestablishment of his majestys Authority at New York to the dispossessing yt insulting forraigner, is at length accomplished by yor Honors Happy arrivall, the which wee heartily congratulate and seeing by virtue of yor Honors Receipt of ye place & Government in behalfe of his majesty from ye Dutch, demand is made of these three Towns in Reestablishing ye constable & Overseers, which were in place of truth amongst us when ye Dutch came to Fort James in July...

"with all due Respect to yor Honor be pleased to understand yt although Fort James was not faithfully Kept for his majesty but unmanlike delivered to him and our Enimyes, whereupon ye poor, naked, unheaded people of severall Townes were forced to subject unto or suffer fury of the Dutch, - yett his Majestys Loyale subjects in these Three Townes, putting their lives in their hands, with expence of great part of their Poor Estates to his Majestys service back'd with ye undeneyable Demonstration of or (now) Associates cordyall Affection, or very loving Neighbor of his majestys colony of Connecticut succeeded by ye Blessing of almighty God they never were in ye Power of the Dutch - Either to be challenged as Conquered by them, or to be delivered to yor Honor our instrumentall saviours having in our Extremity not only protected us also Governed us, Establishing and commissionating Officers here, both civill and Military,

"To whom also we reengaged by ye Oath of God, and formerly by Patent priviledge, by his majestys Express Grant, wee can not either in civility or faithfulnesse doe more lesse without application to these his majestys substitutes that were so ready to take us up, when his Royall Highnesse Lieutenant had left us miserable, without either Aide or Councell, Starr or Compasse, to be vassulaged, would wee have suffered our selves (as they) to have been huft out of our Loyalty, Priviledge, and substance by an Insulting Enimy, but wee would be too Tedious, which might abuse yor Honor..."

November 24. Andros informs a meeting of the Council that East Hampton, Southampton, and Southold refused to make "any returnes upon my Orders sent unto them, for the settling the constables & overseers, nor taken any notice of his Majestie and His Royal Highness' Authority in these parts, after so long time and frequent opportunities."

December 4. Andros writes Winthrop about the prevailing attitude in the three East End towns: "...that I may not be wanting, I send this by expresse, being upon the receipt of a Letter...from the East end of Long Island signed by John Mulford, John Howell, and John Young, who having disobeyed my orders for the settling those parts pursuant to his majesties and his Royall Highnesse Authority, do in the said letter justify the same and would involve your colony with them by making them complices, which I do not at all credit, being confident you will not countenance, much less uphold, them against his majesties service, and not any wayes to obstruct his Prerogative Royall and his Royall Highnesse Right to that part.

"If...there be any pretended engagement between you (which cannot now be valid) I doe hereby desire you (to avoid all misunderstandings that may happen here upon) that you will send to disabuse any such persons at the East end of Long Island being now upon the dispatching of an express thither with my reiterated Orders in his majesties name, forthwith to bee obeyed at their utmost Perrills."

December 26. Andros instructs the Constables and Overseers on the East End "or to any of them who were in Office at the time of the Dutch coming into these parts in July 1673":

"...That your whole Towne may not be involved with them but all his majesties good subjects there may have the benefit of the care his majestie and his Royall Highnesse have taken for the future safety and welfare of this province, and bee secured in their Rights and Property... require you forthwith to put into execution my forms Order...by reassuring yor offices of Constables and Overseers in your Towne; And to all Persons whom it may concerne are hereby in his Majesties name, strictly charged and required to permit you so to do...in the due performance whereof, I doe declare that none of you shall bee any ways molested or questioned for your late omission, except the three Persons who signed the letter sent me as aforesaid, from whom I expect a farther Account."

. This same day, Andros orders Captain Sylvester Salisbury "employed to the East End of Long Island" to carry the above

Warrants and Orders to the three townes, starting at Southold, and staying twenty-four hours in each to receive an answer.

December 28. Two days after he dispatched Salisbury to secure answers to his warrants from the three East End towns, Andros writes Gov. Winthrop that he himself has returned "from settling things at the East End of Long Island the 22nd instant...All things there being settled (quiet) and I thinke to Generall satisfaction, as well as mine ...."

1675

April 6. In a letter to him, the Duke of York responds to Andros' glowing reports: "...I am well satisfied with your proceedings hitherto and that you are in quiet possession of that place but more especially at your conduct in reducing to obedience those three fractious townes at the East End of Long Island."

August 10. The Town agrees that Mr John Laughton "shall kepe Scoole and teach the children to reade and write...to begin... the sixteenth of this Instant and soe to kepe untill the last of December next and then to breake of by reson of the whale Designe untill the first of April next Ensueing and then to begin againe to kepe scoole to make upp the time of one whole yeere for which service the Towne have agreed to give unto Mr. Laughton the full Sum of fortie shilling a month and his Dyet."

October 5. Mosup, Wyandanch's sachem grandson, appeals to Andros for return of the guns that were confiscated during the recent war with the Dutch. Rev. James guides the sentiments expressed and pens the letter for him:

"I and my men understanding that your Honor was pleased to grant Liberty to the other Indians to have their guns returned to them, but a restraint was imposed upon us the Montaukett Indians by reason of some Complyance we have had with Ninecraft the Narbiggom sachem have sent this our messenger with these few lines to Intreate your Honor's favour towards your poor supplicants your honor may understand my father & grandfather have stood always loyal to ye English in ye Pequot wars now towards 40 years since my forefather was a great help to ye English having then this whole Island att his command & since then upon all occasions manifested his faithfulness to the English...& this is known to many of the English yet alive...though of late years we have had some correspondency with Ninecraft yor honor may be assured it was only with regard to our own society we being very weak & few in number & he being great & having woeful experience of the great desolation he made amongst us while we stood in terms of hostility against him but this we understanding is offensive to yor honor we shall forbear for the future only intreate yor honor to take some speedy cause for our security that we may not be molested by the Narhigansets for our dependence is wholly upon yor honor for protection as we hope yor Honor shall find us ever loyall subjects to the king and duke of yorke & to yor Honor & to all authority under you ... now is the usuall tyme of our hunting & to get a little provision & some skins for clothing & if our humble request herein may find a gracious answer, we shall take it as a further engagement to yor Honor & shall rest yor honor's humble servants."

On the other side of the paper, Rev. James adds his opinion:

"... I perceive that delivering up the armes to the Indians doth not relish well with the English, especially since of late we heard of the great slaughter they have made upon the English in other parts of the country. I perceive att Southampton ye English are much troubled ye Indians have their armes...as for these Indians for my owne part I doe think they are as cordiale friends to the English as any in ye country & what is written them is known to many to be ye truth... I leave to yor Honors prudence to act for ye best... "

October 7. Andros issues a directive to "The Aldermen of this City and to Magistrates and Officers in the respective Townes to cause this forthwith to be published and observed:

"An ord Prohibiting trade with Indyans.

"Whereas the General Court of Assizes now in this city, did yesterday make an Order strictly prohibitng the carrying any manner of Drinks or Goods to Traficke in any Indyan Plantaçon or Creeks, or selling any strong Drinkes to Indyans, in the respective Townes or places of Yorkshire upon Long Island & dependencies as also now Powder nor shott, but as is directed by the Law. These are therefore to Publish the same as you and every of you will answer the contrary at yr utmost Perills."

October 13. Coopers on the South Fork petition Gov. Andros:

"The Humble Petition and Addresse of the Coopers of South and East Hampton Most Humbly Showeth

"That there is a company of coopers yearly come in the winter season from Boston to work here that neither pay to Town nor county any Rates and teach young men their Trade for, A winters worke or some small tyme whereby there may be many poor workmen in the Towne which is greatly to the Damage of both Townes & merchants And if any of our Coopers in the Summer tyme when we have noe Employment at homme goe butt to Boston to work if they work under one of these coopers here cannot be permitted to work because hee served not his tyme there whereby it appears that they have A Law that none butt such as have served theyr tymes in that Jurisdiction may be permitted to sett up there.

"Wherefore wee most humbly beseech yor Honor would be graciously pleased to cause an Order to be made for the prohibition of any such that shall come here to sett up that have not in this Government Either served theyr tyme or are inhabitants thereof...And that theyir may bee a sworn searcher and gager that no unmerchantable Barrels may be putt upon merchants as frequently they are whereby the merchant is forced by reason of his Damage with his casque to sett higher prices of his good soo that both Planters and merchants are hereby wronged..."

October 16. Andros writes East Hampton: "Upon ye request of ye sachem of East Hampton & Mr. James ye minister recommendation about ye returning the Indians theyr Armes, It's not thought convenient to alter ye former Resoluçon but as ye Justice of peace & Chiefe Officers shall see cause, they may lett some few have theyr guns for theyr present use, they returning them again in some short time."

October 27. Andros writes to Thomas Baker in East Hampton:

"I have just now received yours of yer 24th of yr Indyans friendly Intelligence & Declaraçons of their Good wills & constant ffriendship which I shall also acknowledge upon all Occasions; & may assure them that if any Disturbance should happen to the Eastward, or any other against the Government, so long as they continue thus, they shall be sure of Protection and need not feare. But I find noe cause or Likelihood of their Intelligence, which I rather believe the ffancyes of some disaffected Indyans who would gladly have it soe, for I have not heard of one English man killed, much less 12...

"If any Trouble should happen you have by your commissions & Places of the Peace and militia sufficient Power to call before you, disarm, & committ any that shall goe about, or (you suspect) would break the King's Peace, not only Indyans but Christians. And if any resist, to make use of all the fforce of your Towne to reduce them. Pray both you and Southampton send daily to see your Indyans in their Plantaccons, and then unless you discover very good cause, bee not at all alarmed to hinder (as above) any you Occasion. I am Your Affectionate Friend."

December 2, Eleven Montauketts "bynde & ingage themselves" with eleven inhabitants (including Rev. James, Thomas

Chatfield, Robert Dayton, and William Edwards) "to goe to sea uppon the Designe of whale killing the present yeare & soe from time to time & at all times, soe long as this company of English aforesaid see cause to employ them...to preserve the boates irons & warpes & to cutt out the whale & bone & secure it so it can bee carted home for wch & in consideration hereof, the aforesd English men doe bynd & engage themselves...to Allow the aforsd Indyans halfe of what they gett both whale bone and blubber...each Indyan to provide one oare for this yeare... "

1676

June 8. In Southold, the Court of Sessions responds to royal instructions received by authorities the day before:

"At the request and uppon the Information of some of ye Considerable neighbourhood of Easthampton this Court Doth order as followeth: "In regards to the scarcity of good Timber in ye bounds of ...Easthampton and the waste thereof frequently made, & yt chiefly by such persons as have none, or very little Interest in ye Comons: it is ordered...no person not having an allotment, and thereby a right in the commons, shall make use of or cut timber in Easthampton...except they have first a lycense in writeing from the Constable and Overseers of ye Towne..."

1677

January 16. Andros writes: "The Magistrates and Officers of the Severall Towns on Long Island: "Whereas I am informed That severall ffamilies from the Eastward, being destitute, intend to come to settle at the East end Of Long Island, You are hereby desired and required to receive all such kindly, and to accomodate them without delay, with some suitable proportion of Land, where vacant and particularly to ffishermen neare the seaside and that they bring their Goods, all ffishing Craft and salt, to bee landed by any vessell or vessells they can procure (being free of all Dutyes) without coming to enter the same here, but with the Officer of the place who is required to give them present dispatch accordingly."

June. The Town petitions Anthony Brockholst, New York Province's new governor, about their plight: "...we are deprived and prohibited of our Birthright, Freedoms, and Privileges to which both wee and our ancestors were borne; although we have not forfeited them by any misconduct of ours, nor have we at any time been forbidden the due exercise of them, by command of our Gracious King, that we know of. And as yet neither we nor the rest of his majesty's subjects upon this island have been at any time admitted since then, to enjoy a general and free Assembly of our Representatives, as other of his majesty's subjects have had the privilege of. But Laws and Orders have been imposed upon us from time to time without our consent, (and therein we are totally deprived of a fundamental privilege of our English Nation,) together with the obstruction of Trafficke and Negotiation with others of his majesties subjects; so that we are become very unlike other of his Majesties subjects in all other colonies here in America, and cannot but much resent our grievances in this respect to the settlement of ourselves and posteritie after us."

1678

June 13. The Constable and overseers order, "noe pson in or belonginge to this towne shall receive or Enteraine any pson yt is alreadie come hither or yt hereafter come above one week unless they have license or libertie from the authority of this towne for ye same and that uppon ye penaltie of paying 5s."

1679

March 24. The Recorder reports today's decision: "Whereas there is different apprehensions concerning ye way of raising pay for a scoole master to teach Chilldren to write & reade which is so nedefull amongst us as well as in other places & therefore for ye deciding of ye same it is by a Major voate agreed uppon yt this towne hath referred ye determynation of it unto ye Right Honorble Governr and high Cort of Assiseth which way is ye most Just & Equallest to be carried on."

June 23. Benjamin Conklin offers to supply East Hampton's militia with Colors, at no cost, in return for being forever exempt from militia duties and from taking his turn at the watch - except during times of trouble. The Town accepts his offer.

1680

May 25. Isaac Mallyns logs the goods taken onto his boat:
"Received on board the barke as followeth: to say one case of tobacco pips one case of linen and woollen; one Case of Iron Ware one truncke with linen; one truncke with linen and sarge; one pack of sarge and Cersey; two barrels of gunpowder four barrels of Oyle, one bundle of whalebone All which goods afore said I promise to Deliver unto Mr. William Darvall or his orders the Dangers of the Sea excepted: he or they paying one

pound eleven shillings and nine pence for freight of the said goods as wittness my hand the day and date above specified.
   "The quantity Reseved the quality unknowne by me."
. Ships have been sailing from Northwest Harbor since the port was established in 1653. From there, merchants ship whalebone and oil, horses, fur, and other goods, in trade with the West Indies, Boston, and Rhode Island. Offshore whalers from Mecox and Sagaponack use the Harbor, too. They find that the trail through the woods brings them to the harbor quicker than the one which goes to the port at North Sea.
   . This year, the first families settle on their Amagansett lands. They are the Barnes, Conklins, Bakers and Schellingers.

1681

January 6. Quauguaheid puts his mark at the bottom of a contract: "I, Harry, alias Quauguaheid, Indian of Montauk, do firmly bind and engage myself to John Stretton, Sr., of East Hampton upon consideration that I am much indebted to him upon former accounts and his present supply of my present necessity do, I say, bind and engage myself to go whaling..."
April 2. The clerk records: "At a Generall Towne Meeting Mr. Thomas James and Capt. Josiah Hobart are chose as committies to meet with the neighbouring towns about sending a Redress to his Royall highness duke of york."

1682

February 19. The Town votes to have Thomas Baker represent its suit against the Indian called Nat for having leased some land in Montauk to Josiah Hobart.
April 9. Seth Parsons and Samuel Parsons witness the agreement that the Town makes with Quasequeg and his squaw. The Indians contract: "To Gin at the East End of the playne & to set their wigwam there Just within the fence & to be Continually there boath Night and day so as to secure horses and other catell from Comeing to doe damaige in the plains untill Indian harvest Next be fully Ended and the towne of Easthampton is to pay and allow being for his payns an Indian coate or ye Vallew of it and to allow and plow for them a akcer of good Land in some convenient place Near where their wigwam is to stand and also to pay them as they shall have occasion tenn bushells of Indian corne as witness their hands."
June 26. The Town clerk records: "Upon information that sundry persons of this towne doe Not only clayme part of the towns Land in that place which is called the Calf pasture, but also have gone soe farr as to stake it out to ther own use

Without any Knowledge or Consent of the towne therr and therefore by the Constable & Overseers to Impower John Stretton senr. and John Mulford to pluck up all such stakes that soe the towne May not be interrupted in Ther...improvement of the sayd prsells of Land according to ther Ingagmnt with Thos. James ther new Minister."

September 2. Thomas Dongan succeeds Andros as governor.

1683

May 10. Josiah Hobart agrees to relinquish all Title, Interest, and propriety in any part of the land "westward of ye Fort Pond & Eastward of Napeague." In return, the Montauk Proprietors agree to admit him as a co-partner and associate, and to have one full share in the Montauk holdings.

August 11. Renock Garrison enters into agreement with Abraham Hawkes and his wife. He binds two of his children to them, John, twelve in September; Anna, three and a half. John, who is to stay until he is twenty-one, is to be taught to read, write, and weave. Anna, who is to remain until she is eighteen, is to be taught to read and write. When they are of age to leave, each child is to receive two sets of clothing from the Hawkes.

August 24. Renock Garrison enters into an agreement with Isaac Mills and his wife. He binds his six year old son, Sam, to the Mills. Sam is to be their servant or apprentice until he is twenty-one. The Mills are to clothe and feed him and teach him the art and trade of a carpenter. When he is old enough to be free, the Mills are to give him two sets of clothing.

September 15. Should Frederick Ellis and his wife be allowed to become inhabitants of East Hampton? The question is raised at a Town meeting. The clerk records the decision:

"...But upon many reports yt are spoken of his loose vitious course of liveing, the constable & Overseers saw cause to warne him out of ye Towne, yet not withstanding this," Ellis brought his goods "to our landing place." None oppose the vote that he not be allowed to stay.

September 24. At a General Meeting, Thomas Talmage, Lt. John Wheeler, Samuel Mulford and Steven Hand are "chosen to meet at Southold, on Wednesday next to join with the committee of the other towns in choosing two representatives for this riding, to meet at York..." to help compose the "*Charter of Lyberties & Priviledges.*"[5]

They are empowered "to stand upp in ye assembly for ye Maintenance of our priviledges & English liberties,....Also, in the town's name, to certify capt. Young, that they do not send these persons in obedience to his warrant, but only because wee would neglect noe oppertunity to assert our own liberties." Rev. James is to go with them, to "advise with them in our concerns." **October 17.** In New York, the Legislature abolishes the three ridings, divides the colony into shires or counties, and, disregarding the Gardiner Island Patent, makes the island part of Long Island. Suffolk County becomes one of the ten counties of colonial New York.

1684

October. New York's General Assembly meets to draw up a Bill of Rights. The document includes the resolve that, as Englishmen, "Every freeholder and Freeman should vote...Trial to be by jury...No tax to be levied but by consent of the Assembly."

1685

June 16. By Major vote, every sheep owner must have one ram for every 20 sheep.

Those who do not comply will "forfeit the value of a good Ram to be bought with ye pay by ye select men & put into ye flock for the townes use."

. Within a few months of becoming king, James II revokes the laws he had sworn to uphold. He calls for direct taxation and an increase in quitrents.

As the Duke of York, he had exempted East Hampton from paying a quickrent, after the Dutch defeat, because the Dutch controlled Lange Eylandt when the town was settled. Now he demands it.

July 13. The Town Clerk records: "Rev. James and Capt. Hobart are chosen by ye Towne of Easthampton to goe upp to Yorke to treat with our Honourable governor Concerning the quitt rent of this towne...Provided you doe in noe way infringe any bound or Priviledge yt is allreadie in our Pattent but only to Procure an Instrument from his Honor which shall assertaine our quitt rent to be Equall with or not Exceedeing our Neighbor townes; And allsoe for a further confirmation of our former right from ye former governors & this you are to Observe as yor Positive Instructions..."

October 1. The Town issues a memorial to Gov. Dongan:

"Whereas at that time the Government of New Yorke was Established under our Soveraigne Lord ye King by collonell Nicolls & those gentlemen sent in Commission with him wee ye Inhabitants of this Towne, soe well as ye rest of the Island, being required, sent our messengers to attend their Honor & then both by word & writeing wee were promised & engaged

the enjoyment of all privelledges & liberties which other of his
Majesties subjects doe enjoy which was much to our Content &
satisfaction. Alsoe after this being required by these his maties
commissioners to send upp our Deputies to meete at
Hempsteade, And there the whole Island being Assembled in
our Representatives wee did then & there uppon ye renewall of
those former promises of our fredome & liberties, grant &
Compact with ye said collonell Nicolls Governor under his
Royall Highness, That wee would allow soe much out of our
estate yerely as might defray ye Charge of Publicke Justice
amongst us & for killing of wolves &c.

"But may it please yor Honor to understand that since yt time
we are deprived & prohibited of our Birthright freedomes &
Privlledges to which both wee & our Ancestors were borne;
although we have neither forfeited them by any Misdemeanor
of ours, nor have at any time bene forbidden ye due use &
exercise of them by command of our Gratious King yt we
know of; And as yet neither wee nor ye rest of his majesties
subjects uppon this islland have bene at any time admitted since
then to enjoy a generall & free Assemblie by our
Representatives as other of his majesties subjects have had ye
priveledge of, But Lawes & orders have been Imposed upon us
from time to time without our Consent and therein we are
totally deprived of a fundamentall Privlledge of our English
Nation Together with ye obstruction Trafficke & negotiation
with others of his Majesties subjects, so yt wee are become very
unlike others of ye King's subjects in all other colloneys &
Jurisdictions here in America, And cannot but much resent our
greivance in this respect & remain discouraged with respect to
ye settlement of ourselleves & posteritie after us,

"Yet all this time payments & performance of what hath bene
imposed uppon us hath not bene omitted on our parts although
ye performances of our Promised priveledges aforesaid have
been wholly unperformed, And what payments from yeere to
yeere this many yeeres hath bene made by us, hath bene made
use of to other purposes then att first they were granted for &
intended by us, so yt wee cannot but feare if ye Publick affaires
of government shall continue in this manner as they have bene,
but hope better, least our freedome should be turned into
bondage & our Antient priveledges so infringed yt they will
never arrive at our posteritie...."

The long memorial concludes with: "if...your Honor should
by reason of counsells & suggestions pursue a contrarie Course
to our humble desires, soe as to continue or augment our
greivances, then we request yor Honor's Pardon & excuse if in

our conscience to God & in Honor & submission to his majestie our most gratious soveraigne wee Prostrate our selves...And can doe noe Lesse in ye meane time but resent our forlorne & bereaved Condition....and humbly make bold to subscribe our sellves his majesties poor depressed though Loyail subjects: And yor most Humble servts."

Rev. James, John Mulford and Thomas Talmage sign, on behalf of the Town.

1686

January 23. By Major vote, the Town orders "yt John Hopping shall have at ye end of his land next to Georgica a little slow land added to his lott & to set his fence by ye pond side ye whole breath of his lott."

May. Dongan offers East Hampton a new Patent. It confirms and expands on the plantation's rights, as set forth in the Nicolls Patent. But the Proprietors view the price asked to pay for it as too high.

May 19. The Proprietors discuss the warrants that have been issued against Rev. James, John Mulford, and Thomas Talmage, for writing the Town's protest to Dongan last October. The men are to appear at York to answer the charges. In the belief that these charges are of public concern, the Proprietors tell the men to get all the help they can to defend their rights, and deputize two of them to seek Town assistance from Connecticut.

June 11. The Proprietors appoint a committee of six "to act in behalfe of the Purchasers & Proprietors in ye Legall Defense of their Just rights in their Lands or for ye Confirmation of their right to stand by them in what they shall Determine upon with respect to ye premises or ye Major Part."

July 29. Gov. Dongan and the Council meet in Fort James. Clerk Jonas Howell records the proceedings in the Suffolk Records: "Robert Cady, John Parsons, Jacob Dayton, John ffields, Samuell Sherry, Oliver Norris, William Hamilton, Daniell Kieff, Simon Hiillyer, John Richardson, makeing their complaints that the town of Easthampton will lay them out no land, as they were ordered in Councill to doe; & it appearing that the said Inhabitants have for more yn the space of fouer yeares payed all dutyes in the aforesaid towns and are become Associates in the same, Ordered that Capt. Josiah Hobart high Sheriff of the County of Suffolk see that a Surveyor lay out for each person of the aforementioned Inhabitants thirty acres of Arable land within the bounds of Easthampton that is not yet fenced or entered and appropriated by any person, they paying the charges which the said Sheriff & Surveyor shall be at in the performance of the same; & giving security not to dispose or sell any of the said land untill it shall be improved by them."

September 11. Dongan issues David Gardiner a patent. It creates the Lordship and Manorial of Gardiner's Island, allows the Manor to hold courts; includes, as part of the Manor, the two long sandbars at either end of the island; conveys all dock rights on the island to its Proprietor (as opposed to the colonial land office in Albany), and prohibits the uninvited from setting foot on the island without its owner's consent.

(At this time, David Gardiner's position is unique in the New World. Nowhere else on the continent does a single person enjoy the power and the privileges that have been granted to him).

October 6. In a warning that is nailed to the Meeting House wall, East Hampton rejects Dongan's July 29 order:

"...And doe hereby forbid and warne the said Kedy &c and Each of them or any others from or under them or any of them from any occupacon of any of the sayd Lands not granted and divided to them by the said proprietors declare unto them and all men hereby that if they or any of them shall presumed to occupy any of the said Lands that wee shall Use the Law against any such occupyer for the defense of the proprietors Right therein to the utmost And this protest we have made to the intent those concerned may not pretend ignorance of the proprietors' Right and Claime in and to the said Lands and may bee lyable to such damages as shall occure if they shall willfully proceed to improve sayd lands and that no persons may purchase or other ways Receive the same from them as good Estate in Law and for the Conservation of the proprietors Right and Claim in and unto the sayd Lands.

This done and published the Sixth of Oct., 1686 By Samuell Mulford by order of the Committee."

October 17. At Sunday morning service, Rev. James attacks Dongan's July order. Reading from Job xxiv, he says: "Cursed is he that removes his neighbours' landmark...As to the land lately layd out here the Curse is against them that acted in it and their order for it is no excuse though it were an edict from the King himselfe as Supreme nay tho' it was establisht by a law yett they cannot be excused from the curse."

Late October. New York's Attorney General, J.A. Graham, files his reaction to the East Hampton protest. He decrees that the protesters "Riotously, Tumultously, Contemptuously, and unlawfully assemble themselves...." and calls the published protest "Scandalous and Libelous."

November 18. The Recorder enters Hobart's information to the Governor's Council: "Josiah Hobart of Easthampton...upon his Corporall Oath Saith That upon the Seventeenth Day of October...Mr. Thomas James minister of Easthampton preacht out of that Text in the Twenty-fourth Chapter of Job the Second Verse the whole Subject of his Sermon was to Show the Evil and pronounce the curses against those who removed their neigbbours Land markes and in his applicacon he brought it to the present matter of this King himself as Supreame nay though it were establist by a Law yet they could not be excused from the Curse and then he went on and blessed God that this was not our Condicon for the providence of God had soe ordered it that our Hon. Governor had made such Restrictions in the order that mens Propieties could not be meddled withall."

. After two more depositions, the Council charges the minister with sedition, orders his immediate arrest, and demands that "the clerk of Easthampton bee likewise here with the bookes of the Town's public affayres."

. Concerned about the way things are going, this same day the Proprietors instruct Samuel Mulford to talk with Dongan about securing a Patent "extending to the east end of the Island, excluding the 30 Acre petitioners, with as easy a quitt Rent...by your discression procured." If the Town cannot exclude Keddy et al, they add: "Let them be moved or setled in common lands within the bounds of the first pirchas of our plantation."

November 19. Dongan commands Henry Ffilkin: "...take into custody the body of Thomas James minister at Easthampton wheresoever hee shall be found and him Safely keepe so as you may have him to answer before mee and the Councill on the first Thursday in December next ensuing unto a certeyne Informacon then and there to bee exhibited against him..."

. Rev. James' arrest leads Mulford and his committee to think it more prudent to petition Dongan for pardon of "their late offenses," before they approach him about the Patent.

Early December. Rev. James petitions Dongan for his release:

"...considering the great charge I have been att for about 3 weeks time since my comeing from home this being the first tyme (for about fourty yeares of my being a minister of the Gospel) that I have beene called to account by any Authority I have lived under, or given any cause for the same...So hoping as God hath got you as a father over this Commonwealth, so you will exercise a fatherly compassion towards yor humble Petitioner, who hath & shall continue yor Excellencies humble Orator att the Throne of Grace. "

. Three weeks after his arrest, Rev. James is freed.

December 9. In a Council meeting at Fort James, Dongan issues East Hampton a Patent. Payment is to be 45s each March 25.

Dongan acknowledges the request of some freeholders "...that I would grant liberty unto the freeholders of said towne to purchase said tract of land off the Indyans and that the ffee and inheritance thereof may only belong unto the ffreeholders... their heires Successors and assignes forever And that I would confirme the premises by Patent under seale of the Province...

"Now Know Yee That I...grant ratyfie release and confirme unto Thomas James Capt Josiah Hobart Capt Thomas Talmage Lieut John Wheeler Ensigne Samuell Mulford John Mulford Thomas Chatfield Senior Jeremiah Conklin Stephen Hand Robert Dayton Mr Thomas Backer & Thomas Osborne freeholders and Inhabitants of Easthampton herein after erected and made one body Corporate and politique and willed and determined to be called by the name of the trustees of the ffreeholders and Commonalty of the town of Easthampton and their Successors all the aforceited tracts and neckes of lands within the limits and bounds aforesaid with all and singular the houses messuages Tenements buildings milnes milnedams fencings inclosures gardens Orchards fields pastures woods underwoods trees timber feedings Rivolets waters lakes ponds brookes streames beaches Quarries mines mineralls Creekes harbours highwayes and casements fishing hawking hunting and fowling (Silver and gold mines Excepted) and all other ffranchises Profitts Commodyties & hereditaments whatsoever to the said tracts and necks of land and premisses belonging or in any wise appartaining or therewithall used accepted reputed or taken to belong or in any wise to appurtaine to all intents purposes and constructions whatsoever as also all and singular the rents arreareadges of rents issues and profits of the said tract of land and premisses heretofore due and payable."

In addition, the Patent

• gives the Trustees license to purchase the land "Commonly called Montauck" and, if the Indians choose not to sell it, decrees that the Trustees and their Successors "shall at all times hereafter be the only persons capable in the law for the purchase of the said tract of land..."

• determines that "the Trustees of the ffreeholders and Commonalty...be and shall be forever in future times persons able and Capable in law to have perceive receive and possess not only all and singular the premisses.." but may plead and defend "...all manner of actions plaints suites Complaints causes matters and demands whatsoever...as any other of his Majestyes Liedge people."

• empowers the Trustees to "have and use a Common seale which shall serve to Execute the causes and affaires...to make such acts and orders in writeing for the more orderly doing of the premisses...so alwayes as the said acts and order be in nowayes repugnant to the laws of England and of this Province which now are or hereafter may be established..."

• orders that there be twelve Trustees, no less than seven to meet, and that the Trustees, two Constables, and two Assessors be chosen each year on the first Tuesday in April.

It concludes with: "WHEREFORE, by virtue of the power and authority aforesaid, I do will and command for and on behalf of his said majesty, his heirs and successors, that the aforesaid Trustees of the Freeholders and Commonalty of the Town of Easthampton and their successors have, hold, use and enjoy all the libertyes, authorityes, (etc) ... without the lett or hindrance of any person or persons whatsoever."

1687

January 24. Management of Town affairs devolves today upon the *body politique*. The Trustees order: "a Rate bee made to the vallue of Two Hundred £ in current money of this Province yt is one Hundred & twentie pounds upon ye allotments of ye Purchasers & Proprietors of this Towne at home according to every mans allotment in devision of land And fourscore £ to bee Raised uppon ye land at Meantaucut according to every mans share or Interest there & this to be Raised to defray charge about the Patten of such as have Interest as above specified & by noe others..."

February 22. Dongan writes to the Board of Trade in London:

"Most part of the people of that Island, especially towards the east end, are of the same stamp with those of New England. Refractory and very loath to have any commerce with this Place to the great Deetr'm of his Ma'tys Revenue and ruin of our merchants ... "

Urging that New York annex Connecticut, he says: "We found by experience, if that Place bee not annexed to that Government, it will be impossible to make anything considerable of his Ma'tys Customs and Revenues in Long Island; they carry away with't entering all our Oyles which is the greatest part of what wee have to make returns of from this Place."

He adds that he closed Long Island's port late in 1686, ordered all ships of trade to clear through New York Harbor, and imposed a ten percent value tax on all goods imported from New England.

July 26. The Trustees sign a deed which permits the Montauketts to plant on Montauk whenever they wish, in return for one ear of Indian corn each year.
August 3. An Indian deed, dated July 25, is executed. It conveys to the Proprietors nearly all the land east of Fort Pond and Fort Pond Bay.
. This year, seven East End whaling companies try out a total of 2418 barrels of whale oil. Each one sells for between 1£ 10s. and 2£.
The companies, two of which are owned by Samuel Mulford, trade with the West Indies and New England, obviating the need for their ships to pass through New York Harbor.
. By year's end, East Hampton's population numbers 502. There are 223 males, 219 females, 26 male servants, 9 female servants, 11 male slaves, 14 female slaves. Eighty-seven men are capable of bearing arms, 2 are merchants. There have been 116 births, 28 marriages, and 57 deaths in the last seven years.

1688
August 7. The Town votes to allot all of Montauk west of Fort Pond.
December 10. James II, England's Catholic king, abdicates the throne in a bloodless revolution.

1689
February 16. William and Mary, Prince and Princess of Orange, accept England's invitation to succeed James II to the throne. Princess Mary is James's daughter.
March. Backed by the militia, Protestant trader Jacob Leisler uses news of the abdication to take control of south New York.
Playing on the fear that, with James II gone, Catholic France may try to invade America, Leisler ousts known Catholics from office, and invites Long Island's counties to send delegates to a meeting of colonial deputies to form a committee of safety.
April 18. With the help of soldiers who have arrived from Maine, Boston rebels react to the abdication by imprisoning Edmund Andros.
(In 1686, James II named Andros Govenor of the Dominion of New England. Two years later, he brought New York and New Jersey under Andros' umbrella).
. To win East End backing, Leisler issues a false alarm. He sends out a report that the fort is about to fall into the hands of James II's followers, and calls for help to secure it.
May 8. Easthampton believes Leisler's message. The Town clerk records the results of a General meeting: "Heard from

New York that the fort is in hands whose fidelity is suspected. Voted that soldiers go to York to assist to reduce the place, that it might be better secured for the safety of the country."

May 10. From Southampton, the County's Freeholders declare:

"Being alarmed by a printed declaration at Boston the 18th last of the Gentlemen Marchts and county adjacent, manifesting the grounds of their seizing the Govr and Governmt into their hands, wishing all others their neighbours to follow them; and our Country of England's example for securing our English nation's liberties and propertyes from Popery and Slavery, and from the Intended invasion of a foraign French design and more than Turkish crueltys, by relation, already acted upon severall of our nation, and other of our neighboures in the West Indies, and particularly Italia

"And we being persons of all others our neighbours, who have groaned under the heavy burdens imposed upon us by an arbitrary power for a considerable time together, without the lest molestation on our parts, and being under the like circumstances of being invaded by a forraign ennemy, which ther other English America is alarmed which moved us to do something at this time for our own self preservation being without any to depend on at present, till it pleases God to order better -

"2. Therefore we esteem it our bounden duty to use all lawful endeavours for securing our headquarters of New York and Albany forts, and all other fortifications, and the same to put into the hands of those whom we confide in, till further order from the parliament in England.

"3. We also think it our duty to use our best endeavours for the redemption and securing of all such moneyes as has been lately extorted from us by the aforesaid power; as also to secure all those persons reputed to be the ennemyes of the peace and prosperity of our country and the fundamental laws of our English nation, as aforesaid till further orders."

May 10/11. From Easthampton, Southampton, and Southold, respectively, Captains Wheeler, Howell, and Platt ride to Jamaica "to demand the Fort to be delivered into the hands of such persons as the county shall chose."

Other men join them, along the way. In Jamaica, they meet with Lt. Gov. Francis Nicholson and Council members. But, after hearing about Leisler's various deceits, they excuse themselves and start the return journey.

.   This month, East End towns oust and replace officials who had been forced upon them during James II's reign.

June 11. In New York, Col. Nicholas Bayard writes in his journal that Lt. Gov. Nicholson left today for England "to complaine against the rebellious proceedings of Leisler and some of the people his assocites."

June 20. In Southampton the majority of Suffolk's deputies refuse Leisler's request and vote to contact Connecticut.

July 9. In a letter to imprisoned Andros, New York City Councilman Stephen Van Cortlandt documents the ongoing rebellion in New York.

He writes that "They have appointed a Committee of safety - 2 out of the Citty, ...2 of Brouckland, 2 of fflatbush, 2 of..., nobody from Suffolk....the rest of the Towns will not meddle themselves."

July 26. The Montauketts and the Proprietors make another exchange. Today, the Montaukets convey all of Montauk Point to the Proprietors. In return, they receive a document which gives the Indians the right to plant corn on that land "soever they have occasion for to plant from time to time when they see cause themselves and their heirs forever, upon the land as purchased of them by us."

July 30. Unaware that Nicholson is on his way to England, a royal order is sent him "to take upon you the government of the said Province Calling to your assistance in ye administration thereof the Principal Freeholders and inhabitants of the same." The document is addressed "To our trusty and wellbelovd Francis Nicholson Esq., our Lt. Governor & Commander in Chief of our Province of New York in America, and in his absence to such as for the time being take care for Preserving the Peace and administering the Lawes in our said Province of New York in America."

August 16. New York's committee of safety appoints Leisler "to Exercise & Use the Power & Authority of a commander in chief of the said Province ..."

September 2. The Trustees authorize a committee to impower Leisler "to secure for this town's use, what monies is to be found in New York unjustly by tax or taxes levied on this town." The committee also is instructed to convey the Plantation's feelings to Southampton, or to his order."

. In London, this same day, Capt. Henry Sloughter tells the Board of Trade: "New York at present lyeth under a loose management being destitute of a Governor and Government seized by the Rable...New York lyeth soe advantageously scituate between the Colony of New England and Virginia, that should it fall into the hands of the French, the trade of all those parts in America would be totally ruined."

September 9. The Town consents "that certain moneys, formerly raised for the public service, might be paid to Leisler **December 9.** John Riggs arrives in New York, bearing two bundles of letters addressed to Lt. Gov. Nicholson. One of them is King William's July 30 letter addressed to Nicholson or, "...in his absence..." Leisler takes this phrase to mean him.

1690

February 20. Leisler issues invitations to the towns of the province to form a new Assembly.

March 5. Southampton's Recorder writes: "At a Town meeting held in Southampton it passed by major voat of the Inhabitants at the said meeting that the paper of grievances drawne up and sent hither from easthampton and now Read in this meeting shall be sent for england to their Majesties on their behalf with others that doe concur in the same, and that they will be at proportionable Charg in sending and Managing the same, that is to say, our proportion of one hundred £ if it be effected."

March 10. Leisler continues his efforts to woo Long Island's East End. This day, Thomas Chatfield, Samuel Mulford, and Samuel Persons write Leisler, "on behalf of ye rest":

"Hon. Sr. having this opportunty wee think it meet Send a few lines to prove our respects to you, and to manifest our great approbation for what you have done for ye Securing of ye place where you live, also understanding you have an Order from his Excellent Majesty the King for ye settleing of matters in point of government which hath been essayed to be imposed upon us in these parts, but could not comply wth being as we apprehend built upon ye old foundation of a power wch we have for this many years groaned under as your Honor Very Well Knoweth in many respects, therefore hope you will not blame us if we doe not willingly Subject to one old bondage againe, but rather use all Lawful means of deliverance from ye same, no in any disobedience to Authourity, whether inferior or Supreame,...

"we are very desirous to let you understand yt we have agreed to send over to his Majesty both a true Narration of ye grievances we have suffered this many years under an Arbitrary power, and a Petition to their Majesties yt we might be rejoined with Connecticut government as formerly, agreeably to the act of Parliament, yt all places being perticularly mentioned shall have the same <u>privileges</u> they enjoyed in ye year 1660, restored unto them, wch doth encourage us to make our Addresse to his Majesty hopeing to obtaine his Royall Favour with other his Loyall Subjects, and in ye mean tyme to stand up both p'sons and Estates in defence of his Majesty's Royall Authority togeather wth other his Majesties Subjects in those parts against all his Knowne Enemies, & if there be need, to afford what assistance we are able not laying ourselves open to danger, therefore humbly intreate your Sr to Consider yt we of Easthampton are a fronteer Plantation & lye most open to danger of any Enemy by sea, and are intended Very shortly to send forth skouts to Montaukett and so to ye end yr Island Eastward yt so if any Shipping be seene upon ye Coasts, tymely notice may be given not onely to our selves but all over ye Island to N.Y. wch hope be of good use for ye publick safety.

"Sr we humbly intreate of you if there hath not been that as you may desire, not to impute it as to any disaffection to your person, much lesse to yor Authority (for ye most part of us) being of ye same Religion, Subjects to the same King, desireing of God your prosperity & good successes in ye place you are in, & that we have a faire correspondence wth you & if you apprehend we are out of ye way, loveingly to convince us of it, & we shall readily harken to ye same.

"So we rest your Very Loveing friends & humble servts."

(New York Province remains the only colony in America without a charter).

March 15. Once again, East Hampton and Southampton refuse Leisler's summons to participate in elections.

May 3. East Hampton resolves to maintain its present course of non-alliance with Leisler.

May 19. A pamphlet is printed in New York. It contains the text of "A Modest and Impartial Narrative of Several Grievances and Great Oppressions That the Peaceable and most Considerable Inhabitants of Their Majesties Province of New York in America Lye under, By the Extravagant and Arbitrary Proceedings of Jacob Leisler and his Accomplices."

The Narrative was to have been presented to the Mayor's Court on January 21. But, as the inside page advises, "the Fury and Rage of this indolent Man Leysler was grown to such height that the day before, by his order, several Persons of Note were violently seized and divers Homes broken open. So as it was not thought safe to proceed in such Method, For which reason its thought well to publish the same, for information of all into whose hands it may come, but more especially for the benefit of our fellow Inhabitants, who are abused by the false Pretentions of this common violator of our Laws and Liberties, as by the following Narrative will plainly appear: Wherein the Courteous Peruser is desired to take notice, it hath been our

Great Care to relate nothing but Matters of Fact, of which we have substantial credible Evidences."

The lengthy discourse summarizes the indecencies vented upon inhabitants by Leisler's men, from imprisonment and torture "worse than the Turks," to loss of work and freedom. It also addresses Leisler's influence on eastern Long Island:

"...The first thing he falls upon was to stir up and animate the people of the East End of Long Island to advance with sufficient force to take possession of the Fort, lest it should be in danger of being delivered up to a Foreign Power this readily took with them whose minds were already heated by the example of Boston, in clapping up our Governor Sir Edmund Andros and after some consultations amongst themselves, they put forward in a Hostile manner increasing as they came along the Island, until they were so far advanced as the Town of Jamaica, being then about eighty in number whence they halted, and sent up three of their principal leaders to discourse the Lieutenant Governor, who upon their coming convened his council the Mayor and Aldermen...into which convention the Persons sent were admitted where after some long debates they seemingly went away satisfied, at least so far as that they and the men accompanying them returned home to their Townes and habitations without doing the least hurt or damage to any..."

. This year, Leisler removes New York Harbor as an obligatory stop for traders. His act gives East Hampton and other towns the right "to transport where they please directly to what place or country they think it fitt, anything their places afford."

October 17. The Lords of Council confirm Henry Sloughter's royal appoinment as "Captain General and Governor in Chief of our Province of New York and the Territories depending thereon in America."

They also give him the various grievances sent from the Province which attest to Leisler's harsh rule, and direct him upon arrival in New York, to "Strictly and impartially, examine and enquire into the severall allegations therein conteyned ..."

October 26. Leisler suspends the court of oyer and terminer, about to sit in Kings County, "until Long Island should be reduced to obedience."

1691

February 13. East Hampton's Clerk records: "Upon information of Governor Slaughter to New York The towns men caused the town to be Called together to concider what Was best be done It was there voted yt Samuell Mulford should (upon Notis of his Honours arivall at New York) Take his

Journey with all convenant speed; to congratulate his Honours happy arrivall In the Towns Behalf with all to make Known ye towns agreveances with Petition for som Redres."

March 19/21. After a rough voyage that took sixteen weeks, Sloughter lands in New York harbor aboard the "Arch-Angel." (Two other English ships, carrying troops and stores, anchored in January, but Leisler has refused to allow anything but supplies leave the ships.)

Sloughter posts his commission for all to see, and demands that Leisler surrender the fort. After two days of intermittent fighting, Leisler surrenders.

April 6. Chidley Brooke, who arrived in New York in January, writes Sir Robert Southwell: "Leisler and Milbourne having been indicted for High Treason have refused to plead it is supposed the Governor will keep them for his majesties disposall of them."

May 17. Sloughter gives in to the demands of the people of New York. While he pardons those who followed Leisler's orders, Leisler and his son-in-law, Jacob Milbourne, are executed.

1692

May 19. Thomas Chatfield records that, at the General Meeting, "phillip Leek Snr did Apeere desireing pmit to travill or go out of the province thereby to seek sum place to settle in: where his wife and fammily might bew: in sum Reasonable safety with Gods providance: Whilst him self being caled forth to serve either king or Country."

1693

April 10. The New York Legislature approves: "...That the Island commonly called and known by the Name of Long Island, shall henceforth be called the Island of Nassau." It is Governor Benjamin Fletcher's wish that William III of Nassau to be remembered in that part of the New World, forever.

1694

May 22. Thomas Chatfield records that the Trusees "have ordered that all Lands that now ly common from the plains westward to the deep Creek of Georgeke that is Known by the name of Osbornes creek and northward to Nathaniell Talmages close in the Northwest plains: and eastward to the Round Swamp & then on a line to the springes and so along to the plaines Eastward: shall be kept and Remain for a common for the use of the proprietors of this township for creatures to feed upon: and order this to be Recorded to that end. Nathaniell Talmage did Declare his dissent against this abov said order: and desired the same to be entered."

June 21. Jacob Dayton certifies "that whereas Ruth the wife of Jacob Dayton doth prove extravagant and refuseth to be Ruled by her Husband or to goe with him unto The place yt he hath provided for there habitation: Therefore I the said Jacob Dayton doe hereby warne all sorts of people whatsoever that they doe not deale with her or trust her any thing upon their perrill for I doe here by declare that I will not pay for it or allow any such dealeings as Attest my hand..."

1695

October 5. The Town issues John Merry a license to sell spirits. It reads: "Easthampton gave to John Merry for the sum of twenty pounds permission to maintain good rule and order in his house, he to suffer no unlawful games or meetings for being permitted by Benamin Conklin and nathaniel Sylvester, two of His Majesty's Justices of the Peace for Suffolk County, to sell wine, rum, cider, beer, and other liquors."

November 20. Aging Rev. James deeds all of his East Hampton property to Lion Gardiner's grandson, John. For this, he is to receive 500£ (half upon signing the deed, the balance to his heirs, within thirty days of his death) and full use of the land during the remainder of his life.

1696

June 2. Majority this day favors repairing the Meeting House instead of building a new one.

June 6. Rev. James dies. (According to his last wishes, he will be buried in the Town cemetery, with his head facing the dead, so that on the day of the Resurrection, he will face his flock).

1697

January 20. Thomas Edwards signs his Last will and Testament. To his "beloved wife Abigaill" he leaves "ye use of my dwelling House for and during the time of her widdowhood and one yeare Longer in case she shall marry also I doe give unto her four of my Neat Cattel which she shall chose And a horse or mare the best I have at her choyse Also I give her half of my household Goods and My will Is that My son Ephraim or hee which Injoyes my home Land shall winter for her four Cattel and pasture for her three Cattel in ye summer time all ye time of her widdowhood as Also a horse or Mare."

1698

May 17. The Trustees Clerk records: "...for the preventing of any persons from becoming inhabitants within the said Township that are of Ill fame or likely to become chargeable unto the said Township that whosoever doe or shall: presume to entertayne any stranger within the township of Easthampton:the sume of five shillings for each and every Weeke that any stranger shall find such entertainment..."
. The Meeting House is enlarged this year.

1699

June 27. After watching an unknown sloop with six cannon laying off Gardiner's Island for two days, John Gardiner rows out for a better look. William Kidd welcomes him aboard the "Antonio." Kidd tells Gardiner that he is on his way to see Lord Bellomont in Boston, and clear his name of piracy charges. Richard Coote, Lord Bellomont, is colonial governor of Massachusetts, New Hampshire, and New York.

(Piracy had been rampant on the high seas for some time when, in 1696, an English syndicate, led by King William III, outfitted the 287-ton "Adventure Galley," Capt. Kidd in command. Kidd was ordered to hunt down pirates on the Red Sea and Indian Ocean, and, because England and France were at war, he was to take French ships as prizes. Somewhere, amid the swells of the seas, it was rumored, the respected mariner turned pirate himself.

In frequent reports to London, Bellomont had warned that Nassau Island - especially its eastern end - was a pirate's haven. In fact he described the East End as filled with people "so lawless and desperate ... that I can get no honest man to venture among them and collect their excise and watch their trade.")

Before the "Antonio" weighs anchor, - Kidd abandoned his other ship in the West Indies, after learning about the charges against him - Gardiner honors his request for cider and six sheep.

Three days later, Kidd returns. This time, he wants to bury some of his belongings on the island. They include a chest and a box of gold quilts. Kidd shows Gardiner where they will be hidden and tells him that, if he does not return, Gardiner may keep them. But, Kidd warns, if he does come back, and his belongings are nowhere to be found, Gardiner, or, his son, will lose his head.

Having said that, Kidd asks Mrs. Gardiner if she would have a pig roasted for him. She does, and for her kindness, he gifts her with a cloth of gold. [6]

July 17/25. Summoned by Bellomont, who has seen Kidd, Gardiner arrives in Boston with Kidd's unearthed treasures. They include three bags of gold dust, one bag each of gold and silver coins, one bag of unpolished gems, one bag of silver rings and precious stones, one piece of crystal, gold bars, one bag of silver buttons and a lamp, 67 precious stones, two amethysts, and some cornelian rings.

On the 25th, Gardiner receives a receipt for "Eleven hundred & eleven ounces Troy wt. The Silver is Two Thousand three hundred fifty three ounces. The Jewels or precious stones weighed are Seventeen ounces three Eighths of an ounce, and Sixty nine Stones by Tale..."

The Eighteenth Century

1700

April 2. This year's election includes, for the first time, the office of Town Supervisor. The position was introduced on Long Island in 1683 when East Riding of Yorkshire became Suffolk County. The Town Supervisors meet at different times of the year. Abraham Schellinx receives the most votes.

1701

June 6. The Town agrees "by a major vote that all persons inhabiting in East-Hampton, being benefited by the common, should all from sixteen years old to sixty, males - servants as well as others - ...go, on the tenth of this June, and so again on the 17th of inst., to cutting bushes for clearing of the common and highways ... "

October 8. In Southold, Suffolk County leaders protest to the New York governor for rejecting Samuel Mulford as a duly elected member of the Assembly:

"We the ffreeholders of this County of Suffolk being mett together according to precept and finding that the writts presented to us for the Election of other Representatives - therein Required do contain an Infringement of our Liberties not allowing us to chuse who we think fittest to trust in that affair, and so may be a precedent for our further thralldom wherefore we cannot at present incline to any further choice having already elected to this Assembly two, sufficient and Legall persons (in our esteem) of approved fidelity to his Majesty and who are no aliens but natural born Englishmen and in their different capacities have served in many Assemblies (in times of wars) of greater concernment than this present Assembly is or can be of and have acquitted themselves as faithful and upright both to the King's Majesty, and to this province, neither is this County yett convinced of any fault that they have committed why we should reject them, on which Consideration we acquise in our former choice of them which hath been free and without Restraint upon our Liberties as Englishmen. So wee bid you farewell."

1702

March 3. The Montauk Proprietors and Montauketts exchange documents. Thirty-two tribe members reaffirm the 1687 deed because "Some people have reported that our deed of conveyance to the said proprietors for the said tract of land was but a pretended deed." The Proprietors give the Indians limited use and enjoyment of certain parts of their former land.

They are to fence in, "as a general field," whatever land they wish to use on Northneck between Fort Pond and Great Pond; "lay and keep open their field or fields" for the town's cattle, from each October 15 to April 5; fence in no more than 30 acres for winter wheat or grass; and maintain their fences at their own cost. They may keep 250 swine (paying for damages their rooting may cause) and 50 head of cattle and horses, and get hay to winter them. The Montauketts and their heirs also may use as much timber as they need for fencing from the woods west of Fort Pond.

April 7. Town Clerk Thomas Chatfield records: "...at a legal Town meeting, it was granted by a major vote that, whereas Capt. Samuel Mulford having erected or built a warehouse at the northwest landing place, and for his encouragement to maintain the same, that he should freely have the full enjoyment of the land it stands on with sufficient addition of land to the same, to set reasonable enlargement of the said warehouse upon, and also a convenient way to pass to and from the same, by cart or travelling, so long as he or his heirs shall continue said warehouse there..."

Major vote also grants "Shamgar Barnes...a garden spot of land at some convenient place upon the common, the same to be to his use and his wife's during their natural lives, or the life of either of them but upon both their decease, the said land to return to the town again."

May 8. Describing the Montauketts as "obstinate and averse to agreement," a Town proclamation empowers a committee of eight men to do what they must, "offensive or defensive in nature," when discussing common pasturage rights with them.

1703

June 30. Edward Hyde, Lord Cornbury, New York's new governor, sizes up East Enders in a letter to the House of Lord's Board of Trade.

After admitting that, for some time, "there has been no Trade between the City of New York and the East-end of Long Island, from whence the greatest quantity of whale oyle comes," he adds, "indeed the people of the East End of Long Island are not very willing to be persuaded to believe that they belong to this province. They are full of New England principles. They chose rather to trade with the people of Boston, Connecticut and Rhode Island, than with the people of New York."

. Cornbury finds his government short on revenue, and a lax Auditor General of the Plantations in office. To augment the loss of ready moneys, he dips and dips into contingency funds. When that is exhausted, he turns to the whalers. He levies a tax on offshore whaling, orders whalers to purchase a license to hunt the leviathan, and demands that they bring him one quarter of all whale bone and oil.

1704
. In London this August, Samuel Mulford tries to have Cornbury's whale tax repealed
October 5. The New York clergy convenes at Cornbury's request, to hear a report on the state of the church in Suffolk County:
"In Suffolk County, in the east end of Long Island, there is neither a church of England minister, nor any provision made for one by law; the people generally being independents, and upheld in their separation by New England emissaries."

1705
June 4 Samuel Mulford takes his seat in the New York Assembly.
June 14. Cornbury proposes that the Legislature pass an Act to "...provide for the Maintenance of some ministers...at the East End of Long Islande where I do not find any Provision has been made yet, for the propagating religion."
July 19. The Legislature passes the bill to support the Episcopalian ministry in New York. Suffolk County is the only county not named in the bill.
. Cornbury continues his campaign to limit East End towns from trading with New England. He orders a sloop to sail Long Island Sound and intercept any ships that leave the East End, laden with whale oil.
. Mulford refuses to obtain a whale license. At year's end, a warrant is issued against him for fishing and his whale oil and bone are seized.

1706
. Among the exports sent from Northwest this year, Samuel Mulford lists in his Journal: "159 muskrats, 70 foxes, 32 raccoons, 2 cats, 3 otters, 1 mink."

1707

. The community of Sag Harbor enters Town records this year.
. Four thousand barrels of oil are made on Long Island, this year. Most of it comes from the East End.

1708

<u>July 1.</u> In a letter to the Board of Trade, Cornbury addresses the change in offshore whaling since Nantucket whalers started to assert themselves: "The quantity of Train Oyl made in Long Island is uncertain... for example last year they made four thousand Barryls of Oyl, and this last season they have not made about Six hundred."

<u>August 24/September 13</u> The Assembly's Grievance Committee, on which Mulford sits, draws up a list of seven resolutions. Five of them embrace East End interests:

"... Every Freeman has property rights

"...Taxation, without Assembly consent, violates peoples' property rights

"...Taxation on imported/exported goods, without Assembly consent, impoverishes the people

"...Mandatory port charges discourages trade

"...Extorting of excessive fees by officers debilitates the weal of the Province."

1709

<u>September 13</u>. The Trustees agree to bar the Montauketts from cutting or selling cornstalks other than for their own cattle.

1710

<u>April 4.</u> Major vote at the annual Town meeting favors "that for the more suitable performing the duty of Assessor according to the intent thereof there shall three substantial men be chosen of the freeholders ... to be in equal power and authority for the levying and making assessments in said Town and have allowance for their trouble, six shillings each."

1711

. The road between East Hampton and Southampton is named Queens Highway, in honor of Queen Anne.

<u>October.</u> Robert Hunter, Cornbury's successor, orders Suffolk County's sheriff to collect 1/20 of whale bone and oil from fishermen, after they deduct their expenses. The tribute is in return for the "privilege" of whaling.

<u>December.</u> Samuel Mulford ignores Hunter's demands. He keeps all the whale oil and bone taken from his catch.

1712
March 15. Arrested for fishing without a license, Mulford and his sons, Mathew and Timothy, are charged with "converting the Queens Goods to their own use."

1713
September 24. The Trustee agree to let the Indians keep three large dogs to protect their fields.

1714
February 5. Three young boys, out fishing, try to cross the outlet of Georgica Pond. A strong current carries their canoe into the surf, where they drown. The loss of Zebedee Osborn, 14, John Hopping, 10, and Joseph Earle, age unknown, has a profound impact on the town. In number, their deaths are the most, at one time, since Easthampton was founded.
April 2. In the Assembly, Mulford rails against government seizure of vessels docked in New York's harbor. (Not only is a heavy duty being imposed on their cargo, inspectors will seize a ship even if only one item hasn't been declared.)

As New York's only printer, Will Bradford, takes down his words, Mulford tells his colleagues:"...not any man was fit for Master of a vessel to go to New York except he were a Lawyer, and then they should not escape except it was by Favour ... We have an undoubted Right and Property by the Law of God and Nature, settled upon the Subject by Act of Parliament; which is not to be taken from them by the Supream Power, without due course of Law. The End of Law is to Secure our Persons and Estates; the End of Government to put the same in Execution, to that Purpose that Justice be done..."
November 3. Mulford addresses the Assembly on the order of electing members. Referring to the house's disproportionate representation and its shift in priorities, from commercial to agricultural, he says:

"...now the Minor Part of the People in the Government have the major Part of the Assembly, and for their Interest Opress a great Part of the People, and they lie under great Disadvantages."

1715
March 15. In a New York Court, Mulford defends his right to hunt whale without a license:

"The custom of the whale fishing is a Free Custom; there is not an Law to prohibit it. It is an ancient custom, to the Third and Fourth Generation. It is more ancient than the colony of

New York and not in any Man's Memory to the Contrary till of late; And in the year 1686, the town of East-Hampton had a Patent to us by the King's Governour, with several Priviledges therein granted to this Corporation, for which we pay 40s. per Annum to the Crown...

"The Whale-Fishing was our Fishing at the time of the Grant, and several years before; so we hold it to be our Right to continue so to do, it being reputed to be one of the Franchises confirmed to us both by Patent, Law, and Reason."

April 19 The Town gives persons without property title in the community "liberty to cut dry wood for firing for the space of one whole year, he or they paying one penny for each load."

June 2. The new Assembly, which now includes representatives from additional districts created by Gov. Hunter, expels Mulford for his speech of April 2, 1714.

.   Mulford is called into Supreme Court, where he is forced to put up 500 English pounds in security. Told to admit that his speech was false, he says, "The worst of it is it was too true."

1716

June 9. Returned to the Assembly by overwhelming odds, in the election to fill his seat, Mulford addresses the House. He denounces Hunter's administration. He attacks the taxes leveled on imports and commodities, the misrule of finances in collecting revenue, and the practice of reserving patronage for those who are members of the high Episcopalian church.

June 21. The Assembly calls for Mulford's June 9 speech to be placed in the hands of the Clerk for recording and action.

.   Mulford has his June 9th speech printed for public reading. This gives Hunter a legal right to sue his sharpest critic in Supreme Court. Using every device possible, Hunter keeps the aging Mulford in one Court or the other, all summer long.

August 21. Responding to Mulford's complaint that, in the past year, he has "been at four Courts, and know not but that it must be from Court to Court so long as I live," the Assembly petitions the governor: "The Assembly, being deeply sensible of the great damage and inconveniency Mr. Samuel Mulford, a member of this house, suffers and undergoes, by reason of a prosecution against him in the Supreme court for printing and publishing a speech formerly made by him in the Assembly, are humble suitors to his Excellency to give orders that Mr. Mulford, in regard to his great age and distance of habitation from the city, and other considerations, may be freed and discharged from the said persecution in the supreme Court."

. Gov. Hunter drops his lawsuit.

September. In spite of his age, Mulford determines to carry his and the Town's complaints to England - and to King George I. Lest Hunter might learn of his plans and detain him, Mulford keeps his agenda secret. He leaves Easthampton in disguise, takes a boat to Newport, walks to Boston and sails for England.

October 2. News of Mulford's departure irks Hunter enough to write about him in a letter to the House of Lords' Trade Board:

"I must do the province the justice to assure you he is the only mutineer within it....He has in all administrations during his life hitherto flown in the face of the Government, and has ever disputed with the Crown the right of whale fishing... judgement has been given against him in the supream court in that case ... "

Hunter tells the Board that Mulford "is now under prosecution for publishing and dispersing a false scandalous and malicious libel..." against the government. Then he speculates on why Mulford left: "...if such as fly from prosecution for crimes & Misdemeanours against the Government can entertain hopes of turning the prosecution against their Governors your Lordships will have much more trouble, & the Governors much less ease, than I am sure you desire they should have."

1717

April 2. As they have in the past, the Montauk Proprietors vote to leave management of Montauk up to the Trustees for a year.

. Work begins this spring on East Hampton's first church. It is 45 by 80 feet. The frame, donated by the Gardiner family, is cut from massive white oak on their island. Beams are 10x10 inches. The sills and posts are larger. The window frames are cedar. The exterior is clapboard.

The church design calls for an expansive auditorium to shelter a high pulpit, a large sounding board overhead, two wide side aisles, side and rear galleries, and box seats. When pews replace the temporary seats, the Gardiner family will have exclusive use of a central pew. To each side of the front door, stairs will lead to separate galleries. Above the front door, a tower will hold a bell and support a hexagonal steeple and spire. The bell is one of several that are sent to churches in America, paid for from a fund called "Queen Anne's Bounty."

June 17. In London, the Board of Trade hears Mulford at its opening session.

(It has taken him this long to gain a hearing. For weeks and weeks after his arrival, he stood at Buckingham Palace's gates during the day, hoping to gain an audience with the king. But, the only attention he got was from pick pockets. After two successful picks, Mulford sewed fish hooks into his rear pocket. Back at the royal gates the following day, he hooked his catch. The piercing cry that rent the air caught the crowd's ear. The reason for the wail reached George I, who made today's meeting possible.)

Mulford tells the Board about Hunter's mandates on whaling. When asked for proof, he says that it is public knowledge, but that he will return with papers he brought to London.

July 31. Mulford brings the Board copies of Hunter's writ of October 1711, copies of subpoenas issued to those who testified that he fished without a license, and copies of his own defense at the trial. (They appear in "An Information," which Will Bradford had printed in New York).

August 14/15. Four witnesses for Mulford address the Board of Trade. Charles Lodwick, a deputy in Cornbury's government "for claiming and taking all...drift whales for the government," tells the Board that whales "killed or taken at sea... used to be "esteemed the property of ye persons who kill or take them... " without a duty imposed.

Mulford and his witnesses tell the Board that they do not mind if a tax remains on drift whales, as long as it is removed from offshore whales.

. In August, Mulford takes his case to the House of Commons, where he distributes a memorial to its members. Called "A Memorial of Several Aggrevances and Oppressions of His Majesty's Subjects in the Colony of New-York in America," its opening lines read:

"Though the Inhabitants thereof were much against being moved from Connecticut to New York, yet it was their Misery and unhappy fate to have it to be so." He contends that if Easthampton had been allowed to remain under Connecticut, none of these problems would have risen.

While citing the honor of being an elected Assemblyman, he attacks the unequal representation: "It is a privilege to have an Assembly if it were as near as may be according to the Number of People in each County...but to have the name and nothing of the Nature, is but a snare..."

Mulford closes his Memorial with a question: "Is the Government carried on for their Majesties Benefit or Good of the Subjects, according to the Laws and Customs of the Colony, and according to English government; or, is it Arbitrary, Illegal, Grievous, Oppressive, Unjust, and Destructive?"

. Mulford also recounts his libel suit to the Board of Trade, and asks the Board to intervene.

August 28. Mulford gives the Board of Trade a petition that Lodwick circulated among London merchants who trade with New York. The signed document states:

"The imports of whale oil and bone from New York have greatly decreased, owing to disputes with the Governor as to a duty demanded for whales catched there. We propose that the inhabitants have free liberty to kill whales."

October 4. To combat any ills that might result from Mulford's actions in London, the New York Assembly submits a formal address to Hunter. The House tells Hunter that the taxes levied in New York are "cheerfully given...towards ye support of ..." the government, and that the revenue was "duly and faithfully apply'd" by Hunter "to ye uses intended, and accounted for to ye satisfaction of the General Assembly during the time of your Excellency's administration."

.   Late in the year, the Lord Justice writes Hunter, "We must observe to you that we hope you will give all due encouragement to repealing the whale tax."

1718

January 20. In another letter to the Board of Trade, Hunter justifies prosecuting Mulford. He calls him a "crazed man," and reminds the Board that the whale taxes are simply a continuation of Cornbury's administration. He insists that, by publishing his speech, Mulford intended to "raise Sedition amongst the people ...and obstruct the settlement of a Revenue or any support of Government."

. The end of January, the Board of Trade steers Mulford to the Committee for Appeals of the Privy Council, and asks the Solicitor General for an opinion on whaling licenses in New York. The council stays all Supreme Court proceedings against Mulford, until it hears his side and Hunter's.

February 25. The Board of Trade writes Hunter:

"You intimate in your letter to our Sec. 22nd Nov. last, that the whale fishery is reserved to the crown by your Patents. As we can find no such thing in your commission, we desire you will explain what you mean by it....

"In the meantime, we have received another petition from Mulford praying dispatch in our report upon the papers our Sec. sent you the 19th of Sept. last, we must desire therefore from you a full answer to those papers; and particularly as to the right of the crown, and that you inform us what quantities of whales are caught in the gov't. whether any persons have paid and continue to pay the dues you demand, and which Mulford complains of what those dues may amount to one yr. with another and how the profit arising by them is apply'd."

April 1. The Solicitor General issues his answer to the Board of Trade: "...if licenses for whale fishing paying such reasonable proportion as the 20th part on importation are warranted at New York by any Act of Assembly, or other authentick order of the Governour and the Council it may be binding to the inhabitants there."

April 23. Mulford appears before the Committee of Appeals, where he reads his response to Hunter's January letter. Referring to Hunter's charge that he is crazy, Mulford tells the Court of Appeals that if "the oppressions and unjust measures taken against me...cannot be redressed...the same may bring thousands...to be crazed as I am." He reissues his charges against Hunter and the easily-swayed Assembly.

June 22. Rev. Nathaniel Huntting leads the first service in the new church. It is the largest house of worship ton Long Island.

July 2. In a joint letter to the Board of Trade, the New York Council and Assembly infer that Hunter's government is "free from tyranny or oppression.." and that they "...know of no grievances in the Province, wch. is in happier circumstances than ever, in great measure owing to the just and mild administration of Brigr. Hunter."

July 7. Hunter answers the Board's request to explain why he claims the whale to be a "royale fish." He bases his argument on the Latin wording of his Vice Admiral Commission. Certain sea fish, including the whale, are mentioned in it.

He adds that 20 sterling is raised per year from whale fishing taxes and finds it "amazing that after all I have sent to the Lords of Trade, to the Agents and others relating to that poor crazed man Mulford I should be still laid under a necessity of sending answers to such odd groundless complaints."

1719

February 24. Rev. Huntting writes in his journal: "This day a whaleboat being alone the men struck a whale and she coming under the boat in part staved in and...before any help came to them four men were tired & chilled & fell off ye boat and oars to which they hung & were drowned."

April 11. The Clerk registers John Hand's ear mark for his cattle: "an Ell on the under side of the left ear, and a crop on the same, and a crop on the right Ear, and a slit in the right ear."

April 15. The Montauketts execute a bond with the Proprietors. Carrying the marks of 14 Montauketts, the bond guarantees they will not allow "strange Indians" to come on Montauk to live or to improve any land there by "taking of a squaw or squaws."

August 20. A problem is resolved. By major vote, the order of seating in the meeting house is defined:

"... the pews in the meeting house shall be seated with men at the West end, and with women at the East end of said home ... Isaac Hedges, Joel Bowditch, and Edward Petty have full power by virtue of said vote, to seat all persons in said pews according to their discretion..." For this, the men are to be paid twenty shillings each.

October 17. After his three year stay in England, Mulford takes his seat in the Assembly. William Burnett has replaced Hunter as governor.

This day, Mulford complains to his colleagues that the colony is 35,000£ in debt and, that Assembly elections were not held this term, as they should have been.

Asked if elections would "prevent" the debt, he answers: "No, but it would Remove the Assembly that had Occasioned it, in some Measure."

October 26. Mulford is expelled from the Assembly for refusing to participate until new elections are held, following the new governor's appointment. 7

1720

February 22. Town Clerk records the Proprietors' decision on all undivided lands in Easthampton:

"agree by Major vote that all ye Common Land that is not yet Layd out to particular persons westward of Meantauk to ye bound line between Easthampton and Southampton Shall be surveyed and Laid out to Each man According to his or their rite in Common the surveying and Laying out of ye same to begin at ye northeast End of Aylewife brook Neck and accabonack Neck... at ye Least, three or four Divisions and to be left to ye Trustees for ye time being where to direct where theire shall and may be Convenient High ways in all places in or about or through ye Sd Land...

"And also it was agreed by major vote of ye proprietors then met together that Capt. Theophilus Howell Theophilus peirson and Abraham peirson Shall be present at ye Drawing of ye Lots for ye Sd Land so that theire may no wrong don in that matter ...no person shall Cut any greene wood for fire wood from ye date above written until ye first Tuesday in April next."

November 1. Gov. Burnett writes the Board of Trade that he has "remitted the five percent on Whale Fishing during my time but require licenses during pleasure to be taken which is asserting the King's right tho I neglect my own profit for the encouragement of that Trade,...this has had a very good effect in the country."

1721
April 4. Major vote of the Proprietors and Freeholders gives Samuel Gardiner "liberty to make a pew in the meeting house for his own use, to him and his heirs, at or on the foot of the East gallery stairs, to do the same on his own cost and charge, not to prevent or hinder persons going up or down the stairs."

1722
April 3. Due to the "great damage and hindrance to the severall small parcels of land laid formerly out in Aylewife Brook Neck and Accabonack Neck," the Proprietors agree, "none opposing ... that the Trustees of this Town may and shall have full power to exchange land with Aron Fithian in the said necks, and also with any other persons as they... see cause."

1723
April 2. Majority vote at the annual Town meeting approves:
   "that a four rail fence three feet and six inches high shall be accounted a sufficient fence in and about this Town, both inner and circular fences. Also, a ditch and ditchbank four feet from the bottom of the ditch to the top of the bank... shall be deemed a sufficient fence."

1724
April 29. Town clerk Cornelius Conklin records the wording on the receipt received from A.D. Peyster, Jr., Treasurer of the Province of New York:
   "Received from...Easthampton in Suffolk County by the hands of Mordecia Hooman the sum of nineteen pounds sixteen shillings and eight pence, being the first payment on the tax for raising and levying the quantity of five thousand three hundred and fifty ounces of plate for the use therein mentioned, and for striking and making bills of credit for their value."

1725
March 25. A question of proper ownership of Montauk lands leads the Trustees to appoint three members to get an attorney's opinion on "our patent & the authority of ye Trustees..."
August 21. Samuel Mulford dies, aged 81.

1726

May 25. Thomas Wheeler sells and "makes over to William Hedges of Easthampton and his heirs and assignes forever all my right in the great swamps at the north end of the Town, as it was laid out by my father Capt. John Wheeler."

Julyy 20. The Clerk records:, "Will Wabeton Indian entereth for his ear mark a hole in the right ear and two half pennies on the under side of the left ear."

1727

February 15. The Proprietors decide to leave management of Montauk in the hands of a committee of five men.

. The Town finally has a common whipper. Richard Syme is the first man seen to be strong enough for the job.

1728

March 22. The Trustees agree to give public notice to free-holders to choose Trustees, Constables, and Assessors according to the Town's patent.

September. Under cover of night, in the first week of the month, pirates invade Gardiner's Island.

They storm the mansion and tear it apart, as they search for valuables, injure aged Lord John Gardiner, who is ill in bed, and bring serious harm to some of his workers. Gardiner prevails upon an Indian, who fishes and hunts for him, to get his family off the island before the pirates find them. (Some of the family had escaped into the woods after hearing the first poundings on the front door.)

The pirates remain on the island for several days, denude it of everything of value, and, before leaving, tie Gardiner to a mulberry tree.

November 8. The Trustees, vote "that all persons indebted to the town upon Any Account whatsoever that shall refuse or Neglect to pay the same be Immediately prosecuted." Clerk Samuel Hudson "is put in to act and doe on the Town's behalf."

1729

May 2. The Trustees decide that there "being two acres of land lying between the fireplace path and Capt. Conklings land at Accabonack Neck it is thought it would be ill convenient for any other man to take up in another division...Cornelius Conkling may take ye sd two acres of land he takeing two acres less than his Right according to his commonage in the next division."

November 20. The Trustees tell Samuel Russell to "make all ye glass sound and good in ye Meeting House, and order a padlock to be bought for ye schoolhouse" and vote "either Right or wrong that the town money in Jeremiah Mulfords hand shall go to ye payment of Mr. Huntting's taxes." (A few people questioned why the Town should pay the minister's tax.)

1730

February 17. The Trustees order Mat Burnet "to get a rope for ye Meeting house bell, that sumthing be dun to ye schoolhouse," and, "by a major vote that natl Dominey take in as much land a joyning to his land at ye harbor as he has alewise brook neck but if in case he dont obtaine a town vote next spring or before for ye land took then he is to throw it out again, and Jeremiah Mulford or natl Baker may go and lay it to him."

March 6. Five years after Samuel Mulford's death, the Crown issues its final ruling on his petitions: "954. GOVERNORS NOT TO CLAIM WHALES AS ROYALE FISH Whereas for some years past the governors of some of our plantations have seized and appropriated to their own use the produce of whales of several kinds taken upon those coasts, upon pretense that whales are royal fishes, which tends greatly to discourage this branch of fishery in our plantations and prevent persons from settling there; it is therefore our will and pleasure that you do not pretend to any such claims nor give any manner of discouragement to the fishery of our subjects upon the coast of the province under your government, but on the contrary that you give all possible encouragement thereto... "

.   A new community of three houses is established a few miles north of the village. It is called Fire Place. The Millers and a Mr. King build on the shore.

The Parsons family settles at the bend of Fire Place Road, so named for the large fires that are burned on the shore at its end. They signal Gardiner's Island that visitors or goods are waiting to be brought over, or, that danger is near.

1731

January 8. To fulfill a need, the Trustees vote to build "a hous for ye towns use ye dimensions of sd hous to be Eighteen feet square and seven and a half between Joynts. And also agreed that sd. hous shall be set up and stand on ye same place where ye school hous now standeth."

December 10. In a major vote, the Trustees order a notice to be placed on a sign post "to warn inhabitants of This town to

assemble themselves at the meeting in order to put them selves
in some method for the support of the ministry for the future
for the Reason of the Great neglect for the time past."

1732

February 16. The Trustees order: "ye Negrows may sit in hind
seat in ye second Gallery on west side.... if they are not voted
down on ye Election day."

February 17. In Southampton, Francis Pelletreau writes
Ettienne Delancey about whale fishing:

"Sir: These few lines are to give you an account of the Whale
fishery in our village and in the neighboring village of East
Hampton, which has been very successful to the present time,
for eleven whales have been killed, 3 large and 8 small one. Of
these 6 have come ashore, and 5 are still afloat, which I expect
will come ashore if the wind continues.

"The six... will make about 220 barrels of oil, and about 1500
pounds of large whale bone, good for London (market) beside
small bone. And if the whales which are still afloat come ashore,
almost all of which belong to our village, they will make about
150 barrels of oil in addition, and a thousand pounds of large
whale bone. And if Mr. Delancey needs anything of this sort of
merchandise I shall always be ready to render him my services.
And I pray you, sir,...in case you have yourself no need for oil
or bone ... do me the favor to let me know the price that I can
pay for oil and bone, for I have no doubt but that it will be
offered to me.."

1733

. Town disbursements this year include payments to individuals
for: "2¹/₂ days at the watering hole,"   "mending the meeting
house glass and school house glass," "warning the Trustees," "2
wild cats' heads," "his man's one day work," "one bull and two
day's work," "committing John Field and Benet."

1734

January 10. The Trustees agree that Timothy Mulford "should
dig up the great gun that he sett in the ground" and that "the
boys or persons who broke the school house glass should be
prosecuted if they can be found by Daniel Osborn..."

1735

April 22. The Trustees "agree to sell the westward Lanes for
grazing to the highest bidder on the twenty-fifth of April at five
a Clock money to be paid in two month after sold." (The lanes,

sold for one year only, are part of the common lands. During the time when they are sold for grazing purposes, the gates to them are closed. People wishing to go through them may do so, providing they close the gates.)

1735/1739
. The South Fork is wracked by an epidemic of "throat distemper."

Worry increases as the two towns are hit with another illness,"lung fever." Together, the often fatal illnesses contribute to over one hundred deaths in three years. When blame for the illnesses is put on the scent of the privet hedges, the order is given to destroy all of them, including those that mark property lines.

1736
April 6. The Town Proprietors vote to divide amongst themselves the common lands north side of Accabonac Neck and Aylewife Brook Neck in the northwest part of town.

April/May. During these two months, the Trustees appoint four men to walk the woods that are to be divided, hire Nathaniel Dominy, Jr. to be surveyor and, with two helpers, to lay out the divisions.

The Trustees instruct the Proprietors to bring their "account of Commonage" to Justice Chatfield's house before May 20; then to "make out their Rights into thirteen acre lots;" and, finally, "to meet on Friday next at 12 a clock Inst to see their lots fairly drawn."

June 4. Forty lots of land are drawn by the fairest method possible. One box contains slips of paper with the names of each Proprietor. Another box holds slips of paper with the numbered lots of land. A name and a number are drawn, the two slips of paper are pinned, and the clerk records the drawing.

June 9 & 10. The Proprietors gather at the Meeting House to learn which part of the *ten acre division* is his. Ten acres of land have been allotted to one acre of commonage.

1737
July 19. The Trustees agree "with John Merry to keep the sheep between the fort pond & the sheep fence as long as the Trustees shall think fit to have them there and he the SD Merry to fold the sheep 24 nights and no more."

1738

September 4. The Trustees agree with George Miller "to keep ye sheep flock at Montauke and to keep them on this side the fort pond one mounth for fourty shillings to be payd in the Mentauke rate."

1739

July 9. John Stretton is to "have Liberty of the school house to teach school until another presents that shall be better approved of or till such time as the trustees shall think proper to discharge him from the school for misbehaviour."

1740

April 1. The Proprietors empoer the Trustees to manage the sheep on Montauk, and to manage Montauk this year.
May 1. The Trustees allow "Elias Mulford to keep a gore of land that he has laitly fenced in near the old brickels and two Rords whide in Amendment of the fore acre division," providing he opens a passage for watering.

1740/41

. The South Fork experiences a religious revival in East Hampton. Credit is given to the controversial Mr. Davenport, who substitutes for the ailing Rev. Huntting. More than 90 new members join the East Hampton church during this period. The revival also brings a number of Indians to Christian belief.

1741

. 162 Montauketts in 34 families are listed in this year's census.

1742/1743

. An epidemic of rampant dysentary plagues the South Fork.

1744

January 23. The Trustees agree "that country produce shall pass for the payment of the Towns and Meantuck Charge for the year 1744 at the following prise (that is to say wheat at 4s. ye bushell; rye at 22/6; indian corn at 2s; oates at 18s; flax and tallow at 6d ye pound.)"
. First House is built on Montauk, to house the keeper of the livestock pasturing in the summer.

1745

November 2. In Newark, the Rev. Aaron Burr, Sr. writes a letter of introduction for the young Rev. Samuell Buell to take to East Hampton: "Dear Sir, These come by Mr. Buell, whom we have prevailed with to make you a visit. It seems a very kind Providence yt sent him into these parts at this time.

"He appears to me the most likely person to unite your people. He is a pious, judicious, and ingenuous young man, and an excellent preacher.

"You will be pleased with him, and find occasion to bless God yt he is sent among you. Mr. Tennent joins with me in recommending him to you, in ye fullness of ye blessings of the Gospel of Peace. We should not have stopped his designed journey to Virginia for any other place...."

(Rev. Huntting's failing health is forcing him to retire after fifty-four years in the ministry. Rev. Buell will replace using the sometimes controversial Rev. Davenport from Southold.)

1746
. Second House is built on Montauk.
September 19. Rev. Buell is installed as rector in East Hampton. His opening sermon is from I Corinthians 11:2: "For I have determined not to know anything among you save Jesus Christ, and Him crucified."

1747
. Third House is built on Montauk.
. The manifest of the home-built sloop "Hampton" shows that she is sailing for the West Indies with a cargo of 70 barrels of beef, 30 barrels of pork, 5 barrels of tallow, 200 bushels of Indian corn, 7000 staves, 20,000 shingles, 1500 hoops, 28 anchor stocks, 500 bunches onions, 12 horses, and 70 sheep. She carries a crew of eight and seven swivel guns.
. With the Rev. Buell as minister, the meeting house/church built in 1717 becomes a member of the Presbyterian denomination.

1748
October 11. The Trustees agree "to give Hannah Tracey 4 loads of wood for taking care to shut ye Meeting House doors" and vote "to lay out North..est Swamps."

1749
January 3. The Trustees order "ye lots to be recorded in the 3 acre Division and...sundry pieces of land to be sold in order to defray the charges of laying out Northwest Swamps and the aforesaid Division."
June 25. The Trustees agree to let Cornelius Pain, Cordwainer, "set up a small house adjoyining to the lot of Peter Murdock on

the southeast side of sd. lot on the town commons and to fence
in one quarter of an acre of land (whar he is to set sd. house)
for a gardin."
. By year's end, all lands considered to be of value "for
improvement" are allotted in East Hampton.

1750
April 3. At the annual Town meeting, major vote gives
Napeague meadow owners "liberty to fence Napeague beach by
running a fence across by Barnes, and across by Amagansett
burying place...and that it shall be lawful to impower all horse
kind and neat cattle that shall be found grazing on said beach
or within said fence...from the first of may to the first of
September...."

1751
May 21. The Trustees order John Mulford and John Parsons to
go to Shelter Island and buy "a sorrel year old stallion of Mr.
Sylvester for Meantauck propriators."

1752
. Parliament enacts a change in the calendar. Eleven days are
dropped from September. Until now, Great Britain and Russia
continued to follow the Julian Calendar, in which the new year
began on March 25. Now the English and the American
colonies will join most of Europe in calculating time according
to the Gregorian Calendar. The Gregorian calendar, which dates
back to 1582, starts the new year on January 1.

1753
. East Hampton's first library starts this year when Rev. Buell
registers in the front of his books, "This book belongs to the
Philogrammatican Library in East Hampton, 1753."
July 5. The Trustees order "7 lb. of powder and 8 lb. of lead
bullets... to Meantuck to be left at Lopers in order to supply ye
Indians in case of an invasion by an Enemy."

1754
June 28. Three days after the Trustees appointed a committee
to meet with the Montauketts about ways to prevent trouble by
other tribes who come on Montauk, the two groups reach
agreement. The Montauketts "forever Debar and Exclude all
mustees or molattos that have Indian Squas to their mothers
Natives of Muntock for to have any Right Right to make any
Improvement of the said lands of Muntock...or to live theair...."

"Further...in case any Native squa of Muntock shall marry any Stranger Indian or forrener she or they shall forfeit and quit all theair Right title or Clame of improveing in any Muntock and neither shall their Husband or Husbands have any Right title or Clame to improve in any manner on said land."
September 12. Josiah Osborn writes his will. "My wife shall have which room in my house her life time to improve...I give my son Jedediah Osborn all my right in the Windmill...my daughter Sarah Osborn and to heirs of her body lawfully begotten 2 acres of land of my home lot which is convenient to seat a house on. To my son Jonathan Osborn my last loom and all my loom tackling and ten Lbs. of York money when he Shall arrive at the age of 21 years....I order that my red cow should not be sold but be kept for my wife and she shall have the best bed and furniture..."

1755
April 15. The Trustees clerk records today's activities:
"Sold ye liberty of pastuering ye Calfe pasture lane for this year to Lemiuel Hedges for 40s 6d & chose John Parsons ye 4th, Jeremiah Conkling & Samuel Parsons pounders for this year for Meantauk, and agreed to have Capt. Nathll Baker take care of ye flock of sheep at Town."

1756
May 6. Rev. Buell directs his sermon to the 38 men in the congregation who leave on the morrow for Lake George, and the French and Indian War. Eight of the men are from East Hampton: Isaac Barnes, Sr., Abraham Dayton, John Field, Jonathan Miller, 18-year old William Miller, Stephen Osborn, Abraham Schellinger, and John Squire.
Rev. Buell takes his opening remarks from I Chron. 19:13:
"Be of good courage, and let us behave ourselves valiantly for our people, and for the cities of our God, and let the Lord do that which is good in his sight."
Towards the end Dr. Buell asks the recruits to consider:
"That the cause you engage in is just and good...
"That a defensive war is frequently necessary as well as lawful, and an offensive war sometimes so...
"That we wage in war upon justifiable reasons... But 'tis so notorious a cause that we wage in war at this time, none need scruple the lawfulness of it - 'tis in defence of our own people, and the cities of our God - 'tis for a land that is ours by the first discovery and priority of possession, which is allow'd to give

title among civilized nations...'tis...for the good of prosperity as well as our own that we now wage in war.

"We learn by experience 'tis impossible to live by such blood thirsty neighbors as the French and their allies in America. They have broken the most solemn traties, made most injust encroachments and committed the most horrid barbarities in a time of professed peace. By their line of forts, surrounding our frontiers by land, they design we shall have but a garden spot in America - and as soon as possibly strong enough, to drive us all into sea - or, subject us to popish tyranny and superstition worse than death...while villainy secures all - our lives, our liberties, our religion..."

1757
July 5. The Trustees agree "to send 7 lb of powder and 8 lb of lead bullets to meantauk to be left at Lopers in order to supply ye Indians in case of invasion by an Enemy."

1758
June 27. The Trustees instruct "Capt. Mathew Mulford to imploy a joyner for to make a pue in the meeting house where ye east dore was and to lay floor in ye bellfre over ye bell."

1759
July 17. The Trustees agree "to send a noate to ye Indians for them to dispose of their dogs & lessen them to three, else we must send men and kill them, (the dogs)." The dogs have been "harming" the cattle.

1760
June 17. The Trustees vote "send twelve men to meantoke to dig & drean ye swamp at ye south end of the deep hollow & likewise for to girdle the trees round sd swamp and to clear ye Indian hogs out of the fatting field."

1761
May 9. Rev. Buell writes Rev. David Bostwick about the young Indian minister, Rev. Samson Occum, who has spent some time teaching the Montauketts: "As a preacher of the gospel he seems to have in view the end of the ministry, the glory of God and the salvation of men; his manner of expression when he preaches to the Indians is vastly more natural, free, clear and eloquent, quick and powerful, than when he preaches to others. He is the glory of the Indian nation."

1762

October 27. The Trustees agree: "...Joshua Parkin have libertey to clear a certain piece of land lying to ye northward of nathan Daytons land by ameganset path containing about one acre and half for to soe with wheat & to take three crops of & to sience all ye stumps so as to kill them & then to take away all his fence & leve ye land for a common."

1763

March 1. The Trustees agree "for two teams to goe down to Joseph Millers family to cart wood for them."
December 22. The Trustees choose Capt. Isaac Burns and Burnet Miller to prosecute the Montauketts for cutting wood "at ye point where they have no Liberty."

1764

March. Prime Minister George Grenville introduces a series of Declaratory Resolves to the House of Commons. To take effect the following year, the Stamp Act will raise revenue in the American colonies through a stamp tax on commercial and legal documents, newspapers, advertisements, and periodicals.
March 17. Dr. Buell writes to Rev. Barber in Connecticut:
"For a week past Heaven and Hell has seemed to meet here and to reign here. My House from Day to Day when we were not in the House of God, began from early morning to be filled with Sinners....Their cries for mercy continued Til ten in the evening. Their cries you might hear in every House as you walked the Streets."
On the third page, Buell tells Barber:
"...I have Scripture Warrant to hope that several of the People in this Town, have experienced a saving change in about a week, or a little more: Many have seemed to others, as well as themselves, to come as it were out of Hell into Heaven! Husbands and their wives, Parents and their Children, hopefully New-born. Among the rest we have a Jew, that I have reason to think is now a true Believer in the messiah, whom he always despised, 'till within a few days."
. The religious revival lasts eight weeks and brings in 99 new members.
May. In Boston, Samuel Adams responds to Grenville's new tax with a series of proposals. They embody the first formal public rejection of Parliament's assumed right to tax the colonies without their consent. The Massachusetts Assembly

adopts Adams' resolves and votes that a circular be issued to
other colonial assemblies, asking for their support.
June. Following review of Adams' circular, the Assemblies of
Pennsylvania, Connecticut, Virginia, South Carolina and New
York denounce Parliament's latest Acts.
  Insisting that, as free-born Englishmen, they cannot be taxed
without representation, they provise that if the king were
formally to ask them to make a contribution from available
sources, they would do so, generously.
. Unimpressed by the American colonies' reaction to a stamp
tax, Parliament passes The Stamp Act.
. Cadwallader Colden, Lieutenant Governor & Commander in
chief of New York Province, receives an undated petition:
  "The Petition of Silas Charles an Indian on behalf of himself
and other Indians Most humbly sheweth...
  "That Your Petitioner & those Indians concerned with him
constitute a Tribe commonly distinguished by the name of the
Montawk Indians, and are the Remains of a numerous Tribe
formerly inhabiting the East End of Nassau Island, and
constitute at present, about thirty families.
  "That upon the coming of the English into this country, the
Ancestors of the present Montawk Indians granted divers
Parcels of their Land to the People, who formed a Township
now called East-Hampton. That this tribe continued to reside in
the Neighborhood; living principally by Planting, Fishing, &
Fowling; gradually wasting away, and those who remain now
occupy a Tract upon Montawk Point.
  "That of late Years these Indians have discontinued their
Ancient Barbarian way of living, and are become not only
civilized, but christianized and are peaceable and orderly, and
willing to behave as good subjects to his majesty King George
the third and his Heirs and Successors, to do the Duty, bear the
Burdens, and be entitled to the Priveleges and Rights of faithful
Subjects. That as such a change of manners, as it exposes them
to a Life of Labour, must introduce an Attachment to Property,
without which they cannot subsist perform the Duties nor enjoy
the Right of Subjects.
  "That they are exposed to, and suffer great Inconvenience
from the contempt shewn to the Indian Tribes by their English
Neighbours at East-Hampton, who deny them necessary Fuel,
and continually incroach upon their Occupations, by fencing in
more and more of the Indians' Lands, under Pretence of sales
made by their Ancestors.
  "That your Petitioner and his Associates are in Danger of
being crowded out of all their ancient Inheritance, and of being

rendered Vagabonds upon the Face of the Earth; and are there-fore obliged to resort to his Majesty's Justice & Goodness, for an effectual Protection, and being advised that they have good Title to the Lands, as yet unsold, by the Law of Nature and Nations, that the Crown has, in all good times treated the Indian Rights, as deserving some Respect, and presuming that his Majesty will be graciously pleased to encourage their Design of becoming his civilized subjects, and their foresaking all the Idolatory of their Fathers,

"they intend to apply for the Royal Grant and Confirmation to them and to their Heirs, that they may also have such a Title as may be maintained in the Kings Court of Law, and afford them a Competent Protection against all Trespassors. But inasmuch as the barbarous and unlettered State of the American Indians rendered it impossible for them to keep Records, & your Petitioners cannot ascertain what Lands have been or remain still unsold

"Your Petitioner now, in Behalf of himself and the rest of the Montawk Tribe of Indians most humbly prays your Honour to give Directions for Prosecution of Intrusion, against all such as occupy any Lands between Montawk Point and Sagg Harbour to discover what Lands remain unsold, unless the Inhabitants of East-Hampton do, by a Day to be fixed, shew before your Honour, how far their Indian Purchasers, bona fide, made, do, or ought to extend; And that your Honour would be pleased to grant and confirm to said Indians (who will afterwards give in their Names) all the lands on Montawk-Point, that may appear to be still unsold by their Ancestors."

1765

. A post road is laid out this year. Riders on horseback will carry the mail on the 239 mile-long route which starts in New York. From there, the rider will go to Brooklyn, Jamaica, Smithtown, Riverhead, Southold, Shelter Island, Hog Neck, Sag Harbor, East Hampton and Southampton, stopping at villages along the South Shore on his return to New York.

1766

February. Parliament repeals the Stamp Act. It has become quite apparent to the English government that the American colonies will not submit to arbitrary taxation.
April 16. The Trustees agree with Siness Dibbel "to ring the bell and to shut ye meeting house doors and to have a care of the boys to keep them from playing around ye meeting house."

1767

January. Parliament passes tax laws that have been drafted by Charles Townshend, the new Chancellor of the Exchequer. Variations of earlier statutes, these set a tax on specific imports to the colonies. One of those imports is tea.

Summer. Parliament passes Townshend's Mutiny Act. The decree orders all colonials, on demand, to furnish quarters for British soldiers stationed in their town, and, when needed, to provide them with supplies.

. When news of the Mutiny Act reaches America, the New York Assembly refuses to comply. It lets it be known that the necessities will be provided at its own discretion. Parliament responds to that by abolishing the Assembly's powers. Undeterred, its members continue to meet and legislate, until the governor formally dissolves it.

1768

April 1. "By major vote," the Trustees "give Jacob Wickham liberty to cut timber on the parsonage land near grassee hollow for house & shop; likewise order advertisement to be put up that the calf pasture lane is to be hired to the highest bidder at the next meeting; and furthermore agree with Jeremiah Conkling to live at Montauk this year, etc...."

Summer. Parliament's Acts lead to an ever-widening breach between England and the American colonies. Over the summer, Merchants in the leading towns agree not to import British goods until the Townshend Acts are repealed.

In addition,

. Colonial women organize Daughters of Liberty associations, promise not to drink tea and only to wear homespun clothes.

. In Boston, Samuel Adams petitions the king and circulates letters to all the colonial assemblies. He calls for repeal of the Acts, and a return of the colonies to their previous status.

. Lord Hillsborough, the Crown's new Colonial Overseer, sets up Boston as an example. He orders the colonial assemblies to ignore Adams' circular, and dispatches two frigates and a regiment of soldiers to Boston.

. Adams realizes that there is only one road left. The colonies must declare their independence from the crown, unite together, and seek friends in foreign alliances.

Early October. Two regiments of British soldiers land in Boston.

A week later, Adams sends out a series of letters under the signature "Vindex." He advises that "a standing army within the kingdom in a time of peace, without the consent of Parliament, is against the law...and that the Americans, as they were not and could not be represented in Parliament, are therefore suffering under military tyranny."

. A Glasgow printing firm publishes a slim volume of two Narratives by Rev. Buell. The second Narrative, "...the Surprising Work of God's Grace. Begun at East Hampton March 1764," suggests why it happened:

"... Our remote situation from the continent, I suppose, hath in some measure been a means of preservation from those errors in doctrine; those amusements by controversies; and those corruptions in morals by vitious examples, ordinarily most prevalent in populous places ...

"There are about two hundred families belonging to the town of East-Hampton. The body of the town is so compact, that several hundred people live within hearing of the ringing, in a season tolerably calm and serene. Living thus compactly, hath been of advantage for the more swift propagation of a religious concern in the late day.

"There are belonging to the town two villages, the one about three miles east, and the other as far west, from the body of the town. I have been informed by the aged among us, that the first inhabitants of the town came from both Englands, and that some of them were very pious people ....

"About four or five years after my installment, I had what I have ever since called a small harvest of souls."

1769

January 4. The Trustees agree to cut the women's seats lower in the meeting house.

February 8. The Trustees agree to let the Proprietors erect a grist mill "in the street on the hill near Chatfield's house, or where the pound is."

. Parliament's attention remains on American affairs, this spring. After several influential members call for repeal of the Townshend Acts, Townshend's successor, the young Frederick, Lord North, proposes a compromise. He suggests repealing all of the Acts, except the tax on tea. He reasons: "America must fear you before she can love you...I will never think of repealing it until I see America prostrate at my feet."

Isaac Barré replies: "To effect this is not so easy as some imagine; the Americans are a numerous, a respectable, a hardy people...For my part, the America I wish to see is America increasing...prosperous...able to consume your manufactures, support your trade, and pour wealth and splendour into your towns and cities...Unless you repeal this law, you run the risk of losing America."

Parliament ignores Barré's warning. The tea tax remains.

May 10. Meeting in Williamsburg, Virginia's House of Burgesses condemns the tea tax, declares that taxation only can be levied through representation, urges the American colonies to unite in protest against the violation of their rights, warns the crown of serious consequences should it bring any American to trial in London, and orders copies of the declarations sent to every colonial assembly.

1770

January. Lord North resigns as Chancellor of the Exchequer to become Prime Minister.

February 12. The Trustees grant forty men permission to build a wharf in Sag Harbor. Nine men are from East Hampton, one is from Sag Harbor, the rest are from Southampton. The Trustees note that "trade and commerce are in general a benefit to mankind and in particular to the inhabitants of this town." The wharf is to start "at Southampton on East Patent line where Southampton grant for said wharf ends, and to run northerly thirty rods." The Trustees stipulate that the men must form a company and that its capital must be "divided into forty shares at 20 pounds each."

March 6. The day after four Boston men die in a clash with British soldiers, patriots hold a meeting. Samuel Adams leads the cry for the troops to leave. By sundown, their order for the troop removal is delivered to the British. It is refused.

1771

April 25. Thomas Foster, cooper, conveys a half share interest in the new long wharf at Sag Harbor to victualer Daniel Fordham.

August 7. The Trustees grant Jeremiah Conkling the right "to plow his wheat stubble again this year for which he is to drive ye cattle out of ye hither woods to ye point woods."

1772

May 28. The following ad appears in the New York Journal;

"First Long Island Stage Coach. The subscriber being much encouraged, proposes to erect a station wagon to drive from Sag Harbor on Long Island to Brooklyn once every week in summer and once every fortnight in the winter season...

"The Stage will set out from Brooklyn Ferry, with Passengers, at Ten O'Clock in the Morning of Monday, the 4th of May, and will that Night put up at Samuel Nicoll's on Hempstead Plains, where a Waggon will be ready for their reception on Tuesday Morning to carry them to Epinetus Smith's at Smith's Town and there exchangers; and then proceed to Benjamin Havens's at St. George's Manor; and on Wednesday Morning will set out from thence to Sag Harbour, where a Passage Boat will be ready to carry all Passengers to New London; likewise, stages are established in the different Towns in Connecticut and Rhode Island Governments, to carry Travellers to Boston.

"Terms for passage are as follows: From Brooklyn Ferry to Samuell Nicolls, 4s. each person; from Samuel Nicolls to Epinetus Smith, 4s; from Epinetus Smith to Benjamin Haven's, 4s; from Benjamin Haven's to Nathan Fordham's, 5s; Goods per Hundred, 1 penny per mile; and Baggage as usual.

"Thus a Passenger may, in three days, be conveyed 120 miles on a pleasant road for 18s., in a convenient Waggon, and meet with the best Entertainment.

Samuel Nicolls, Benjamin Havens, Nathan Fordham"

(Afternoon arrival in Southampton is followed by a slow, arduous ride to Sag Harbor. The last miles are traveled through darkened woods, with an Indian guide, lantern in hand, leading the way.)

August. George III orders Parliament to change a law that will have the Crown, not the colony, pay the judges' salaries in Massachusetts. (As it is, they serve at his pleasure.)

October. News of Parliament's latest Act infuriates the colonies. In Boston, Adams moves for the appointment of a Committee of Correspondence to deal with the political crisis.

The Committee would consist of "twenty-one persons to state the rights of the colonies and of this province in particular, as men and Christians and as subjects; and to communicate and publish the same to the several towns of the world as the sense of this town, with the infringements and violations thereof that have been made, and from time to time, may be made."

(The idea for a series of Committees throughout the colonies evolved from a letter that Rev. Jonathan Mayhew wrote in 1766 to Boston lawyer and patriot, John Otis:

"Cultivating and understanding and hearty friendship between these colonies appears to me so necessary a part of prudence and good policy that no favourable opportunity for that purpose should be omitted...You have heard of the *communion of churches*...while I was thinking of this in my bed, the great use and importance of a communion of colonies appeared to me in a strong light, which led me immediately to set down these hints to transmit to you.")

In adapting Mayhew's suggestions, Adams recommends that a regular system of committees of correspondence be organized throughout each American colony, and that they keep in touch with each other, linked in a common defense of their rights and freedoms. (This marks the genesis of the united colonies.)

1773

February 8. The Pennsylvania Gazette addresses Parliament's latest Act: "What the Parliament could not fleece from us by Taxes, the Crown will by Monopoly."

The Tea tax will grant the debt-ridden East India Company exclusive right to by-pass London's auction houses and ship tea directly to America. The new law enables the company's tea, even with a threepence tax added, to be cheaper than that brought in by the Dutch or, even by smugglers. The tax is only to be collected after the tea is put ashore.

September 5. The Trustees agree to consult a New York lawyer "on account of ye writings concerning Meantuck," and to forbid the picking of cranberries at Napeague before the first Tuesday in October and none to be picked "before sun one hour high." Offenders will forfeit the berries or their value to the Town.

Early October. Tea that has been stored for a long time in London warehouses is loaded on ships sailing for America.

November 10. The Trustees order the calves to be brought off Montauk on the 18th.

November 22. Committees from five Massachusetts towns meet at Boston's Faneuil Hall. Everybody agrees that no tea may be unloaded from any ship in the harbor, and that letters, asking for support, should be sent to other towns.

. The first ship laden with tea sails into Boston's harbor the end of November.

December 15. The Trustees' vote is unanimous: "...if any person or persons Shall set up innoculation of the small pox in the bounds of East-Hampton or that shall bring any person or persons from any other place or places in order to have the small pox after they are innoculated into Sd Township after the Date above he or thery shall be liable to...fines...and every person that shall be innoculated in Manner as above sd, for the small pox shall be liable to the like fine of the Sum of five pounds."

December 16. After more tea ships arrive in Boston's harbor and requests that they depart are ignored, nearly 7000 people

gather in and around the Old South Meeting House. A final
plea for the ships to leave is sent to Governor Hutchinson.

Hours pass before the rider returns with his answer, but nearly
everyone stays to hear it. The request denied, Adams quietly
tells the candlelit assemblage: "This meeting can do nothing
more to save the country." Less than two hours later, 342 chests
of tea are afloat in the harbor.

1774

February. News of the Boston Tea Party reaches London. An
infuriated Lord North seeks revenge through new measures that
he defines to Parliament. But, he finds unexpected opposition
in the House of Lords. Among the more outspoken members is
the Duke of Richmond, who rises from his seat to say:

"I wish from the bottom of my heart that the Americans may
resist, and get the better of the forces sent against them."

March 25. Opposition to North's vendetta is not strong enough.
Parliament approves his Acts. The Boston Port Bill closes the
port to all traffic until Boston indemnifies the East India
Company for the loss of its tea, makes Marblehead the new port
of entry, and Salem the new seat of government. The
Regulating Act strips the commonwealth of all power and
rights, bringing it under complete control of a crown-appointed
governor. The Acts are to become law on June 1.

May 10. Reports of North's Acts reach America.

May 12. At Faneuil Hall, Massachusetts Committees approve a
circular letter that Adams drafted. It calls on the American
colonies for support and sympathy.

June 17. East Hampton responds to Adams' circular. Clerk
Burnet Miller records the decision: "At a meeting of the
inhabitants of the town of East Hampton, in the county of
Suffolk, legally warned by the Trustees of said town, the 17th
of June, 1774,

"1st voted, That we will, to the utmost of our ability, assist and
in a lawful manner defend the immunities of British America;
that we will cooperate with our brethren in this colony, in such
measures as shall from time to time appear to us the most
proper and the best adapted to save us from the burdens we
fear, and in a measure already feel, from the principles adopted
by the British Parliament, respecting the town of Boston in
particular, and the British colonies in North America in general.

"2nd voted, That a non-importation agreement through the
colonies is the most likely means to save us from the present
and further troubles.

"3rd voted, that John Chatfield, Esq., Col. Abraham Gardiner, Burnet Miller, Stephen Hedges, Thomas Wickham esq., John Gardiner, Esq. and Capt. David Mulford, be a standing committee for keeping up a correspondence with the City of New York and the towns of this colony; and if there is occasion, with other colonies, and that they transmit a copy of these votes to the Committee of Correspondence for the City of New York. Voted Unanimously, not one contrary vote."

. This same day, the Massachusetts Assembly meets in Salem. Before reporting a suggestion made by the Sons of Liberty in New York, Samuel Adams asks that the doors be locked. He then calls for a Continental Congress to be held in Philadelphia on September 1, appoints delegates to attend it, and offers measures for the relief of Boston.

Summer. Colonial reaction to Adams' May circular is similar to that of East Hampton - with one exception. Pennsylvania clings to the hope of a reconciliation with England and the belief that dumped tea should be paid for.

Throughout the summer, droves of cattle, sheep, and other livestock; barrels of sugar, wheat, and maize, and cartloads of other provisions are taken to Massachusetts from American towns, including East Hampton.

(In Virginia, General George Washington declares, "If need be, I will raise one thousand men, subsist them at my own expense, and march myself at their head for the relief of Boston.")

September 5/Octoeber 26. Meeting in Philadephia, the First Continental Congress adopts the Articles of Continental Association. (In declaration, they parallel East Hampton's June resolution, which calls for non-importation of British goods.)

Congress adjourns on the 26th, after agreeing to reconvene May 10, 1775.

September 13. The Trustees agree that "no cranbres be picked on Nappege Beach until the 10 Day of October next every person picking before shall forfeit five shilling per bushel and all the Cranberies he or she shall pick; the one half of the fine to go to the town the other half to the informer or Informers."

November 15. The Committees of Correspondence from each Suffolk town meet in Riverhead. Clerk Ezra L'Hommedieu records the decisions:

"1. Voted That we recommend it to the several towns in the county to set forward a subscription for the employment and relief of the distressed poor in the town of Boston, to be collected in such manner as the committees in each town shall judge proper; to be in readiness to be forwarded early next spring.

"2. Voted That John Foster have the care of procuring a vessel to call at the several harbors in this county, to receive and carry the above donations to Boston.

"3. Voted That we fully approve of the proceedings of the late Continental Congress, and recommend it to the committees of the different towns to see that the Association by them entered into on behalf of themselves and their constituents be strictly observed."

1775

April 11. Meeting at 6 p.m. the Trustees agree...

"with John Hand that he should have the liberty of Drawing the Sain at Elwive brook Sololy to himself for this Season he not Debaring people from Catching fish to Eat in their familys for which privilege he is to Give two Dollars..."

"with Benjamin Hedges to live at the hither end of Meantock for one year to take and account of all cattle, etc."

"with Jeremiah Conkling ye 4th to live at meantauk at fatting field for one year to take care of said field."

"with Jacob Hand to live at the fort pond at Meantauk ..."

April 19. The first shots between British soldiers and colonial minute-men are fired in Lexington, Mass..

April 20. Deputies from the Committees of Safety of nine counties, and from the Council of Safety of the State of New York, meet in New York to form a Provincial Congress and draw up a set of laws.

April 29. The Town votes to adopt New York County's Articles of General Association which it has distributed:

"Persuaded that the Salvation of the Rights and liberties of America depends, under God, on the firm union of its inhabitants, in a vigorous prosecution of the measure necessary for its safety; and convinced of the necessity of preventing the Anarchy and confusion, which attend the dissolution of the powers of Government, we, the Freemen, Freeholders, and Inhabitants of East Hampton, being greatly alarmed at the avowed design of the Ministry to raise a Revenue in America, and shocked by the bloody scene now acting in Massachusetts Bay, do, in the most Solemn manner Resolve never to become Slaves, and do associate under all the ties of Religion, honour, and Love to our Country, to adopt and endeavor to carry into execution, whatever measures may be recommended by the Continental Congress, or resolved upon by our Provincial convention, for the purpose of preserving our

Constitution, and opposing the execution of the several
arbitrary and oppressive acts of the British Parliament, until a
reconciliation, between Great Britain and America, on
Constitutional Principles, (which we most ardently desire) can
be obtained; and that we will in all things, follow the advice of
our General Committee, respecting the purpose aforesaid, the
preservation of Peace and Good Order, and the safety of
individuals and private property."

The document ends with the notation that it contains the
signatures of "*every male in the Town ... that are capable of
bearing arms.*"

May 10/August 2. The second Continental Congress convenes
as an advisory committee in Philadelphia.

May 27. New York's Provincial Congress recommends that the
counties and towns within New York appoint committees.

June 22. John Chatfield, Chairman of East Hampton's
Committee of Correspondence, arrives in Philadelphia with East
Hampton's signed copy of the Articles of General Association.

It is a singular document, the *only* copy to carry the
endorsement of every able man in a community.

June 26. Continental Congress endorses the wording of New
York County's Articles of General Association.

June 28/July 28. Men from Southampton and East Hampton
enlist in a company being organized by Captain John Hulbert, a
wealthy Southampton farmer and merchant.

July 22. The Provincial Congress Clerk records: "Thomas
Wickham, member of the Provincial Congress from Suffolk,
produced a certificate from John Chatfield of East Hampton,
showing that every male inhabitant of the town capable of
bearing arms, had joined an association for resisting the
measures of Great Britain; and, on 5th July following, the
people of the town represent to Congress that they have not
less than 6000 livestock on Montauk exposed to the enemy,
and request that troops should be stationed there for
protection."

July 31. Provincial Congress approves a letter to be sent to East
Hampton and Southampton:

"By the enclosed copy of a letter from Gen. Washington to
Gen. Wooster, we think not unlikely the designes of these ships
may be to take provisions from different parts; as Montauck,
and other parts of the east end of Long Island are much
exposed, we judged it proper to give this intelligence, that you
might take such methods for securing the stock there, as you
shall judge necessary. Hulbert and Griffing's companies can be
employed for that purpose till otherwise ordered."

August 5. Ship owner John Foster advises Provincial Congress "that the committees of several towns in Suffolk County have resolved not to permit any cattle or livestock to be shipped from Suffolk County." (Word has come that cattle austensibly destined for the West Indies market is going to the British in Boston.) In his letter, Foster asks for permission "to take a cargo of livestock to the West Indies and return with military stores for the benefit of the Colony."

August 7. Provincial Congress sends a letter to John Chatfield:

"Sir, We have received your express and request you would use your best endeavors to prevent the ministerial army from taking off the cattle from your island...Powder will be sent you immediately with four companies from Gen. Wooster's camp.

"P.S. It is requested that the officers you may employ in this service be under Col. Fanning's command, that you would provide the troops with all necessaries." (Wooster is encamped in Harlem. Fanning is in Southold.)

August 8. Thirteen British ships sail into Gardiner's Bay. They include seven transports, one armed schooner, two men-of-war, two brigs, and one scow. In addition to their regular crew, the ships carry two hundred soldiers.

Abijah Willard, the British commander, wants to buy stock and provisions from Gardiner's Island, but Abraham Gardiner refuses to let him have any. (Gardiner was warned in late July that the English might try to plunder the island. Instead of taking the advice given, he argued that the family should not have to pay for the cattle's removal. Gardiner is the guardian of the island's owner, the minor John Lyon Gardiner.)

August 9. The Trustees agree "not to have any cattle go on to Meantauk till ordered as they were brought off on account of a fleet that appeared off ye point amd went to Fishers Island after Cattle."

August 10/11. After British negotiations with Gardiner fail, Willard orders his men to remove the best of the island's stock and provisions. It takes three days to take off 1200 sheep, 60 head of cattle, 30 hogs, 13 geese, 16 shoats, 1000 pounds of cheese, and seven tons of hay. Total value is almost $4000.00. Before his ship weighs anchor, Willard pens Gardiner a letter:

"Sir: As we have got loaded all the vessels, I can't come to your house, according to your promise. I send you account of what I have got off your island, viz: sheep, eight hundred and twenty-three; fat cattle, fifty-nine; cows, three; calves, three - one of the calves got away; the cheese I will take account of. Send me some pigs, fowls, potatoes, and ducks, and some bread; and when you come to Boston I will secure your interest to you, if in my power. I am sorry it is not in my power to come to your house; but so good a wind we can't stay. The hay you must send an account of by Capt. Lawrence.

"Sir, I am yours, Abijah Willard.

"August 11, 1775, 12 o'clock at night."

(He has been less than honest in the number of livestock that he has had removed, and less than honorable in infering that he and Gardiner enjoyed an amicable relationship, and that he was a welcome guest at the now-deserted island. Willard leaves his letter on a table in the living room. Soon after his fleet sails out of the bay, Gen. Wooster's troops land on the island.)

August 14. Committees of East Hampton, Shelter Island and Southampton hold a hurried meeting in Sag Harbor to determine the implications in Willard's letter. Each witness testifies that Gardiner is loyal to America and took a strong stand against Willard's demands. Concluding that Willard's letter was a deliberate attempt to bring Gardiner trouble for resisting him, the examining committee issues the following:

"We, the said Committee, having examined evidence under oath, and considered every circumstance relative to said affair, do unanimously conclude, that the said and other executors are entirely clear from all such imputations, and that all such reflections were entirely groundless."

August 16. Continental Congress orders "several companies of the troops of this Colony raised in Suffolk County (to) proceed with all possible dispatch to join the Continental Army under the command of major General Schuyler."

It also writes Gen. Wooster: "...as it is probable future attempts will be made by order of General Gage to take the livestock from the east end of Long Island and the islands near it, it is conceived by the Congress that to prevent such degradations it is proper that you should continue there with your troops till further order, which you are hereby desired to do accordingly."

August 24. William Johnson Rysam signs his will. In addition to legacies made to his children and grandchildren, the English-born sea captain leaves East Hampton 200£ "to be put out to interest and the interest...to be applied to the schooling of such poor children as the parents are not able to pay for schooling of their children, and the town trustees to be the guardians and judges of such children that may be objects of poverty."

September 7. Capt. Hulbert and his men march off Montauk with borrowed guns. They are on their way to New York and, from there, to Ticonderoga.

September 9. In Bridgehampton, David Pierson writes the Provincial Committee of Safety on behalf of East-Hampton and South-Hampton's Committees:

"Gentlemen - Your favor of the 25th of August we duly received and note the contents. We would cheerfully comply with your request in respect to raising two companies of minute men for the defence of the stock at Montauk, but we think it entirely out of our power, as we are but a small number of men here; and a considerable part of our strength is already gone in the service.

"We have called a meeting of the joint committee...this day, and have voted to call our militia together in the second battalion, in order to enlist a company if possible, to send directly off to Montauk, as it is at present without even a soldier to guard it, and we are fearful we shall not have sufficient ammunition amongst us to fix out one company; and should General Gage's troops come upon us in this destitute condition we shall be absolutely under the disagreeable necessity of complying with their terms. Therefore, gentlemen, we must beg the favour that we may have two companies sent here as soon as possible. It is the opinion of Gen. Wooster that we are in the most defenceless condition of any part of this Continent."

. Provincial Committee of Safety writes David Pierson:

"Sir - Your favour of the 9th current in behalfe of the united committees of East and South-Hampton came to hand this morning, in answer to which we advise that a number of men not exceeding twenty-five, be placed upon Montauk, with orders to drive the cattle off in case a fleet from Boston should arrive to rob at that end of the island again.

"We recommend it to you to be diligent in embodying your minute men, that should an attack be made upon any part of your county, they may be ready to march immediately. You will see by the regulations which the Congress have published for the militia, that the minute men, when called out to service, will be upon Continental pay. We can say nothing to you on the subject of ammunition, further than that we are not able to supply you with any."

September 23. The Recorder enters in the Committee of Safety's journal: "It being presented by this Committee that Capt. John Hulbert of the 3rd Regiment of the troops raised in the Colony and Capt. Daniel Griffin of the said regiment with their respective subaltern officers are all in the City of New York, and unable to proceed to Ticonderoga for want of money to defray their expenses, Resolved and ordered, That Peter V.B. Livingston, esq., as Treasurer of this Congress, pay to Capt.

John Hulbert 37£ 6 shillings and 9 pence....to enable them to proceed to Ticonderoga, or elsewhere to join the army under the command of General Schuyler ..."

September 25. Provincial Committee of Safety alerts Easthampton and Southampton's Committees:

"Gentlemen - One of our boats (employed to watch the motions of the fleet and army at Boston) is just arrived from the eastward, and inform us, that on the 21st inst., in the morning off the harbor of Chatham, near Cape Cod, they saw a large ship of war standing to the westward; and about three hours after, they saw four ships, one brig and 1 schooner, all standing the same course, over the shoals.

"Our boatmen could not, with any safety, go near enough to make a perfect discovery, but we apprehend they are part of a fleet destined for Suffolk county, for the purpose of getting more stock...The Colony troops raised in your county, being ordered by the Continental Congress to join the army to the northward without excuse or delay, you will therefore be under the necessity of acting with redoubled vigilance and resolution. Please - send copies of this express to the committee of Southold and Shelter Island."

October 13. Before he abandons his office in New York, Governor William Tryon writes the following, "This date considered as the close of royal authority here." He boards the "Asia," anchored in New York harbor. From there, he keeps in touch with the mainland.

late October. Hulbert's company escorts the British prisoners from the Lake Champlain region of hostilities to Philadelphia, where they are presented before Continental Congress. (Reports spread that Hulbert's march has done much to lift morale and speed up enlistments in the continental Army.)

1776

February 8. The joint committees of East Hampton, Shelter Island, and Southampton meet in Sag Harbor to draft a memorial to Provincial Congress: "Gentlemen - In the strongest confidence of your benevolent purpose of raising and stationing an armed force, with sufficient ammunition, who, with our minute men and militia, may, at all events with heaven's blessing, deliver and defend us from British attacks and ministerial vengeance, we have in low capacity but in high spirits, presumed to the utmost of our power to embargo; strictly prohibiting the sale of and exportation of all provisions on any pretence whatever until the 1st of March ensuing, or until we have the sense of provincial Congress.

"Now gentlemen, if your honourable house can condescend to our politics and think with us that it will best promote our great, our common cause, to retain the provisions which is now amongst us, rather than to permit them to be sold and exported, and consequently our army supported with provisions purchased, and perhaps, with great difficulty imported, when, as is menaced, our unnatural enemies shall invade us by land and sea; we say, if you can adopt our sentiments, by all that is dear to true zealous sons of liberty, we beg you will not compel us to flee before our enemy, but detach to our defence such ample number of troops, sufficient in conjunction with our own, to answer this important purpose, and in your wisdom, continue and confirm the above mentioned embargo. Signed by order of the committee, Maltbey Gelston, chairman

"P.S. The desire of this part of the county is that some method be fallen upon to establish a post from New York to the east end of this island that we may be favored with the earliest intelligence."

February 24. Provincial Congress approves the embargo memorial, and recommends it to the entire county.[8]

February 28. The Trustees agree "to let people turn horses & sheep to Meantauk...ye 5th of March" and appoint Abraham Mulford and Jeremiah Gardiner "to stake out a small Garden for John Gan adjoining his house ..."

March 4. Provincial Congress writes to John Chatfield in Easthampton and to Thomas Cooper in Southampton:

"Sir - this covers a resolution of Congress directing the committees of East and Southhampton to station suitable persons on the most proper places for observing the approach of a fleet. From some intelligence we have received, there is reason to expect that the British army are about to leave Boston, and as it is probable that they may attempt to take possession of this Colony, we therefore entreat you to use all possible despatch to carry this resolve into execution."

March 22. John Chatfield alerts the Provincial Committee of Safety: "This day about ten o'clock in the forenoon, our guard stationed at Montauck saw twenty sail of square-rigged vessels; five of them appeared to be large, and two sloops, bearing about SSE from the point of Montauck, about nine or ten miles to sea; the wind SSE the weather something thick and hazy, steering about NE by N, and sailed to the eastward of Block Island, and supposed by the course they steered that they were going into Rhode Island ... As we are a frontier at the east end of Long Island, I am destitute of men to defend us, and have but little ammunition."

April 7/8. Armed British ships appear in a fog off Montauk's north and south shores.

Throughout the shrouded day, the dispersed men-of-war keep track of each other with barrages of cannon fire.

. Worried about the livestock on Montauk, Easthampton's Townsmen call on young Jonathan Dayton to take 40 men, and do whatever he can to keep tthe British from landing.

On Montauk, Dayton orders his men to march around the hill, in full view of the fleet. Behind the hill again, and out of British sight, Dayton tells the men to take off their jackets, turn them inside out, put them on again, and march around the hummock, once more. The different look of their uniform may lead the British to believe that a large patrol is deployed on the barren land. His ruse works. The fleet weighs anchor after an aborted attempt to land.

April 16. The Trustees agree "with William Conkling to sweep the meeting house ring the bell and shut the doors and windows for one year for three pounds."

May 1. Fifteen hundred head of sheep and cattle are driven on Montauk. The sheep are sent to pasture on land between First and Second Houses. The beef cattle go to Indian Field; cows and calves, to the fields between Second and Third Houses.

May 4. The New York Committee of Safety orders all Suffolk County committees to disarm "disaffected persons" and turn over their weapons to Col. Henry B. Livingston.

. The order to disarm is carried out. Abraham Gardiner is relieved of his arms by Abraham Loper and John Davis of East Hampton, and Dan Collins of Guilford, Conn.. They remove "130 Fire Arms Bayonet Cartuch Boxes and 3 Silver Headed Swords, and taking from Coll. Mulfords 3 Casks of Powder and 2 Boxes of Lead Delivered to Coll. Livingston."

May 15. Continental Congress's resolution calls on the colonies to form independent governments. In a preamble, John Adams writes that no American in good conscience can take an oath to support any government whose authority comes from the Crown.

May 20. The Trustees agree to give Abraham Conklin 40/ "to enable him to transport two of his children into the Jerseys."

July 2. Twelve of the thirteen American colonies approve the Declaration of Independence. New York does not vote because its delegates have not received instructions.

July 4. This evening, the Declaration of Independence is adopted by twelve colonies. The New York delegation still is without orders.

July 9. New York formally adopts the Declaration.

July 12. Provincial Congress approves the written reply to the July 5 letter from Easthampton and Southampton:

"Gentlemen - Taking into consideration your letter of the 5th ins. applying to us for directions relative to the preservation of the stock at Montauk. Since the date of your letter, you must have understood that Col. Livington, the Commander in that quarter, has applied to the county Committee for their advice and assistance respecting the preservation of stock, and making necessary defence in your quarter.

"We also understand from Messrs. Dearing and L'Hommedieu that persons are appointed by the Commisssary-General to lay up all the stock in those parts fit for use, and also, boats to be provided to remove the rest in case of danger; viewing things in this light, we hope your fears are subsided. In case they are not from the measures already taken, we shall expect to hear from you, and shall not be wanting in supporting all the friends of the common cause of America."

July 16. The Trustees give the Widow Emma Miller "three £ to enable her to get over to Connecticut with her family."

July 20. Provincial Congress resolves that every Long Islander is to keep a small number of livestock and drive the rest to concealed places. Congress orders the militia, or the minute men, to kill livestock in danger of being taken by the British.

(In a letter to Gen. Washington, informing him of the resolutions passed, the Provincial Congress chairman adds:

"I cannot conclude without expressing my wishes that the detachment under Lt. Col. Livingston may be continued at their present post, for that part (South Fork) of the island is so much exposed to be insulted by the enemy's cruisers, that I fear the inhabitants would totally abandon the country should those troops be drawn off.")

August 26. The British land on western Long Island.

August 27/28. The Battle of Long Island last two days.

August 28. Provincial Congress asks Trumbull to send a thousand Connecticut troops to help Long Island, since most of Long Island's fighting men are with Washington.

August 29. Britain's Brigadier General William Erskine orders the Long Island committees to dissolve, lay down all arms, and turn over all livestock and wagons to the British army.

He ends his memorial with a warning intended for Suffolk County inhabitants: "...unless they show a dutiful submission in all respects, and an immediate compliance with these orders respecting the cattle and wagons, I shall be under the necessity of marching the forces of my command without delay into the

county, and lay waste the property of the disobedient, as persons unworthy of His majesty's clemency."
. This same day, Provincial Congress resolves "that it be recommended to the inhabitants of Long Island, to remove as many of their women, children and slaves, and as much of their livestock and grain, to the main, as they can; and that this convention will pay the expense of removing the same."
August 30. Washington abandons Long Island to the British.
August 31. From Sag Harbor, Rev. Buell writes Gov. Trumbull:
"...The Western Counties upon this Isle are already in their possession. With about 300 Horses and a foot company they are about to penetrate into this county I this hour came from our Committee who have desired me to record their request to your Honor: That if possible you throw a number of troops upon this island as soon as possible...We are the rather encouraged to hope for this favor in our present extreme emergency....We have three companies stationed here consisting of 90 men each, together with a 3rd part of our militia, who are ordered to march immediately up the Island. About 15 miles from here our people are erecting a strong breast work. Where this part of the island is, but about 50 rods wide... 200 men may oppose 2000. As one half of our militia is already in the army, we extremely need some assistant without any Hyperbole.
"There are ten thousand people with all the stock in this county which will probably fall into the hands of the King's troops, unless we have some assistance. Your Honor will take a full view of such shocking consequences and doubtless be assured that it will greatly tend to intimidate the enemy to hear that there is an army marching against them from the Eastward and much befriend your Honor's great confident, the excellent General Washington. But I need not multiply words."
. In the next days and weeks, boats cross and recross Long Island Sound, taking Long Islanders to safe refuge in Connecticut. Among the refugees from Easthampton are Dr. Aaron Isaacs, his wife, and their eight children. They depart with 3 loads of Household Goods, 8 loads of Goods, cattle and horses, 2 hogs, 9 loads of hay, 2 loads of corn, 15 bushels of oats, 1 Riding chair, 56 sides of leather, 20 calves skins, 2 pots of butter, 1 bag of copera, 1 yoke of oxen, and 2 fat cows.
September 1. Major General Delaney orders Long Island residents to take an oath of loyalty to the Crown.
September 5. David Gelston of East-Hampton, who is active in helping the Long Island refugees, writes to the New York State Convention from Saybrook, Conn.: "Can only tell you the

distresses which I hourly see and hear from Long Island, are beyond my power to describe."

September 7. Abraham Gardiner writes Trumbull: "In consequence of a report prevailing in town that the people of Connecticut are coming to take away our Livestock and effects, the Trustees, who transact the business of the town have met early this morning, and unanimously agreed to send an express humbly requesting Your Honour's Prohibition of such measures, as apprehensive, if prosecuted, we shall be involved in perplexities and sufferings, far beyond those we are now the subjects of, in that it may be constructed, we are somehow accessory thereto, (which we are not) being subjects of His majesty King George and therefore mean not to act a part exposing us to his displeasure. We have therefore thought proper to request Your Honour's interposition, as we judge in our favour...we are your honour's humble petitioners."

Rev. Buell appends a memo:

"Sir, The Trustees have desired me the subscriber to signify to Your Honour my acquiessence in the above request which I now do and in testimony thereof, Subscribe myself Your Honour's humble and obliged petitioner."

. Gen. Erskine issues a requisition to Suffolk County residents:

"You are hereby ordered to preserve for the King's use ___loads of hay, ___bushels of wheat, ___of rye, ___of barley, ___of indian corn, and all your wheat and rye straw; and not to dispose of the same, but to my order in writing, as you will answer the contrary at your peril."

September 8. Livingston, whom Washington has appointed to command the east end of Long Island, writes Trumbull:

"Since I wrote to Your Honour the People of East-Hampton and Southampton have almost universally taken an oath of Allegiance to George the third, King of Great Britain. It was tendered to them by Col. Gardiner since I came here. They are now driving their Cattle into the woods in order to hide them from us. They had brought them from Montauk Point to East Hampton in order to drive them westward to the Enemy in Compliance with a Proclamation issued by General Erskine who is appointed Commanding Officer for the Eastern Part of Long Island by General Howe.

"The want of whale boats is a great inconvenience to us as a retreat is almost impracticable without them should any Vessels of force be in the sound.... I have just received a letter from him (Gen. Washington) desiring me to endeavour with all my Powers to distress the enemy as much as possible But not to run any Risk of the Detachment by suffering my Retreat to be cut off...the bearer (of the letter) Captain Conklin has offered his services to cruise off Montauk Point to give intelligence of the enemy's motions, if he can be furnished with a swift-sailing vessel he has in his eye at New London... "

September 10. In a letter to Trumbull, Livingston absolves David Mulford of East-Hampton of any Tory complicity:

"I have just now received your favors of yesterday since which I have taken Colonel Abraham Gardiner who tendered the oath of Allegiance to the inhabitants of South and East Hampton. I am told he, with a party of men, surrounded the house of Colonel Hedges at Sagg and Colonel Mulford at East-Hampton and obliged them to take the oath much against their inclination."

September 13. The day before he sails again for Long Island "to harass and distress our Enemies," Livingston writes his mother from Saybrook, Conn..

"...Being deserted by the Militia of Suffolk County whose fears got the Better of their Patriotism I was obliged to make a retreat from the Island. I have taken Col. Gardiner and some other Prisoners; they are to be detained on their Parole at Colchester...The Inhabitants of Long Island who were wont to live in affluence are now obliged to quit their Habitations and depend upon the Charity of their Neighbors in Connecticut for subsistence. I have procured a number of vessels for their Removal at Governor Trumbull's request."

September 15. Livingston writes Trumbull that, following Gen. Howe's order for enlistment and impressment of 2000 Long Island men, "the Sag Harbor wharves are packed with men and families seeking refuge in Connecticut."

September 22. In another letter to Trumbull, Rev. Buell responds to rumors that the governor has ordered all East End residents to depart with their goods or, be judged and punished, as favoring the enemy. Buell agrees with Trumbull's sentiments, but he feels that to uproot the people completely would not be fair because Southampton and Bridgehampton already are stripped bare. He uses a pseudonym at the end:

"When of late I have wrote your Honor, it has been seized and stopped by the way...reports...have been ventilated that Your Honor had given positive orders for the removal of the people from the east end of this island, with all their effects, and those who obeyed not must be judged inimical to the general good of America, and expect to be utterly laid waste and destroyed....

"In this their distressed situation the people have their waiting eyes lifted up to your Honour, requesting and supplicating that if possible, a stop may be put to these last-mentioned oppressive methods of procedure. They look upon themselves as a people given up by the continent and know they must obey the orders which are given them, or abide the infinitely shocking consequences of a refusal... Notwithstanding emigration there now are at least a thousand in the town of East-Hampton. Tis impossible for them all to remove to the continent with their effects. Many families would be ruined as to worldly substance in so doing. The people in their present distressed and perplexed situation would yet hope that they may not be as a torch on fire at both ends, which must necessarily have a quick consumption. Considering the times in which we are fallen, your Honour will please to excuse me if I only add your Honour's etc etc   Incognito"

October 1. Howe orders all livestock and grain on Long Island to be taken from the rebellious residents.

October 21. East-Hampton's Committee of Correspondence dissolves itself with the following declaration:

"We, the Committee of East-Hampton, in the county of Suffolk, being thoroughly convinced of the injurious tendency of our former meetings and resolutions, and willing to manifest our hearty disapprobation of all such illegal measures, do hereby dissolve this committee and as far as in us lies revoke and disannul all former orders and resolutions of all Committees and Congresses whatsoever as being undutiful to our lawful sovereign, repugnant to the principles of the British Constitution and ruinous in the extreme to the happiness and prosperity of this country."

(Other town committees in Suffolk County have drawn up similar declarations and sent them to Gov. Tryon, who has set up headquarters in Southampton.)

November 18. The Trustees vote to have Jacob Hand take care of the sheep "and defend them from the Indian dogs."

December 10. Rev. Buell writes Tryon:

"Sir Yours by Mr. Hedges came safe to Hand with the Proclamation of Viscount Howe and Williame Howe Esq. Which publicly read after Divine Worship. - and which I am very sure was very universally assented to, and acquiesced in. - And can assure You, Sir, that inhabitants honestly design to remain in a peaceable Obedience to his Majesty, and will not take up Arms, nor encourage others to take up Arms in Oppposition to his Authority: - At the same Time - be equally assured, that should they be compelled to take up Arms against the Continent this east End of the Island is absolutely ruined and Destroyed. - We are so situated that our condition is insular and extremely critical. We can't defend ourselves - should the King's troops attempt, we expect they will soon be cut off - shipping can't block up the Sound so but that Continental Soldiers Cross. - They and Privateers, at Pleasure and there are many of each at, or between us and the Opposite shore who visit us often and suddenly - and have already greatly oppressed us -

"I assure You, Sir, this moment while I am writing I hear of a Number of continental soldiers just come into Town. - what number there is at Sagg Harbour I can't yet find out, nor their design - Judge You, sir, what our poor soldiers must do who were designing to set out tomorrow morning to wait upon his Excellency Governor Tryon: - some I suppose will not now dare to go - others perhaps will,- tho' they stand a chance to be transported to the continent immediately upon their return. -

"I am persuaded, sir, you pity us in this our unhappy Situation, and You will I doubt not use your Interest and Influence that we be not necessitated to procure the Resentment of the Continent to our utter Ruin. - We have great confidence in the Benevolence and clemency of the King's officers - hoping that at present we may be suffered to abide in a peaceful subjection to his Majesty - without becoming active so as to produce our own Destruction.

"Sir, You propose in Yours, that I inform Col. Gardiner and other Friends in New England, concerning the Proclamation You sent me and Benefits to be enjoyed thereby. This I can freely do - and doubt not but the Militia that are gone from us, for fear of being pressed, would with others, gladly return to us, though they stole away, could I assure them, they shall not be pressed into Service - that may cost them their Lives, and in the issue prove the ruin of this End of the Island - could Mr. Hand and You, Sir, (our representatives) obtain such a privilege for us? - Happy for us it would indeed be! -

"As to my own Self, Sir, - I feel myself, a Subject of King George and honestly mean to act in character - I have been so active in getting the Fat Cattle to General Howe - and have so warmly opposed Peoples leaving the Island, etc. etc. - that I have been seased and carried to Sagg-Harbour in order to be transported to the main - but Indisposition prevented - I now stand upon a Parole of Honour. - I am however most of all concerned for my Dear People. We often hear Prophecies fom the other Side of the Water, that we here shall have an oppressive dreadful winter - I boldly confront those Prophecies - relying on *British honour* - and fail not to comfort the fearful - I trust not without sufficient Grounds - If I am mistaken, I shall be confounded and must remain for ever Silent.

"But tis now after midnight, and I shall weary You, Sir, with reading as well as my Self in writing - However, I have to add, that I write at the Desire of the Principle men in Town - am not without fears, this Letter will be stopped before it goes out of Town - Such are the Times in which we are fallen - You will therefore excuse me, if I subscribe to Yours - etc., etc. Incognito"

December 24. In Southampton, Tryon writes Lord George Germain, Secretary of State for the Colonies, that he reviewed Suffolk County's Tory militia earlier in the month. Some of the 800 men who came and took the allegiance were from Southampton and East-Hampton. More, he adds, would have come, if rebel parties had not been on the east end. Tryon encloses Buell's December 10 letter to him, noting:

"Mem. The above wrote by the Rev'd. Mr. Buell, Presbyterian Minister... of East-Hampton - a favorer of the Rebel Rank, until converted by the victory of the 27th of August."

December 25. Gen. Sir William Erskine leads British soldiers through a blinding snowstorm, into Southampton.

1777

. Food is scarce on the East End during the early months this year. Troops from both sides plunder available provisions, each side rationalizing that if it does not take them, the other will. Raid after raid is made on sheep and cattle, and farmers are forced to kill their milk cows in order to feed their families.

April 20. New York State's Constitution is adopted.

Article XXXVI addresses previous Patents granted to communities within the state: "...be it further ordained that all grants of land within this State, made by the King of Great Britain, or persons under his authority, after the fourteenth day of October, one thousand seven hundred and seventy five, shall be null and void; but that nothing in this Constitution contained shall be construed to affect any grants of land within this state made by the authority of the said King or his predecessors, or to annul any charter to bodies politic by him, or them, or any of them, prior to that date..." The Dongan Patent remains in effect.

May 23/24. Secret dispatches from the South Fork have kept the militia in Connecticut apprised of events on Long Island. A surprise attack is planned after news arrives that the enemy broke camp at Southold, and left for New York on May 21, and, that the British have considerable provisions stored in Sag Harbor.

Lt. Col. Jonathan Meigs and 170 continental soldiers (some of them from East-Hampton) embark from Guilford, Conn. for Sag Harbor. They sail across Long Island sound, tote their boats across the beach to Peconic Bay, and push off. It is midnight when they land about four miles from Sag Harbor, hide their boats in the woods, and set off on foot.

Meigs' attack is a success. British supplies, on shore and in ships at anchor, are destroyed and, without loss of life on either side, ninety British soldiers are taken prisoner. Twenty-five hours after leaving Guilford, Meigs, his men, and their prisoners are on Connecticut soil.

May 29. In a letter to Gen. Parsons, Gen. Washington responds to news of the Meigs expedition:

"Dear Sir: I am just now favored with your letter of the 25th by Major Humphrey. The intelligence communicated by it is truly interesting and agreeable. And now I shall take occasion, not only to give you my hearty approbation of your conduct in planning the expedition to Long Island, but to return my sincere thanks to Lieut. Col. Meigs and all the officers and men engaged in it......"

. The War Board report on Meigs' raid leads Continental Congress, then sitting in Philadelphia, to recognize his success with "an elegant sword to be provided by the Commissary-General of Military Stores and presented to Lieut. Col. Meigs."

June 12. The Committee of Safety receives a petition from Long Island refugees in Connecticut: "Our distress is daily increasing, our wants constantly multiplying, the strictest prohibition of passing to Long Island to get over anything to support ourselves on and little or nothing to be had here for paper currency and hard money we have not. Harvest is approaching and some of us have bread Corn (on Long Island) and we desire permits to pass and repass to take over to the Relief of our families that forage that will otherwise fall into the possession of more than savage Enemies."

. Gen. Erskine sets up headquarters in the Gardiner house on Main Street. Across the road is the publick house which the widow of Rev. Huntting opened, following his death in 1751. It was the only means she had of supporting herself and her family. The house was built for the minister in 1699, on property bought by the Church of England. The Huntting house is considered neutral ground by both sides of. the war. Here, British soldiers off duty can relax, as can the townsmen.

June 26. Connecticut's Committee of Safety resolves: "On the presentation of John Mulford Esq. of Long Island, now resident in Stonington, shewing he is very infirm, has no means of support in this State, that he hath an estate on Long Island and is desirous to return with his family and some stock, for the recovery of his health and support of his family &c; ... the said John Mulford Esqr., and wife be permitted to return to Long Island, taking with them one horse and one cow."

September 2. Sgt. John Parsons, a member of the 5th Co. of the 4th New York Regiment, is killed.

October 10. The Trustees vote to write a letter to the captain of a British ship that is anchored off Montauk "about his taking off the stock at so low a price."

November 15. Continental Congress adopts the Articles of Confederation. The agreement, which will have to be ratified by every state, defines the relative powers of Congress and individual state responsibilities.

December 29. The Trustees agree to notify Dr. Lawrence, David Russill and the people of Southampton that they are not to set up innoculation in East Hampton. If they do, "they must abide the consequence."

1778

March 21. In New York, Guy Johnson, Colonial Superintendent of Indian Affairs, addresses a letter to: <u>Montauk on the East end of Long Island:</u>

"Whereas the Indians of Montok &c have represented to his Excellency the Commander in Chief here & to me - The hardships they labor under through the many restrictions laid upon them by the Inhabitants on the East End of Long Island, particularly in the articles of fishing, hunting, and other things necessary to providing a Sustenance for their families, as well as respecting they are circumstanced about their Lands which has been long considered & represented by them as a Grievance - I am therefore authorized to require you will take these matters into Consideration and that you will Afford these Poor People such Liberty and Indulgence as they have reasonably required as it is his Majesties' Pleasure to give all Protection and countenance to those Indians who by their Fidelity are entitled to the favor of Government."

October 10. Rev. Buell writes Gov. Trumbull about his recent "personal interview" with Tryon. When Tryon was on the East End, he suggested that Buell propose "exchanging a variety of commodities ... such as Rum, sugar, molasses, tea - whatever may please the ladies - in short, any kind of bartering, excepting salt and military stores. His Excellency supposed such an Exchange might possibly be agreeable, as useful to both sides; and as tending to remove distances....Your

Excellency will determine whether it is expedient to return an Answer to the above proposal by the present medium of conveyane, or otherwise.

"In converse with his Excellency, Gov. Tryon, he repeatedly made mention of burning, laying waste property, and distressing the Inhabitants upon the Sea Coast, as what was talked of in the past Government....Whether this is held up to view *in terrorem* or fully designed,...I am permitted to make mention of it to your Excellency....His Excellency appeared to wish for the proposed Effect, in consequence of apprehension, rather than putting so shocking a plan in execution."

Buell adds that Tryon wrote him, "I find our Political creeds are as opposite as light from Darkness. "Then, he sums up his own credo: "I cannot afford oil to those springs which seem to move and accelerate or retard the Wheels of State as on one Side or the other...at whatever Bar of the Public I may stand - and perhaps stand impeached, for my conduct in the present Day - I am not anxiously concerned - if Wisdom sits at the helm of Government and Justice tempered with clemency, holds the Balance of retribution...secure within myself, am incomparably more concerned for the Weal and Prosperity of my Native Country and the Public."

1779

May 10. The Trustees order Christopher Hedges "to tag the sheep on Thursday the 13th Instant and to keep all the sheep to the westward of the fort pond till further orders."

June 10. Provincial Congress votes that the Governor grant Aaron Isaacs, who has been living in Haddam, Conn. with his family since September 1776, permission to return to East Hampton "and bring from thence his horse and a quantity of flax he has there."

August 16. The Trustees agree "to send two men to Montauk to look for wounded cattle and provide the best they could for them."

August 23. The Trustees agree to buy a stallion from Ebenezer Hedges for 22£ and "to send one man to New York to inform General Tryon that "the Kings troops hath taken a number of cattle of the land of Montauk by way of plunder ..." and to send "one man to Montauk to watch the motion of the Kings ships."

1780

. In September, the British fleet anchors in Gardiner's Bay.

September 26. British Admiral Marriott Arbuthnot reciprocates his recent dinner at Abraham Gardiner's house with a party aboard the flagship "Royal Oak."

His guests are the Gardiner family, Rev. Buell, and others from the Village. They dine on curry, boned fowl, and hotly seasoned "The Devil." Wine is plentiful. This leads the minister to recite a poem and muse about the fruit and women on board, and to wonder what the consequences might be. Arbuthnot is quick to reply that, with "thanks to God, no Eves are aboard."

1781

January 23. While in search of the French fleet, the "H.M.S. Culloden" runs into an intense gale and is driven ashore east of Fort Pond Bay in Montauk. Her rudder breaks in two and all attempts to free her and turn her around fail.

January 26/February 14. The Culloden's crew works to dismantle their ship of her cannons (at least 46), masts, and anything else which is salvageable for use on other damaged ships.

March 1. The Articles of Confederation are ratified. (Virginia, the sole holdout, agreed to it after New York, Connecticut, and Maryland agreed to deletion of the article which would have left ownership of western lands to those states that already had claimed them).

October 19. Gen. Cornwallis raises the white flag in Yorktown.

December 31. The Trustees' clerk records:

"Whereas Government hath demanded forty tons of hay of the inhabitants of the town the Trustees did assign each man the quantity that he should procure for Government."

1782

February 4. The Trustees agree "to give the widow Esther Filer one bushel & half wheat..." and that "lui Osborn should go to Southampton to confer with the Doctors respecting their assisting Daniel Dayton in the innoculation of the small pox."

1783

March 14. The Trustees agree that the horses can go on Montauk on the 24th and that no bulls, three years old or older, can run on Montauk unless the ends of their horns are blunted.

September 3. The permanent Treaty of Peace between England and the thirteen United States of America is signed in Paris.

November 25. The British evacuate New York.

. Soon after the Americans take possession of New York, East Hampton receives orders to call a town meeting and elect Town officers under the State of New York. The Town Clerk records, "we accordingly did and chose all those that were chosen the preceding April."

1784

April 1. The Town votes "that all children not inhabitants of East Hampton, but sent here from other towns for the purpose of schooling shall pay school house at the rate of six shillings per year each child."

December 6. The Trustees agree "to pay Zebuon Howell £8 for going to New York in the year 1776."

December 28. At the urgings of and under the guidance of Rev. Buell, the future of East Hampton Academy is assured when the Proprietors meet to consider its incorporation.

The Academy, the first to be chartered by the new State Board of Regents, will offer advanced education to students ot East Hampton and beyond. Its teachers and students are to be governed by the laws the Proprietors draw up. Jabez Peck is to be master of the classical school. William Payne is named professor of the writing and English school. ($5,000 has been raised to build the three-story, forty window Academy.)

1785

January 2. The following notice is published:

"East Hampton Academy being now completed for opening on the first Monday in January, the proprietors inform the public that they have founded their edifice for the benefit of society as a Seminary of education upon the most liberal and effectual plan. It is provided with the most approved masters for reading, writing, English, Grammar, and elocution, also, arithmetic, book-keeping and navigation, surveying, geography, and all the most useful branches of the mathematics; also, the Latin and Greek languages, and the principles of French, and whenever sufficient encouragement shall appear a professor of that polite and useful language will be provided.

"The building is spacious and elegant and perfectly calculated for the design. The utmost attention will be given to establish such plans of discipline and modes of instruction as will fix the attention and give the complacency of the pupils while they inform the mind, improve the manners, and rectify the heart.

"Good accomodations for scholars are provided on very moderate terms the price of board will not exceed one dollar per week that of tuition will be according to the hours of attendance and the branches taught - reading, writing and arithmetic will not exceed two dollars per quarter. Such are the peculiar advantages of situation and other circumstances, as to give the utmost reason to believe that such as may make a trial of the Institution by sending their youth for education will be perfectly satisfied with the experiment."

1786

February 2. The Academy issues an advertisement:

"A spectator of the late annual exhibition at the East Hampton Academy says that of nearly 50 youths who made their appearance on the stage in the course of the day and the evening, there were not five whose present accomplishments in speaking would not be an ornament to the pulpit or the bar -

"Declamation in Latin, Greek, and French were elegantly spoken. The examples of penmanship were rarely excelled. What is remarkable is the number of young ladies and little misses who presented themselves with all the ease and elegance of an Assembly room, joined with the elocution of a theatre."

June 26. The Trustees agree "to give a Bounty of four shillings for every old Fox and two shillings for every Young Fox that shall be killed in the Township of East Hampton."

1787

April 3. Major vote at the annual Town Meeting calls for the three Overseers of the Poor to: "... bind out as apprentices all the children of such parents belonging to this town, as are unable to maintain them, and also to compel all such persons to work as have not any visible means of gaining an honest livelihood, agreeable to an act of the Legislature of this State passed the 17th day of April, 1786."

November 5. The Trustees favor "to send Doc. Gardiner and Phineas Hedges to Sagg harbour to lay out a highway for the use of our town."

1788

March 2. The New York State Assembly and Senate vote to annex Gardiner's Island to East Hampton.

August 20. By Act of Congress, Sag Harbor is made New York State's second port of entry.

The law stipulates that "The district of Sagg Harbor shall include all bays, harbors, rivers, and shores within the two points of land which are called Oyster Pond Point and Montauk Point."

1789

March 4. Superceding the Articles of Confederation, the Constitution of the United State becomes the law of the land.

June 29. The Montauk Proprietors appoint a committee of five to work with the Trustees on the problem between the Montauk tribe and Jonathan Hedges, and others. The Proprietors give their representatives full power "to support the said Indians in defending their privileges at Montauk provided they can have security for the payment of moneys expended in said business."

1790

August 10. Meeting in New York City, the U.S. Congress makes Sag Harbor a federal port of entry.

Chapter XXXV is "an act to provide more effectively for the collection of duties imposed by law on goods, wares, and merchandise imported into the United States." The district of Sag Harbor will be all waters and shores between Oyster Pond Point and Montauk Point.

1791

May 10. David Frothingham publishes Long Island's first newspaper this Tuesday in Sag Harbor. *The Long Island Journal* shares space at the foot of main street, near "The Landing," with his printing shop, book store, and bindery. Frothingham's principle, "Eye nature's walks, shoot folly as it flies, - and catch the manners living as they rise" appears under the masthead.

1792

March 5. The Trustees vote to give Henry Dominy 8£ to build a school house at Northwest.

October 17. The New York Chamber of Commerce appoints a committee of five men to hire someone to determine the best location for a lighthouse on Montauk Point.

November 1. In a letter to the Chamber committee which hired him, Ezra I'Hommedieu reports his findings. He advises purchase of 13 acres at Turtle Hill, including the beach to highwater mark, "seventy-five feet above the level of the sea at highwater, and two hundred and ninety seven feet from the shore. The hill is equally high to the Bank and the land equally good for a foundation... being to appearance gravel, stone, and marl, with clay...we find it necessary to take in this quantity of land in order to have a dwelling place, well and garden, below the hill westward.

"Not withstanding the height of this hill, above the water, there are others at a distance near the sea, something higher, which will make it necessary...to have the Light House seventy or eighty feet above the top of the hill, so that the same may be seen over the land by vessels which may be to the westward near the shore. On the north side there is no obstruction. We could see Plum Island, Gardiner's Island, and Fisher's Island very plain.

"... as the Bank is washed by the sea in storms, we suppose it best to set the Building at this distance ....The Proprietors are content to take six pounds per acre for the land, provided the United States fence the same, or such part thereof as shall be unproved, at their own expense. They will also grant the privilege of landing on any part of their land, and carting through the same, whatever may be necessary for the Light House. The title must come from the Proprietors, and not from trustees, who have no power to convey....."

At first reluctant to sell the Montauk land, the Proprietors agree, on condition that additional construction is confined to the keeper's cottage. Price, in U.S. currency, is $15.00 an acre.

1793

March 2. After debating the issue of a fifth lighthouse, Congress sanctions $20,000 for Montauk Light's construction.

September 2. Arbitrators Nathan Fordham, Jonathan N. Havens, and James White set a precedent when they decide how to end the dispute between David Russell and the Proprietors on the meadows next to Russell's property in Little Northwest Neck:

"... it would be beneficial for all parties concerned to lay aside the old passing highways mentioned in the records, and in the room of them to establish new passing highways for the conveniency of the Proprietors of the meadows ... all such parts of old recorded roads running on each side of the neck ...ought to be considered as private property of the said David Russell after the said new roads are laid out..."

1794

June 15. John Lyon Gardiner records a conversation that he had with his overseer's mother:

"Mrs. Miller remembers well when they first began to drink tea on the east end of Long Island. She tells a number of curious stories about their awkward manner of using it. One family boiled it in a pot and eat it like samp-porridge. Another spread the leaves on his bread and butter, and bragge of his having eat half a pound at a meal, to his neighbor, who was informing him how long a time a pound of tea lasted him. She remembers the first tea kettle that was in East Hampton. It came ashore at Montauk in a ship, the 'Captain Bell.'

"The farmers came down there on business with their cattle, and could not find out the use of the tea kettle, which was then brought up to old 'Governor Hedges' some said it was for one thing, and some said it was for another. At length one, more knowing than his neighbors, affirmed it to be the ship's lamp, to which they all assented."

(Gardiner, 7th Lord of the manor, is Rev. Buell's grandson.)

September 11. Charles Burrall, Assistant, Postmaster General, writes Samuel Isaac Parsons from Philadelphia:

"You will prepare yourself to commence your first ride the 1 of October next or as soon after that date as you can be prepared." Parsons is to carry the mail between New York and Sag Harbor.

1795

January 1. Suffolk County's first post office opens. It is in the home of Henry Dering, its first post master. Until this date, Sag Harbor mail has been delivered to and picked up from the local tavern. If an address was off the rider's route, it was not unusual for mail to be left in the crevasse of a tree.

1796

. The Montauk lighthouse is built this year. Specifications call for it to be octagonal, made of stone, measure 28 feet in diameter at its base, and rise 80 feet high. 137 steps will wind around the central shaft. The floor under the lantern is to be three feet thick. The lantern is to be lit by sperm oil.

May 9. The Trustees decide "to let Thomas Baker get pump sticks in the hither woods for the Light house bell."

November 4. Jared Hand becomes the first keeper of the Montauk light.

1797

April 4. Majority vote at the annual Town Meeting gives the Trustees "...full power and authority in case application should be made to them by any poor person for assistance to remove from this town to some other part of the world, to advance so much money on the credit of the town as they shall think best for the removal of such persons..."

April 10. The Trustees vote to take down the upper galleries in the Meeting House.

July 3. The Trustees agree "...that the House to be built at the Fort Pond at Montauk be 7 by 27 Feet one story high."

June 27. The Trustees agree "by major vote to let James Field move his famely into the house that his father formerly lived in at the Head of three mile Harbor & to continue them there for the space of three months for which he is to pay one Dollar."

August 7. David Fithian informs the Trustees that one of his heifers in the Field has calved, and asks to be hired a Right for the calf. The Trustees grant it.

August 8. The Trustees agree "to allow three gallons of Rum to raise the Haus at Fort Pond."

1798

July 19. Rev. Buell dies.

. In "Notes and Observations on the Town of East Hampton," published this year, John Lyon Gardiner characterizes the Town: "Beef and flaxweed are the principal articles of exportation among the farmers. Till within about thirty years, Boston has been the place for a market for this part of the County - New York is now. The people are more properly Graziers than farmers, they raise large droves of cattle and sheep for sale; but very little else except flaxseed and cordwood; the wood will soon be done unless it is preserved by Legislative authority."

November 28. Rev. Lyman Beecher arrives at the dock in New London, Conn. with his horse and, packed in a small trunk, his worldly belongings. It is Thanksgiving morning, and he is sailing for East Hampton, where, upon recommendation, he has been invited to be its new minister. It will be his first parish.

(When he read about Rev. Buell's death, earlier in the summer, the recent Yale graduate assumed that Tutor Davis, who has friends in East Hampton, might be asked to take the pulpit. After a visit there, Rev. Davis told him that "many" in East Hampton were skeptical and that the young of East Hampton did not like the minister who was attending them.

Though East Hampton always had supported its church and ministers, the era of skepticism crept in with two of the teachers who were hired to teach at the Academy. In Rev. Beecher's words, "It was the age of French infidelity."

Recounting his visit to East Hampton to Lyman Beecher, Davis quoted East Hampton's wishes, as expressed by one of its residents: "Davis, we want you to get a man that can stand his ground in argument, and break the heads of these infidels.")

1799

February 4. The Trustees agree "with Jonathan Skellinger & Company to Build a House at the hither end of Montauk for two hundred and fifteen pounds, to take their pay in wood at

Montauk which they are to cut & cart down and sell for one
Dollar per Cord for their Labour..."
February 1. Rev. Beecher writes Roxanna Foote, whom he is to
marry in September: "Before I came an attempt had been made
to settle a Mr. _____, whom Dr. Buell, before his death,
recommended. All the Church, except one, united with him, and
many of the sober people. The young people almost
unanimous against him. They meet. Both sides very warm. The
minority too strong to be opposed; the majority to sanguine to
yield.

"Finally it is agreed to hear another man, and in this state of
things Mr. Beecher comes. On either side the combatants recoil,
suspend their strife to gaze at Mr. B.. The young people
conclude that I must be a pretty 'starchy' chap. Every Sabbath
has been stormy, so that few have heard me. So I lectured and
visited, and visited and lectured, and was nicknamed the snow
bird for flying about so in the snow-storms...."
February 10. In another letter to his fiancée, Rev. Beecher
writes, "My preaching seems not to move. I speak against a
rock. The people continue to watch me as narrowly as a mouse
is watched by a cat, and I continue to mind my business. There
are some who would be glad to lay hold of some fault; but, if
God enable, I shall keep clear. If I would baptize all the
children, as Dr. Buell used to do, I could unite them; but that,
you know, I can not."
April 2. Majority vote at the annual Town Meeting gives the
Trustees "full power to sell the sea weed that may be cast on the
shore at Sag Harbor."

On other matters, the Trustees decide that "the cattle may go
to Montauk friday 5th ins."
April 23. Two years after they voted to take them down, the
Trustees vote "to have the upper Galleries put up with
Banisters."
July 5. Rev. Beecher enters in his diary:

"This morning, about half past eight, I performed an act
probably as important in its consequences as any in my whole
life...I subscribed to a covenant, in which I promise to the
people of East Hampton to settle with them, and carry on the
work of the Gospel ministry among them; ..."
September 5. Rev. Beecher writes of his ordination, earlier
today: "This important day will ever stand prominent through
the days of my life, and probably through the days of
eternity...After the ceremony...received the right hand of
fellowship from all the male members of the Assembly. An

exceedingly pleasant, tender, and affecting ceremony...After ordination, my first business was to organize a session.

"Dr. Buell had always belonged to Presbytery, and the Church called itself Presbyterian; but they never had an elder, never sent up any records, never had any to send. Dr. Buell was Church and every thing else. They were Congregational up to the hub; got along in an easy, slipshod way."

November 15. In a letter to her sister, Harriet, Mrs. Beecher writes, "As for Mr. Beecher, he is every body's man. I will tell you a little how it has been...

"Mr. Beecher has preached seven or eight times a week the whole winter. Last week, for example, he preached twice in town and two lectures, besides a funeral sermon on Gardiner's Island, and five sermons to the Indians and white people down at Montauk. He every week lectures at some of the villages adjoining: Wainscott, four miles; Amaghansett, three miles; Northwest, seven: The Springs, seven; and another place with an ugly Indian name. Some weeks at two or three of these places; and when not..meetings afternoons and evenings, and sometimes in the forenoon. I have not in the least exaggerated, and you may therefore suppose he has not had much leisure to attend to other business.

"My principal business has been to prepare three meals a day, and now and then to put my house a little in order....This uncommon attention to religion has brought a good deal of company. We have not passed above one or two evenings without visitors since I have been here, and they commonly stay till eleven o'clock..."

The Nineteenth Century

1800

January/February. In the course of six weeks, East Hampton experiences a religious revival. Of the 80 persons who are converted, 50 unite with the church.

April 7. The Trustees Clerk records the end of a quarrel:

"Whereas a dispute has arisen between the Trustees and John Huntting concerning the Pew in the meeting house where the said John now sits which he claims a right to by reason of his Great Grandmothers building said Pew and for ending said dispute forever hereafter the Trustees have agreed to let him the said John Huntting have the use of one half of said pew for three years and at the end of three years from the date hereof he agrees to give up all Right & title to his family to said pew forever."

April 28. The Trustees agree to let Josiah Hand plow and plant a certain portion of land on the northeast side of the lighthouse for three years at a cost of 50s per year.

August 14. Rev. and Mrs. Beecher move into their salt box on the five acres that they bought last spring. Their property abutts the Huntting publick house, south of it. Like the few houses that are on the main road, its gabled end faces the road. Its front faces south, to capture as much of the sun's warmth as possible. Following custom, the firewood is piled next to the front door.

(To Beecher, the seldom-traveled road is "two ruts worn through the green turf for the wheels, and two narrow paths for the horses..." and "generally covered with flocks of geese."

The road's extreme width led to a comment of the time that "the projectors of such a road supposed themselves possessed of a continent, a large portion of which they would never need to cultivate." The only trees are a line of poplars between two large properties, and one large elm.[10)]

August 18. The Trustees give Abraham Miller permission to buy all town-owned cranberries at Napeague for $18.

1801

March 26. David Fithian is charged and fined 12s. for cutting two trees "in the hether woods of East Hampton."

October 12. The Trustees agree "to paint the upright part of Meeting house of a Light Red or Peach Bloe." Also, "to hire some days of the Indians to put the fat cattle in their field" and appoint Jeremiah Miller Jr. to handle the negotiations.

November 15. After deciding two weeks ago "to circulate subscription papers for the purpose of painting the Meeting house," today the Trustees agree "to drop the idea of painting the Meeting house this season."

1802

January 25. The Trustees vote to give the widow Bower "five loads of wood & Josiah Dayton to cart it at nine shillings per Load," and for Jona S. Conklin to "get one Load Wagon spokes out of the point wood out the old treess...at 3/ the set."

. Amagansett's first school house is built between the two sets of cart ruts that comprise the main road.

May 10. The Trustees name a committee "to agree with any persons that may apply to purchase the Water belonging to this town at Sagharbor to Build a wharf and also with Capt. Rysam for a Quantity of water adjoining his wharf at Sagharbor agreeable to a Vote at our last annual town meeting."

November 29. The Trustees order the Clerk "to settle with Mr. Beecher his salary up to the 4 day of September and to pay him the Ballance due him out of the money for Pew rent."

1803

February 3. East Hampton forms a society to "restore to the town its ancient purity of morals."

April 4. The Town gives Springs residents, and those living near it, the right to establish a public pound in which to hold livestock found running at large.

April 11. The Trustees agree "to notify the Montauk Indians that they are to ring their hogs..." (for which purpose, the Trustees have bought the wire).

1804

April 3. Among the resolutions approved at the annual Town meeting, voters agree that, "Whereas it is thought to be advantageous to the inhabitants of this town to have a Canal cut through the foot of the Beach adjoining Russells neck known by the name Stratton Beach and whereas John Mulford now owner of the Meadow at the foot of said Beach is willing a canal should be cut through it on consideration that the Town will give him all the sedge and meadow Grass that shall make out from said Beach in consequence of said Canal being cut Therefore voted that John Mulford shall be entitled to all the meadow Grass and sledge that shall hereafter grow or make out from said Beach in consequence of said canal being."

1805

April 2. Fifteen issues are approved at the annual Town Meeting. Among them:

"5th. That all the meadow grass between Indian well and the foot of the highland be hired out for the year ensuing, to be mowed and not pastured and hire it to Jonathan Barns Jr., for 5 pounds 14....

"11th. That it shall not be lawful to dig up and carry away the turf or ground in the town street, and if any person or persons shall..., such person or persons shall forfeit and pay the sum of five dollars for every such offence, unless they previously obtain liberty of one of the commissioners of highways...

"12th. That the front seats in the lower gallery in the meeting house shall belong to the singers and those persons that do not sing at meeting shall move out of said seats and make room for those who do sing....

"13th. That no person or persons not inhabitants of this town shall get and carry any sea weed from the beaches or common land belonging to this town without liberty from the trustees, under penalty of one dollar per load, to be sued for, recovered, and appropriated by the trustees of this town in such manner as they shall think proper."

April 8. The Trustees authorize the clerk "to advertise to hire the Pews out at Public Venue on Monday at 3 months credit."

.   The East-Hampton Library Company is founded this year. Inside each book, a sticker tells the borrower that "This Book belongs to the East Hampton Library Company to be returned on the first Monday of April, June, August, October, December, and February."   Fine for tardiness is one cent a day, including Sundays.

The second sticker advises: "Books cannot be given out to families in which there is a contagious disease. Books which have been exposed to contagion will not be received at the Library, but will be considered as lost books, and a fine will be required of the person to whom the book is checked."

1806

January 13. The Trustees agree that "every person or persons who shall apply to the Trustees for any Wheel Timber, Cow Troughs, Maple or Waggon Timber shall pay the Trustees for the same when they make application... "

.   "Morse's Geography," a small, leather-bound book for children published this year, names East-Hampton the principal town of Suffolk County.

September 17. The Montauk Proprietors meet to vote on a proposal made to the Trustees by a Mr. Tudlow, on behalf of the Montauketts. The Indians want the Proprietors to rescind all claim to, and return to them and their heirs forever, close to 3000 acres on Montauk. The land encompasses Hog Creek and half of Hither Woods.

Citing the deeds of purchase made and confirmed in the past hundred years with the signatures of their ancestors and those of the Indians (or, their marks), the Proprietors deny the Montauketts' request. They provise that they "are ready as we always have been to compromise in a fair manner any disputes in reference to the Indians or any others." They affirm that they will defend their titles to this land and instruct the Trustees to so do, if necessary, "with full power and authority."

This same day, the Trustees appoint a Committee of Five "to defend the title of the proprietors of Montauk before the Legislature or any other court in such manner as they shall judge most proper." The five are Jonathan Dayton, John Lyon Gardiner, David Hedges (of Bridgehampton), Abraham Miller, and Nathan Sandford.

September 24. The Town votes to add $100 to Rev. Beecher's salary. It is "to be annually collected, raised, and levied in the same manner as his present salary is."

1807

March 6. Springs residents sign a covenant to build a larger schoolhouse for their community. The new 18x24 foot school will be built on property owned by George Asa Miller. The first part of the agreement reads:

"We, the subscribers, considering the very great importance of securing to the rising generation the benefits of a good education....also the very great privilege and convenience in having some central place of common resort for the worship of God in future days and for religious conference - do agree...to build a house such...for...a schoolhouse and a House for occasional publick worship..."

Signers include the names of Bennett, Field, King, Leek, Lester, Parsons, Penny, Talmage.

July 20. The Montauk Proprietors appoint a committee of three to respond to Indian grievances by presenting their deeds to the commissioners of the State Legislature. They also authorize the Trustees to make a new agreement with the Indians, subject to their ratification, and appoint a committee of five to fix the boundary between the town and the land at Montauk.

1808

January 4. The Trustees agree with Phillip Hedges that he is:
"to live at the hither end of Montauk the year ensueing to take an account in writing of all the Cattle Horses and Sheep that are put on or taken off of the said land of Montauk the year ensueing Also to keep the proprietors line of fence that runs from the corner of the home lot where he now lives to Mulford's Stage in good Riypair so as to stop Cattle Horses Sheep and to keep in the said line of fence a good swing Gate of sufficient breadth to ride through on horseback....And to find two men to look up the sheep at winter and bring them to Town, and to drive all the Cattle and Horses that are left to the westward of the ditch plain after the common stock are put in the fatting field..."

1809

December 16. Rev. Beecher writes his sister-in-law, Esther Foote: "I shall, I think, without doubt, be dismissed from my present charge the next spring. I can not rear my family upon $400 a year, and not more than half the people are willing to give more, and are beginning to discover that we have no sort of economy...In what part of the vineyard I shall be called next to labor is to me utterly unknown. I have this comfort, that there are few places at this day that give less than I receive now...."

(Beecher wants his salary raised to $500 a year and for the church to pay $500 worth of bills. The church agrees to pay the bills but, denies the increase.

Those who have not been converted have lost influence in East Hampton, and have ceased to subscribe to the church. As a result, church income is lower than it used to be. When some of these people turned against him, Beecher considered showing them how infidelity is more exposed to ridicule than religion. At Yale, he had written what he called a "whimsical dialogue to take off infidelity." He revised it and was planning to have it performed at Clinton Academy. But, the "skeptics" banded together and called a meeting of the Trustees, who voted to prohibit the skit.)

1810

.   The federal government's arsenal is built this year in Sag Harbor.
April 16. The Trustees agree to have a box with a lock built in the upstairs gallery of the Meeting House to hold Mr. Dimon's psalm book and pitch pipe.

April 10. At a Presbytery meeting on Shelter Island, Rev. Beecher reads a statement of his circumstance and the terms that would allow him to stay, instead of accepting the invitation to become the minister in Litchfield, Conn. Neither he, nor the congregation, is seen as at fault for its decision to grant his request for dismissal. The Presbytery resolve is unanimous that "he is hereby recommended to said association as a minister of the Gospel in good and regular standing..."

(Before leaving for his new position, Beecher remarks, "if I were going to be a missionary, it would be to the poor, not to the rich.")

1811

February 6. A special Town meeting is held at the Meeting House "pursuant to public notice for the purpose of settling on a minister of the Gospel."

A committee is appointed "to wait on Mr. Phillips to know his terms and report the same to the meeting." For their part, the Inhabitants vote "That we will give Mr. Ebenezer Phillips a Call and that we will allow him the use of the Parsonage Lands, including an eighth part of a share of Montauk and furnish him with twenty cords of fire wood annually and pay him three hundred and fifty dollars per year during the time that he shall remain our Pastor."

A majority of the church Deacons and Elders are to "sign a Call to Mr. Phillips agreeable to the...vote in Behalf of this meeting" and be part of a committee "to draft a Covenant and circulate it for the people to sign."

April 11. After considerable turmoil between Rev. Phillips' wishes and what the church fathers understood them to be, a covenant is drawn between them:

"...with the unhappy differences which has recently taken place between us respecting a certain agreement relating to the Suffolk County Recorder, The Public have become acquainted from a late lengthly conversation on this unpleasant subject and also from information derived from other sources, we are fully convinced that the difficulty has originated entirely from a misunderstanding of the agreement - on this grounds of mistaken views in relation to the said contract, we do not hesitate thus publically to exonerate each other from any allegations which either of us has or may have made in any way against the other. While at the same time, justice to ourselves obliges us to state that we acted according to the agreement as we understood it. - which of us was mistaken in our views of the

agreement is a mere matter of opinion - Here the thing must rest and we feel willing that here it should forever rest."
. Over a period of several summers, Yale college President Timothy Dwight travels through New England and New York State. His intent is to write about what he sees and, through his writings, to refute present foreign opinion about America. This year, he writes Letter III of "Journey to Long Island." Of East-Hampton, he writes:

"....A general air of equality, simplicity, and quiet is visible here in a degree, perhaps, singular....Their moral and religious character, also, are much above the common level...a society has been voluntarily established here for the express purpose of strenghtening magistrates in the prevention and punishment of petty crimes...They have not merely formed a constitution...but have executed their resolutions in a manner highly honourable to their character. Equally honourable...their industry and frugality...exemplary behaviour at church...spirit of good neighbourhood...mutual decency and respect...and the interest which they take in the enjoyments and sufferings of each other ...they have their faults: but I can truly say, I wish that the inhabitants of this country, generally, had as few."

December 11/12. The 11th is unusually warm for December, and most of the farmers on the South Fork decide to leave their cattle in the fields through the night. Fog starts to roll in during the evening. By 2 a.m. on the 12th, snow begins to fall. The temperature drops to eight degrees. The wind picks up and escalates to near tornado strength. The snow falls and falls and falls. Farmers who try to save their cattle cannot find them beyond the white wall in front of them. Ships are tossed on shore. Twenty-four hours after it began, the storm ends, taking with it lives and property.

1812

January 28. Jared Hand succeeds his father, Jacob, as keeper of the Montauk light.

(In 1803, the elder Hand had written President Thomas Jefferson, asking that his son be his successor. Jefferson replied, "I have consistently refused to give into this method of making offices hereditary. Whenever this one actually becomes vacant, the claims of Jared Hand may be considered with those of other competitors." Earlier this month, after Jacob had informed Henry Dering, Superintendent of the Lighthouse, that he no longer could continue in the job, Dering wrote Secretary of the Treasury, Albert Gallatin, and proposed Jared as the appropriate successor.)

May 15. Dr. Ebenezer Sage writes Henry Dering from Washington. Sage, who moved from Easthampton Village to Sag Harbor in 1798, was elected to Congress in 1801.

"I lament with you the signs of the times, present and to come in Suffolk. The county is broke in pieces, and will never again unite in that harmony, for which they have heretofore been celebrated. The people are honest, politically but they know but little of what are commonly great men, which are nine in ten great rogues. Could the people be made sensible of the causes of the present distracted situation of the State of New York, one election would put things right, but this they neither will- nor can know. I am sick & disgusted with what the popular clamor calls great men, give me honest men.

"All our troubles originate from these great men. Men of talents, as they are called, nine in ten of whom are impudent, unprincipled, speculators upon the honest simplicity of the people, whom they gull by hiring newspaper makers to sing hosannahs, until the people really believe they are Demigods & fall down & worship them. These great men playing upon the credulity of the multitude have destroyed the liberties of man in all countries, and the day I fear is not far distant when our country will share the same fate..

"Burr was a great man, but he could not be President at the time he chose, & attempted to sacrifice the peace of his country to his revenge. Randolph is a great man but Jefferson did not choose to send him as Minister to France & he has ever since sought his revenge in attempts to subvert the government. Giles is a great man, but Mr. Jefferson did not choose to employ him in his Cabinet, & he is now pursuing the same cause of Randolph.

"Bob Smith was a great man but Madison wanted a better & put him out of office, & in his wrath he wrote a book to pull down the Administration. L. R. Bradley, Granger & Pope are great men, the two first wanted to be Judges, & the last a secure retreat in some fat office from the vengeance of the Kentuckians who are denouncing him for advocating the U.S. Bank, now labouring at the dirty work of intriguing the little man out of his office to give it to some one who will reward them with loaves & fishes. I could name twenty other - but enough of this depravity of great men."

(Five days earlier, Sage had written Dering that Washington politics was nothing more than "a matter of bargain and sale, like mercantile speculations... scratch my back and I will scratch your elbow."

June 18. War is declared between the United States and Great Britain.

July 18. Gov. Daniel Tompkins writes to Major Gen. Stephens:
  "The Artillery Company at Sagg Harbour are indispensable for the security of that exposed part of our Frontier and, therefore, no part of them ought to be ordered to New York. The company alluded to have unanimously volunteered their services for the defence of Suffolk County & it is to be hoped that the Artillery of New York will make up the detachment of 450 Artillerists for the defence of that place without calling a few scattered men from Sagg Harbour; and it is my wish that you dispense calling the drafts from the Sagg Harbour company to New York and in their stead order out an equivalent number of the New York Artillery."

. This month, men who are exempt from the draft organize an artillery command in Sag Harbor.

July 31. Britain's Commodore Sir Thomas Hardy writes John Lyon Gardiner:
  "...as it is probable that the Government of the United States may call you to account for permitting refreshments to be taken by the British Squadron from your place, I think it necessary for your satisfaction, and to prevent you from experiencing the censure of your Government for me to assure you that had you not complied with my wishes as you have done, I should certainly have made use of force and the consequences would have been the destruction of your property, yourself a prisoner of war, and whatever was in possession of your dependents taken without payment. But it is not my wish to distress individuals on the coast of the United States who may be in the power of the British Squadron."

1813

April 6. The Town votes to raise money, through taxes, to equal the amount which the State has allocated to East-Hampton for schools. (An 1812 State law supports education.)

May 3. The Trustees adopt for their common seal "a plain one with the words East-Hampton on the margin." They resolve "that no one shall draw any seine in any of the ponds belonging to the Town...without...liberty of the Board of Trustees."

May 20. One Village cow owner writes another:
  "It is with greaf that I am obliged to inquire into the causes that has induced you to spread A report through the town that we willfully cheated you in swapping cows last September.

  "First, Did you not act your pleasure certainly you did for we never should have given you 1 cent to have swapt and should never have thought of it had you not have asked Stratton if we would swap any of our cows away for your black cow secondly you say that we told you that the cow was 8 years old and no older to this I answer that I told you the cow was 9 or 20 years old and I did not know which If I made A mistake and the cow (as you say) Mrs. Chatfield says was calved in 1802 it now being 1813 which will make her 11 years old it was no more an intentional error in me than it was in you to tell me at the time we swapt and now last winter that your cow would calve in March (which I never have indulged one thought was an intentional error in you) but found that you labored under a mistake the cow however has not calved nor does she yet spring bag...."

June 12. A number of British ships remain off Gardiner's Point. On this day, Brig. Gen. Rose writes Henry Dering:

"We are at present in a very disagreeable situation, the enemy very plenty in our waters (eight ships in number yesterday)... have been on Montauk twice for food and water and have taken ten cattle. Our militia, even our most easterly regiment is scattered from twelve to fifty miles from Montauk....It seems the British left pay for what they took, which was considered a bad thing as it has a tendency to cool our patriotism..."

July 11. At two a.m., five barges from the British fleet start their attack on Sag Harbor. They commandeer three American ships and set fire to one before the militia repulses them and the ships are forced to retreat beyond cannon range.

December 6. The Town's commissioners of common schools resolve to divide the town into eight school districts. Gardiner's Island is to be included in the lst District.

1814

. In an undated letter, Congressman Sage writes a friend:

"This place (Sag Harbor) has been built up since the Revolution by honest industry in catching whale and codfish...The Orders in Council put an end to all our prosperity and war is fast making them poor and wretched....

"We formerly had 20 or 25 coasting vessels employed in southern trade, and in carrying wood, &c. to market. 3 or 4 of them only remain, some of them have been taken to Halifax, others burnt and others so often taken and ransomed that the owners are unable to keep them in repair, and...they are either sunk at the wharf, or laid up to rot in creeks and inlets...

"Nothing to be seen but houses stripped of furniture...no happy countenances among us, but children from want of reflection and soldiers made happy by whisky; but for our clam beds and fish many would go supperless to bed."

April 5. The Town authorizes the Trustees to apply to the Governor "for a military force to guard this town," and to index the Town Records "or transcribe them in order that they may be rendered more legible and of easier comprehension."

April 14. Town Clerk Abraham Parsons records the following determination made this day by Abraham Miller:

"I,...one of the judges of the court of common pleas, in and for the said county, do hereby certify that Isaac Plato, a black man of East-Hampton, in the county aforesaid, aged about forty-seven years, and about five feet nine inches high, hath exhibited satisfactory proof to me, that he was born free and that he is now a free man, according to the laws of this State."

June 4. Nancy Dominy, a student at Clinton Academy, writes to her brother, "...I have heard that there was a company going on Montauk next week. Tuesday - there is a number of British ships to Montauk - they expected they would come on shore today for Cattle there was a party of soldiers from the harbor went on last night and a number of men out of town... I am much pleased with the parasol you sent...the marriage of Caroline S and Hedges Miller was in our paper a week or two past Caroline I believe thought you had put it in, they are not married as yet. "

December 24. After several months of discussion on the wording, American and British representatives sign a peace treaty in Ghent, Belgium.

1815/25

. The war over, Sag Harbor resumes its place as a port of importance on the east coast. In agreement with the Trustees, ship builders pay for wood that they take from the woods on Montauk and in East Hampton.

Sloops, schooners, barks, packets, and brigs take shape. Soon, the port again is crowded with arriving and departing sails. Some of the ships are laden with cargo (including farm produce, and wood cut by East Hampton farmers from their lands). Others return from a season of whaling half way round the world.

July 12. Tons of pig iron and a 32 lb. cannon from the wreck of the "Culloden" are pulled out of Fort Pond Bay by a diving machine.

September 20. A hurricane hits the South Fork, sending the ocean inland and the beach sand into ponds and creeks. Crops are ruined and trees are driven to the ground.

1816

April 2. Eleven issues receive majority vote at the annual Town Meeting. No. 10 provides Joseph Dimon with Sunday dinners at town expense if he will conduct the music at church.

December 14. Sarah Gardiner of Gardiner's Island signs two declarations which are witnessed and recorded with the Town. In the first one, she releases from slavery "my negro man named Pomp, being of the age of thirty-four years, and able to gain a sufficient livelihood and maintenance." In the other, she frees William, aged thirty-two.

1817

January 9. Residents of the Port of Sag Harbor, as they address themselves, meet to counter the presence of the "Infidel society." The all-male group establishes the Sag Harbor Moral Society. Its purpose is to suppress vice and liquor and to promote moral thinking and moral behavior.

1818

March 2. The Trustees agree "to sell a small piece of Common land in Sagg Harbor which lies between the East corner of Robert Fordham's house lot and the highway,...to send David Talmage to Montauk to warn the Indians to leave the hither woods....to sell the towns Poor house which stands in the hook..."

1819

August 28. Capt. David Van Scoy orders Capt. John Hedges to "warn all those men in your district to appear at the store of Mr. Eli Parsons Jr. on Monday night at 9 o'clock the evening of Sept. 4 Compleat in arms as the law directs for military improvement."

1820

May 22. The Trustees appoint a committee of themselves to build a stone wall at the south end of Fort Pond in Montauk. They are afraid that unless the wall is built to raise a sand bank, the surf will cut through at low tide and, in time render Montauk Point an island.

1821

August 27. The Trustees agree to sell underwater land, at the end of the Sag Harbor wharf, to New York State. Cost for the water lot is $125. The State will build a 300' x 165' wharf, to be known as "The State Pier at Sag Harbor."

1822

April 18. At 7 this evening, the Trustees meet at the Town
bouse. They agree "to hire two bulls for the use of the Town
until the cattle on Montauk are put into the fatting field.. to hire
out the Pews in the meeting house at public auction on Tuesday
the 16th at 5 O'Clock P.M....to sell Abraham Hedges some pine
wood for the purpose of making coal..."

1823

April 1. Thirteen laws are passed at the annual Town Meeting.
They include:
"2nd. That so much of the money arising from the hire of the
pews and slips as have been hired out as is necessary, be applied
for the purpose of repairing the belfry, and that the trustees be
authorized to do the same..."
"4th. That a committee of three be chosen to procure the
standard of weights and measures for this town..."
"7th. That the yards of Lewis Edwards, Nathaniel Hand, Jr.,
and Elisha Osborn, Jr., be public pounds.
"9th. That the width and boundaries of the town street be
ascertained, in order to know whether encroachments have been
made on the same or not."
"13th. That all the meadow grass between indian well and the
foot of the Highlands, be hired out to mow for one year, and
not for pasture."

1824

.   Early in the year, Edward Dayton of Hardscrabble Farm (at
the corner of Stephen Hands Path and the Sag Harbor Road)
pays fifty follars for a Pleasure Wagon. Embarassed by his
self-indulgence, Dayton keeps the Jerusalem Dilly in his barn
for three months.
   When he finally rides in it to the village, it is the first wagon to
be seen there that is suspended on springs. Its body and the
rails of its two padded seats are curved, and the back of the
front seat can be moved forward, for access to the seat behind.

1825

April 11. The Trustees Clerk records: "...hired out the pews and
slips for the sum of $153.30...agreed to put up at auction the
fencing of the sandhills....that Elisha Osborn Junr. wait on
Sylvester Hand, in order to ascertain whether he will lead the
psalmody for a few weeks on the sabbath provided the trustees
will   provide him with a dinner on each   sabbath...that the

people of the district at the Springs be provided with a bull at the public expense untill the cattle are put in the fatting field...."
June 6. The Trustees appoint "their clerk to procure dinners for Mr. Sylvester Hand on Sundays, while he leads the singing."

1826

February 27. The Trustees vote to give the widow Polly Talmage "one Bushel of Corn, one Bushel of Rye and half a bushel of Wheat, and the same to be procured by the Overseers of the poor." They also agree "that thos persons residing in the southern district of this town, who have not carted wood for the Rev. Mr. Phillips this Year, be requested to cart on Tuesday the 7th Day of March next, and that their Clerk give notice thereof by public advertisement."
April 24. The Trustees agree to hire John Mulford's bull for town use for one year, and to pay him six dollars. They order the clerk to record the regulation made several years earlier about bulls pasturing on Montauk:

"Any proprietors of Montauk can put a bull Calf in the field the whole season, the same bull when a yearling has a right in the field the latter half of the season; when he is two years old he has a right outside, and also carries one beast on with him: when he is three years old the same privilege; when he is four years old he has a right in the field, and one right for a beast outside."

1827

January 29. The Trustees agree:
"Samuel A. Stedman, Oliver Rose, Raymond Dickens, Wanton Allen to put up a hut near the point of Montauk at a place to be approved of by the trustees for which privilege they are to pay one Dollar per week for each and every week they occupy the same...but they are not permitted to erect said hut untill they prove...that they are men of good moral character."

1828

February 6. The Trustees direct that the Town's one copy of Silas Wood's "History of Long Island," "which has been presented to the Town by the Author, be put in the Care of the town Clerk, and to be let out a week at a time only, and returned every Saturday night, subject to a fine of one cent for turning down a leaf; three for every drop of tallow on the said book, six cents if not returned by Nine in the evening on the returning days, and I cent a day until returned."

May 19. The Trustees agree "to let Emmeline Filer keep School in the town house, on paying one shilling pr. Schollar pr Quarter, and repairing all Damage the house may Sustain in consequence of Such school...to purchase a cow for the Wid. Mary Talmage and appointed...a committee to procure said Cow."

1829

April 7. The Trustees resolve "that public Bulls be procured for the use of this town as heretofore has been the custom..." and "that North West, the Springs, Amagansett and Wainscott districts, have each one public Bull, and that the town Street and its contiguous vicinity have two public bulls."

December 7. The Trustees agree "to let Mr. Potter of Brooklyn erect an ice house on Montauk for five dollars, per year.... resolve that those inhabitants of Block Island and also those inhabitants of Shelter island who have built fish houses on Montauk be required to pay $6 per year, for each house so erected, as long as they shall occupy the same."

December 18. Twenty-five year old David Johnson Gardiner, eighth Proprietor of Gardiner's Island, dies unmarried and intestate. This state of affairs breaks the line of primogeniture, making him the last Proprietor to receive Gardiner's Island by entail. Ownership of the island passes to his younger siblings, Sarah Diodati, John Griswold and Samuel Buell Gardiner.

1830

January 18. Because no one attended the December auction, to bid on building a stone wall on Montauk, and because the Trustees could not find any man to contract 50 rods of it, on this day, the Trustees agree that "on the 20 the Trustees go to Montauk and build stone wall on the Beach against the further Plain."

February 8. The Trustees agree "to employ mr. Sylvester Hand to lead music on the Sabbath and teach a School until the last of march 2 nights in each week..."

The singing lessons will take place in the town house and the students will get the firewood from the parsonage woods at Jericho.

The Trustees also pass "an ordinance that a Town Meeting should be called agreeable to the request of the Reverend Ebenezer Phillips to take into Consideration his separation from his people on account of ill health on his part."

April 6. The Trustees agree "to hire out the Pews in the meeting house on Wednesday the 14th Inst" and to raise the back seats in the gallery for "an easy view of the person speaking."

1831
November 13. Jonathan Mulford Jr. writes to his son, who is on a whaling expedition:

"Dear Henry, I have written you two letters before this - One by the ship Phenix - one by the ship Washington and this third letter I send you by the Franklin, Capt. Fordham bound on a Whaling Voyage...We got in the remainder of our Hay and all our Wheat in most excellent order. We have finished gathering Corn and Stored it - we had a good crop of Corn - we are at present engaged getting fire wood at home - and cord wood at North West shore. We   received your letter dated August 4 -...it gave me inexpressible happiness to hear you were well - that you had got along as well as you expected -

"I was likewise happy to hear that you could make yourself contented at home another year. You know I never approved your going to Sea. I know by experience a Seaman's life is a very hard Life. I would advise you to obey the Orders of your Superior Officers - your Captain and Mate you will hold high in your estimation. I can assure you that they are descended from very respectable Ancestors. I wish you to take good care of your constitution. A broken constitution is seldom ever restored.

"I wish you never to make use of any profane Language but always consider yourself in the immediate presence of your God - A God who has the Winds, the Seas, the Oceans, and all things at his Sovereign Control ...

Your affectionate father"

1832
February 6. The Trustees agree to grant "James Edwards permission to draw a seine in Georgica pond and cove and...to support Mr. Edwards in case he is prosecuted for drawing seine in said pond" and for David Talmage to "furnish the Widow Ann Bennett with one load of wood."

1833
. This year, John Griswold Gardiner buys out his siblings' shares in Gardiner's Island, and becomes the island's ninth Proprietor.

1834

May 6. The Trustees agree "that Abm Van Scoy call on Jona B. Mulford for the manure due on the parsonage land according to agreement."

1835

. The first Amagansett post office opens in the home of Eleazer Mulford Conklin. He is its first post master.

April 7. The Town votes "to grant James M. Huntting one seat in a pew or slip wherever he pleases to hire it, as a compensation for his services of singing in church, and the trustees pay for the same out of the pew money."

1836

March 7. The Trustees agree to let Capt. David V. Scoy "carry a stack of hay home from the parsonage on the condition that he carry two loads of manure for each ton of hay and spread the same..." They also sell "the old trimmings of the pulpit to David Sherry for one dollar.

1837

March 22. East Hampton representatives attend a County-called meeting at Sag Harbor's Presbyterian Church in Sag Harbor, to discuss education.

At the meeting, one of several throughout the county, a resolution is passed, "That in the opinion of this meeting, our common schools ought to be greatly elevated in their character, and may be materially improved without increasing the time and money expended upon them....That this meeting recommend the formation of districts, or town associations, for the improvement of common schools."

1838

April 2. The outgoing Trustees vote: "...the one hundred dollars received of Isaac Williams last spring for the privilege of catching oysters in the oyster pond on Montauk for four weeks belongs to the town of East Hampton..." They order it credited "accordingly."

(This is contrary to past administration of moneys received for the right to gather wood, stone, pasture, etc. on Montauk. Such moneys have been used for the benefit and improvement of Montauk and, if any is left over, as dividends for the Montauk proprietors, those individuals who own shares of Montauk land. The Town does not own the land.)

. This year, John Howard Payne writes about Easthampton. Of its fisheries, he records: "A horn is sounded at daybreak, whenever the sea gives promise of abundance, and all the men hurry to the beach in their boat toggery; the boats pull off, and ere long all hands are pulling at the netropes, waist deep in the water, and the sands are swarming with heaps of fish of every description, the greater of which are used for the purpose of being left to decay upon the fields for manure....

"Such is the inspiration of the sound of the horn-call to the sea, that all the male creation of the village rush forth on the instant. A Connecticut notion-monger who announced the arrival of his peddling cart by the sound of his horn, was astonished to find every house suddenly depopulated of all the holders of the purse strings. The signal had been mistaken for a call to the seine-drawing."

1839

April 1. Nine Trustees resolve and three dissent that "the one hundred dollars received of Ebenezer Story and others for oysters taken from the oyster ponds of Montauk belongs to the freeholders and Commonalty of East Hampton." Again, Board majority ignores true ownership of the Montauk lands.

1840

January 1. Following another boundary dispute between the two South Fork towns, and Southampton's request that the State Surveyor General look into the matter, Surveyor General O. Holly issues his decision:

"the line heretofore usually known and recognized as the line of division... is the line intended and established by law as the true line of division between the said town of Southampton and East-Hampton."

1841

March 5/6. Isaac Willetts of Hempstead leaves Brooklyn at 6 p.m. on March 5. His destination is Montauk. His goal is to win the bet he made with Gilbert B. Miller of Brooklyn: that he can reach the easternmost point of Long Island in less than twenty-four hours, with a pair of mares pulling a 300-pound wagon.

In spite of the thick snowstorm that envelopes the South Fork during the last two hours of his ride, Willetts completes the 130-mile trip and enters his witnessed arrival in the lighthouse log: 5:02 p.m., March 6.

November 8. James Madison Huntting writes in his journal:
"... the day very dark; required candles lighted."

1842

April 5. Among the laws passed at the annual Town meeting:

"...all geese and goslings found running in the street between Abraham Parson's mill and Samuel Osborn's corner, shall be liable to be impounded, penalty 25 cents per head for every goose or gosling so impounded, with cost of suit, one half of the money to be retained by the pounder, the other half to be paid to the overseer of the poor; ...."

(Many families raise geese. When the fowl are strong enough to sustain themselves, they are let out of the yard. Ivariably, they wend their way to the village pond.)

1843

February 15. James Madison Huntting enters in his journal:

"This day according to the predictions of the Israelites is the day when the dissolution of the world is to take place; but nothing at present has occured to the natural eye in the heavens above or on the earth beneath."

April 4. Sixteen laws are passed at the annual Town Meeting. They include:

"that the Commissioners of Excise be, and they are hereby requested, not to grant any licensing for retailing spiritous liquor in that part of the town belonging to Sag Harbor."

"that the same number of pews and slips be hired out the ensuing year as were the last, and the moneys arising for the rent of the same be appropriated to defray the necessary expenses of the meeting house, and the overplus towards the payment of the clergyman's salary."

"that the act respecting the geese be repealed."

. Rev. S.R. Ely again allows Episcopal services to be held at the First Presbyterian Church on summer Sunday afternoons.

August 30. Rev. Beecher and his two minister sons are in East Hampton, to participate in services conducted by neighboring ministers. During the day, each Beecher leads worship. Edward gives his sermon in the morning. His father is heard in the afternoon. William preaches in the evening.

That night, James Madison Huntting records his impression of this Wednesday: "Today Doctor Lyman Beecher administered the Sacrament. It was indeed a very solemn, interesting and delightful occasion. His two sons were also present. Their parting addresses, winged with much Christian love and affection, will long be remembered, and as this day was appointed as a day for visitation of neighboring ministers, no less than 9 or 10 were present. The day is pleasant, although warm."

1844

February 28. New York State Senator David Gardiner and his daughters, Julia and Margaret, are among President John Tyler's guests aboard the frigate "U.S.S. Princeton."

As it nears Mt. Vernon one of the ship's cannons, the Peacemaker, explodes on firing. Death is instantaneous for two members of the President's Cabinet, for Tyler's mulatto servant Joseph, and, for Senator Gardiner, all of whom were on deck.

(Gardiner and his family lived in Easthampton, from 1816 to 1825, when he leased Gardiner's Island from Mrs. John Lyon Gardiner, his cousin's widow. Gardiner wrote "Chronicles of the Town of East Hampton," which was serialized in the Sag Harbor Corrector in 1840.)

June 26. Following a four-month courtship that began after her father's death, Julia Gardiner marries President Tyler. (The country's tenth President is thirty years older, and a widower with grown children.)[11]

July 19. The Long Island Railroad opens its line to Greenport on the North Fork. This will enable South Fork-bound mail to be brought there by train, then by ferry, to the South Fork.

1845

. During the summer, Columbia University student, Morgan Dix, keeps a journal of his family's holiday in Easthampton. They have rooms at Abraham Candy's boarding house on Apaquogue Road:

"There is a charming custom which is, I believe, almost without exception universal here. It is that of training ivy and honeysuckle over the house, and filling the little spaces in front of them with beautiful flowers. The effect is indescribably pleasing.... 0 fair Easthampton, long mayest thou remain in thy ancestral simplicity!...before the sacrilegious band of speculation, the pitiless axe of utilitarianism, the merciless standard of IMPROVEMENT dare to invade thy precincts. This is my hearty wish. May heaven grant my prayer."

Another entry: "Upon the eastern outskirts of Easthampton village is a collection of houses, mostly fronting on a wide and barren common, which bears the name of Free-Town...the inhabitants there being emancipated slaves, who have come to this part of the world to settle."

Two houses catch his eye in Amagansett. One of them "has an immense chimney rising portentously above the dilapidated roof, and a crane extending from one of its gables, apparently to draw up food from the outside in case of a blockade."

On a day in August, Morgan, his parents and another boarder ride to Montauk. His journal entry describes Napeague as "an immense plain ...covered mostly with sand... a scanty crop of coarse grass, destitute of trees...a dismal spectacle... the spot where mosquitoes 'most do congregate.'... one of the most comfortless places ... "

He finds Montauk "a remarkable place... no road is visible but a few marks of wagon wheels upon the greensward... Here and there huge stones, or rather rocks, are seen, sprinkled as it were along the surface of the ground...now and then a reedy pool, abode of ducks, around whose water a herd of wild, and often fierce, cattle reposes. Before and behind extends a narrow strip of land; on either side grumble the deep-sounding billows of the Atlantic. Here at length you may imagine yourself to have reached the very limit of creation."

September 22. E.V. Homan's flyer heralds:
"NEW ARRANGEMENT
MAIL-STAGE & RAIL-ROAD

"The U.S. Mail-Stage will leave Easthampton Monday, Wednesday, and Friday at 5 o'clock a.m., leave Sag-Harbor at 6 a.m., Bridgehampton at 7 a.m., Southampton at 8 a.m., and pass through the villages of Canoe-Place, Good-Ground, and Flanders, to Riverhead, where it will intersect a train of cars for New York.

"Fare from Sag-Harbor to Riverhead	$1.00
"Bridgehampton to Brooklyn	$2.371/2
"Southampton to Brooklyn	$2.371/2

RETURNING
"Passengers must take take the accomodation train which leaves Brooklyn at 91/2 a.m. to intersect the stage at Riverhead, for any of the above-named villages."

November 13/15. Close to midnight on Thursday, fire erupts on the West side of Main Street in Sag Harbor. Abetted by a high west wind and rainless days that have left rooftops very dry, the conflagration moves fast. Soaring flames turn night into day, as they whip down Long Wharf, incinerate whale ships anchored alongside, and spread to East Water Street.

By the time the fire burns out, late on the 14th, the harbor business area is in charred ruins. Over one hundred buildings (including hotels, shops, businesses, and every cooperage and smithy building on East Water Street) are destroyed. Nonetheless, residents start to rebuild at once. The morning of the 15th, lots on Wharf Street are selling $100 per foot front.

1845/1846

. Work begun on the Sag Harbor/East Hampton turnpike in 1845 is completed in 1846. Travel rates are posted at the toll house, which is about a mile from Sag Harbor Village:

"For farm wagon or cart drawn by two horses, mules, or oxen, 5 cts. one way or 9 cts. both ways ...

"For stage, wagon, or coach, for the transportation of passengers, drawn by two horses, 10 cts ...

"For every chaise or other two wheeled pleasure carriage, or small wagon or other four wheeled pleasure wagon drawn by one horse, 4 cts. for one way or 7 cts for both ways; 3 cs. for every horse and rider ...

"For every sled or sleigh drawn by one horse, mule, or ox, 3 cts..."

1847

January 18. The Trustees give Alexander Smith and Abraham Austin "the privalidge of drawing seins on Montauk on the North and South Shores also to build an ice house and Shanty to live in and to put fish in the money pond and to draw them out again for 5 years at Sixty dollars per year..."

1848

March 1. A Parish meeting is held to incorporate tbe Presbyterian Society and name it the First Presbyterian Church of East-Hampton. Six trustees are chosen. (This ends the Town Trustees' role in governing church affairs.)

August. The first Trustees of the Methodist Episcopal Society contract with Benjamin Glover of Sag Harbor to build a church in Amagansett. The village's first church is to be 34 feet long, 26 feet wide, 16 feet one inch high, cost $650.00 and be ready in three months.

1849

January. This month, the "Iowa," captained by William Howes, prepares for a new kind of voyage. Instead of going after whale, she and her passengers will head for the west coast. She is the first ship sailing from Long Wharf for California and Eldorado.

(Its passengers will not be the first from the South Fork to pan for gold. Polly Swett and her husband, who left Sag Harbor for the west coast, in 1838, were raising sheep near Santa Rosa when news of Sutter's Fort excitement reached them. In his first week of panning, Polly Swett's husband mined $1600 in gold.)

March 19. The Trustees agree "that those of the Trustees who were opposed to giving a deed of the parsonage property to the First Presbyterian Church have their names entered upon this record as being opposed to the said deed To whit, Frederick King, Hezekiah Edwards, Schuyler R. Conklin, Thomas Osborn.

"Also instructed the Clerk to transfer the money received of George Hubbard for the privilege of gunning on Montauk from the acct of the Proprietors to the acct of the Town."

(Again, Trustees credit the Town with moneys that should go to the Montauk Proprietors).

April 2. Today, the Trustees reverse one of their March 19 resolutions. George Hubbard's payment for gunning is voted to be transfered "from the account of the Town back to that of the Proprietors."

June 11. The Trustees grant the U.S. Government permission to establish a Life-Saving Service in Amagansett on a lot "16 by 28 feet to be located on the Further Plain near the sea shore."

The government is given a 25-year land lease for "$30.00 payable in advance for the whole time. The land to be used for no other purpose except for a site for erecting Life Boat House and receiving the Life Boat & using the same-...whenever used for any other purpose ... the lease to be void."

July 28. Isabel Mulford Dominy writes to her husband:

"Dear Nat The day after you left us, it appeared as if half of the house was gone. I never was so lonesome before in my life .... I have spent $5 and have a list of the articles I have bought and when you return you can judge for yourself whether it has been spent for unecessary things. I am going to send my flour bag to the mill today for the first time since you left Uncle Levi's cow has dried up so that Aunt Nancy can't let me have butter and I get it at the store....Thomas Isaacs brought me a few sticks from the woodpile which lasted until he could get Sylvanus Osborn to cart a load from Grandfather's woodlands ...now for the news of the day....George Mulford and the Widdow are waiting impatiently for the year to be up. I believe the wedding dress is already made. John Dayton is quite devoted to Leib and it is thought that they will be married in the fall....Thos Parsons has his house full of boarders and has had between too and three hundred application for board Mr Candy and Grandfather Miller haven't any Esther Jiles hog pen took fir Tuesday and burnt up her hog it caused a great sensation for a short time for people thought her house was burning down it took fire from some ashes that she had put in it.... Your affectionate wife."

September 1. Attorney Daniel Lord renders an opinion on Montauk ownership and right to partition. After memorializing the Nicolls and Dongan Patents, the deed transfers between the Indians and Proprietors, and the agreements made by the Trustees, on behalf of the Proprietors, he concludes:

" ... land of Montauk embraced in all Indian deeds and in the 2 Pats are vested in fee in Pro's of Montauk, so called, and that trustees of E.H. have no right, no interest, therein."

His reasons are:

"1...incontestible evidence that this was private property of the purchasers who were inhabitants, whether purchasers or holding purchasers rights and not corporate or common property of the town. These facts are contemporaneous and therefore sure guides to a true understanding of the...charter.

"2nd. That the Fisheries and all other incidents to ownership in fee of land confirmed by the Sovereign to a subject citizen belong to those Prop's.

"3rd. Trustees of E.H. can have no legal control of the lands without consent of the prop's.

"4th. There is no legal objection to a partition as soon as prop's obtain possession. If Trustees will not surrender lands as they have set up rights inconsistent with the trust, a suit in equity to account and settle the rights of the parties and to preserve the property during suit is proper."

1850

May 7. The Trustees agree to hire counsel to examine, and issue a written opinion on, all deeds, conveyances, etc. that relate to the different purchases of Montauk lands from the Montauketts.

November 15. On behalf of the Montauk Proprietors (who number, in all, about one hundred and twenty-five), Henry P. Hedges, Maltby G. Rose, John T. Dayton, Wilkes Hedges, S.B. Gardiner, and David H. Huntting sign the complaint which George Miller of Riverhead has drawn up.

The lengthy affidavit identifies the various deeds enacted between the Montauketts, as sellers, and the Proprietors, as buyers, of Montauk lands; and affirms 'that the Trustees managed Montauk, at the pleasure of the Montauk Proprietors, "solely for the benefit and account of the several proprietors of Montauk as individuals and tenants in common." (The "last straw" in Montauk's management was the Trustees' March 19, 1849 vote.)

December 17. Jennie Lind, known as the "Swedish Nightingale," gives a concert at the huge, new National Hall in

Washington. It was built especially for her concert on the grounds of the fire-ravaged National Theatre.

Seated in the audience are many of the nation's leading dignitaries, including President James Fillmore, Daniel Webster, Henry Clay and John Howard Payne. With cries for an encore at the concert's end, the singer turns towards the composer and sings "Home Sweet Home."

December 18. The Brooklyn Eagle reports on the Swedish Nightingale's concert and her first encore:

"Before the first line of the song was completed the audience was fairly 'off its feet' and could scarcely wait for a pause to give expression of its enthusiasm...the undemonstrative sort clapped, stamped and shouted as if they were mad, and it seemed as if there would be no end to the uproar.

"Meantime all eyes were turned upon Payne, a small sized elegantly molded, gray-haired gentleman, who blushed violently at finding himself the centre of so many glances."12

1851

March 20. Julia H. Miller writes to her niece, Henrietta Mulford :"....We have had no snow till this month which has been more severe than the winter, two snow storms and a long spell of eastwardly weather, rain, and wind. Old ocean broke its bounds and tumbled its banks into Hook Pond....One solitary sleigh yesterday, the 'East Hampton Daily' which you know must go -...

"You imagine us seated by our old chimney fireplace as you left us, but not so. We have a Franklin stove and sheet iron fireboard which make the old room warmer than ever and we save a good deal of wood as the stove is brought pretty well into the room.... I have endure it not withstanding my aversion to stoves in all shapes..."

July 14. The Trustees appoint "Baldwin C Talmage and Isaac B. Miller in connection with the clerk a committee to obtain evidence respecting the suit now pending between the Trustees and the Montauk Proprietors."

July 19. Commanded by Captain George S. Tucker, the bark "Martha" sails from Sag Harbor for Japan. On board is America's first Consul to the Far East nation.

September 8. A verdict rendered in Suffolk County's Supreme Court ends the tangled dispute between the Trustees and the Montauk Proprietors.

The significant decision gives ownership fee to the Proprietors. The Court cites the Dongan Patent, which stated that the Trustees could manage and buy Montauk lands for the "tenants in common," meaning, group of people.

When the U.S. government bought a portion of the land for the lighthouse site, the "tenants in common," not the Trustees, conveyed title in their name and shared in the purchase price. None of the money went to the Town. The Court orders the Trustees to execute a release and surrender the premises under their corporate seal.

1852

January 6. Rev. Samuel F. Johnson, Methodist minister at Amagansett and Middle Island, writes in his diary:

"Stormy weather prevents us from holding our meetings at evenings. Perhaps it would be in vain to hold them for it seems that we (especially myself) are so unfaithful that we need expect no blessing on our plans."

March 9. The Trustees order their Clerk to give David Huntting, representing the Montauk Proprietors, "all papers and documents relating exclusively to the land of Montauk, and also to fix their corporate seal to the Release..." and agree to appoint a commitee that will consult with the proprietors "to reestablish the boundary line between Montauk and Naupeag...."

1853

February. This month's weather is cold enough for Gardiner's Bay to freeze, enabling horse teams to walk the distance from Fireplace Road beach to Gardiner's Island and from Shelter Island to Greenport.

April 3. At the annual Town meeting, the Trustees are told to secure a legal opinion on the Town's liability, as a corporation, for the debts that it incurred in its suit with the Montauk Proprietors, and to determine who owns title to the sea weed at Northwest. If the Town is held responsible, the Trustees are instructed "to dispose of any or all of the common property of the town within the coming year, as they think best."

1854

March 20. "On the request of the people in the Wainscot district for liberty to enlarge their burying ground," the Trustees agree "that they have liberty so to do But in no way to interfere with or dicomode the regular or common communication to Abner Strong's land adjoining - "

November 15. Two thirds of Suffolk County's Board of Supervisors favor an Act to preserve "good or eatable fish in the

waters of the Town of East-Hampton." The Act specifies that:
"No person or persons other than the inhabitants ... shall
hereafter take or catch any fish, commonly called eatable fish,
with seins or nets in any of the creeks, bays or waters of the
Town of East-Hampton, nor shall any person or persons other
than the inhabitants ... take or catch any eels, clams, oysters, or
shell-fish of any kind upon any flats or in any of the creeks,
bays or waters of the Town." Violators will be fined $50.00.

1855

January 15. Trustees Clerk Daniel Dayton records that the
Trustees offered for sale "in accordance with public notice
previously given the common land at Napeague between the
Montauk line and Napeague Harbor and Gardiner's Bay and
the line set up by the Trustees. Terms Cash to be paid on
delivery of the deed ...Said land not sold - ."

March. Innkeeper Nathaniel Huntting ignores his cousin's
request to move his woodpile from the edge of his Main Street
property. Road Commissioner David H. Huntting, who lives
next door, is surveying the street before it is made an even
width.

Cousin Nathaniel argues that the road is wide enough, that it
is the custom for a woodpile to be part of the fencing of one's
property, and that its present location is a handy spot for
unloading wood, after it is brought from Northwest Woods.

In addition, Cousin Nathaniel points out that others down the
road dug potato storage holes so far out into the road that, on
his daughter's wedding day, the bridal party carriages had to be
driven out into the middle of the road to avoid them.

August 9. An East Hampton visitor writes to the Troy News:
"After much tribulation and fasting, clouds of dust and great
heat, we are here. The first two above mentioned are due and
charged to the Long Island Railroad, which is universally
acknowledged the most gigantic swindle on record and takes
more than five hours in which to do ninety miles of travel....
East Hampton has a population of about one thousand. In the
fashionable season its number is swollen from thirteen to
fourteen hundred. It has but one hotel which is poorly
patronized, as all the visitors prefer stopping at private houses....
The first church is still standing...inside (it) rejoices in a super
abundance of stove pipe running in all directions and
disappearing through the roof....the key to the front door
weighs two and a half pounds ...

"They have one Justice of the Peace here. He is as blind as a bat and cannot write his own name. He employs a little girl to do his writing and seeing for him....We have it from good authority that the birth of an infant in this town is considered a matter of greater importance than the independence of Mexico...Capitol police would die from want of employment, there being no bars and no drunkards, no singing women. There is no barber, taylor, hatter, stationer, harness maker, banker, baker, or druggist, and there is no likelihood of there ever being any such in the place. There are several burghers here and a few from Troy, and they all bathe in the same ocean, which is about the only thing they have here worth having - and which knocks the aristocracy of Troy about just as ruthlessly as it does the plebeian burghers. Excuse haste. "

August 19. Fanny S. Huntting writes in her Journal: "The weather pleasant but rather dusty been to Church morning & afternoon. Mr. Talmage, a brother of Mrs. Mershon, preaches this morning & Mr. M in the Afternoon....I did not attend...Sabbath after Sabbath passes away and very soon the last Sabbath with me will be forever passed....Mrs. Phebe Barnes died this afternoon truly we live in a dying world."

1856
March 11. D.B. Van Scoy of Amagansett writes to Town Clerk, David Baker: "Dear Sir: - This morning there was porridge ice on the south side opposite this village, extending from the shore to the main bar. From the shore outwards, some three rods, the ice was strong enough to bear a man."

May 20. The case known as the Town Seaweed suit is settled out of Court. Edmond Rogers and his mother, Caroline Rogers, both of Southampton had sued the Trustees for "taking and carrying away seaweed from the Shores and Beaches adjoining the Mulford farm of the said Edmond Rogers and Caroline M. Rogers at Northwest."

This day, they not only agree to discontinue the suit, but "further agree that no other suit of a similar nature shall ever be commenced or carried on by them against the said Trustees of the Town of East Hampton."

1856/1857
February 4. The Trustees' Clerk records: "Meeting lost for want of a quorum...very cold."

. Due to heavy snowfalls, the Long Island Railroad is unable to provide service to the South Side from December 23 until mid-February. The Atlantic Ocean is frozen for a mile out.

1857

__August 31__. In a series of letters to a friend, P. Van M. now in his sixties, writes on his growing up days in East Hampton.

"The old town has become quite a watering place. Some two hundred people quiet, sober, and refined, gathered here for a six weeks' sojourn. I do not think you could well find a better society. It is eleven o'clock and they are all upon the beach, a motley and curious-looking assemblage, in their gay bathing-dresses. Here at least is no standing upon ceremony. How the long, rolling swell comes tumbling in, breaking and combing over some hundreds rods from the shore.

"Do you know how to bathe in it, Diedrich? I do assure you it is not every man who can get a comfortable bath in the surf. First of all, having donned your attire let it be plain flannel by all means, and cut off at the elbows or knees take a sharp run up and down the beach, of say ten rods: it will start your blood, so that you get not the fragment of a chill. Then watch the roll of the surf, take a run into it and jump over the first one you meet at knee-high; go on now, there is a monster to meet you. It looks mountain high to you, and as if it must hurl you like a chip to the shore, and so it will, if you meet it not bravely. Stand still until the top of it begins to comb over, and when it strikes you it will roll you in the sand like a tub; but you will neither stand still nor wait its coming, but clasping your hands above your head, dive straight into it...

"I am told that some of the natives display astonishing skill and agility in their combats with the waves, but I could never persuade one of them to go in, either from a natural dislike of the water, or from the fact that they have mostly been on sea voyages and so have enough of it."

1858

__January 1.__ The Montauk light is changed from a steady beam to a flash beam. Thirty miles west, the new Ponquogue lighthouse is lit with a steady beam.

__February 20.__ In the early morning hours, on the second day of a thick snow storm and pummeling winds, the clipper ship "John Milton" smashes into rocks five miles west of Montauk.

__February 21/28.__ In the continuing storm, Jefferson Mulford leaves his Amagansett home on the 21st and rides east, along the shore. It is his job to look for possible wrecks·and call out volunteers when he finds them. (Every five miles on the beach there is a shelter to house a boat and tackle for such emergencies.)

Beyond Great Plain, Mulford finds a frozen body on the shore. Further on, another...and another...and another, until he nears the "John Milton" and hears the muffled ring of her bell. Dislodged from its mounting, the bell is wedged between two beams. With each swell of the waves against the battered hull, it tolls in the snow-smothered air.

Mulford alerts townsmen, who hasten to the beach. As more dead are found over the next days, their remains are placed on farm wagons and brought to the village. There, in the coroner's carriage barn on Newtown Lane, twenty-two bodies are laid side by side, in case someone can identify them. The bell is taken to the church.

. News of the disaster overwhelms East End residents. Many, from both Forks, make the arduous pilgrimage through deep snow to pay their respects to the unknown crew.

Two Sundays after the storm, a funeral service for them is held at the First Presbyterian Church. Rev. Mershon takes his sermon from Job xxvii:20, 21: "Terrors take hold on him as waters; a tempest stealeth him away in the night. The east wind carrieth him away, and he departeth: and as a storm hurleth him out of his place." Mershon tells his congregation, "...we have come to bury the stranger. No father, no mother, no wife, no sister attends this burial to moisten the gravels cold earth with their tears...The members of this community, whose home is washed by the wave of the ocean, and much of whose interest is upon the sea, will weep at the sudden and untimely end of those who have perished in its waves, almost within our hearing."

Following the service, young men from the village lead twenty-two horse-pulled wagons in a solemn procession down main street to the South End Burial Ground, where all, but Capt. Harding, are buried.

. (A theory behind the "John Milton" catastrophe develops after the Sag Harbor whaler "Washington" anchors in home port on the 22nd. She was off the Long Island coast about the same time as the stricken ship. "Washington's" Captain Henry Babcock took readings of the sun at noontime on February 20. He knew where his ship should be, but the steady beam that he saw from a lighthouse made him feel that something was wrong. He did not believe that they could have reached Montauk that quickly. Against the pleas of his entire crew, Babcock ordered his ship to be tacked and stand offshore.

Dawn proved him to be right. The steady beam came from the new Ponquogue light. Neither he, nor Captain Harding, who had sailed out of New York harbor a year earlier, knew that the

Montauk light had been changed from steady to flashing during their time at sea.)[13]

June/September. Sixteen hundred dollars is raised this summer, mostly from the season's sojourners, towards cost of building an Episcopal church. (For the past three years, lay reader John Wallace and Rev. Samuel Gardiner of Sag Harbor have led Episcopalian services at Clinton Academy.)

July 23. In a letter to his students' parents, H.H. Benjamin records the past five months of school in District No. 4 (up on Fireplace Road):

"It is the humble opinion of the writer of the foregoing that there is a deplorable lack of interest among you for the educational welfare of the children under your charge. This has been made strikingly manifest to your humble servant in the extreme irregularity of attendance which characterized the pupils during the past term. Irregularity of attendance is one of the greatest obstacles to a child's advancement up the rugged hill of science. It indicates a want of interest which you display toward no other subject connected with that child's well-being. You are careful to have him or her well fed and clad; while you seem content that the mind should become a barren waste. Be assured that in proportion, as you exhibit an interest in the intellectual development of your children, in the same ratio they will strive to advance themselves.

"Therefore, being desirous to promote the intellectual welfare of the children of this District, as well as of all others - as I was once a child, myself - I beg leave to suggest that the parents or guardians of the said children visit the school at least once, during the term, and that more send their children."

July 24. While visiting from Newark, New Jersey, Aaron Carter describes East Hampton in a letter to his brother, Horace:

".. I will try to tell you what kind of a place I am at. It is 5 miles from Sag Harbor, 15 from Green Port, about 110 from NY but, from the way they are behind the times, should think they were about 5000. There is not a steamboat within 5 miles, nor a locomotive within 15 miles, the nearest telegraph office is at New London! There is no place where rum is sold in town. It is the most quiet and orderly village I have seen in a long time.

"It is an old place ...There is one street, very wide, & almost covered with grass, with here and there wagon tracks. The houses on either side of the street are occupied by farmers & the farms stretching from the road in both directions. The land is rich. I have not seen such beautiful fields in many a day, which speaks well for having been cultivated for 200 years.

"I imagine that Newark was once very much such a place as this, those good old days of yore, when there was life, fashion, & more comfort than now. When people were 'passing rich' at 40 pounds a year...But just so sure as they get a Rail Road to this place, the whole character will be changed... Board is now $7.00 a week & that will rise & then it will become a fashionable resort. I think it exceedingly refreshing to get out of the way of steam for a little while & live more as they 'of old time' used to. The farmers were busy fishing for...bunkers yesterday....they use them for manure."

1859

April 1. The first regular mail stage run from Amagansett to Sag Harbor begins. Jerry Baker is its driver. He leaves Amagansett at 8:15 a.m. for East Hampton. From there, he drives to Sag Harbor to meet the noon mail train from New York and the steamer from New London. Mr. Baker charges 25 cents for each passenger.

July 10. St. Luke's Chapel, East Hampton's first Episcopalian church, is consecrated by Rt. Rev. Horatio Potter of the Diocese of New York. (Dr. Alfred Wagstaff, a major contributor to the building fund, was asked to name the church. He chose to honor the physician St. Luke.) The wooden chapel is on James Lane. Plans are to have visiting ministers lead the summer services, close the church in winter, and for lay reader John Wallace to conduct the winter services at Clinton Academy. [14]

August 21. This day, Rev. Charles Beecher preaches in the Presbyterian church. Afterwards, he visits with Mrs. John Lyon Gardiner, widow of one of his father's former parishioners.

In conversation, he asks her: "Were you, Madame, a member of father's church?"

"Oh, no," she answers, tears coming to her eyes, "not till after he left. It was his leaving that was the cause of my conversion. I thought when he went that the harvest was past, the summer ended, my soul not saved."

October 7. Referring to Rev. Mershon's proposal for a new church, James Madison Huntting enters in his journal: "Today we have had a Parish meeting in relation to a New church. 4th meeting. Every meeting apparently lessens prospect of accomplishing the object. Every meeting increases in number..."

December 6. Huntting records: "A Parish meeting held this afternoon. It was voted to accept the lot of an acre which I purchased of David W. Huntting for the sum of $1500 and present to the congregation for the purpose of erecting a church edifice (provided the congregation raise the means for building a church) (the sum of $9300 already being raised) several efforts having before been made."

1860

March 17. Harriet and Thomas J. Mulford, and Phoebe and Marcus Hand deed a small lot in Amagansett to the Trustees of the First Presbyterian church of Amagansett. The Trustees pay them $350.00 for the deed which stipulates:
     " ... for the purpose of erecting a Presbyterian church and no other purpose." The lot borders Main Street.
August 23. Amagansett's first fair is held at the Hand farm on Hand's Lane. The $150 raised will go towards cost of building the village's Presbyterian Church.
September 8. The Trustees resolve "to appoint a committee to investigate the matter respecting the house and other obstructions which Nathaniel Dominy has recently placed in the hook on *common* land between the wind mill and school house and get such counsel as said committee may deem expedient and prosecut said Dominy..."
November 15. The First Presbyterian Church of Amagansett is dedicated, with Rev. Alonson Austin Haines its first minister. Rev. Mershon opens the ceremony, reading from the 1 Kings 3:13, "I have surely built thee a house to dwell in, a settled place for thee to abide in."
December 28. The wires are strung on the telegraph poles between Sag Harbor and East Hampton.

1861

April 11. An expensive horse, sent by its owner to pasture on Montauk, was found dead in a marsh. The owner of the alleged $5000 horse (said to have been quite thin when it came on) is suing the proprietors for improper care of his mount.
     In a letter to attorney William P. Buffet of Bridgehampton, Henry P. Hedges attempts to explain how care is provided for the livestock. The litigator had thought that his horse would be watched over, at all times. "The duty of the Keeper at the first house is to enter <u>all</u> the cattle in the common pasture List - to keep in repair certain fences, etc.. The duty of the Keeper at the Second House is to see to the sheep.
     "The duty of the keeper at the Third House is to keep the field list - to take the general care of the whole stock on the land, and to pay particular attention to heifers and calves & to ride Tuesday & Friday in each week among the cattle - to keep the cattle in their proper fields."

April 12. At 4:30 a.m., Confederate troops start firing upon Fort Sumter, set on the shoal at the entrance to Charleston, S.C.. Thirty-four hours later, the bombardment ceases, the federal troops leave, and the War of the Rebellion begins.

May 21. Excitement occasioned by news of war courses through town. The American flag is run up on the liberty pole, which has been placed in the middle of Main Street, between Nathaniel Huntting's Inn and Samuel Buell Gardiner's house. In the afternoon, villagers gather around the pole to hear John Wallace, Rev. Mershon, and Lawton S. Parsons speak on the country's future.

. As part of its effort to blockade Charleston's harbor, the U.S. government forms the *stone fleet*. It is to be made up of ships that no longer are serviceable. After the government buys them, valves are inserted in their hulls, and the ships are towed or sailed to Charleston. There, the valves are pulled and the ships sink quickly. The special fleet includes three whalers from the port of Sag Harbor, the "Timor" "Emerald," and "Noble."

June 18. At a meeting in the Town House, the Sea Spray Guard is formed, 27 men enroll and the by-laws are drawn.

One by-law states: "No person shall be accepted as a member of this Company without the approbation and consent of a majority of all the officers of said Company, anything in the constitution to the contrary, not withstanding."

September 1. Rev. Mershon leads the last service to be held in the 1717 Meeting House. His sermon is on "Our fathers have told us what work thou didst in their days, in times of old."

. The new Presbyterian Church is of Romanesque Revival design. Two sets of arched double-doors form its entrance. Unalike square towers flank the front doors and, above them, six narrow-arched windows.

The smaller tower, on the left, is crowned by a steep, four-sided spire. Vertical louvered belfry openings surround the third level of the taller tower. Above each one is a clock, nestled into the truncated mansard roof.

1862

May 5 . The Trustees resolve: "S.M. Osborn & Edward Dayton as a Committee go to Northwest and see Josiah Kirk, (who owns the Mulford farm) as he has obstructed the passage on the shore against said Kirk's premises, by erecting a fence from his land, on land belonging to the town into the water, thus making it impossible to transport seaweed or any article on the shore, and act according to their judgment in the matter."

August 21. , Vote is unanimous on three proposals made at a special Town meeting:

The Town will offer $100 to each man who has responded to, or who will answer President Lincoln's July 2 call for 300,000 soldiers to serve for three years or until the war ends.

A military committee is named "to look after and supply the families of the volunteers." It is to pay the soldier's wife three dollars a month and one dollar extra for each child.

Volunteers and draftees are to be exempt from taxes.

October 23. In a special meeting, a committee of six is named "to call on each man whose name is enrolled and raise what money they can to procure substitutes for the war; that the quota which this town is to furnish may be filled and thus evade the draft" and the Supervisor is asked "go to New York to procure the requisite number of men as substitutes to fill up our quota under the late requisitions of the president for 600,000 men."

1863

February 14. Twenty-three year old Charles E.Loper is killed on board a gunboat at Roanoke island.

April 13. The Trustees appoint Edward Dayton to "confer with the Trustees of the First Presbyterian Church in said Town of East Hampton in order to ascertain on what terms the old church and lot on which it stands can be purchased."

September 1. Suffolk county begins to draft men.

1864

June 23. At a Town meeting, the Board of Town Auditors is authorized to issue bonds to finance the bounties for the men who enter the army or navy. This is in accordance with the "Bounty Law" passed by the State on February 9.

October 11. Vote at a special Town meeting empowers the Supervisor to pay a "bounty," not to exceed $400, to each man who answers President Lincoln's July 18 call for 500,000 men, and a proportional bounty "for every volunteer or substitute so accepted (in the army or navy) for any less period of time."

October 31. In Wainscott, Sarah Hopping writes her brother, Aaron : "My dear Brother -... I know a sailor's life is a hard one but hope it is not so hard as a soldier's. I suppose you will like to hear about the draft, well it is over and no one gone as yet.

"They only wanted 9 men out of East Hampton and drafted 18 as many again, to make allowances for those who might be exempt, and they only got five or six men out of the 18 so they had to draft again for the other three and I guess they will not get any out of that crew by the looks of that list of names...this time, about everyone that is drafted is either sick, dead, or too old...There has also been a draft for the State Militia which took most every body. I do not know what they are going to do with them. I guess not much but make them drill once a month, or pay a fine if they don't.

"Monday evening November 7th...There is a great political meeting in the old church tonight... it is Election day tomorrow, and I suppose we shall soon know who is President. I wish it might be McClellan but am very much afraid it won't and if Old Abe is elected again I expect it will be nothing but drafts for the next four years. Everybody has been full of politics for the last two months. There have been meetings somewhere most every night for three weeks back. Sace"

Brother Jake adds his message, at the bottom of the page:

"It is Election day today but I think East Hampton is a good democratic town yet if your Ship's crew had been here, I think it would have gone stronger yet...

" I think Old <u>HONEST</u> Abe will be reelected. I hope we shall be fortunate enough to reelect Governor Seymore if we do I think we shall be allowed free press & free speech in New York state a while longer. I hope this <u>Nigger</u> war will be over before you get home ... the prospect is as dark now as ever ... it will be as long as it is an abolition war."

<u>December 5.</u> The Trustees resolve that the "Clerk place notices in the town notifying any inhabitant of said town who may cart <u>sea weed</u> from the shore adjoining the Farm formerly known as the Mulford farm, that they will indemnify them from any damage which may arise therefrom."

1865

<u>January 2.</u> The Trustees grant William M. Tuthill's request to enter into fish oil manufacturing on Napeague, and for John Swany "the privilege of erecting an oil Manufactory near Goffs point on Napeague, south of Luce & Brothers..."

<u>January 29</u>. Rev. Mershon's sermon today is on "Dancing as a Social Amusement for the Professing Christian." Tracing the presence of dancing back to antiquity (but, not into the Garden of Eden), midway through, he says that dancing "leads the professing Christians to forget the vows which they have taken upon themselves."

He concludes with the honest admission that, "With all my decided views on this subject, this has been an unpleasant task imposed upon me."

April 3. Gen. Robert E. Lee surrenders to Gen. Ulysees S. Grant at the Appomatox Courthouse in Virginia.

1866

March 15. The Town Trustees conclude a lease agreement with George W. Miles and Co. of Milford, Connecticut. For forty dollars, the company will use Oil Manufacturing Station Nos. 1 and 5, on Napeague,...for the manufacture & sale of fish oil."

1867

January 26. Winter weather embraces Long Island.

Today's issue of The Corrector reports: that "The East End of Long Island is literally 'left out in the cold'...

"For several days, not even our neighbors of the Hamptons sent us the cold comfort of a winter's greeting and Shelter Island was as silent as a snow image...The world is lost to us...."

1868

March 12. Following a special meeting with the Southampton railroad committee, East Hampton's Town Board resolves that: "the Supervisor and his successors in office issue interest-bearing bonds to help pay for the extension of the south side railroad, ...from the west end of Southampton to Sag Harbor; to offer the money, should Southside decline it, to whichever company will build that extension or a line from Riverhead to Sag Harbor, or, one from Sag Harbor to East Hampton."

March 26. At another special Town meeting on three unresolved issues, the Clerk records: "We are opposed to calling any more meetings... as we are desirous of attending to our own business and allowing other people to attend to theirs."

1869

. In the spring, some Wainscott residents decide it would be a good idea to build a bridge across Georgica Pond. Their plan is not without merit.

Not only will the bridge shorten the distance to East Hampton, it will be an improvement on the rutted, sandy road through the woods. The only alternate route to town is across the Georgica bar to, and along, the beach.

The amateur road builders embark upon their project almost as soon as they conceive it. Unfortunately for them, they toil alone for months. Nobody in East Hampton feels like giving them a hand, even though they too will benefit from its construction. Not until the bridge is nearly ready for travel, do some villagers contribute money and muscle towards it. [15]

August 12. This issue of the Sag Harbor Express notes:
"Old Clinton Academy has been hired to the Catholics for services for a few weeks."

1870

February 7. The Trustees, clerk records: "Information having been given of the opposition of Mr. Josiah Kirk of North west to the taking of seaweed from the shore opposite his land & of his threats and acts of violence to several persons but especially toward Mr David S. Sherry It was Resolved that the committee on suits be directed to defend any person or persons in any suits that may arise involving the title to the seaweed on any part of the shores of N west between the highway leading down to the Bay along the south side of Scoy farm to the point of cedar point beach."16

February 28. The Trustees report that David Sherry has sued Josiah Kirk "for unloading seaweed from his waggon which he had taken from the beach at North west in front of said Kirk's premises and that Kirk had set up a plead of title as a defense."

1871

March 25. Appleton's Journal includes an article on East Hampton, with illustrations by Harry Fenn. The writer tells the reader: "....Of all the original places in that old-style land, and of all the places that date back into the seventeenth century, none so now retain the customs and relics of the past in their perfectness as East Hampton....The wide street is simply a great lawn, richly green with a thick matt of grass, common to all, and through it run several tracks for vehicles....

"Just a half mile from the straight, wide street runs parallel to it the ocean beach. Down to it is a carriage road and a foot-way, the latter, by the old records, called the Mill Road, because near where it left the street stood the first mill - which we are informed was run by ox-power..."
. The writer John Heartt, who is summering in Wainscott with relatives, writes about the local people:

"The people of Wainscott are more conservative in their habits and ideas than the inhabitants of other east end towns, unless we except East Hampton. Some are more conservative than others and there is one individual residing in the hamlet - a descendant of old Puritan stock who came over from England in the "Mayflower" in December, 1620, who is so conservative in his ideas politically, religiously, and civilly that he will not have a stove of any description in his house.

"The cooking is done over a fire built on the hearth, and his estimable wife does her baking in one of those large commodious ovens of the type 'Dutch ovens.' This oven she heats once a week, at which time she bakes all the bread and good things that are necessary for the consumption of the family during the week. In winter the rooms are warmed by huge logs laid over immense brass andirons."

July 17. The last time the brig "Marva" left Sag Harbor, she returned from the South Atlantic waters with $32,000 worth of whale oil and bone.   On this day, as the wind fills her sails and she heads out into Gardiner's Bay, she becomes the last whaling ship to leave Long Island.

September. Montauk is featured in an unsigned article in Harper's New Monthly Magazine: "the eastern extremity of Long Island is...comparatively unknown, except to a few sportsmen attracted thither by its very wildness, and to such tourists as find special charm in its seclusion, and in the bold and picturesque scenery of its defiant promontory, upon which the wild Atlantic incessantly beats, and sometimes with tremendous violence. We had been informed that these tourists had a 'hard road to travel' leading, after all, only to a 'wild, desolate country,' infested by mosquitoes and snakes ....Napeague, from ocean to sound, must remain the waste that it is; but the land east, for about eight miles in length by a width of a mile or more, some day not far distant, will become a place of summer resort for the dwellers of the main-land."

1872

July 28. Mrs. Anna Stratton Parsons writes to her young married daughter, Julia Parsons Sherrill, in Kansas: "...Church was filled it appeared as if they were nearly all strangers. The town is just full of them. And also Amagansett. Charlie Parsons, the Davenports and Kelloggs have been here the past two weeks I should think the girls would get disgusted with them.

"They are riding around in Nat Dominy's farm waggon with side boards and a frame with green cambric covering and a flagg with goose quill Brigade for their motto. They look as much like Rowdies as any comparison I can give them. They went on Montauk last week and stayed two nights. I have not heard from there since they came off."

1873

June 27. A visitor at Third House writes in the guest book: "Montauk grand glorious Montauk!   Ask me to name its equal in romantic scenery, & I will tell you of the far off Pacific coast you will not find it there, & away beyond in the isles of the Sea still you find it not. No, it is not to be found, only here. There is but one Montauk."

August 4. In another entry of the Third House guest book, the visitor writes, "Oh, Governor Dix. If you are great on vetoes, Why don't you put one on the bills of Napeague mosquitoes?"

1874

May 26. David Huntting, a scholar at the First Presbyterian church's original Sunday school, addresses the school on its fiftieth anniversary. Reflecting on its early days, he says:

"The sessions of the school were at first, and for many years, held only during the warm season of the year; for be it remembered that at that time no artificial heat was deemed necessary to temper the atmosphere of your church, or suffered to smother and quench the spiritual fires rekindled from week to week upon its altars.

"No smoke from ill-seasoned cord-wood or suffocating gas from burning anthracite marred the devotions of church-going adults or moistened the eyes and choked the lungs of children. The time-honored 'morning service' brought to your church a company so few in number as to provoke from even a Beecher the remark that he could not preach out his people to a decent attendance on that service. With such habits on the part of the people and such meager and inadequate provisions for the comfort and even health of the children, it was not advisable nor indeed possible to continue school through the winter months."

October 29. George Lansing Taylor's newspaper article on Eastern Long Island praises East Hampton: "...one of the best specimens of unaltered Puritan life and manners in existence is still presented by the people of this town....In the War of American Independence, there was not one Tory in the Town...If we had such a spirit of loyalty throughout the nation or even the Northern States today, such events as the late mob-revolution in New Orleans would quickly be at an end."

1875

February 6. The Corrector's front-page features an article on Easthampton by Prentice Mulford. He finds it: "a fine old village ...full of boarders. The principal street a sort of elongated hotel; farmhouses broke out with new piazzas; Irish nurses; tourists; city mammas and daughters walking that street every morning, and looking, with dignified curiosity, into everybody's front windows."

. Close to a million and a half cattle and 6150 horses go on Montauk for the summer. Some of the 200 calves are carried in wagons. The cattle are in good condition, several horses are sick, and the pasture is green but overrun with grasshoppers.

April 6. The new Trustees call for "a Special Town Meeting to raise money for the prosecution of suits and to deliberate in regard to the suit now pending between the trustees and Josiah Kirk,."

They also resolve to "maintain and defend all the rights and privileges of every description granted unto the Freeholders and commonalty...by the several Patents..."

1876

April 13. The East Hampton Glee Club gives "A Greate Concerte." Written in old English style, the program notes on the front page inform: "To be Attended at ye Meetinge House

"Ye doors openeth at early candle light w is 7 by ye clock

"Ticket price is Two York shillings (a.k.a. 25 cents)."

Back page advice includes:

"N.B. All those who are so blessed as to have good lungs and religious training are expected to stand up and help sing ye last Hymne.

"N.B. For as much as ye younge womenne that singe are shamefaste ye younge menne are desired to look awaie from them whenever they do singe, that they maye not be put to confusion and make mistakes.

"N.B. Giddy girls that come to ye concerte with their steady company are requested not to talk to each other and thereby disturb ye singers."

The singers are: "Temperance Pearson, Charity Hopvine, Freelove Jerusha Ladde, Sunlight Buttermore, Bassett Bumpus and many others if they don't have colds." Plus: "Valiant Easygoer, Ichabod Tubbs (no relation to wash Tubbs), Recompense Dewsnapp, Obed Pettugill and a little boy."

1877

March 8. Adelia Anna Parsons Sherrill writes in her diary:

"Mr. Cartwright and a brother of Mr. Hutchinson have varioloid in a light form - while Emma and Frank have real pox, Frank being very sick.

"Pantigo is fenced off at Amie's Lane - and this end by the mill. Churches are closed - also schools. - the stores also - no public gatherings allowed in the village. The streets are quiet as on a Sunday - some of the young people have gone to Bridge Hampton to church tonight, Anna among them."

(One young man dies. Both of East Hampton's physicians come down with the illness, but survive it.)

March 12. Fanny Huntting, James Madison Huntting's sister, enters in her diary: "A solemn day, such a day as never occurred in the memory of the oldest inhabitant. The Board of Health has closed the church."

1878

June 16. Members of the Tile Club, a group of young artists who live primarily in New York, rollick through East Hampton on a self appointed mission to learn about an area that is little known to them. On Montauk, they stay at Third House, run by Mr. and Mrs. E. S. Stratton, and fill four pages of the guest book with ink drawings.

Walter Paris tops page 86 with his signature. Below it is a sketch of Third House, followed by Earl Schinn's notation, "The reprehensible defilers of this Blank Book are the New York Tilers." Underneath that, Schinn sketches a pensive man whom he identifies as "The O'Donovan Possibly the Noblest."
. This year, L. Clarkson writes "The Shadow of John Wallace." He tells his readers that East Hampton: "... is a quaint and lovely town of one long street; a grassy avenue so broad, that over its green expanse meander two or three unpremeditated roadways, worn at different points to suit - so at least it seems to the eye of the peregrinating stranger - the varying convenience of the inhabitants. On either side is a walk bordered by huge elms and sycamores and horse-chestnuts; and these same great trees shelter the picturesque little houses that stand, in their uncalculated simplicity, close upon the road.

"They are two centuries and more old, some of them shingled cottages, whose roofs take so steep a slant, and whose color is so delicious a gray, that it is no wonder the artists have settled down upon the place and claimed it for their own... the little settlement wears an untroubled and time forgotten aspect. From end to end its long avenue is as tranquil as though no echoes of the nineteenth century turmoil had yet reached its fair green highway. The old Town Pond still lies far out in the bed of 'the street' and the geese and ducks are paddling about in happy unconcern of the passer-by."

July 6. Justice J. O. Dykman renders his findings on the suit brought by Robert M. Grinnell and his wife, Sophie, against the Montauk Proprietors.

(On May 1, 1877, the Grinnells paid James P. Mulford five pounds for an undivided interest in the Montauk lands. Soon thereafter, they sued for partition.

Matters of fact addressed and confirmed include the five land transactions between the Proprietors and Montauketts.)

Among the several subjects he addresses, Dykman says: "The effect of a judgment for the plaintiff in this action has not been overlooked. It will interfere and break up a system venerable for its antiquity, and throw open to division, occupancy and improvement, a large tract of land heretofore uncultivated and wild."

In Conclusion III, he says, "The rights and priveleges of the Montauk tribe of Indians constitute an incumbrance or lien upon the said land which is superior to the rights and interests of the said tenants in common, and of the persons claiming through or under them and the said land must be partitioned or sold subject to the rights and privileges of the said tribe."

Dykman appoints Sag Harbor attorney, Everett A. Carpenter, to act as referee and submit his decision.

September 23. The Town Trustees review the application of the Trustees of school District No. 4 the Springs "for the land which they now occupy as a site for their schoolhouse bounded by three highways." The Clerk records that he "is authorized to execute a deed for the same unto the said Trustees of said school District for the sum of $3."

1879

February. Scribner's Monthly features "The Tile Club at Play" this month. East Hampton's main street is described as an "immense *tapis vert o*f rich grass, green with June, and set with tapering poplar trees...bordered on either side of is broad expanse by ancestral cottages, shingled to the ground with mossy squares of old gray 'shakes'. The sides of these ancient buildings, sweeping to the earth from their gabled eaves in the curvets of old age, and tapestried with their faded lichens, were more tent like than house like... Not the warwickshire landscape, nor that enchanted stretch from Stratford to shottery which was Shakspere's lovers walk, is more pastorally lovely."

Of the town, which the artists call "a painter's goldmine," Arthur Quartley (named 'Marine', in the article), says: " ...some neighborhoods are very strongly marked with the artistic consciousness. They combine well. They set out their milk pans to drain in beautiful compositions...They are all the time posing for effect. Easthampton is one of them."

May 1. A meeting is held at George A. Conklin's store to decide on the name of the post office that will open on the 17th. Mr. Conklin suggests "Promised Land." Charles C. Miller recommends "Land of Promise." Conklin's name wins.

May 30. The Montauk Proprietors decide not to appeal Dykman's July decision. Instead, they vote to raise funds to bid on the land, should it be put up for sale. They assess $500 on each eighth share, for a total of $140,000. Some of the East Hampton Proprietors feel that this is not enough. (Since 1875, men from New York have been buying shares from descendants of the original owners.)

. The East Hampton Lawn Tennis Club is founded this summer.

.   Arthur Benson of Brooklyn begins negotiations to buy Montauk. This is the same man who founded Bensonhurst, further up the island.

Benson believes that, through inter-marriage, the Montauketts have lost their legal status as a tribe, and therefore no longer have rights to any Montauk land. On the other hand, the Montauketts are convinced that they will retain the fishing and hunting rights that were provided in earlier transactions with the Proprietors. Acting under that belief,the Indians sell Benson the little land that they have left. Their payment is ten dollars for each tribe member and Benson's promise that he will pay them a like amount each year.

September 20. Saturday's edition of The Signal carries "Doolittle"'s article on Montauk Point: "Extending out into the Atlantic Ocean, rock-bound and surge beaten, it differs in structure and topography from the rest of Long Island. Gradually, the land begins to rise, and grow into irregular bluffs, and the hills terminate in abrupt cliffs on the ocean side, at the base of which is a narrow beach strewn with huge boulders and rounded pebbles."

October 22. The Montauk Proprietors gather at the house of Jehial K. Parsons to vote the sale of their Montauk lands.

Proceedings begin on the porch at 2:30 when referee, E.A. Carpenter, stands on a chair and reads the Supreme Court decree authorizing the sale. Four men are there to bid.

The starting bid of $50,000 is followed quickly by $75,000, $85,000, $100,000.

From there, bids rise at $1000 increments.

Judge Henry P. Hedges, who represents the Proprietors, drops out at $130,000. Gen. James Van Allen, on behalf of the Grinnells, stops at $150,000.

$1000 more, and all of Montauk goes to Benson. (With auction costs expected to reach $11,000, the Proprietors will net about $508 each.)

After the sale, a New York Herald reporter asks the new Montauk owner, "What do you intend to do with Montauk?"

"Why, my boy here wanted to be a farmer and this is just the thing for him," Mr. Benson answers.

"Don't mind him," Mr. Carpenter tells the puzzled reporter. "he has something else in view which he will not divulge."

1880

April 5. Fanny Huntting records in her journal: "Rather a stormy Town Meeting. The effects of liquor were visible."

August 7. The chapel in Springs, built on land donated by the Miller family, is dedicated. Its bell is a gift from Capt. Sineus M. Edwards, who brought it from New London on his schooner.

1881

April. Mary Nimmo Moran, artist wife of the painter, Thomas Moran, is admitted to the Royal Society of Painter-Etchers. The Diploma, signed and red sealed by Queen Victoria, is the first one to be awarded to a woman. The work which won her the Diploma is "The Goose Pond - Easthampton." It is part of an invitational exhibit of American artists in London.

Mrs. Moran's etching is of the village pond and its semi-permanent residents. In the background are the South End Burying Ground, the old windmill, and the house which is thought to have inspired "Home Sweet Home," by John Howard Payne.

July 24. Fannie Huntting's room gives her an unblemished view of Main Street. Fom her window, she misses little. What she sees often finds its way into her journal. Today, she writes:

"This morning I counted 60 persons coming from mass which is held every other Sunday in the house of Patrick Lynch. I think the Catholics feel pretty well set up, as Mrs. ex-President Tyler is of that denomination and is a regular attendant."

1881/1884

. Arthur Benson's plans to develop 220 prime acres of Montauk into an exclusive fishing and hunting resort take shape during these four years. In letters to a select group of friends and acquaintances, he proposes that they buy property on the high bluffs that overlook the Atlantic Ocean, and there, build their summer "cottages."

Benson's idea finds acceptance. The Montauk Association is formed. Its members retain the noted landscaped architect Frederick Law Olmsted to create the site plan, and the young New York firm, McKim Mead & White, to design their houses.

Though visible to each other, Olmsted sets the seven houses far apart, in a cohesive, but, seemingly random-like fashion, around the clubhouse. Each has a spectacular ocean view and enjoys the sea breeze. Access to the houses is by trails over the salt marshes.

The shingle-style architecture which the architects have revived and which is gaining favor in east coast resorts, is employed here. Neither as extravagant in size, nor in amenities, as those expected to be found in Southampton and Newport R.I., each of the houses, nonetheless, is exquisitely detailed.

With Napeague a mosquito haven, the summer residents prefer to arrive on Montauk by yacht. Extra luggage comes by train to Bridgehampton or to Sag Harbor and, from there, by wagon.

1882

. W.W. Munsell's History of Suffolk County, New York is published. Of Napeague, he writes, "What was once a desolate and uninhabited place is now a village of 'fish factories,' as they are called, and a business has sprung up involving over $500,000 capital and affording business to hundreds of men...

"The first factory was started in 1878 by Hiram Dixon and Brothers, and at the present time, there are ten companies in full operation with an assessed value of $104,000."

December 4. Seven Town Trustees members resolve "To sell water lots or any of their remaining interest in any of the undivided lands of the town according to their discretion."

December 14. For the sum of *one hundred dollars*, the Trustees "remise, release, and quit claim to" John A. Bowman of New York, "his heirs, and assigns forever, all and singular...that certain tract of land situate, lying and being in the town of East Hampton...bounded and described as follows: On the west side by the boundary line between the towns...on the south by the Atlantic Ocean, on the east by the Amagansett road to the Ocean at Indian Well...and on the north by the fence line of owners of adjoining uplands...said tract being six miles in length between the east and west bounds aforesaid.

"Also, all the right, title, and interest...to all that certain tract...bounded on the north by highwater mark on Gardiner's Bay, on the south by the line of fences as they now stand of the adjoining upland owners, on the east by land formerly conveyed by said trustees to John B. Terry, and on the west by and including Louse Point Beach or the East Beach of Accabonac creek to the mouth of said Accabonac creek. Also, all the right, title, and interest...of, in, and to all and singular the

several lots, tracts, pieces, or parcels of land, being the
remaining undivided common lands lying above highwater
mark...westward of Montauk to the Southampton line,
wheresoever the same may be...which have not heretofore been
sold or conveyed..."
. This year's copy of The Long Island Railroad guide book
describes Amagansett as "...even more retired, if possible, than
East Hampton. The ocean and surf bathing, the sailing, and
fishing are the great inducements for the holiday seekers."

1883
January 15. A letter printed in today's Long Islander, a
Huntington newspaper, conveys his portrait of East Hampton:

"To see East Hampton, in its primitive purity, one should visit
the town in the dead of winter, when the summer strangers have
departed. The cold is intense when the winter wind shrieks and
wails from the ocean across the bleak level, on which the village
stands, raw and chill, as if winnowed through ice and snow, all
the way from the land of the wild Esquimaux.

"At this season of the year, the only amusements are quilting
frolics, sewing circles, and dramatic societies. The old custom of
warming the beds is still in vogue. A large earthen jug filled
with boiling water, and securely corked, is placed under the bed
clothing...The isolation of East Hampton is seriously threatened
by the invasion of the Long Island Railroad Company. Several
routes from Bridgehampton have been surveyed through East
Hampton to Montauk, and the shriek of the locomotive will
soon wake up the Rip van Winkle slumber of the past. A
beautiful country lies here undeveloped, destined, at no distant
date, to be both populous and popular."
April 3. A stormy debate rages at the annual Town meeting
over the Trustees actions the past year, especially the land sale
to Bowman.

Since the Board's election the previous year, record-keeping
(such as it is) has been sloppy, repetitive, almost sophomoric.
Trustees Clerk Seymour Tooker has governed the Board as if
he were an autocrat. And the Board has done his bidding. If
Tooker found a State law not to his liking, he ignored it and the
Board followed, agreeing "if necessary to contest the
Constitutionality of a law passed by the Legislature." Time and
again, resolutions have been made and passed, only to be
revoked at the following month's meeting.

At today's meeting, Tooker is asked to read his report on the
recent land transactions made by the Trustees. After he finishes,

the report is deemed unacceptable to the majority of those present. On motion, it is refused.

Tooker replies that deeding the bottoms of harbors and creeks on the north side of East Hampton was made to him and to other Trustees, "in perpetuity and in trust for the benefit of the people."

Trustee Nathaniel Dominy reads one of the deeds issued to Bowman, warns the assembled that capitalists are buying up the individual commonage rights, that the people's privileges are slipping away, that the Trustees thought it best to make these conveyances (reserving the Town's rights to fishing, nets, seines, and seaweed), and that he does not think the buyers got very much.

Outraged by his comments, the Townsmen resolve "That a committee consisting of Jehiel K. Parsons, Samuel P. Osborne and Charles Dayton be and are hereby appointed, with plenary power, to investigate acts of the trustees of the Town for the last two years...and ascertain what they have sold and what disposition has been made of the money realized from such sales and report to the next Town Meeting."

April. East Hampton is dubbed "The American Barbison" in this month's issue of Lippioncott's Magazine. The publication carries a long article by Charles B. Todd, some of which recounts his vision of last year's summer scene:

"In every quiet nook and coigne of vantage, an artist with his easel, fair maidens trudging afield with the attendant small boy bearing easel, color box, and other *impedimenta,* sketching classes setting out in great farm wagons carpeted with straw...

"At sunset and sunrise, herds of sleek, matronly cows with barefoot boys in attendance wind through the street; scythes and sickles hang in the willows by the wayside, and every morning the mail coach rattles into the village with a musical flourish of the driver's horn, stops at the post office for the mail-bag, calls all along the street for bags, baskets, and parcels, and at last rumbles away toward the railway station, seven miles distant."

1884

. Work begins on building painter Thomas Moran's house and studio which will overlook Goose Pond. Much of the material for the main street house, from the interior staircase to the leaded panels for the front door and many of the windows (no two of them the same size), comes from a razed New York City building.

April 1. At the annual Town meeting, the twelve Trustees are voted out of office in favor of a new slate.

April 24. The Trustees appoint Clerk David J. Gardiner and D. Egbert Talmage to be a committee "with instructions to employ counsel and to procure their written opinion about certain irregular or illegal proceedings of the board of Trustees for the years 1882 and 1883 and to report the same to this board at their earliest convenience."

June 5. The Trustees resolve that "the committee on suits be instructed to further investigate and prosecute at their discretion all illegal or improper proceedings of the Board of Trustees of 1882 and 1883, and to report the same as seems proper."

June 23. The new Board of Trustees resolves that its clerk demand "of the old Board both individually and collectively that they render to this board an account of all moneys received or controlled by them or either of them in their recent capacity as Trustees or officers of the Board and that they do within one week pay to this Board or to clerk thereof all such moneys belonging to the town which have not been legally and properly expended by them and especially including the moneys received by them for sales of land to John A Bowman, Brinley D Sleight and Robert J Power."

November 10. Joseph S. Osborne writes to his brother, Edward, who has been homesteading in Kansas with two friends:

"My dear Ned -   I have talked with Mother and she has talked with Father and while they are willing to have you come home, and always glad to have you here and now wish you to feel welcome to come and stay, yet they do not feel that they ought to stand in the way of your doing what seems best to you and in the end most desirable.

They both feel as though they hold out small inducement to offer in the way of a living, but you will be welcome to come home and live at home and make what arrangements we can for working in the place and for living... mother wants you to do just as you prefer in the matter.

"If I thought there was a real good show for you to make anything here for a term of years I would write you now to come for we could get on nicely no doubt and do much as we wished to yet after all the thinking and talking of it over and planning etc. there still stands firmly the question where is the living to come from? I will send you a few figures concerning the receipts and expenses of the farm as they appear to me and wish you to look over and see what I have omitted or how far wrong I may have estimated expenses of operating the farm.

"We all want you home so much and yet can really see so little inducement to call you here, that you can readily see how difficult it is to say anything more than this, or than we talked of at the station, so you must decide what you consider best in the long run and remember you are entirely welcome here, altho we do not, because we can not, offer strong inducements to return....I take the best year for instance as it is altogether a fair sort of a year tho not so good as many seasons. The whole value of our

Wheat	127 bush @	90	114.30
Oats	275 "	40	110.00
Potatoes	25 "	50	12.50
Corn	200 "	60	120.00
Stalks	10 loads	4	40.00
Straw	5 Tons	10.00	50.00
Hay	15	15.00	225.00
Pork	1,000 lbs.	.07	70.00
1 old sow	400 lbs.	.05	20.00
Pigs sold			80.00
Calves sold	(4) @12.50		50.00
Butter & milk	(4 cows) @25.		100.00
Eggs & fowls sold & used			125.00
			1116.80

"This is a money estimate only, of course it is not entirely accurate. Now as we would want our horse anyway, we will call his keep for a year $100 - would have to hire carting wood etc., if we did not keep a Team (say) $15.

_____highway tax $132.00 and then the convenience of a Team no money value but very handy and some other conveniencies which no one can readily enumerate ----

Now as to the expense of producing the above

help will cost	8 months about	20	100.00
board "	" 8 "	" 10	80.00

_____help extra for farm work will be, say,(with board)
60.00

we would not need so much if we did not
operate the farm as we do now

threshing   78.00

Sundry help for butchering, cutting corn, oats, etc. etc.
60.00

Repairs to harness, wagons, etc. etc.   20.00
Blacksmith   10.00
Hay necessary to feed cows & horses 10 tons   @15
150.00

Straw for litter etc. 4 tons   @10   40.00

Stalks	10 loads @ 40	40.00
Corn for pork & pigs		120.00
Corn & other grain for fowls & eggs		50.00
Oats for team say	200 @ 40	80.00
Manure bought		80.00

Labor of family not counted
Trouble and risk of loss of cattle and   1248.80
    horses not counted   <u>988.00</u>
      Approximate receipts   260.80

"Now if we did not operate the farm we would keep fowls
same as now and by them make the amount   75.00

  cost of feed also by keeping a sow and raising a litter of pigs
we might make a little say   10.00
would keep a cow which would be worth say   <u>20 00</u>

"These would make manure enough for our
    garden , ETC.   105.00

"This amount (105) would about keep one horse, so <u>whole</u>
actual project would be for one year. I don't know how to
figure any better than this. The manure we make is all used to
produce the crops, so I have not noticed that in either debtor or
credit. I suppose we would not think of renting the place or
working it on shares and if we gave up farming we would still
work the home lot and grow a few potatoes and a little corn and
some things as we could operate without much expense and do
some of the work ourselves, turning & plowing etc.

"Now Ed do just what seems best for you in the circumstances
I won't feel you are crowding me out at all if you decide to
come home - I can probably support myself outside of the
farm and am willing to do so, but you see all the farm pays us
will not keep Father, Mother, and Ella, and if we fail to rent the
house any season, why we run behind in our accounts -

"This year we shall not pay our bills by $500 I guess or more
- Our house rent is quite an important factor in our income and
somehow our expenses for all sorts of things seem to be very
large."

1885

<u>April 7.</u> At the annual Town meeting, the Supervisor is
"authorized and instructed to insert in the next annual tax levy,
the sum of four hundred and fifty dollars, and pay the same to
David S. Sherrill, David I. Gardiner,and D. Egbert Talmage,
who are hereby appointed and constituted a committee on the
part of the Town, to prosecute to a final determination the suit
now commenced for the recovery of moneys now withheld or

misappropriated, entitled, "Trustees of the Freeholders of and commonalty of the Town of East-Hampton, against Marcus B. Hand and others."

April 9. The new Board of Trustees resolves "that the committee on suits is hereby instructed to prosecute any and all suits now pending and any suits that may come up in the interest of the Board and to report to this Board at their pleasure."

October. Lizzie W. Champney's article on "The Summer Haunts of American Artists" appears in this month's Century Magazine. She calls East Hampton "...a true artist colony, and perhaps the most popular of adjacent sketching grounds for New York artists. This popularity is not entirely due to its accessibility, for its attractions are as pronounced and as varied as those of any of its more remote rivals...Here are rural nooks for the landscape-painter delightfully English in sentiment. Here are beach and sea panoramas, storm cloud-battles, or shimmering calm for the marine painter...Here are costumes of the last century and fascinating faces for the figure-painter; and here are salt sea breezes and sunshine for all."

December 19. Arthur Benson informs East Hampton of his plans for next year's summer pasturage on Montauk. He writes:

"I have decided to alter the present arrangement of dividing the Montauk pasturage into fatting and outside fields; and shall, next summer, throw all into one field, extending from Fort Pond to the Point, and from the Sound to the Ocean. The charge will be three (3) dollars for one cattle right, and for a horse right, double that sum. No bulls of any age whatever are to be allowed on any part of Montauk."

(When the livestock come off Montauk in November, most of them are shepherded along the main road. Some of them are driven along the beach. In Amagansett, they are herded between bars that go up across Main Street. There, they stay until their owners arrive and pick them out, according to their earmarks.)

December 26. East Hampton has its first newspaper today. On an inside page, The Easthampton Star's proprietor and editor, George H. Burling, tells his readers that the weekly will be "devoted to the welfare of the town" and that he aims to make it "a first-class family paper."

The Star's office is in Will Racket's former carriage house, which he had moved to Main Street. The newspaper is printed in New York City, save for one page, which arrives blank. Burling plans to fill it each week with local news and, in time, also with advertising. The only trouble with that is there is not much to advertise in the Town. Most of the shopping is done in Sag Harbor or, even in New York. East Hampton shops are limited to a butcher, greengrocer, plumber, and the like.

1886

January 2. The Amagansett column of The Star reports on a recent discovery by Life-saving Captain Madison King. On the beach, he found a bottle with an enclosed note: "I write this to inform all whom it may concern that I do not want to remain in this world longer and am about to commit my body to the depth of the sea. To all my friends, I leave an affectionate farewell and entire forgiveness of the wrong done me.   Marian C. Stokes"

July 10. Under the headline "Saline Salutatory," The Star announces: "The first bath of the season was taken by Dr. Herrick on Tuesday. Since then the popular pastime has become so general that the bathing season may be declared as fully opened." (Beachgoers at the foot of Ocean Avenue wait until Dr. Everett Herrick measures the water temperature with the aid of a large thermometer, before wading into the ocean.)
. An idea is proposed this year to enlarge Clinton Academy so that dances may be held there. The prospect appeals to many of the summer people, who start a fund to pay for the renovation.

1887

January 8. The Amagansett Telephone & Telegraph Company is founded by five men. It is one of the first such companies on Long Island.

February 16. The Highway Commissioners meet to discuss the AT&TC's application to erect poles along Main Street in East Hampton to, and through, the village of Amagansett, and to string and run telegraph and telephone lines from pole to pole. Saying that everyone will benefit, they give permission, on condition that the highway is kept free and that no poles are placed in front of dwellings.

March 19. The Trustees' Committee of Suits reports on the three-year series of lawsuits against the Trustees of 1882/83. The case against Nathaniel Dominy, former "leader" of the embattled board, and Harry Bisgood is clear. Through then-Trustees Clerk Tooker, Dominy conveyed under water lands to Harry Bisgood. In turn, Bisgood signed them over to Dominy.

The report states that other members of the 1882/83 Board testified that they never approved such a transaction, and Bisgood testified that he only was a "go-between" and did not profit from the transaction. The report concludes that in May

1886, the court found for the Town and set aside the deeds, a judgment being rendered against Dominy.

At this same meeting, the Trustees resolve that the committee in charge of the Town House is "instructed to make all necessary repairs on the stove pipe in said Town House."

April 23. Amagansett items begin to appear in The Star with the by-line "by telephone."

. The fund to enlarge Clinton Academy continues to grow.

. A number of Main Street residents plan to install oil lamps near the front edge of their homes this year. If they do, they will be able to deduct $6.00 a year from their highway tax. (An 1884 State law grants this deduction to anyone who does not live in a city or in an incorporated village).

September. Evening dances at Clinton Hall (Clinton Academy's new name) leads one conservative soul to write:

"This year, tennis is not the chief end of man. Perhaps the new village hall is responsible for the inauguration of something heretofore unheard-of in East Hampton - i.e. late hours. One cannot battle the surf in the morning, play tennis all the afternoon and dance all night, and live. Tennis has suffered. The long and the short of it is, that East Hampton isn't what it used to be. Late hours and ultra-fashionable tastes are out of place here. Let us all come here another summer to have a good time, but a restful one, and refrain from getting on the rack or going on the racket, and have more of the racquet."

October 15. A Connecticut doctor advertises in The Star:

"Dr. A. N. Sweet, Barrister of Middletown, Conn. can be found in Sag Harbor, at his office in Mr. John Homan's residence the FIRST THURSDAY of every month in the year, regardless of weather - weak and deformed joints as well as fractures and dislocations a specialty. Consultation fee...$2."

1888

March 12. This Monday, after a night and morning of rain, snow starts to fall at noon. By nightfall, the wind picks up strength. Telegraphic reports from the western end of Long Island say that much of it is impassable. The temperature drops to zero. The sleet is blinding. The wind, rising to near-hurricane intensity, creates snow drifts ten feet high.

March 15. The train that left Sag Harbor March 12 at 7 a.m. arrives at Hunter's Point Thursday afternoon.

. During the era of summer boarders, bath houses painted from a palette of bright colors are wheeled to the beach in June, and removed in October. In the morning, horses and shays from Homan's livery or, Osborne's boarding house, pick up beach-bound individuals along Main Street, deposit them at the foot of Ocean Avenue, and repeat the trip. "Everyone" is at the sea shore by eleven o'clock.

Children play on the beach in bathing suits, while the fully clothed adults socialize under tents or decorative umbrellas, a carpet or throw rug under their feet. Only after Dr. Herrick takes his large thermometer to the water's edge, dips it in, and signals that it is warm enough to enter, will they step into their bath houses and change into their bathing attire.

The women's bathing suits are almost as full as their dress outfits (long stockings, long sleeves, skirt below the knee, the only bared skin a "V" at the neck). For the ride home, the wet bathing suits are dropped into one of several wooden pails of water that are tied to a luggage rack, at the back of the carriage. One pail for each bath house. Lunch may be soon, but the carriage often will stop at a nearby farm, long enough for its passengers to drink a glass of buttermilk.

At noon, the various boarding house bells are rung from the middle of the street to announce serving of the day's main meal. The ringing is as much for the laggard boarder as it is for the "mealers." (The latter are summer's overflow, people who have found rooms in private homes, but who must take their meals at a boarding house. When a mealer is sick, a tray of food is taken to him or, her, from the boarding house.)

July 28. The Star's founder appeals to his readers: "A Village Improvement Association is Needed. We would suggest that the property owners and others interested in the welfare of our village form an Improvement Association similar to the one which has been in operation in Southampton the past six or seven years...much might be done to beautify our village and make it still more attractive as a place of residence...This is a matter in which all of our residents are interested - summer as well as permanent - and we believe very few would hesitate to become members."

July 30. The Trustees resolve "That the committee on suits and privileges have the authority of this board to commence an action immediately to set aside a deed known as the Bowman deed if after a conference of counsel such an action may be deemed expedient. Cried unanimous." 17

1889

January 1. Benjamin Van Scoy, Joseph S. Osborne, and David J. Gardiner organize the East Hampton Lumber & Coal Company. For the present, the company's yards will be the red sheds in the rear of the Osborne house property on Main

Street. The lumber and coal will come by carts to East Hampton, after being unloaded from trains at Bridgehampton. Mr. Osborne, who is very active in many areas of East Hampton, was only 22 years old in 1874, when he was elected Town Clerk.

November 13. Henry P. Hedges writes the introduction to Volume 4 of 1734-1849 Records of East Hampton. Of the men who lived there during the past century, and those whom he has known, he writes: " ... few streets, even in the great cities of the land, presented a higher constellation of minds than East-Hampton Main Street. In her palmy days it may be doubted if the Senators of East-Hampton would compare unfavorably with the illustrious Senate of the Roman Republic."

1890

June 28. Edward Smith Boughton, who became manager of The Star on June 2, buys the paper.

. Mrs. C. H. Aldrich is selling ice cream from her Egypt Lane residence, this summer, "by the plate or quart."

November. The Journalist editor Allan Forman writes: "It makes all the difference in the world whether you spend your summer vacation on the North, the Sound Fork, - or the South, Ocean shore. On the South Fork, you wear fancy blazers, dress a good deal, play tennis and attend hops; on the North side, you wear an old flannel hunting shirt, go fishing, and you don't hop unless a crab catches your toe...The South side abounds in cottages and summer boarding houses. The North, with farm houses, the best fishing, and some of the worst hotels in America."

1891

March 1. A letter to The Star, signed "Tax-Payer," offers road improvement. ideas: Level Wind Mill Hill, use the earth to fill up the street; extend Lily Pond Lane westward to the Town line (crossing private property can be had "for a public highway free of charge").

He warns that if the roads are not in good condition, the time will come when "the public and poor residents of this town will be deprived of all water privileges for either profit or pleasure."

June 4. East Hampton's Highway commission grants Mary E. Dayton and Patrick Lynch permission to plant shade trees in front of their Main Street homes "at a greater distance from the outside line of the highway than is usually laid down as proper and right."

August. The New York World reports on East Hampton's summer social scene: "The city dames have their days at home, serving tea, ices, etc.. There is a Tennis club to which nearly everyone belongs, and once a week one of the matrons serves tea in the little barn on the grounds, which is tastefully decorated with greens, tennis nets, goldenrod and other wild flowers. There is quite a cotterie of collegians, hence a baseball nine.

"Everyone meets everybody else on the beach of a morning and there is a town hall where every Saturday night a dance is given, where the men wear evening dress and the belles display last winter's evening dresses."

August 28. The Star reports that some men are interested in starting a club in East Hampton. Possible sites for the club are to be scouted before the first meeting, in September.

September. The Ladies Home Journal features "From My Cottage Window," a regular column by The Rev. T. Dewitt Talmage, minister of the Brooklyn Tabernacle Church.

In this month's issue, Rev. Talmage write: "Our summer house is a cottage at East Hampton, Long Island, overlooking the sea. From (my) window, seventeen vessels are in sight - schooners, clippers, hermaphrodite brigs, steamers, great craft and small...the sea hums us to sleep at night....This place has always been a resort of good morals...East Hampton, instead of being two hundred years behind, is two hundred years ahead. Glorious place to summer! Spencer and Huxley and Renan and Ingersoll have not been through here, yet. May they miss the train the day they start for this place."

September 12. Founders of the proposed Maidstone Club hold their first meeting.

They choose, as the site of the new club, eighteen acres which overlook Hook Pond and, beyond it, to the dunes and ocean. (This land was allotted to Thomas Chatfield in 1653.) Purchase price is $14,000. Five acres will be for tennis courts, on which work is to start at once, and a baseball lot. The clubhouse is to be finished in time for the 1892 season. A spokesman for the club tells The Star:"The committee wishes us to particularly emphasize that one of the fundamental rules is that no intoxicating liquors will at any time be allowed upon the premises." No games may be played at the club on Sundays.

October 28. The Maidstone Club is incorporated. Annual dues are set at $15.00 for a member, his wife, one child under ten, and one guest. Each additional child or guest is $5.00.

Autumn. A writer on "Artists of East Hampton" bemoans: "Alas, the spirit of the times is creeping over this restful place.

There is so much talk of a railroad. A race course has been established; tennis grounds; new additions have been put on the old Clinton Academy; now there is to be a new Maidstone club. Why did they not select some poetical Indian name for the club?..."

1892

March 2. The Georgica Association is incorporated. Members are summer home owners whose properties are on the Wainscott side of Georgica Pond. Each member has one vote for every $1000 of real property listed in his name on the Town Assessor's tax role. The purpose of the Association is to maintain a quality of life within the community. The area, named Georgica by the early settlers, is being developed by William B.S. Wood, who bought the land and is selling acreage to friends.

July 17.   Eighty-three people stop by Mrs. Dominy's Ice Cream Parlor during the day for her homemade cream.

August 13. The Maidstone Club opens this afternoon with the serving of afternoon tea (and lemonade). An evening dance follows. Four hundred and fifty members and guests attend.

October 15.. Dr. J.A. Todd's descriptive letter about Montauk is published in today's Tarrytown Argus.. Of the Montauk peninsula., he writes that it "presents as wild and weird an appearance of treeless, windswept hills and tortuous sandy valleys as a traveller in any civilized country is likely to see....

"Within a short time past ten summer cottages have been built on the high bluffs overlooking the ocean, about three miles west of the lighthouse, and in connection with them, a club house with stables attached for the accommodation of those occupying the cottages. By a rule of the Association having control of the colony, no cooking is allowed to be done in the cottages.

"The people in the cottages can take their meals only in the club house....there is...something about this wild land and wilder sea, in their weird solitude, that makes one think of genies and fairies, spirits and hobgoblins."

1893

April 26. One week after telling East Hampton that he will extend the railroad tracks eastward from Bridgehampton, LIRR's president, Austin Corbin, tells the Town that he will build the track within 60 days, if the Town can secure right-of-way between Bridgehampton and Benson's line in Napeague.

LIRR will provide first class cars, low fares for those who buy 1000-mile books, and, in time, take the line through Montauk.
October. The Sag Harbor & Bull's Head Turnpike Company sues LIRR. Demanding that the company change its route, the suit claims that the present railway crossings are injuring the Turnpike's value traveling capacity. (Before the month is over, the Supreme Court dismisses the suit.)
September. This month's issue of Long Island Magazine carries William Wallace Tooker's article on "Some Supposed Indians Names of Long Island." Quoting New England authors of the 17th Century, who refer to "wainscot" and "Wayscot" as oaken timber, Tooker, who lives in East Hampton, dismisses the idea that Wainscott was an Indian name.

He writes of "a body of fresh water, covering some sixty to seventy-five acres, extending from the main road or common at the school house to the ocean bluffs, and known from a very early period of the town's history as the Wainscott - or as it is designated in 1670, 'The Wayinscot Pond.'

"It differs from neighboring ponds of Georgica and Sagaponack in never having an inlet from the ocean within memory, and in having a bottom composed of a thick deposit of mud, which in some places is several feet in depth, which made it eminently suitable for the purpose of preparing *Wain'scot.*" He writes that wainscott is made after oak is cut, cleared of its branches, and the trunk is pitched "in a muddy place in a river, with the head downward for sometime;…when seasoned sufficiently they saw it into boards for wainscot…"

Referring to 1652, the year when Wainscott's name first appears in Town records, he asks, " What was the cart-way for unless to cart the wainscot or oaken timber from the pond to East Hampton?…There is no doubt that the land around was once well wooded with trees growing in the pond…stumps still stand to be seen under water at the head of the pond."

1894

April 14. Rev. Lawrence J. Guerin, pastor of St. Andrew's Roman Catholic Church in Sag Harbor, records an agreement he has made with George E. Halsey of Water Mill: "…the said George Halsey agrees that he will on or before the first day of September make, erect, and build and finish in a good substantial and workmanlike manner and with good and substantial materials a church on the lot owned by the Bishop of Brooklyn at East Hampton, New York. In consideration whereof the said Lawrence J. Guerin agrees to pay the said

George E. Halsey to the same, the sum of four thousand, seven hundred dollars (4,700)." The church lot is on Buell Lane.

. Golf comes to East Hampton this summer when the Maidstone Club lays out three holes.

. Asa O. Jones' new house on Newtown Lane is the first one in Town to contain a bathtub. (When a bathtub was installed in the White House, in Washington D.C., thirty years earlier, doctors decried its presence. They said it would be harmful to the human body to immerse it daily in water. In fact, in Boston, you need a doctor's sanction to take a daily bath.)

August 11. Over 500 people take part in East Hampton Village's parade to celebrate acquisition of its first street-sprinkling carts.

The afternoon parade starts at the bend of Ocean Avenue and makes its way up Main Street and past its decorated houses. Colonial-dressed B.Z. Griffin leads the way on his mount, followed by a wagon carrying the Southampton band; fifty cyclists on festooned wheels, some of them from Montauk, some of them costumed; the watering carts; thirty firemen marching behind their Hook and Ladder, and, finally, Capt. Nathaniel Dominy and his crew in the Georgica Life Saving Station lifeboat, on a float pulled by four horses.

Among the more spectacular floats are those of mason Teunis Barns who, with assistants, is seen building a chimney on his horse-pulled wagon, and that of green grocer William Jones. Jones' display is banked with vegetables. Red and green tomatoes on one side spell out his name. On the other side, a different colored *legume* for each letter spells VEGETABLE. Wreathed with garlands of flowers, fruits, and/or vegetables, 100 horse-driven carriages, complete the procession.

(The sprinkling carts are an important addition. For two years, the awful dust of Main Street has been a frequent topic of conversation and, a possible threat to the village's loss of summer boarders. The $900 raised to buy the carts came from the summer colony.)

. Nebraska summer visitor Dr. Horace P. Holmes writes about his impressions of East Hampton for the Omaha Bee:

"Queer, quaint, quiet East Hampton....the artist's retreat, the tourist's mecca, the tired man's haven....To the westerner, it is unique. Antique, in every fact, its buildings old and gray, vineclad and moss-covered. You visit dwellings and sit before broad fireplaces built over 200 years ago, and drink from wells dug by compatriots of the Pilgrim fathers...The sand dunes, running like giant earthworks thrown up for Titan's battle grounds, are covered with bayberry....Crabs in season are plentiful, and it requires but a few minutes' work to get a basketful...Among the artists who make East Hampton their summer home are C. Y. Turner, who sold his painting "On the Beach at East Hampton" for $30,000...St. John Harper, Howard Russsell Butler, O'Donahue....A railroad will soon be extended ...East Hampton deservedly holds the prophecy of a very successful future."

August 12. The New York Herald Tribune article on Rev. Dewitt Talmage's new home in East Hampton starts thus:

"Down on Long Island there is a lovely spot which is fast becoming known as Clergymen's Retreat. It is filling up with beautiful villas built by the wives of clergymen for luring their spouses away from the heat and fatigue of the city, before it becomes time for the annual trip to Europe or the mountains."

(In East Hampton, this assemblage of summer homes has led to their locale being tagged Divinity Hill.)

September 1. A reporter for Troy, New York's daily files a piece on Amagansett. It is "...quaint and curious...crime is unknown... people have neither locks to their doors nor bars to their windows - a reproduction of the Acadian village of Evangeline and Gabriel. If one wishes his shoes shined, he must exert himself with the brush which will be found ready for all comers at the post office. You ask for a barber and are referred to 'Hand's Barn,' where razor and glass await you, if you see fit to avail yourself of them."

September 2. On his twenty-fifth anniversary as minister of St. Luke's chapel, Rev. Charles H. Gardiner speaks at Sunday service of the church's early history.

He tells the congregation that efforts to raise funds to build an Episcopal chapel were "considered a doubtful experiment at the start...encouragement...amongst the native population was scant ....The good people of the town said, 'it will be a church for the summer boarders...and will probably do no harm...pity everybody in the village cannot conform to the faith of our Fathers - the old Puritan sires....the old Meeting house is good enough for me.' I am repeating actual comments."

Rev. Gardiner describes John Wallace "as an educated gentleman" who "would occasionally favor the congregation with an original sermon of his own, and his efforts were often more acceptable than the selected sermons he was authorized to read."

Of the congregation, Rev. Gardiner says:

"As was originally thought when the chapel was erected, this congregation has been almost entirely composed of summer visitors. Episcopacy I regret to say, does not seem to flourish amongst the native inhabitants of eastern Long Island. But we are not persecuted."

September 16. St. Philomena's Church, East Hampton's first Catholic church, is dedicated by the Most Rev. Charles E. McDonnell, D.D., Second Bishop of Brooklyn. (Father Guerin has named the church after the obscure Virgin-Martyr Saint and in memory of his sister, Philomena, who died when she was very young.) Among the large number of people at the service is Rev. Father Donahue of Greenport, who travels by ferry and bicycle to reach East Hampton.

October 5. An ad in The Star advises on travel to East Hampton:

BOATS

Steamers of Montauk Steamboat Company
leave Sag Harbor Monday, Wednesday and
Friday at 4 p.m. Leave New York Tuesday,
Thursday and Saturday at 5 p.m.
Steamer Long Island leaves Sag Harbor for
New London daily, except Sunday at 6:25 a.m.
and 12:20 p.m., arriving at New London 9:30
a.m. and 4:00 p.m. Leaves N.L. at 10:00 a.m.
and 4:00 p.m., arriving at S.H. at 12:00 and 7:30
STAGES
Rackett & Edward's line of stages, connecting
at Bridge Hampton with all trains, leave stables
at 1:10 and 5:50 p.m.
Stage leaves East Hampton post office daily
(except Sunday) for Sag Harbor at 9:45 a.m.,
returning leaves Sag Harbor at 1:30 p.m."

1895

January 11. The Star editorial wonders "...what that fellow has been eating who dreamed of building a $20,000 boulevard from Brooklyn to Montauk. He should come out on the east end for subscriptions and his enthusiasm will receive an Alaskan chill."

March 21. Springs' largest single day's shipment of fish, in years is recorded: 65 barrels and 8 boxes of flat-fish, totaling between 7 and 8 tons, are shipped from Barnes Hole Landing.

April 9. The Town receives a letter from the LIRR. The site of the railroad station has been decided. It will be on David J. Gardiner's vacant lot on Race Lane.

April 24. The Town's Highway Commissioners grant David J. Gardiner permission to "lay, construct, and maintain a Railroad switch crossing over and across the highway known as Race

Lane.....said switch to be put in for the accommodation of the East-Hampton Lumber and Coal Company...on condition that repairs and maintenance shall be at the expense of said D.J. Gardiner or his heirs or assigns."

April 25. Construction locomotive "F.H. Clement #" arrives on a flat-bed trailer pulled by eight horses. It is taken to the proposed railroad crossing at Newtown Lane. Round-the-clock work starts on completing the track to Amagansett.

May 3. The Star's "Village Town News" column reports: "Main street has sacrificed another of its trees for the moving of an old building. As to value, the tree was worth more than the house."

. This day, Frank E. Raff, Superintendent of LIRR's stations, writes to A.A. Topping, Assistant Agent in Bridgehampton:

"... I would like you to go to East Hampton for a few days until the regular man gets there. You will have only a flag house for an office and wire will be cut in Saturday morning. There will be very little business handled until stations are built.

"You will sell tickets from single and excursion books as there will be no room for a case. Take good care of your money and pay close attention to your wire."

June 1. Thirty years after the railroad line first stretched across this country, railway service to East Hampton begins. Engine No. 4, pulling one baggage, one express, two parlor cars, and four passenger cars, arrives at 7 a.m.. The road beds remain rough and uneven, and most trains arrive late this day. The noon train is the exception.

June 3. Commencement ceremonies for the first class to graduate from East Hampton's Union School are held in Clinton Hall. The class numbers five students: May Conklin, Bessie Gay, Ettie C. Hedges, Mary Strong, and Edmund Tillinghast.

June 7. In its local notes, The Star suggests: "The town clock should now be regulated according to railroad time, which is about five minutes faster than town time. Any one depending on the town clock for time to catch a train might get left."

June 9. Subhead of the Brooklyn Eagle's article on Arthur Benson and Montauk reads: "He secured 10,000 acres at auction in 1879 for $160,000 and his son has just sold 4000 acres to Corbin and Pratt for $200,000."

June 17. Jerry Baker's forty years of delivering mail to and from Sag Harbor ends today.

From now on, all mail (except between Amagansett and Springs) will be put on mail cars of trains, and sorted en route. Baker's square-topped, two-horse stage will continue traveling between Amagansett, East Hampton, and Sag Harbor, carrying passengers and items which he has been asked to buy for someone. But, the sound of his bugle, announcing arrival of the evening mail, now only will be heard between Amagansett and Springs.

October 20. On his way to Washington, D.C. Wyandanch Pharaoh stops at the Brooklyn Eagle office. He tells a reporter,

"I am afraid of the white man...my ancestors once owned all this country and it was taken from us by force and fraud...There are from 100 to 150 of our tribe still left, and although they are scattered all over the country, from Montauk to California, they are all interested in this suit. So, you see, I am not the last of the Montauks."

In Washington, he plans to look into the records concerning the rights of his tribe to remain on Montauk. (Corbin has ordered them off).

November 1. Seven years after The Star's founder urged East Hampton residents to form a village association that would address the best interests of the community, the weekly begins a series. Originally printed in the Brooklyn Eagle, each article is about a different   improvement society on Long Island. Today's article features Southampton's improvement society. Founded in 1884, its membership is mostly male.

November 22. Three weeks after The Star began the series on village improvement societies, a notice appears in this week's issue: "All the ladies who are interested in a village improvement society are requested to meet in the annex at the Hall on Monday evening at seven o'clock."

The ad's presence in The Star brings an editorial comment in the same issue:

"Good! We trust the ladies will go ahead And begin the grand work of improving."

November 30. Inclement weather kept all but five interested women from venturing to the Clinton annex, on Monday. Twenty-two show up this Saturday for the rescheduled meeting, and all but one decides to be a founding member.

The women name their new group the Ladies Village Improvement Society of East Hampton, draw up a constitution, elect officers and determine the organization's objectives. The society will focus on improving "the highways, sidewalks, cemeteries of East Hampton and any other work for the general interest and welfare of the village."

Dues will be fifty cents.

December 17. The LIRR's first public passenger train to Montauk makes its initial run. A number of persons, some of them with winter picnic baskets in hand, board the train at

Bridgehampton, East Hampton, and Amagansett for the short ride to Montauk. There, they have an hour and a half to picnic and sightsee before making the return trip.

December 26. Meeting in the Town House, five of the six Trustees agree "that the Beaches opposite the inlets of the ponds known as Hook Pond and Georgica Pond be reserved for the purpose of draining said ponds." A unanimous vote approves reserving special privileges for the Town in the quit claim sales of South Beach property.

The Town will reserve beach rights to fishing, landing, packing and carting fish; landing boats, seins, nets, and fishing tackle; spreading and drying nets and seins; landing, cutting up, and carting whale; shooting and hunting; erecting Bathing houses, safety lines, and arbors (but not to obstruct public travel on said beach); and to "pass and repass, to walk or ride, sit or stand, or lounge on said premises." (The fishermen have kerosene-lit shanties on the beach. With built-in bunks and pot belly stoves, the structures give the men a place in which to rest and in which to cut up some of their catch.)

1896

January 10. After deciding on future fund raisers - a dramatic entertainment in the spring, and a musical, in a few weeks, LVIS members listen to Mrs. C.E.C. Homan read a letter from William H. Barnes. A city engineer in Kansas and former East Hampton resident, Barnes has replied to a request from Mrs. Homan, on ways to improve Town Pond and the village green.

To keep the pond from evaporating in a dry season, leaving mud on which to gaze, he suggests digging down deep enough to take out all grass roots; then, to line the bottom and sides "with a good puddling clay." After being leveled, he recommends that the pond bottom be compacted by "'milling' a herd of sheep or young cattle on it for two or three days. A few boys and cattle would add much to your work of retaining the water. The above method is used by engineers in canals and reservoirs."

Homan proposes that the common be made into an enclosed park, "with a hawthorn hedge running from the north cemetery steps to about opposite the church, then by a graceful curve turn and run to the east and upper side of Mill Hill, thence around the road and pond, keeping upon the edge of bank when possible, until you reach the cemetery steps at the south end....The common is well situated to make an attractive and romantic spot, linking as it does, the present with the past."

He also recommends planting low-spreading trees and some evergreens, and creating walkways, after the trees are more mature. Barnes ends his letter with the thought that Main Street should be bordered by thirty foot wide lawns in the residential area, and that a bicycle path be added. This, he added, would "tend to keep lots of dust out of the residences and also protect the roots of the shade trees which I saw were badly exposed.... Sidewalks are needed in winter; if you can create a sentiment, the property owners will do the rest in most cases."

January 28. The LVIS holds a well-attended New England supper and Klondike auction to raise funds. The LVIS needs money to support the long-term task it has taken upon itself - to light Main Street and, keep it lit.

February 5. Austin Corbin appears before the Senate Committee on Ways and Means, in support of the bill introduced on January 13. The bill, which has the support of Congress' Shipping Committee, authorizes "the establishment of a free port at Fort Pond Bay, or elsewhere in the waters of Long Island in the State of New York." In closing, Corbin says:

"...If it is not successful the loss will fall upon the proprietors and not upon the public. Fort Pond Bay affords the ideal conditions for the first experiment. It is a deep water harbor at the end of Long Island, from which it is reasonably certain there will be lines of steamships running to Milford Haven, England, or to other European ports, shortening the time of transit between New York and London so that it will be five days instead of six days.

"The harbor has been...practically unused with little commerce and with the shore line and the title to the lands adjacent in a few hands...The water line and sufficient land area for a free port can be laid out and the port surrounded and established, with its walls, wharves, warehouses, and factories, under the most favorable conditions..."

June 4. Austin Corbin is killed in New Hampshire when his horse-drawn carriage flips over, and his head hits a stone wall.

August 23. The Eagle reports that Montauk's first steel pier is "nearly finished and ready for steamers." The 400-foot long structure is in Fort Pond Bay.

. (If anybody thought that the initial enthusiasm of LVIS members would wane soon after the society's founding, a review of its first nine months would put the assumer to shame.

In its commitment to beautify the village LVIS members literally donned garden gloves and took shovels in hand, to set over 100 honeysuckle plants into the ground around the fences of both village cemeteries, to seed the banks of the railroad extension, and improve the station's look with a planting of Virginia creeepers. Through subscription, socials, and the society's first fair, held in Clinton Academy this summer, the LVIS has $1000 in its treasury. Some of the money will be used to buy lamps, wooden posts on which to place them, oil, and the salary of a lamplighter.)

1897

March. The Court of Appeals rules against the Town's five year legal battle to have Fort Pond Bay declared town waters and off limits to non-resident fishermen.

The Court reasons that the bay's shape precludes it from being owned by the town under the terms of the Dongan Patent. It cites the measurements of the entrance to the bay, as the basis for its ruling: "...had it curved so as to make it narrower than the body of waters contained within the boundaries the Court would have decided that Fort Pond Bay was a harbor of the town conveyed under the patent."

June 7. The new Clinton Cycle Club meets at Clinton Hall in the evening to draw up a constitution, a set of by-laws, and to elect officers. The second floor of A.M. Payne's new building on Newtown Lane will become the club's future meeting room. The club's purpose is to promote general interest in cycling, determine and protect the rights of cyclists (who also are called "wheelmen"); and spur improvement of highway conditions. The constitution permits club membership for those between the ages of 16 and 18, who are of good character.

. From May through July, the LIRR adds special horse-and-carriage trains. The semi-weekly runs, which leave Long Island City at one p.m. on Tuesdays, permit summer residents to bring their team with them, and for others to stay overnight on the South Fork, and make a tour.

For commercial fishermen, the railroad now has a regular fish train that leaves Montauk at 6 p.m., in time for the fish to be in the New York market by daylight.

June 25. Van Scoy, Dayton, & Stratton's ad in The Star offers a $10.00 reward "for information that will lead to the discovery of any store that is furnishing better and more stylish hats for the same money that we are putting out." There is a 1/3 to 33 1/3 price reduction on all hats, trimmed and untrimmed, starting June 19.

It concludes: "As our contract with our trimmer expires soon, don't put off getting a hat too late if you wish it trimmed."

December 18. Lighting Main Street is the main subject under discussion at today's LVIS meeting. A vote shows that seventeen members are for it, and "two are for darkness." The majority   agrees to appropriate funds to light the street and keep it lit.

1898
. The Clinton Cycle Club builds bicycle paths along the sides of Main Street and Newtown Lane.

February 7. The LVIS buys 56 street lamps and posts, and lamp oil for $161.75, and hires a lamplighter for $190 a year.

April 20. President William McKinley signs the Spanish-American War resolution at 11:23 a.m.. The news reaches East Hampton twenty-two minutes later, when a Brooklyn Eagle reporter calls the telephone station at the village drugstore.

August 3. The War Department announces that Camp Wikoff is to be established on Montauk and made ready in four days, to receive soldiers, many of whom fought in the just-concluded brief war in Cuba. The camp will be both a recuperation center and a debarkation point for 22,000 to 25,000 troops. Great Plain, the camp site overlooking the ocean, is co-owned by the Corbin estate and LIRR's vice-president, George Pratt. The soldiers will be quarantined until the ill are identified.

August 3/7. The LIRR makes Camp Wikoff accessible by laying 122,795 feet of track and building the first of 14 storehouses.

August 6. One hundred and five carloads of horses arrive on Montauk from Florida. (Due to transport problems, most of them never accompanied the U.S. cavalry to Cuba.)

The Quartermaster ships 150,000 lbs. each of hay and oats, 250,000 lbs. of straw, and 50 cords of wood. Schuyler Arsenal in Philadelphia ships clothing, 10,000 each of bed sacks and blankets, and 147 hospital tents.

The U.S. Post Office borrows LIRR's postal car No. 24 to serve as Camp Wikoff's post office.

August 10. Between afternoon and late evening, three trains bring troops on Montauk. In spite of heavy rain all day long, when the trains stop in East Hampton, women are on the platform, ready with coffee, sandwiches, fruit, tobacco, etc..
. The army's major problem at present is the water supply. Initially, the water is taken from Fort Pond. Healthy soldiers who drink it become ill. Wells are dug but the water is brackish. Standard Oil and Union Tank contribute four large tank cars, each one to hold 6000 gallons of water.

August 12. The following LVIS ad appears in The Star: "Notice; Will the lady who ordered a broom-cover at the fair, and to whom it has not been delivered communicate with Mrs.W.A. Hedges."

August 14. A disinfection barge, "Protector" lies alongside the transport "St. Louis" at Montauk. Soldiers and crew are given disinfective baths on that barge before going to another one for fresh clothing. The discarded clothes are left on the transport.

August 15. The ship "Miami" berths at the LIRR pier in Montauk. Col. Theodore Roosevelt, his Rough Riders, and the Third Cavalry troops debark and march through the village, past a cheering crowd, to the white-tented camp. Five other troop ships dock behind the "Miami."

August 18. Mrs. Washington A. Roebling, Director of the Woman's National War Relief Association, notifies The Star about the extreme privation of the troops.

She appeals for East Hampton women to make apple sauce, which, "would be a good substitute for butter," and points out that, while the Rough Riders and other troops have received packages from families and friends, the Ninth and Tenth Cavalries (made up of non-white soldiers) have received nothing.

. The Star reports that Amagansett is enjoying its busiest summer, to date. Seasonal boarders have filled every room in the hotels and every room available to them in private homes. Rates are at a premium.

August 23. The Telegram reports that there are 225 cases of typhoid among the Rough Riders, and, that the surgeon in charge refused to allow the Red Cross "to furnish, at its own expense, distilling plants."

August 24. A concerned East Hampton resident writes an unsigned letter to The Star on conditions at Camp Wikoff:

"...It is no exaggeration to say that some of the food sent down by me yesterday saved life and I beg everyone in the name of humanity not to relax their efforts...It is worse than no use to send things down by express and freight; take them direct, go to the first camp you come to...don't ask for an officer but show that you have food to give ... you will be surrounded by all who can walk, and generous fellows who will carry what you give them to those too sick to leave their tents.."

August 26. The Star editorial comments on Camp Wikoff:

"There must be a screw loose somewhere when Uncle Sam's soldiers, backed by a country of unlimited resources, are allowed to starve on transports and compelled to depend on charity for food when they land upon our shores."

. By month's end, Camp Wikoff has 6300 tents, each with five beds, 5000 horses, 2000 mules, and 24,000 men. With the troops are their mascots: Teddy, an eagle with a wide wing spread; Josephine, a mountain lion; Toral, a Spanish pony; and Dabney, a young runaway in major's stripes, whom Col. Roosevelt befriended.

September 3. President McKinley arrives on Montauk for a 27-hour "inspection" of Camp Wikoff. During his visit, a woman gets his attention long enough to describe the deplorable conditions. But, an officer dismisses her as "an hysterical woman." The selected sights for the president to visit do not include the tents where the Regulars lie, unattended and dying.

September 9. This week's Star editorial headlines:

"Remember Camp Wikoff

"...the truth will out, and every day some influential paper contains an editorial or a letter which adds to the tide of popular indignation that is beginning to sweep the continent... righteous indignation...that sooner or later will break at Washington and sweep the men who are responsible for the crimes of the camp into outer darkness.. President McKinley's famous visit to the camp was a farce...If the women who are actually saving lives in the camp in spite of the officers are hysterical, then we say God bless the hysterical women."

September 10. This week's Harper's Weekly includes W.A. Rogers' condemning report on Camp Wikoff. In part, it reads:

"The soldiers who come up on the ordinary transports usually arrive famished. Upon arriving at the dock, they have to tramp a mile or more in heavy marching order to the detention camp. At the dock it is their good fortune to meet a kind friend. Mrs. Valentine Mott stands, day after day, early and late, with milk, beef extract, and sandwiches to brace the poor weak fellows for their weary march over the hills...

"The one cheerful feature of the camp is the black soldier. He, as a general thing, came through but little the worse of the pestilent climate of Cuba, and coming of a race used to privations stood the starvation rations better than his white brother .... There is no exaggeration in the current stories of the starvation and neglect of these, our returning heroes......"

. Following orders from Washington, evacuation of Camp Wikoff begins mid-month.

October 7. "MOVING PICTURES" at Clinton Academy. This evening, the Academy's room is crowded with those who bought tickets to see the Edison Projectoscope exhibit moving pictures "as true to life as though the actors were on stage before you." 'The Great American Wargraph, with its pictures of the Spanish- American War, is on view, too.

October 15. The last troops leave Camp Wikoff.

October 30. The New York Times' Illustrated Magazine features an article on "East Hampton The Restful." Its writer records: "...the real centre of East Hampton for its Summer folk lies on the seaward edge of the town; it is the bathing beach. It is not a fashionable beach like that of Naragansett Pier, or Southampton, a score of miles to the southwest, but one where men, women, and children go to bathe without caring for looks or asking what is the correct thing in bathing.

"Right and Very Reverends, authors and artists, clergymen and lawyers, old men and women, matrons, hordes of college boys and half-grown girls, children and babies, shout, shriek, dip, and swim, while...a beachman with cork jacket around his body stands... by the edge of the surf to give confidence to timid bathers...

"East Hampton is restful not only because people have so far avoided the absurdity of repeating in Summer the same things they do in Winter, but because the moist atmosphere predisposes to quiet, acting soothingly on excited nerves...."

1899

February 4. In a letter to The Star, a summer resident protests plans to introduce electric light to East Hampton:"...There is no reason because a 'boom' has struck East Hampton, why at once it should be necessary to turn it into a typical up to date, American village, probably the most hideous thing of its kind in the world, with arc lights, trollies, cobble stones, and terrible architecture....having an electric plant ... is pretty sure to lead to the worst abomination of all - the trolley. This...would be the 'last straw' for many...a large number of houses would be for sale cheap; among them that of one of the many lovers of East Hampton As It Is."

April 2. The last annual town meeting is held at Clinton Academy. (State law has mandated that they become biennial).

May 20. The Brooklyn Eagle article on "Building and Real Estate in East Hampton" reports: "Work commenced on May 17 by a New York contractor on two new summer cottages...for Mr. Thomas of Manhattan, who, with his family, has been a summer resident at East Hampton for many years... owing to the large number of advance engagements made at the most desirable boarding places...this spring, Mr. Thomas was unable to find accommodations during August for his family. Consequently, he decided to build at once."

September 14. Concerned about the continued deplorable state of Main Street - a dust path in summer, an uncrossable mud strip in winter, the LVIS holds a special meeting to organize a

Road Committee. Vote is unanimous "that we should start by making a thoroughly good road as far as we can til the money fails, beginning at corner of Newtown and working up the street..."

To prepare for this eventuality, the Road Committee will travel the length of Long Island, to talk with various road engineers about the best way to pave Main Street.

. During the course of their autumn excursion into road information, a reporter for the Brooklyn Eagle asks a member of the Road Committee why the women have undertaken this task. She replies, "The men wouldn't, so we will."

September 25. The artist Mary Nimmo Moran dies at the Studio, of typhoid fever. Two weeks ago, she was told that her daughter, Ruth, whom she had been nursing through the fever, would die of the contagious disease. On hearing the news, she collapsed and fell ill herself. On this day, Ruth is recovering.

The Twentieth Century

1900

March 17. With no fire lit in the Town House and "the day being cold," the Trustees adjourn to the Town Clerk's office. There, "to correct any misunderstanding concerning the title to property along and adjoining the South Beach...and to perfect title for those who may wish to use the Banks or Dunes for residence purposes....," they resolve to quit claim "to any owner of land adjoining said South Beach, from Georgica Pond on the West to old Egypt Lane highway on the East."[18]

Quit claim requests must be made within six months, each deed to cost $25.00. The boundary line "is to conform to the general line of grass growing." A proviso requires that "boats and seines may be allowed to lie upon the banks or grass, for a distance of 50 feet on either side of the highway."

September 29. Today's Brooklyn Daily Eagle covers the opening of Temple Adas Israel, in the East Hampton part of Sag Harbor: "Twenty years ago, it would have been difficult to find a representative of the Hebrew race in Sag Harbor, but the establishment of the Fahys watchcase factory has brought large numbers of Poles and Russian Jews to the village to seek employment in that manufactory....

"In business, the Jews have pushed rapidly to the fore in Sag Harbor. They control the clothing and fruit trade, and upon the main business thoroughfares 15 large stores testify to their industry. This does not include the number of wagon and pack pedlars who work the surrounding country, making the village their headquarters."

(In 1882, Joseph Fahys went to Ellis Island to hire newly-arrived immigrants. Forty-odd Jewish families came to Sag Harbor, as a result. Their numbers grew. In 1883, they formed the Jewish Association United Brethren. In 1890, they paid $50 for cemetery land on Route 114.)

1901

January 22. A group of Village women meet at the home of Florence Nightingale Osborne to organize a literary society. They decide to meet once a month, autumn through spring, to pursue literature, especially that of travel, whether here or abroad. Once a year, discussion will center on a particular phase of East Hampton. The women name themselves "The Ramblers."[19]

April 12. "The question of the Beach Banks, East of Egypt Lane, not having been finally disposed of previously," the Trustees resolve that a strip of land, "not less than one hundred feet wide along the South Beach and as near the Ocean as practicable, extending from Egypt Lane to the highway at Amagansett, be dedicated for a public highway." Two Trustees are appointed to work with the Clerk to examine the beach and determine the highway's boundaries and widths.[20]

August 9. Shortly after midnight, the Maidstone Club burns to the ground.

August 10. Afternoon tea for 200 is served on the Maidstone Club lawn

August 23. The Star notes that Le Roy Edwards is out on the street nearly every day with his Locomobile. Horse owners hire him to run up and down the street while they accustom their animal to the machine.

1902

March 14. The Trustees dedicate the strip of beach land for the planned Atlantic Highway. The road will run along South Beach, as close to the ocean as possible, from Georgica Pond to Wainscott.

September 4. The Trustees hear that Wainscott residents, whose properties face on the beach, oppose the proposed beach highway. This is the first opposition.

1903

January. Summer resident Charles de Kay's article, "Summer Homes at East Hampton," appears in Architectural Record.

He writes: "It is rare to find city folk building with so much feeling for the landscape as one observes in East Hampton.... The charm of this scenery is not easy to define, but persons of very different character bow to it....

"A prevailing type of summer home is a smallish frame dwelling shingled, without paint or stain, having a deep porch cut out from the ground floor, or, to put it the other way, the second floor brought forward over the porch. They are houses that cost $8 to $12,000....They are almost without exception, simple developments not from the colonial manse, but from the colonial country dwelling of wood, only the dwelling is generally more liberal in porches and loggias than the early settler's house, as befits the home that is for summer only....

"As one passes along (Main Street) individual trees surprise one by their size and grace. Eastward toward Amagansett and westward toward Georgica Lake the old farms open out and villas are seizing possessions far and near of what used to be pasture or arable land. The air is loaded with the perfume of rose and honeysuckle, sweet scented grass, lilacs, and syringa, and whether one drives across the island by the grand avenue through the classic region called Hardscrabble, and winding through the sandy wood-roads comes out on the distant stretches of Gardiner's Bay, or, skirting Georgica, ploughs through Wainscott and Sagaponack, the same friendly yet severe landscape is about one, with here and there the glimpse from a rising ground of some dune-framed slice of the ocean."

. This year, Austin Culver and Ulysses Lee build The Three Mile Harbor Pavilion for picnics and dances.

July 6. The LVIS minutes record today's animated meeting:

"...it is thought necessary by some of our summer people to run the (street sprinkling) carts on Sunday. The Secretary believes she is voicing the sentiment of almost every member of this society when she asserts that the LVIS of East Hampton will not stand for any such arrangement."

1904

January 8. Readers of The Star are advised today:

"Unless Pepsikola Cures your Dyspepsia, E.J. Edwards will Pay Back the Money." The amount is twenty-five cents.

Everett Edwards is described as "too busy a druggist" and his reputation as "worth too much" to risk recommending a product that doesn't do what it is meant to do. This one is said to have "performed some cures in East Hampton that border on the miraculous." Besides doing wonders for sour stomach, nerves, wind belching, digestion and eyes (it clears them), Pepsikola "is almost sure to increase your weight."

1905

April 5. Majority vote at the biennial Town Meeting favors replacing mass Town Meetings with an election district system. (The increasing Town population netted the need to change the "old fashioned way" of voting.)

While the majority also approves "That the twelve candidates receiving the greatest number of votes for the office of town trustee on the ballots cast at this town meeting be the town trustees as provided in the East Hampton Town Patent," it defeats four propositions that called for the sale of liquor by saloons, hotels, storekeepers, or, as a prescription, by pharmacists.

(Passage of the Raines Law, regulating Excise tax, required the propositions to be placed on the ballot.)

1906

<u>April 10.</u> The State Legislature passes an Enabling Act. The bill gives the Montauketts a standing in Court, as a tribe (a position hereto denied them), and the right, as a tribe, to initiate legal action. (Previous attempts to sue for return of their land failed, when the Court ruled that they had no standing in Court.)

<u>June</u>. Sunday golf is permitted at the Maidstone Club after 12:30 p.m. - and, only after a circulated petition was returned with many signatures, including those of the clergy.

. This year, Everett Edwards builds an addition to his pharmacy on Main Street. It will house the town's first central telephone office.

1907

<u>April 4</u>. By a seven vote majority, Town vote sanctions licensing pharmacists to sell medically-prescribed liquor.

<u>Summer.</u> News that Gustav Buek has bought "Home Sweet Home," the house said to have been the inspiration for John Howard Payne's song, is reported in countless papers across the country.

The property first belonged to Ralph Dayton, an early Town settler. He left it to his son, Robert, who built some sort of structure on it. Conjecture is that it probably consisted of two rooms, the kitchen and the one in which the family slept on straw covered with blankets.

Robert, who died in 1712, bequeathed the eastern part of the house to his widow (provided that she did not remarry) and the remaining part to his grandson.

There appears to be a large gap in history about the house, between the death of this grandson, also named Robert, and when the merchant Aaron Isaacs acquired it, in the 18th century. It is thought that Matthew Mulford lived there for a time before Isaacs, after the farm house next door was wrecked in a storm.

1908

<u>November 10.</u> Five men from Cincinnati and New York City form The Gardiner's Bay Company. They plan to create a summer colony for themselves and to "...purchase, lease, or otherwise acquire" property and water rights, extending from Promised Land to Fresh Pond.

The community will comprise "hotels and innkeepers, caterers, keepers of livery stables and stables for horseless conveyances of all kinds, warehouse men, tobacconists, dealers in provisions, wine and liquor dealers, barbers and hairdressers, newsdealers and proprietors or managers of theatres, opera houses and other places of public entertainment...to build, own or purchase or otherwise acquire railways and railroads solely in connection with the business of the Corporation."

(The partners have each commissioned a Mediterranean Revival Style house to be built for their summer home, making them the first large estates in Amagansett.)

1909

September 13. The Springs Village Improvement Society holds its first meeting. The Society wants to buy the unused red brick school house across the road from the Springs Community Presbyterian Church, to be used for the community-at-large.

October. The new Springs Society buys the old school from the Springs School Board, for one dollar "and other considerations." The Society must make the building available to the community-at-large; the deed is in the Society's name, but it cannot sell the building, and should the Society ever disband, the building reverts to the Springs School.

The Society names the building Ashawagh Hall. *Ashawagh* is the Indian word for "place where two roads come together."

December. Reporting on Suffolk County events since January, the Riverhead Review has this to say:

"The big Montauk steamship proposition keeps bobbing up and if it was but a dream at one time, the phantasm has appeared so many times and to so many people, that it is today looked upon as certain to materialize....

"While we are waiting for the Montauk steamship work to take definite form, there is activity in the Montauk region that augurs well for future developments at the East End, steamship or no steamship...residential development at Devon and Amagansett and East Hampton and Three Mile Harbor is of a character to make any observer take notice and it means that homes of the highest type are to be established in considerable numbers thereabouts."

1910

April 23. Voters approve creation of a police district. Hiram Sherrill is elected Justice. The three Commissioners are voted in, unopposed.

May 22. The first service is held in the north transept of the new St. Luke's Church. (The larger church is going up behind the original one. Its architect, summer resident James Nash, based his design on churches that he studied during a trip to Maidstone, Kent.)

. Nine hundred and twenty-four 25 x l00 foot lots on land just west of Napeague are for sale. The property, being developed by Herbert A. Weeks, runs from Main Road to the ocean. Brokers in New York City and on the island have received over sized four-page prospectuses which tell the reader:

"...the American public are through being fooled by Wall Street manipulators, and are rushing in flocks to buy Real Estate. They are right if they buy right. Buy cheap and hold it for a couple of years and you will make fortunes. Read this opportunity:

"LONG ISLAND ATLANTIC AVENUE OCEAN LOTS

$50	Easy Payments
AND UP	$2.50 per month
	10% Discount for Cash

"Never in the history of Real Estate Development has a man of moderate means had an opportunity to own a piece of land fronting the Atlantic Ocean. It has always been the rich man's luxury....Here is an opportunity, with a little cash and patience, to get rich."

July 23. The Trustees resolve "that it shall be unlawful for any person or persons to take from the waters...any escallops with dredges or Dredging in any other manner than from a Boat propelled by oars and not more than one Dredge from a Boat can be lawfully used, at one time."

October 10. Justice Abel Blackmar hands down his decision on the Montauketts' legal efforts to regain their "rights." He has rested his conclusion on a detailed study of the Dongan Patent and Town history. Blackmar determines that the Patent gave the Town's Proprietors exclusive rights, and that when Benson bought Montauk from its previous owners, he became the sole, absolute owner.

Blackmar supports his decision by quoting a passage from the 1687 Indian deed: "..in token thereof we have digged up a piece of earth and delivered it as our act and deed into the hands of the inhabitants of East Hampton"

In denying the Montauketts rights or standing, he concludes: "Prior to the purchase of the Indian rights by Mr. Benson there was a number of Montauk Indians in the enjoyment of tribal rights in Indian field and a sufficient tribal organization to preserve to them those rights. There is now no tribe of Montauk Indian. It has disintegrated and been absorbed into the mass of citizens. If I may use the expression, the tribe has been dying for many years. Separation of the members due to the purchase by Mr. Benson gave it the final death blow. But I hold that the purchase was a lawful act and there is no consideration of justice which makes me loath to find there is no longer a tribe of Montauk Indians."

October 11. The Brooklyn Eagle comments on Blackmar's opinion: "...with the help of the Supreme Court in Brooklyn the remnant of the old Montauk race - whose tribal name has been given to so many things, from theatres and 'swell' clubs to prize-fighting arenas, and 'buy-your-own-home' town lots -..has been driven by law off Long Island.

"WHERE CAN THEY GO?

"From the point that bears their name, and which they thought they owned, they may go into the sea. Elsewhere, legally, there is no place for them."

1911

January 5. The Riverhead News records the Court finding on an East Hampton man:

"Wm. H. Jones...was indicted this week for endangering the life of a child, and the story as told by the man's wife reveals a most inhuman state of affairs....Before the justice she testified that her husband compelled her to keep their little daughter, less than two years old, in a cold, tumble down kitchen, day and night. No heat could get into the room, and during all of the cold weather in December the infant was confined there alone, lying on a bundle of filthy rags....She stated, too, that when she didn't treat the infant this way her husband beat her... Doctors testified the child was in a pitiable condition...sores, scabs and abrasions...teeth already badly decayed, some of them down to the gums. One of the baby's arms had been broken and never set.

"As the case ranked only as a misdemeanor from a legal point of view, Jones could not be sent to State Prison. Pleading guilty... he was sent to the county jail for ten months."

February 1. The County Review reports on a Star editorial:

"The East Hampton Star says that the time will soon be here when there will not be much shorefront property that is not owned by out-of-town speculators.

"That is true and for that reason every town in the county should immediately make provision for a local shorefront park. The inhabitants of each town are entitled to the privilege of free access to the water-front at some point and it is incumbent on the trustees of every town to see that such privileges are assured them for all time..."

November 24. According to The Star, large deposits made at East Hampton, Southampton, and Sag Harbor banks the last few weeks "show the prosperity of the farmers...who have completed the harvest of the potato crop...prices paid for stock have established a record."

1912
. Winter sports include horse and sleigh races from the flagpole on the snow-covered green to Newtown Lane.
June 26. At 10 a.m., The East Hampton Free Library opens for the first time in its new quarters. The Board of Managers has invited the public to participate in the day-long celebration. Tea is served at 4. The door closes at 9 p.m.. (For the past decade, the library was cramped in one room at Clinton Hall. Its own building is the gift of Mary and Lorenzo E. Woodhouse.)

1913
July 7. The LVIS Secretary records in the minutes:
    "We received an invitation from Mrs. Manson to hold our Fair on her lawn and in her house if she could have a booth for the advancement of the women's suffrage Movement." The society accepts the invitation.
August. The Town Board hears and denies a request by some residents to build a dancing pavilion at Maidstone Park.

1914
August 1/4. Declarations of war are made between Germany and Serbia, Germany and France, Great Britain and Germany.
December 3. Ruth Gordon Stratton of East Hampton joins the American Red Cross.
April 11. Dr. Herrick dies. A Maidstone Club founder and its only president to date, he leaves it a conditional legacy of $7500. The Club can never serve liquor, must maintain its present character, and all of its tennis matches must be decided by three sets out of five, not by two sets out of three. Should the Club choose not to accept these terms, it must turn over his bequest to the East Hampton Free Library.

1915
May 7. Morning newspapers in the United States carry a warning from the Imperial German Embassy that Americans should not book passage on British ships.
    . In an address before the Order of Colonial Lords and Manors, Sarah Gardiner Tyler gives a picture of Gardiner's

Island as it was on the threshold of the American Revolution:

"The estate had become a garden of beauty. From eighty to one hundred attendants kept it trimmed and blooming; some two thousand loads of hay were stored in barns every autumn; three hundred or more cattle grazed in its sunny pastures, and ten times as many sheep with an annual yield of thousands of pounds of wool.

"The dairy produced butter in large quantities, and cheese averaged as many as a hundred and twenty pounds per day for the season. The lord of the Island rarely stabled less than sixty horses, the finest in the country.

"He raised annually a hundred hogs; wild turkeys hovered about in great numbers, coming to yards daily to be fed with the tame fowl. A large herd of deer roamed at will among the old trees. Thus Lion Gardiner's legacy has descended, an Island quite unspoiled by time, a lovely solitude which no Caucasian ever called his own unless he was called by the name of Gardiner."

. This spring, a cinder road is built across Napeague. It will improve the long ride to Montauk.

June 15. The Maidstone Club accepts Dr. Herrick's legacy.

September. Women are allowed to play tennis at the Maidstone Club on Sundays - in mixed doubles only.

October 2. The Town Board appoints councilman Hiram Sherrill a committee of one to confer with Westhampton sculptor, Theophilus A. Brouwer. The sculptor would like to give the Town one of his large sculptures, for outside display.

1916

July 3. The major issue at today's LVIS meeting is Brouwer's offer to the Town. The women agree to petition the Town to refuse his statue.

July 8. Town attorney, H.G. Stephens, reads LVIS's resolution to the Town Board:

"The Ladies Village Improvement Society at a regular meeting held July 3rd by a majority vote adopted the following resolution, which resolution it begs to respectfully submit to the trustees of the village.

"Whereas, the charm of this village has ever been recognized to be largely in its unique and perfect simplicity, and the village in this particular has always remained true to its early traditions, and whereas any large statue erected in any conspicuous place in the village would tend to mar this simplicity, therefore be it

"Resolved, That the Ladies Village Improvement Society would most earnestly request and respectfully urge ...to decline any offer of a statue or monument for a public position, now or in the future."

July 13. The Town Board responds to recent petitions calling for stricter legal measures to lessen the chance of infantile paralysis "getting a foothold in this community." It authorizes the Health Officer to perfect such measures as may cause an inspection of all children coming into the Town in any manner and that he be guided as to authority by Section 24 of the rules and regulations of the Town Board of Health."

August 7. The Town Board hears Brouwer's reply to its letter, advising him not to proceed with his gift: "...as there is opposition to its reception the project is at an end. I only can add that it is with the deepest regret that I recall making the offer of my time and talents. I have given much careful thought to the perfecting of a design which would be in keeping with the surroundings and the colonial history and quaint character of Old East Hampton ....

"What pains me is the utter misunderstanding shown by the Ladies and others objecting. To tell an artist of any character that his work will interfere with the charm of simplicity is to insult his work to the limit. All over Europe it is customary to collect and highly prize all works of art in memory of the givers and these art objects constitute the great attraction of many otherwise uninteresting places.

"East Hampton has many men of great ability as its guests and in no instance has it retained the smallest remembrance such as a painting, sketch, bit of carving, sculpture or any work with the single exception of the most brainless one of the lot who out of a sick heart poured forth a sad lament, and yet this one remembrance has done more for East Hampton in an advertising way than any other one thing.

"If a suitable gallery had been provided and the request made every one of the long list of painters, sculptors, etc.. would gladly have given an example of his work to be held in remembrance of him and East Hampton would certainly have been the richer, the more unique. Its 'simplicity' would not have been marred but if any work had been done out in the open it would have added to and not have taken away from the quaint charm of the place.[21]

"When I lived there I was one of the strongest in condemnation of any innovation or change that would modernize or injure the true beauty of the town and yet when I visited it this summer I find a vast increase in money expenditure but a total lack of the simple, unique, beauty to be there seen some twenty years ago. You have made a modern town, but old quaint colonial East Hampton is no more ...

"When I made the offer...I had in mind what I have suggested above as to retaining a parting gift from the painters and other art workers. I am not in need of advertising.

"The Ladies Village Improvement Society is in error if they imagine that they were to do me a favor by accepting my gift."

August 24. Responding to public concern about infantile paralysis, the Town Board adopts sixteen recommendations.

Among them, arrival of any child under sixteen must be reported; nobody under the age of sixteen may attend public or private gatherings of *any* kind; a visible placard is to be posted at the entrance of a house, in which a case of polio existed within two weeks; anyone who dies from polio is denied a public funeral.

August 26. After a tribal meeting of the Montauketts, Chief Wyandanch Pharaoh writes a letter to The Star. In part, he writes, "Even if there isn't any tribe, whoever there is living that was born and brought up on Montauk, it is right that they get what belongs to them - just the same as if a citizen dies and leaves children...their estate...This being a queer world, it really seems as though the poor Indians were never meant to have what belongs to them. Plenty of law, little justice."

September 2. The Town Board resolves that "... no schools, outside of incorporated villages, shall be opened until Sept. 25th, 1916, pursuant to recommendations of the State authorities."

September 9. The Town Board receives a bill for $25.00 from Raymond G. Blydenburgh of Hartford, Conn.. He writes that it is for expenses incurred in returning his family to Hartford after health authorities would not allow his family to enter the town with a child. The Board moves to reject the request.

September 30. Town Board majority calls on the Board of Health to rescind all special regulations except that of Section 2 which reads: "Every hotel proprietor, boarding house keeper and all other persons will report immediately to the local Health Officer the arrival of every child under the age of sixteen received in their hotel, house, or household."

October 24. The Brooklyn Eagle editorial predicts: "Montauk Point will be the seaport of the western world's shipping. Freight service will be transported direct from the West through tunnels under the North and East Rivers...thence to the wharves at Montauk Point. The wharves will accommodate the largest boats and trains will run out on the docks and be loaded direct to the boats without rehandling of freight."

November 1. Town barbers raise the price of a haircut from 25 to 35 cents. Increased rents and supply costs demanded it.

November 2. The barbers rescind their price increase. Patrons threatened to have their wives take up the scissors.

. Today's Brooklyn Eagle editorial comments on the newly-opened highway from Amagansett to Montauk. It notes that 28 motorists made the round trip opening day, and predicts that, by spring, daily travelers across the strip will average 280.

1917

February. The United States breaks diplomatic relations with Germany.

February 19. Seventy women meet at the Huntting Inn to organize a Red Cross Chapter for war work. Many join the Red Cross at the meeting.

April 6. The United States declares war on Germany.

. Walter Benjamin enlists in the U.S. Navy. He is the first young man from Amagansett to enlist after war is declared.

April 13. The Star's front page lists the names of 140 East Hampton residents who responded to President Woodrow Wilson's request that Americans sign the loyalty pledge.

In the same issue, the Springs column notes: "Ford autos are quite the rage now and it looks as if horses are to become a thing of the past except for farm work. George A. Miller and Clarence E. King are among the recent purchasers of cars."

. The first steps towards organizing a volunteer Home Defense Guard on the South Fork are taken in East Hampton. West Point graduate Lt. Stephen Sherrill consents to drill the new company during his vacation.

April 21. A Naval Reserve enrollment branch of the New York Navy Yard opens in Amagansett. After encouraging her son, Herbert, to enlist, Mrs. Herbert Barnes opens the ground floor of her Amagansett home to sailors, during their free time.

. Some East Hampton residents meet at the library to discuss ways to make the town more self-supporting during the war, while also helping the nation.

Proposals are made and accepted to promote the conservation of food stuffs and encourage local agricultural production on a larger scale, and to spread the cry for both, through mass meetings and patriotic speeches.

May 1. Pasturage on Montauk is open to cattle grazing. Owners are to drive their cattle to John Dickinson's farm outside East Hampton, and pick them up there in November. Season rates are $5.00 for beef cattle and cows, $10.00 for horses, and $2.00 for calves under one year.

May 14. Secretary of War Newton Baker orders the 19th and 20th Field Artillery to use Montauk Point as a staging area. Recruits from New York join army regulars who came there from duty on the Texas border.

May 18. Two hundred and sixty men come to the High School to hear about organizing a Rifle club. More than half sign up.

May. The U.S. government lays out Napeague Bay and Block Island Sound as torpedo practicing grounds.

May 23. The Long Island Railroad sends its exhibition train to Amagansett. Part of the Long Island Food Reserve Battalion's efforts to interest women in preserving and canning, the train includes one car, in which illustrated lectures are given; a baggage car, containing the canning equipment, and a business car which serves as headquarters for the Battalion's directors.

May 24. An ad in The Star reads:
"WANTED FOR HIRE tents for women's land army for summer. Communicate Box 604."

May 26. The Osborne Bank opens in the Village.

June 19. The Rifle Club, now numbering 160 members, becomes a unit of the Suffolk County Home Defense League.

July 1. A U.S. Aviation camp to train pilots is started in Montauk. Hangars under construction include one for a dirigible and another to house three hydroplanes.

August. Everit Albert Herter, a promising young artist, enlists in the camouflage corps, Company A, of the 40th Engineers. Adele and Albert Herbert's son is the first volunteer for the corps since it was authorized by the War Department.

December 18. Ruth Gordon Stratton arrives in France where she reports to the American Red Cross Headquarters in Paris. She receives instruction about what she and other social workers can expect when they are sent on active duty in the provinces.

December 24. A flag with 63 stars is stretched across Main Street on a cable. Its stars are to remind passersby that 63 men from East Hampton are in the war.

1918

January 29. State Court of Appeals upholds Justice Blackmar's 1910 decision which denied tribal rights to the remaining Montaukett descendants. Writing for the Court, Justice Burr asserts that evidence given during Appeal failed to show that the descendants rarely, if ever, met as a tribe.

June 6. An electric chandelier is installed on the new isle of safety at the east end of Newtown Lane. The nine-foot high fixture with five lights is expected to lessen the number of accidents where the lane intersects Main Street.

June 12/13. Sergeant Herter, who arrived in France in January, is mortally wounded at Château Thierry, where he is supervising the camouflage of American batteries.

He is promoted to Lieutenant on the day he dies.

August 7. "Indians Made White Men by Ruling."

Under the headline, The Sun's article profiles the numerous Appeals that followed the Court decision in the case Wyandanch Pharaoh, as chief and tribe of Indians, plaintiff-appellant, vs. Jane Ann Benson and others defendant/respondent."

August 31. The swimmer Annette Kellerman gives a talk at the Village Hall to benefit the American Red Cross. She also holds a diving and swimming exhibition at the Devon Yacht Club, to benefit the local chapters of the American Red Cross.

November 11. The world lays down its arms. Peace is declared.

November 12. News of war's end arrives for many with the arrival of the early morning train, its whistle blowing non-stop.

Within a short time, the electric light plant whistle is blowing (and does so most of the day), a parade is planned, and posters, heralding an evening meeting and dance are placed around the town. Robert Appleton lends a huge 20x40 flag to hang across Main Street on a wire, strung from The Star office to a large elm.

December 11. Dorothy Hamlin, who enlisted in the American Red Cross last month, arrives in Paris, where influenza is rampant. A Red Cross Canteen worker, "Dolly" is one many young women who responded to the urgent plea for people to replace exhausted volunteers in Europe.

1919

January 13. "Dolly" Hamlin succumbs to influenza in Paris.

Her dying wish is to be buried in East Hampton. Unable to fulfill her wish at this time, the Red Cross gives her a funeral, followed by burial in the American Cathedral Cemetery in Paris.

February 12. The first flight of the C-4, the country's largest dirigible, takes place at the Montauk Naval Air Station where it was assembled.

The test flight is run from Montauk to Block Island, from there to Amagansett, and back to its hangar. The C-4 carries a crew of six and is capable of carrying 3000 lbs. of bombs. She is nearly 200 feet long and has a cruising speed of 600 miles.

(Dirigibles hangared in Montauk during the war were kept busy. Through their frequent "bombings" of eastern towns with quantities of War Loan literature, they were given large credit for the Drive's success.)

November 6. Voters defeat three of four local options on the sale of liquor. Majority vote favors prescription sale from pharmacists.

November 7. South Fork residents crowd Bridgehampton's Atlantic Hall to hear Montauk summer resident, Zella de Milhau, recount her experiences as an ambulance driver in France, during the war.

November 25. Men and boys jam the school auditorium to hear Dr. Arthur R. Guerrard speak on "Plain Facts about Venereal Disease and Their Prevention."

One of the pamphlets distributed at the lecture heralds "Do Your Bit to Keep Him Fit."

1920

January 23. Today, Dr. Helen Williamson talks to women and young ladies about "Plain Facts About Venereal Disease and Their Prevention." Among the pamphlets handed out after her talk is "Your Country Needs You - a Talk with Girls."

July 4/7. Swans on Georgica Pond see and hear a lot of Enrico Caruso this week-end. The famed tenor and his family have rented a house in Georgica. He likes taking a boat onto the pond and sing his loudest. Rather than flap their wings for an encore, the swans take momentary flight.

September 25. In a special election, village residents vote, 166 to 57, to incorporate East Hampton Village.

November 11. Daniel E. Grimshaw, lc, U.S.C.G., receives the Navy Cross from President Wilson "for extraordinary heroism in an attempt to save the coal-laden steamer "Wellington" after the vessel had been torpedoed on September 16, 1918." (Seaman Grimshaw was one of several volunteers who spent hours aboard the British ship off Calais, trying to keep her afloat.)

1921

August 13. The East Hampton Historical Society is founded. Its purpose is "to foster interest in local history..." and "...to preserve local relics and works of art, to the end that the history, as well as the physical and scenic features of East Hampton might not be lost to future generations."

. Mr. and Mrs. Woodhouse have agreed to underwrite the cost of restoring Clinton Hall, (to be known again as Clinton Academy) before it is turned over to the new Society.

May 31. A new set of ordinances is passed today by the East Hampton Village Board of Trustees. They include:

No. 14. No animals of any kind are allowed to run at large on the streets. (Cats and dogs are not on the village list.)

No. 16. No team of horses or other animals may be tied or hitched to any shade trees along the streets or sidewalks.

No. 17. Bathing nude is not allowed in village waters between sunrise and 8 p.m.

No. 19. Using sling shots and throwing balls, stones, snowballs, or balls of ice and snow is not allowed on village streets or sidewalks.

No. 27. Nobody may drive or operate a vehicle on or upon any public road in the village faster than one mile in four minutes.

November 10. East Hampton is growing and prospering but, unlike their predecessors, today's voters reject allocating funds for support of the town poor.

1922

August 13. Two weeks after a spectacular fire destroys the second Maidstone Club, its board members decide to build the third clubhouse at a new location. They select club-owned land, next to the golf course, overlooking the dunes. A tennis clubhouse, and additional courts, will be built on the burned-out site (at the end of Maidstone Lane, which is off of James Lane.)

1923

January 2. Calling its action "purely technical," the Village Board rejects the War Memorial committee's Dec. 11 request that it delegate the committee "full power, without obligation of any kind, to the village, to improve and maintain the" Hook Mill green as "a memorial worthy of the sacrifice which it represents."

The Board also votes to recommend to the Hon. Henry A. Wallace, Secretary of Agriculture, that a memorial to Theodore Roosevelt, who died in 1919, be built in the form of a national highway from New York to Montauk.

June 22. The Maidstone Inn (not to be confused with the Maidstone Club) is run by the LVIS this entire day. In an extraordinary gesture, the owners of the remodeled inn have turned over their entire operation, including all of today's income, to the organization.

In addition to the three meals served under LVIS guidance (Mrs. N.H. Dayton supervising the kitchen), a cake and candy sale is held in the morning, a card party is given after lunch, four o'clock tea precedes a baseball game, and the evening is marked by a dance in the new ballroom.

July 21. Adele and Albert Herter open their Georgica home, "The Creeks," for a week-long exhibition of their own artwork. It is their first show in twenty years. Their paintings, many of them portraits, are hung against backdrops of brocade.

Visitors are encouraged to walk through their Italian-style villa and to enjoy the gardens. Laid out when the house was built in 1899, the gardens (one of them filled only with white flowers, another, in blooms of different blues) are the first formal gardens in East Hampton.

(After the Herters bought the 55-acre Halsey property, they camped on it their first summer there, to determine the perfect site for their house. Made of stucco mixed with beach sand, the U-shape house surrounds a waterfront terrace that looks straight down to Georgica Pond and the ocean. Every room enjoys a water view. The property includes a boat house, in which Mrs. Herter keeps a gondola. She uses it at tea time, to visit her pond-front neighbors and friends.)[21]

September 11. The Town Board resolves that any individual or corporate owner or, keeper of cattle, must tuberculin test them when they are six months or older, non-tested cattle cannot pasture with other livestock, and no cattle may be brought into town that were not tested within three months of entry. This ordinance, which sets a fine not to exceed $50.00 for violators, exempts any territory within the incorporated village.

1924

February 18. East Hampton haulseiners join others from Long Island's fishing industry at a mass meeting in Greenport's town hall. They are there to protest a proposed bill now before the State Senate. If passed, Bill No. 309 would decimate every aspect of the industry, from commercial fishing to boatyards, sail makers, and the Fulton Fish Market in New York.

The Raebenold bill seeks to remove the term "migratory fish of the sea" wherever it appears in present fishing law, give the commissioners absolute power to determine the mesh size for fishing nets, and ban the use of any kind of trawl in State waters.

If passed, Bill No. 309 would end virtually all commercial fishing, except by string tied to a pole. Though they do not believe the bill will pass, the men decide to send a protest committee to Albany on the 20th. They are not willing to risk the outside chance that a majority of the State legislature bends to the will of the powerful sports fishermen's lobby.

.   Twenty summer residents found the East Hampton Riding Club, and Robert Appleton finds the right property to buy for its clubhouse and stables. It is the old John Dickinson farm and 17th century house on Pantigo Lane. Membership is in two categories: *holding,* permanent, is for the original founders and those who help fund the property's purchase; *associate* is elected annually and limited in number to 46.

July 5. Maidstone Club's new clubhouse opens. Unlike the shingle-style architecture of its predecessors, this one is of stucco, its design reflective of Normandy farmhouses.

.   Plans are formulated this year for a series of state parks on Long Island. The idea, which includes linking them together with a solid ribbon of beautiful highways, came from Robert Moses. The 35-year old protegé of Gov. Al Smith, Moses heads the recently-organized Long Island State Park Commission. He has the governor's assurance that moneys to finance his plan will be available next year, from the $15 million bond issue which voters are expected to approve in November.

Moses is given authority to choose the park sites and negotiate their acquisition. Should negotiations fail, he can seize them under the State Conservation's right of eminent domain. Hither Hills on Montauk is his first choice. He enters into talks with the Benson Estate for 1700 acres of Hither Hills and 158 acres near Montauk Light. The price is said to be $75 an acre

The news catapults Miami Beach-builder Carl Fisher into offering the Estate more money for the same property. Benson Estate's administrators sever their talks with Moses, and sign an agreement with Fisher.

August 11. Moses reacts to the Benson Estate-Fisher dealings by seizing 1842 acres on Montauk. He intends to keep Hither Woods, the open downs, and the beaches in their natural, wild state, while making the new park available to the public.

September 8. The future look of Main Street is of utmost concern at today's LVIS meeting. At issue are what some people see as ugly buildings and what others view as an overabundance, in size and quantity, of signs on buildings and along the roads.

Realizing that more than the LVIS must be involved if Main Street is to be free of visual discord, the Society calls for a "Save Main Street Association." Its members would come from influential organizations in the community, namely the Lion's Club, the Mason's, the Village Trustees, and the LVIS.

September 14. Mary Hamlin carries the LVIS plan to a meeting of the Lion's Club: "That more foresight was not shown in the development of businesses along Main Street twenty-five years ago is to be regretted.... It is plain to be seen that, unless such an idea as that of zoning the village is adopted, the development is going to be haphazard and not at all to the advantage of anyone, be it the summer resident or the business man."

November 22/23. Federal Prohibition agents make their first serious move against the flow of liquor from secret storage points on Montauk. After placing their car in the middle of the road on Napeague Beach, they stop any car which looks suspicious. Even people returning from work on Montauk are detained. This effort nets the agents thirteen men among eleven carloads of liquor.

November 24. The Brooklyn Eagle comments on the week-end raid by Federal agents: "...last week's arrests reveal no sudden leak...it is common knowledge that liquor has been cheap and abundant in and about Montauk for two months....It also is common knowledge that for the past two months booze has been coming in at Montauk Point in large quantities."

(In spite of over 3000 prohibition agents in Suffolk County alone, the agents have little success rounding up the highly-organized bootleggers. Tipsters stationed at Brooklyn Federal Court alert the smugglers by phone, whenever district agents are in Court on a case. The "all-clear" signals allow liquor-laden trucks, which may have been hidden since their cargo was taken from a ship, to travel the roads in daylight. Agents also surmise that telephone operators are on the bootleggers' payroll. Rarely are they able to make an arrest after receiving news about activity. For their part, the majority of the feds' informers are members of the Ku Klux Klan).

1925

March. The Long Island and Pennsylvania Railroads release their findings on the soundness of developing Fort Pond Bay into a deep water port for transatlantic steamers. Hired to do the study, Will A. Lyford reports that neither time nor money would be saved by making the Bay the primary harbor.

He suggests that the idea be tabled for twenty years, but recommends that the federal government research having immigrants debarked and detained at Montauk Point, instead of at Ellis Island.

. This month, Carl Fisher informs the New York Telephone & Telegraph Company that Montauk's summer population will rise to 150,000, in four years, and its winter residents will number 50,000. If he is right, the company will be forced to undertake the biggest expansion program of any in the state.

May. The year-long crusade to rid East Hampton Village of commercial signs concludes this month.

The LVIS received pledges from offending real estate "signers" not to put up a sign for five years and, to allow removal of those now visible. On a May morning, LVIS members set out in their cars to remove the "For Sale" and "For Rent" signs and return them to their owners.

May 19. East Hampton's Village Board of Trustees adopts the proposed zoning ordinance. (State law, of recent vintage, allows the governing body of a community to divide it into zones and determine building restrictions and requirements.)

The local law divides the Village into four zones (fire, commercial, manufacturing, and residential), and requires building permits.

The Village Board also passes a health ordinance. Milk no longer can be sold raw. It must be pasteurized or, come from cows that were tuberculin-tested within a year of sale.

. Summer residents found a social organization, complete with a Constitution and By-Laws. The purpose of *Old East Hampton* is "to maintain the associations and friendships, and to preserve the standards and ideals of the original summer residents of East Hampton."

There are to be two classes of membership, *active* and *associate*. The latter now summer elsewhere. As for the active, "The roll may not contain more than ninety..." and "The privilege of voting is confined to active members."

The Constitution calls for "at least four social meetings between July 1 and November 1, and such other meetings as the executive committee may arrange for." Under the By-Laws, immediate relatives who are visiting a member of this group are entitled to all the privileges of Old East Hampton - save that of voting.

In addition, "The Group shall be entertained at meetings arranged by the executive committee;" "no member may entertain the group or use the term, 'Old East Hampton' in extending invitations, except by the authorization of the executive committee," and "Suitable guests, in sympathy with the purpose of Old East Hampton, may be invited to any entertainment at the discretion of the hostess."

July 4. During the night, someone stakes a six-foot high Ku Klux Klan cross at the south end of the Village green, and ignites it. The cross burns for some time before it falls over and leaves its charred imprint on the grass.

September 11. Carl Fisher buys over 5000 acres on Montauk from the Montauk Company. The price exceeds $1 million.

The land between Fort Pond and Third House, includes miles of ocean shore and high rolling hills.

September 23. Carl Fisher confirms the rumor which has circulated for months: He has bought 9800 acres (1300 under water) on Montauk for $2,500,000, and plans to make Montauk the Miami Beach of the north. There will be thirty miles of roads, a bathing pavilion with 1000 private lockers, and four golf courses within the next two years.

They will be followed by three glass-covered tennis courts, polo fields, a barn to stable 200 ponies, a half-mile gentlemen's driving track (which will surround a sprinting and running track), 20 miles of bridle paths, a winter ice skating rink, boat lines to New York, New London, and Boston; and a one-to-two hour train ride to New York City. A 287-room hotel will rise and land-locked Montauk Lake will be opened with a 300-foot long channel to the Atlantic Ocean, for private yachts to enter.

Also on his elastic horizon are schools, churches, and squash courts. Fisher says that his development is being undertaken in cooperation with the LIRR which promises to install the finest club cars on its service to the East End.

. Fisher's announced plans for Montauk spurs a high number of real Estate purchases this month. Properties bought range from large tracts of farm land to water front acreage. Among the sales is the Hand farm in Wainscott. The fifteen room house and sixty acres goes for $27,000.

November 2. After what is expected to be the last time that cattle will graze on Montauk lands, the livestock are driven off.[22]

December 1. Montauk's largest industrial plant opens. The Fowler Sea Products Co. expects to employ as many as ninety men during the summer months, to buy nearly all the Montauk catches, and those of the town's other fishermen. The company aims to sell its filleted products, chilled, direct to buyers across the country.

1926

. Considered without value by voters in 1923, Northwest property now commands $1000 an acre for waterfront land and from $250 to $500 an acre for property on recorded highways.

January 10. In an interview published in today's New York Times, East Hampton summer resident Edward E.. Bartlett credits Florida's seasonal resorts for the present real estate development on Montauk. According to Bartlett, wealthy families have been looking for a summer retreat with weather similar to Florida's winters. While they want it to be closer to

New York City, it must be distant enough "not to be overrun with an undesirable element."

Convinced that Montauk will be their Eden, Bartlett adds that if the railroad had run through to Montauk when Southampton first became fashionable, pleasure seekers would have learned earlier of East Hampton's "ideal conditions" and Southampton would not be as large as it is today.

January 20. The artist Childe Hassam pens a note to Bartlett, who has bought his painting, "Adam and Eve Walking Out on Montauk in Early Spring":

"This spring landscape of mine, the spring of the year and the springtime of life (according to our early teaching anyway) is Montauk as it looked for untold ages at that time of the year. There is no more beautiful or classic stretch of landscape anywhere; most barren-bare places if you will are always beautiful - they are like the nude, they contain the essence of beauty and are therefore classic."

January 26. T. E. Ringwood, the engineer in charge of the Montauk development, tells the press, "I can see no reason now why the people of Long Island or any other part of the United States should feel dubious as to the ultimate outcome of the development at Montauk."

February 6. Increased interest in Montauk leads The Star to inaugurate an eight-page supplement to its regular weekly issue of eight pages. The addition features social events and news from Montauk and Amagansett, a wrap-up of real estate news on the East End (especially on Montauk), and ads from most of the real estate brokers. (The idea originated with young Jeanette Edwards Rattray, who will do most of - if not all of - its writing.)

February 19. Fisher's Montauk Beach Development Co. takes title to 10,000 acres of Montauk land. The price is $3 million.

February 26. Today's issue of The Star carries Fisher's answer to a telegram. He was asked his opinion on the future of Long Island.

From Miami Beach, Fisher calls Long Island "as perfect a living spot in summer as Miami Beach is in winter...an intensive study of climactic charts on Long Island indicates that the eastern point is as favorable as any spot in the entire United States, seven months of the year.... Long Island will see, with the coming years, a logical trend of advancement that will amaze. It will be the 'Florida of the North.'"

May. For the first time since the mid 1600s, cattle are not driven on Montauk for pasture. In their stead are 1000 sheep,

brought from Wyoming to crop the grass on the new golf
courses.
November 8. Work begins on one of the Montauk polo fields
and the half-mile driving track to encircle it. The track is to be
used for competitions between amateur horsemen. Both track
and field will be part of the polo village that now is on the
drawing boards. It is similar to the one Fisher built in Miami.

1927

April. The LIRR announces that $100,000.00, is being invested
on a new Montauk terminal, and that sleeping car service
between Montauk and Pittsburgh will run from June to
September.
May 18. The LIRR's summer schedule starts today.
   In addition to the "Sunrise Special," which became a daily
summer feature last year, the company has added the "Montauk
Special," to address the pronounced increase of travel to East
Hampton and Fisher's developing dream. The Special will run
on Fridays and Mondays, with a through parlor car to and from
Washington, Baltimore, and Philadelphia.
October 15. In a special election, Village voters approve
appropriation of $60,000 in bonds, to insure that the structure
known as "Home Sweet Home" is not removed from the
Village. Vote count is 152-52.
   When the bonds are sold, the money will repay the
anonymous group which, calling itself the John Howard Payne
Memorial Association, bought the house from the Buek Estate.
The Brooklyn Museum was about to buy it, and there was talk
that it might be dismantled and moved.
   Postcards mailed earlier in the week to Village tax payers
carried seven reasons to vote "yes." The first was:
   "We are known as the 'Home Sweet Home' Village. Could you
bear to lose that proud distinction, or see it go elsewhere?"
October 18. In Bedford Hills, N.Y., Thatcher T. Payne Luquer
writes to the New York Herald Tribune, "I have the honor to be
a grandnephew of John Howard Payne and have in my
possession many family letters and records. The song 'Home
Sweet Home' was not written in the house in East Hampton, L.I.,
nor did Payne ever live in it... I have often tried to correct the
false traditions clustering around the so-called 'Payne House' at
East Hampton, but with little success. I cannot, however, let
money be spent to perpetuate a falsehood without making an
effort to let those concerned know the facts. I am sending a
copy of this letter to the president of the village of East-
Hampton."

October 20. A New York Times article addresses the controversy over "Home Sweet Home." It notes that "Residents of this village declared today that the stories discrediting the legend that John Howard Payne lived here in the 'Home Sweet Home' cottage would not interfere with its purchase for $60,000... "

. This same day, Village Mayor Samuel E. Gregory writes Luquer, "...we make no claim or pretense whatsoever that John Howard Payne was born here or that his song was written here but...I think that you might consistently, in view of all the facts, agree with me, first, that he had in mind as home his native land of America; second, that he had in mind the location of his mother's birthplace and home, East Hampton; and third, that he had in mind the 'Lowly Thatched Cottage,' the house in which his mother lived, and that if so, we are justified in our desire to preserve for all time, not the birthplace, nor even the home in which he lived, but rather the home which furnished him with the inspiration for that song which the world...will continue to sing so long as the cherished word 'home' remains a part of the English language..."

(Was Isaacs' grandson, John Howard Payne, born in East Hampton, or in New York? He was born two or three days after his father and four siblings left by boat for New York, where his father was going to open a school. Would his mother have accompanied them on such a hard trip, if she was soon to give birth? Maybe not. Then again, perhaps his birth on June 9, 1791 was premature, a result of the long journey. That might explain why he was sick, as a child.

Information records that he attended the Dame School in East Hampton Village until he was twelve, when he joined his parents in Boston. Since he was sickly, it is possible that his mother or, a relative of hers, thought it best that he be near the salt air. Where did he stay, then? Possibly, at the Isaacs' house. Perhaps with an aunt. Even if he didn't live in the house called "Home Sweet Home," his grandparents were alive. So, it is safe to assume that he spent time there, off and on, during those early school years.

Why, then, the mix-up between this house and the Osborne house, where he also is said to have lived? Isaacs was a wealthy man, the owner of considerable property around East Hampton. When his daughter married William Payne, who taught at Clinton Academy, they lived in a house that Isaacs owned. That house is where Osborne has his office. The house, with a Main Street address, is the second house east of Dayton Lane, but to the rear of the property.)

1928

February 4. This afternoon, Hamid Bey (known on the Loew's theatre circuit the last fifteen months as the "Egyptian Mystery Man") puts Lola de la Morje to sleep in a window on Main Street. The window belongs to the Edwards Theatre, where Hamid Bey and his troupe are performing. At nine o'clock, he picks up the sleeping woman from the window and carries her to the stage of the Edwards theatre, where he takes her out of a six-hour trance. (His East Hampton appearance is the first one outside Loew's network of theatres across the country.)

July 28. The Maidstone Club's new beach cabanas and swimming pool open. The pool plaza is just below a broad grass terrace that overlooks the ocean, and where afternoon tea is served. Some of the beach cabanas, complete with their own sunyards and shower, are up, with more to follow. (The additions are to satisfy some of the club members who had threatened to leave and build their own club, which would have beach amenities.)

1929

January 20. Today's London Observer carries St. John Ervine's article on his visit to East Hampton in 1928.

Writing about the controversy that has simmered in the Town the last two years (summer residents would like East Hampton returned, in name and in style of architecture, to its English heritage), the English critic says:"...The singular fact about this lovely village, lying placidly under its elms and close to the Atlantic Ocean is that, although it was founded by Englishmen, and made beautiful by trees that were born in the kentish Weald, it does not suggest England. It seemed to me to be intensely American. East Hampton is native; New York is foreign. East Hampton is American; New York is cosmopolitan. East Hampton is a western village; New York increasingly becomes an Oriental town.

"I do not know how much of the founders' stock survives in East Hampton, but the founders themselves have left their mark on it; and that mark is lovely. The individualism of the English who will not submit to any authority but their own is apparent in this place, for though the founders came from Kent and brought live memorials of Maidstone with them, they were not content to repeat Maidstone.

"They made a new village and made it American. The sentiment which is expressed in the reproduction of Maidstone Parish Church and in the effort to alter the name of the village is entirely modern. The pioneers preferred to start afresh."

August 22. Today is a milestone for the East Hampton Free Library. The formal opening is held of The Gardiner Memorial Room, a gift of Mary Gardiner Thompson and J.T. Gardiner, and of the new board room and cloister, the gifts of Mr. and Mrs. Woodhouse. The Morton Pennypacker Collection of 18,000 volumes on Long Island history is housed in the fireproof Gardiner Room. The Star calls this collection "the most important thing that has happened to our village since 1784..." (when Clinton Academy was chartered).

October 1. The LVIS protests to the Town about the airplane noise on Further Lane. The society asks the board to select a proper landing place in town, in the vicinity of the village.

October 11. The Star reports that the "Realty Market Continues Active." During the last six weeks, $250,000 worth of land and homes has been sold. According to the article, Cortland Godwin approached his purchase with considerable thought. Before deciding to buy on Appaquogue Road, he alternated the last four summers with rentals in Southampton and in East Hampton.

In this same issue, a Massachusetts firm offers lots for resale on Mill Hill, Talmage, and Miller Lanes. They are described as:

"The only restricted property in East Hampton, and the only properties sold during the land boom where the people got their money's worth."

November 4. Representative members of the Village community gather at the East Hampton Free Library to witness formal Village acceptance of a gift of property. Mr. and Mrs. Woodhouse have donated acreage at the corner of Dunemere Lane and Main Street for a cultural center. The gift includes $100,000 towards its construction and maintenance.

The center will be called Guild Hall, Its gallery will be known as the Thomas Moran Gallery. The small theater will be named after the late John Drew, a prominent stage actor who was well-known and loved in East Hampton, as a member of its summer community. The Woodhouses want the center to be used primarily by year-round residents, not the summer colony. However, of the 150 names listed on the initial committee today, better than 100 of them winter elsewhere.

November 13. East Hampton's first holdup takes place on Main Street. Two young, fairly short men pull up to a parked car, point their guns, order the occupants to get out, take ten dollars from Kenneth Edwards' pocket, and head west.

November 22. In Sag Harbor, Harry D. Sleight writes the introduction to Stephen L. Mershon's treatise, "Shore Front Rights." Sleight affirms "the very serious problems relating" to

Long Island's shore front titles. For example, "The Town of Southampton, after three centuries of existence, is uncertain of the ownership of long stretches of beach and bays within its boundaries, over which areas its early settlers and their immediate descendants moved with every confidence of ownership and well-defined views of true proprietorship."

On the other hand, "The Town of East Hampton, after centuries of existence, halts, hesitates, and then gives quit claim deeds or limited leases to sand dunes of great potential value in its beautiful residential districts fronting upon the broad Atlantic."

1930

May . The new horse barns and other additions at the East Hampton Riding Club are completed this month. The 54 stalls, most of them deluxe in size, are also "rich" underfoot. Peat moss from Germany covers the concrete floor.

July 4. Lead column of The Star's front page addresses the growing need for an airport in the town.

Up to now, summer home owners and visitors have been landing their planes wherever space is made available to them. That space used to include Robert Appleton's field on Further Lane, until the noise became too much for his neighbors. For the length of time that it was available, the Gardiner property across the street from the Huntting Inn was an ideal touch-down spot. Less so, but used, nonetheless, is the Sag Harbor Road.

The Star article warns that the people of this town "lack vision" if they do not face the need for an air field, and points out that an airport will "advance the prosperity of the village by affording the proper facilities to plane-owners."

Census returns show that East Hampton Town's population has increased 34 percent in the last decade. Preliminary figures list a population of 6519 (74 of which are unemployed) and 54 farms.

July 17. East Hampton Village pays tribute to Samuel A. Gregory, with a testimonial dinner at the Oaks Inn. More than 150 people, including summer home owners, share in the celebration. Mr. Gregory has just retired as its mayor of four years. Among the many salutations offered this evening is his permanent imprint on the physical beauty of the village. During his administration, zoning was introduced and lands were acquired and dedicated as public parks.

September 12. In spite of the petition's 1000 sigantures, the Village Board of Trustees rejects the request that the movie theater be open on Sundays.

1931

March 13. "Home Sweet Home" opens to the public for the first time since the Village acquired it. Among its many valuables is the carved chest which Thomas Osborne brought to East Hampton in 1649; a rare Canary luster teaset; a rocking chair (said to be the first one made in America); and "Water Bibles," small brown china bowls, shaped like Bibles, with a cork hole at one end. They were used to warm the hands and feet in church during the long sermons.

. After highway signs start sprouting up again, in and on the way to East Hampton, the LVIS orders stickers printed with which to seal envelopes. They carry the legend, "East Hampton favors products not advertised on the landscape."

July 17. The front page of The Star carries a letter from Village Trustee Scott McLanahan, in which he explains why the Board changed its collective mind about Sunday movies:

"....I am not personally, and never have been, in favor of Sunday movies in our village, simply because I would much prefer the village streets to be quiet and uncrowded on Sunday and in keeping with the traditional character and atmosphere of a simple country village on that day. On the other hand, I believe that a majority of our voters (be their judgment good or bad) are in favor of Sunday movies and would and will vote in favor of them if there should be a village election on the issue. There is no doubt in the minds of those who know the situation, that if no concession whatever is made to this majority sentiment, the issue will be raised in a village election and candidates chosen and controlled by the movie interests nominated and, in my opinion, elected.... The influence of those interests, if controlling in the board, would be most unfortunate in many ways.... "

August 19. Standing backstage, in the hallways, and in the aisles of the theatre, nearly 1000 people crowd the late Wednesday afternoon opening of Guild Hall.

The long-awaied celebration includes a short concert, speeches, and dedication of the John Drew Theatre and of the Thomas Moran Galleries. A formal tea follows in the galleries. Most of the art on exhibit is that of Moran's contemporaries, who discovered East Hampton in the last quarter of the 19th century.

September 29. In a letter to Robert Moses, Carl Fisher offers his Montauk holdings to the State Park Commission for one million dollars less than he paid for them.

December 2. The Town Board enters into lengthy discussion on the advisability of creating a Planning Board. Two of the

three Justices are not in favor of zoning the town. The third
Justice, Clifford C. Edwards, says that the town would be wise to
look ahead to the day when there might be zoning. He presents
the names of five people who would be willing to serve on this
board. The motion to place these names on record is not
carried.

1932

. Mrs. Charles Sabin, who sumnmers in East Hampton, initiates
the Woman's Organization for National Prohibition reform.
May 6/26. Fisher's Montauk Beach Development Corp. goes
into temporary receivership on the 6th.   Twenty days later,
permanent receivers are appointed. Corporation assets are
valued around $9 million, liabilities at $6 million.
.   For the first time since 1920, the LIRR's through-to-
Washington-and-Pittsburgh parlor cars are not added on for the
summer season.
December 12. The Town Board resolves to thank the Zoning
Commission for the time it spent in drawing up and presenting
a plan for zoning the town, and discharges it from further
concerns in the matter.
    The Board cites the four hearings that were held in each of
the Villages on the Commission's proposal. It notes that in each
village, opposition to zoning "in any manner whatsoever" was
over 90 percent.

1933

May 24. East Hampton voters approve repeal of Prohibiton.
June 1. Town law, as codified by the State, is changed. The
Clerk no longer can vote with the Board
September 1/2. President Franklin D. Roosevelt arrives at
Montauk aboard Vincent Astor's yacht, "Nourmahal." Rain and
heavy waves keep him from plans to board Capt. Herman
Gray's 45-foot sloop, "Orca," for some fishing. Saturday's
fishing only produces one small tuna, a few sea bass and some
porgies. The yacht leaves Fort Pond late Saturday evening,
escorted by two destroyers.
October 23. C. Louis Edwards & Co, on Main Street in East
Hampton Village, is having a special showing this week of the
latest 1934 Philco Radios. They have been in short supply for
some time, due to an unprecedented demand.
November 7. Democrats win control of the Town Board for the
first time in many years. Republican Supervisor Nelson C.
Osborne loses to Capt. Herbert N. Edwards by 45 votes.

1934

January 1. The Town Board majority opposes proposed State legislation that would ban net fishing in certain County waters. The resolution stresses the financial investment in East Hampton's commercial fishing industry, the number of jobs and satellite businesses generated by this industry, and the incredible hardship that the law, if passed, would heap upon East Hampton.

Spring. In New York City, Clifford H. McCall, the Maidstone Club's treasurer, reminds a fellow member that the club will not be able to take advantage of Prohibition's repeal because it is still bound to the terms in Dr. Herrick's 1914 will. The next day, McCall receives a check for $7500, made out to the club. In turn, as stipulated in Herrick's will, should the club decide to serve liquor, McCall issues a check from the Club to the East Hampton Free Library, in the same amount.

June 11. The Maidstone Club applies for a liquor license.

1935

. Nine years after she bought the old Hedges House on James Lane, Mrs. Hamlin opens a renovated and enlarged inn. Each bedroom has its own bath, a luxury in this town. Furnishings are authentic Sheraton and Chippendale, with hand-blocked Chinese paper on the walls. The large dining room opens on to a terraced Swan Garden, named for its 100-year old fountain.

An inn brochure announces: "For those enjoying fresh dairy products and certified eggs for breakfast, these are received daily from Mrs. Hamlin's Stony Hill Farm at Amagansett." As she has promised, Berry, her English butler, and Marianna, her cook, are in charge.

October 24. The Star celebrates its fiftieth year with column after column of reminiscences. Among the many contributors, Ruth Bedford Moran recounts her family's love affair with East Hampton. Ninety-six -year old Charles Osborne recalls the days before the Town had a newspaper. Henry M. Williams, in California and unable to see, takes a memory walk through the Village, naming every house and business along the way.

Composer/conductor Victor Harris heralds East Hampton's beauty and its residents' responsibility to help maintain it. He writes, "I have been in every part of Europe except Russia, and I would rather spend one summer here, in East Hampton, than a dozen anywhere abroad."

November 14. Montauk Manor, the Island Club, and other Montauk properties belonging to the Montauk Development Co. are bought at a tax sale.

1936

. Early this year, Pocahontas Pharaoh records her mother's oral history. They are in East Hampton, where eighty-eight year old Maria Pharaoh, last "Queen" of the Montauketts, has lived, since her husband died many years ago.

Maria Pharaoh speaks of a man who came to see her the year before she moved to East Hampton: "He offered me so much money and told me such sweet lies...he would give me eighty dollars a year...as long as I lived. It was to be always. I got it a few years and no more. This gentleman's name was Frank Benson."

She recalls a time when oysters "were plentiful" in Oyster Pond. "My father used to get lots of them, and come off and sell them and trade them for flour and kernel; our corn meal was made in Amagansett, East Hampton.

"We used to get all our food in the summer for the Winter, our barrels of flour and sugar, potatoes and beans and turnips. We also raised pigs for Winter. We never ever went hungry at no time."

February 17. The Town Board hears that cost of building the proposed airport in Midhampton would amount to $74,000 for two 2500-foot runways and terminal building. The Town would be responsible for $22,000, most of it going for rental of equipment.

August 6. Commenting on the local impact of Summer Society, as it emerges from the Depression, The Star editorializes:

"...Our storekeepers and contractors, however, will have to accept two fundamental changes that have come with this transitional period. The four months season and a summer colony which, to a very large degree, is indifferent to the costs of goods and service, is gone forever."

September 11. *Old East Hampton* president Harry L. Jefferys writes to the chair of the society's Admissions Committee:

"Dear Mrs. Donoho, I am glad that you admitted Mr. Gus Cordier to membership in Old East Hampton. A daughter is of course eligible. but if she is married or living apart from her family, her name must be passed on by the Admissions Committee. Otherwise, we might get some very undesirable husband or other 'in laws.' Gus Cordier is of course included with his wife."

1937

January 14. Three days from now, Warner Brothers' "The Gold Diggers of 1937," opens here. As part of the film's promotion, Warner's publicity department has scattered fifteen "hidden treasures" throughout the village. Clues leading to them are among The Star's pages today. The treasures are of cash or, tickets to the Edwards Theatre.

1938

September 21. At 2:45 p.m., a 100-mile hurricane whips across Long Island and through East Hampton. Brutal winds uproot many trees, including Main Street's canopy of elms; rip off rooftops, peel away sides of houses, and lift structures from their foundations.   The ocean surges over the dunes, rages across lawns and highways, pours into basements and floods houses, leaving residents stranded on tabletops and second floors, until rescue arrives. When it reaches the tracks in Napeague, Montauk becomes an island until the tide recedes.

"Ocean View," the menhaden fishing steamer out of Promised Land, sinks with six of its crew. Four fishermen off Gardiner's Island and two fishermen off Montauk drown. Montauk's fishing village is blown away, and a Montauk man, at work on his harbored boat, is swept overboard. At 6 p.m., Dr. Arthur H. Terry's barometer registers a low 28.55.

1939

. W.O. Stevens' "Discovering Long Island" is published this year. In his chapter on East Hampton, he says, "The Postmaster General and the President of the Railway Express Company have issued formal decrees that East Hampton shall also become one word. But who or what are they?"

He informs readers that East Hampton is "...of such intimate and picturesque charm that it can be appreciated only by sauntering along its wide, shady avenue," and that *green* "is a highly appropriate word to use in describing the village.

"There is so much of that color reflected in the pond from trees overhead and trim lawns that run right into the water that, from certain angles, the pond looks like a huge plate of pea soup in which you half expect to see giant croutons afloat."

Stevens calls the village "a monument for the rest of the country to study, to see what can be done by intelligent citizens. Its unique beauty is due to the two associations of public-spirited people, Garden Club and Village Improvement Association."

September 1. Germany invades Poland without any prior declaration of war.

September 3. Great Britain and France declare war on Germany. World War II begins.

1939/43

. During the war, numerous artists flee Europe for refuge in
the United States. At the urging of Sarah (nee Wiborg) and
Gerald Murphy, who knew many of them during their years
abroad, they find their way to East Hampton and the beachfront
Wiborg estate, next door to the Maidstone Club.

Among them are the Lebanese artist, Lucia (the only name
she uses). She stays with the Murphys the summer of '39, meets
and marries the inventor, Roger Wilcox, and settles in
Amagansett.

Lucia, in turn, draws others to Long Island's eastern end: Max
Ernst, who is married to Peggy Gugenheim, the American art
patron who helped him to escape, Salvador Dali and his Gala,
Jean Helion, who escaped from a prisoner of war camp,
Fernand Leger, Arshile Gorky, Jimmy Ernst, Marcel Duchamp,
and the writer Anais Nin.

Also in summer residence during these years is the entire
Spanish Republican government-in-exile. Most of its members
stay at the Sea Spray Inn, at the foot of Ocean Avenue.

1940

July 4. The Star notes that the nomination of Wendell Willkie
for president "has met with such widespread public approval
that Republicans the nation over as well as many, many
Democrats are full of confidence these days that the eight long
years will soon be over."

October 16. The first peacetime registration for compulsory
military service is set up.

1941

December 7. Five East Hampton men are among U.S. armed
forces personnel stationed at Pearl Harbor when the Japanese
attack from the air at 7:10 a.m.. They are Mario Sireci, Jay
Collins, Morris Hettiger, Dick McCarthy, and David Gilmartin.

December 22. The Town Board hears a letter from the County
Clerk. He is asking each town to establish centers, to which
people can bring their old automobile license plates. The metal
plates will be used for defense material.

1942

Spring. The U.S. Army commandeers the Maidstone Club
without prior notice. The club is to serve as an observation post.
Two soldiers pitch a tent in the parking lot and hook up
communication to the club's telephone line. Club officials

propose that the army build a sentry box somewhere else on club grounds.

June 13. At midnight, Coast Guardsman Second Class John C. Cullen begins a six-mile patrol of Amagansett's beach. An hour later, on this foggy Sunday night, a German submarine surfaces 500 yards off Amagansett beach. Its presence goes undetected by the radar installed in a series of wooden towers along the coastline, from Montauk to Westhampton.

Four men debark U-boat 202 for a rubber boat and paddle towards what they believe is East Hampton Village. On shore, they bury their small craft, and supplies that include a suitcase of explosives. Minutes after the spies have changed into civilian clothes, Cullen happens upon them, three miles from the Coast Guard Station. One man engages him in conversation.

He tells Cullen that they came from Southampton to fish, but have been beached by the fog. He says that they will set off at daybreak, when the fog should lift.

Cullen is suspicious. Wartime restrictions limit fishing to daylight hours. Local fishermen know that. He suggests that the men come to the Station, where they can have coffee and remain until light. The thin-faced German responds with a question.

"How old are you?"

"Twenty-two. What's that got to do with it?"

"You got a mother and father? You want to see them again?"

The German who speaks English well offers Cullen $100 to forget that they are here. He increases the bribe to $300 and orders Cullen to look him in the eye.

"Would you recognize me again? Maybe we'll meet sometime in Southampton."

"No," Cullen answers, as he takes the money. The German releases his grip. Cullen, who is armed only with a flare, turns around and slowly walks eastward. As soon as he is lost in the thick fog, he races back to the Station. Fom there, a search team is dispatched to the beach, as the Germans, having discovered their true position, head on foot for Amagansett's railroad station.

While one of the men changes clothes outside the station and tosses the discards into a bush, another man buys four tickets from station agent Ira Baker. He tells Baker, "The fishing hasn't been very good out here...because of the fog. I guess I'll go home." They take the first morning train to Jamaica.

At dawn, another Coast Guard patrol returns to search the beach for some sign of foreign presence. Any skepticism about Cullen's story vanishes when a pack of German cigarettes is

found on the beach and, next to it, a trail of damp sand. At
trail's end, a few yards off, the patrol sees an area of wet sand
amid the dry. Buried underneath are a canvas bag stuffed with
German uniforms and four tin boxes. Back at the Station, they
find one box filled with explosives, detonators, and bombs disguised as clumps of coal

June 27. After two weeks of rumors, FBI Chief J. Edgar Hoover
announces the arrest of the German spies who came ashore at
Amagansett. While not revealing what led to their capture, he
allows the public to believe that diligent FBI accomplished the
feat. He does say that the men had enough survival and bribery
money and sabotage equipment to last two years.

   Special targets for destruction were the Chesapeake & Ohio
Railroad (a major coal carrier), the Aluminum Co. of America,
the cryolite plant of the Philadelphia Salt Co., Hell Gate Bridge
and Pennsylvania Railroad's terminal in Newark, New Jersey. [23]

September 18. The Town Clerk tells the Town Board that the
gasoline and tire shortage is imposing great inconvenience to
Montauk residents who want to get hunting or fishing licenses.
A motion is made and passed to empower Frank Tuma, who
owns a fishing and tackle shop in Montauk, to issue the licenses
there. He is made a Deputy Clerk for these purposes only.

1943

. A U.S. Naval Torpedo Testing Range is built on the shore of
Fort Pond Bay, and the hurricane-wrecked fishing village is
bulldozed to make way for government construction.

1944

June 1. During the war, The Star is mailed to American
outposts around the globe. A feature each week is a letter
addressed to "Dear Boy," from "One of the Mom's."

   In today's issue, she recounts that, "In the past two weeks the
leaves have burst forth on the trees along our Main Street. The
violets have never been so plentiful; the lilacs have just
blossomed out; the dogwood trees are especially lovely this
year. On the 'loop,' the road from Amagansett to East Side and
Springs, the winding road and the white blossoms, mingled with
the green of the woods, make the countryside an enchanting
fairyland.... "

 December 7. B-29 gunner John Day Jackson, who spent
summers in Amagansett with his parents, is lost in a raid over
Japan.

   (For his senior year thesis at Yale, in 1942, Jackson wrote on
Montauk and its distinct land ownership. "Two Centuries and an

Age," subtitled, "The story of the curious survival of the manorial common pasture system at Montauk," is on file in the Long Island Collection of the library.

1945

April 10. The Trustees agree to tell the Bay Constable that "If he hears that anyone is arrested by a State Conservation Officer for taking clams from Town waters without a State license, he is to tell the alleged offender to fight the case, that the Trustees will uphold his rights and defend them."

August 14. At seven p.m., President Harry Truman goes before a bank of microphones in the White House to announce Japan's unconditional surrender to Gen. Douglas McArthur, and the end of World War II. Within minutes of his news coming over radios in East Hampton homes, Main Street and its sidewalks are crowded. The night air is filled with the sound of horns, whistles, firecrackers, clashing tin pans. By eleven p.m., Main Street returns to its normal pace for a night in May.

1946

August 13. Village Mayor Judson Banister and Town Supervisor Herbert L. Mulford, Jr. issue a joint proclamation. They "appeal to everyone to destroy immediately, before it flowers, all ragweed, commonly known as black weed, and thereby assist in the prevention of hay fever."

1947

October 8. Meeting in executive session, the Town and Village Boards declare 1948, not 1949, to be the 300th anniversary year of East Hampton's founding.

December 15. The Brooklyn Museum enters into contract with Harrison Mulford. It will pay him $3500 for two rooms of the ancient vacant dwelling next door to "Home Sweet Home." The museum will remove the rooms, one up, one down, which are considered exquisite examples of 17th century architecture. (The property once belonged to Josiah Hobart and, after he died, to Samuel Mulford.)

Three years ago Mulford's descendant had offered to sell the farmhouse to the LVIS for $5000, if it would have it moved. Harrison Mulford wanted to build a new house on the land. The LVIS expressed serious interest, on condition that the house could remain there for three years, while the society sought a suitable site. for what would become its headquarters.

No agreement was reached and, the following year, after refurbishing the old barns, Mulford opened The Mulford

Riding Stable on the grounds. He later raised the purchase price to $25,000 for the entire property. But, nobody wanted it.)
. Preparations have been underway since last summer for the Town's 300th anniversary. High spirits drop in the spring, when the Brooklyn Museum's plans are confirmed. Most of East Hampton is appalled by the news. Besides being one of the Town's very few remaining 17th century houses, it also was going to form part of the natural backdrop for the pageant to be performed this summer, on the Village green. Pleas to delay cutting it up until summer's end produce nothing.

A campaign to keep the house where it is accelerates on Mary Hamlin's return in April. Believing that the Village will agree to hold a special referendum on buying the house, and that voters will favor it, Mrs. Hamlin (as she had done with Home Sweet Home) and fellow LVIS members Mrs. Percy Schenck and Mrs. Edward Gay Jr., take an option on the house. Five local organizations petition the Brooklyn Museum to withdraw its commitment. Letter after letter in The Star urges against the purchase.

To allay taxpayers' fears, the LVIS votes at its May meeting to provide $5000 for the farm's maintenance, and, for the next ten years, to pay both the Village and the Town the equivalent of the Mulford Farm's 1947 property taxes.

June 15. In spite of the LVIS's clear commitment to the Mulford Farm taxes, Village voters reject buying it.

June 24-29. Continued concern over the Mulford house leads summer resident and East Hampton League member Percy Ingalls to contact Mulford. Mulford says the farmhouse can stay where it is if Ingalls can raise $25,000, in two weeks.

Ingalls holds a special meeting on the 24th. Three of the people invited are from the LVIS, three are from the Garden Club. Ingalls, John Cole, and Jackson Starke represent the League. A list of possible donors is drawn up, their names are distributed among the fledgling "Mulford Farm Committee" members, and the campaign begins.

A meeting on the 27th proves that the full amount can be raised. Everybody possible is approached. TWA president Juan Trippe stops at each Maidstone Club cabana to make certain that no one is missed for a "touch."

Ingalls, Starke, and Cole take over the $100 option and underwrite the $1000 for the June 29 contract signing.

After the signing, Ingalls writes summer resident Mrs. Sterling Peters: "The subscriptions reported as having been promised was considered very satisfactory...Preservation, in this case, means anything from making the building water tight to a certain undetermined amount of restoration, all of which would depend upon the amount of money subscribed."

The Committee originally planned to turn the deed over to the LVIS. But, Ingalls tells her, the LVIS said that it was not tax-exempt, a fact important to contributors. Instead, it will go to the Historical Society, with the proviso that the LVIS is to share equally in all decisions governing Mulford Farm. The LVIS also is to oversee ground maintenance, restoration, furnishings, and provide the docents when the house opens to the public.[24]

June 28/29. The Town celebrates its anniversary with a series of events. Among them, a parade down Main Street, with float after float depicting the Town's history, and pageants performed on the village green. Part of the pageant's natural scenery is the old Mulford farmhouse.

1949

. In the last week of April, work begins on landscaping Mulford Farm. During the winter, LVIS and Garden Club members, Mrs. A. Wallace Chauncey, Mrs. Percy Ingalls, and Mrs. Hamilton King researched 17th century planting and farm life, and drew a plan where every bush, tree, and flower would be. The specimens selected were available in the 17th century. The first to be planted are the start of an apple orchard between the house and barn; an elm tree, behind the house; a pear tree, behind the picket fence at the front of the property; boxwood bushes, dogwood trees, firebushes, and groups of lilacs.

1950

July 28. The Secretary of the East Hampton Group of Alcoholics Anonymous writes The Star a note of thanks for "the splendid cooperation that you have shown the East Hampton AA."

Twenty-two months ago, "4 alcoholics met one evening on the front porch of a local home. This was the start of the East Hampton Fellowship of Alcoholics Anonymous .... last week we had the largest closed meeting, and Tuesday the largest open meeting since the start of AA in East Hampton. We believe that this is due to the unstinted publicity, complete and understanding cooperation that you have given us."

1951

October 19. The Dongan Patent, as it applies to the rights of East Hampton's people, has been discussed at previous Village Board meetings. To get a clearer picture, the mayor asked

lawyer Leo Koenig to research the Patent and report on it.
Koenig gives his opinion at today's meeting:
The Indian title to this land, he says, "was not recognized in
law. The Indian tribes in the new world were regarded as mere
temporary occupants of the soil, and the absolute rights of
property and dominion were held to belong to the nation by
which any particular portion of the country was first
discovered.

"While the early settlers did acquire deeds from the Indians,
the purpose of the deeds was merely to secure peaceful
relations with the Indians. The deeds were never recognized in
law as passing title to any individuals."

On the English title: "English possession of Long Island
rested upon the right of discovery. Discovery is made for the
benefit of the whole nation, and the land is disposed of by that
organ of the government which has the power to dispose of the
national domain. That organ was then the King of England,
whose grant to the Duke of York included Long Island. We
must look, therefore, for the origin of the title to the land within
the town of East Hampton, to the royal charter issued under the
government of the Duke of York."

1952

April 7. With the help of the State's Conservation Department
Commissioner, Perrry Dureya, representatives of sports
fishermen, who surf cast for bass, and those of local commercial
fishermen, who shore seine for bass, sign an agreement.

The preamble records that the commercial fishermen
recognize that sports fishing "adds to the health and recreation
of those who participate in it, as well as contributing
importantly to the economy of Montauk," and that the sporties
recognize "that commercial fishing for striped bass from shore
is a method of harvesting this species which has been employed
by the commercial fishing industry for more than seventy-five
years, and that such fishing contributes to the general economy
of the State, and importantly to the economy of Montauk in
particular."

For their part, the baymen agree "to discontinue seining from
shore and further agree not to engage again in any such seining
during the life of this agreement in that part of the Atlantic
Ocean from Shagwong Point to Montauk Point and from
Montauk Point to Gurney's Inn, located on the ocean side ...
that the areas described... shall be known as a 'Surf Caster's
Sanctuary.'"

In return, the sporties agree "that they will raise no objection, or attempt to influence others to raise objections, and will oppose and use their influence to dissuade any person or persons who attempt to raise objections to the operation of seines from shore in areas of the town of East Hampton not herein described and known as a 'Surf Caster's Sanctuary.'

The agreement also calls for both sides, "if it is desirable," to sponsor and support legislation of this agreement, which would be effective from 1953 through 1957. The present agreement expires the last day of the year.

September 6. LVIS members hear that 2360 trees are being cared for under their sponsorship, and that the Mayor would prefer bricks (to be supplied by the LVIS) rather than hedges to run along the sidewalk of Main Street's shopping district.

1953

January 12. Sarah Diodati Gardiner's will is Probated in New York City. Miss Gardiner, who died on the 5th, has left East Hampton Village her Main Street "White House" and a $40,000 trust fund for its maintenance. She would like it to be known as the "Gardiner Memorial Building," to be used "for literary, artistic, educational, charitable or park purposes, or for such other exclusively public purpose" as Village officials decide.

The house stands on the grounds of the "White House," where Julia Gardiner Tyler lived when she was in East Hampton. After the hurricane winds of 1938 uprooted 123 fruit trees on the grounds and rolled back a tin roof at the rear of that house, then-owner Fannie Gardiner Collins sold the property to her relative. Miss Gardiner had the White House torn down and replaced it with a white-washed brick mansion.

February 7. At a special meeting, the Village Board of Trustees declines the gift of the Gardiner house. The Board reasons that income to be generated from the trust would not be enough to maintain the house and warrant removing it from the tax rolls.

August 21. The East Hampton Free Library's new reference room is dedicated at the annual afternoon tea given for the public. Dayton Hedges, who now lives in Cuba, underwrote construction of The Hedges Room, which has been named in memory of his relative, Judge Henry P. Hedges.

Hedges commissioned Jeanette Edwards Rattray to write the just-published "East Hampton History and Genealogies." Forty-five families are represented in the genealogy section. Proceeds from the book's sales will go to the library. (In 1897, the late Judge Hedges, who had spoken at both the 200th and

250th anniversaries of the Town's settlement, published a
history of East Hampton that included 25 genealogies.)
December. The Long Island Fishermen's Association Bulletin
reports on the Atlantic States Marine Fisheries Commission's
opposition to fishery legislation that is rooted solely in social
merit: "There are many state laws..(and) ... local ordinances
now in being that have not only caused a hardship on
commercial fishermen but has resulted in less fish for the
angler, who, for the most part, was responsible for enactment of
the laws. Practically all lack scientific support. They were
adopted or passed to satisfy a group of people who, because of
their selfish attitude, exerted pressure on their governmental
representatives....Legislators would do well to give all proposed
fishery legislation a thorough check before they are called
upon to vote in law a bill..."

1954
June 8. Mail delivery within a mile of the post office on
Newtown Lane starts today. With its arrival, cost of mailing a
local letter becomes the same as that of sending one out of
town. Up a penny, to three cents.

1955
May 4. The first in a month-long Civil Defense Training
Course is given in the Court Room. The weekly lectures will
cover nature and the effects of radiation. A call is issued for
volunteer ground observers.
July 2. The restored Mulford Farmhouse opens to the public in
an afternoon preview. It has taken seven years to raise the funds
necessary to complete the interior work.

   In 1948, the house lacked plumbing, heating, electricity, and
furniture. Some of the rooms were in bad shape. One upstairs
bedroom floor was so rotted that it had to be replaced. The
house, fully furnished with period pieces lent or donated for the
occasion, will be open every summer day. Members of the
LVIS, dressed in clothing of the 17th and 18th centuries, will
serve as hostesses.

1956
August 11/12. A little after 10:00 p.m., Saturday night, a 1950
green Oldsmobile convertible speeds along Springs Fireplace
Road. As the coupe nears a gradual bend in the road, its right
wheels hit the soft shoulder. Turning the steering wheel sharp
left, to get the car back on the road, the driver loses control.
The

Olds veers across the road, skids 172 feet, and comes to rest over two young trees. near telephone pole #91. The rebounding saplings flip the convertible over. Tossed out of his shoes and seat, the airborne driver slams into a tree, head first, and drops into bushes,12 feet away. The first to arrive on the scene find one of the headlights illuminating the branches above.

The woman passenger in the front seat is hurled into the road. The woman in the back seat is killed. Her death and that of the driver, Jackson Pollock, are two of ten highway fatalities this week-end, on the South Fork. (Nassau and Suffolk Counties are the State's worst offenders in the number of auto-related accidental deaths.)[25]

August 23. An article by Mrs. Thomas M. Day, chair of the LVIS's Tree Committee, is published on the front page of The Star. It addresses Dutch Elm disease which has attacked "three very distinct and serious areas in this village."

Mrs. Day writes that the source of the trouble is "dead or dying elms on private property." In late May and June, when the disease-carrying bark beetle emerges as an adult, the trees are particularly susceptible to the disease. Mrs. Day calls the problem "epidemic" in East Hampton, and says that the Society will do what it can to prevent further transgression of the disease. She encourages individuals to care for their trees, remove them at once, if they are diseased, and take the diseased wood to a specially reserved area at the Village Dump.

1957

. This spring, volunteers are needed to man the air observation towers that are in place in East Hampton, Bridgehampton, Southampton, and Hampton Bays. In this Cold War era, the United States coastline is streaked with lines of warning for possible Russian attack. To be operational twenty-four hours a day, each Civil Defense tower needs a total of 164 persons to volunteer two hours of duty, once a week.

July 13. East Hampton's first professional art gallery, The Signa Gallery, opens at 53 Main Street. Its owners are the artists John Little, Alfonso Ossorio, and Elizabeth Parker.

It has been twelve years since Jackson Pollock forsook a downtown Manhattan studio and, with his bride, Lee Krasner, removed to an uninsulated farmhouse on five acres overlooking Accabonac Creek. Their presence drew fellow artists, for visits. In time, some of them became part- or full-time residents, too. The gallery's statement of principle appears in the opening's broadside: "With so many artists living and working in this area, the Signa Gallery has been established for the purpose of showing new significant contributions to the painting and sculpture of today."26

September 9. Thirty years after the word "zoning" was first introduced at a Town Board meeting, and five years after a Zoning Commission was named to draw up a zoning plan and many public hearings followed, the present Board adopts zoning. The new ordinance creates a Zoning Board of Appeals, whose members will represent each of the school districts.

1958

February 19. Long neglected and hidden away behind the Methodist Church, the Old Town House is returned this day to Main Street on a flat-bed truck.

It is placed next to Clinton Academy, on land that formerly housed Otto Simons' plumbing shop. The Town Trustees gave the small structure to the Historical Society in 1956, Summer residents raised the money for the Society to buy the property and the plumbing shop.

May 24. Guild Hall's exhibit, "The South Fork Writers," opens in the Moran Gallery with an afternoon tea. The gallery walls are hung with manuscripts, book jackets, illustrations, photographs, notebooks, etc. from thirty Southampton and East Hampton writers.

Among them are Robert Alan Aurthur, Betsy Barton, Hoffman Hays, classicist Gilbert Highet, New Yorker writer A. J. Liebling, suspense writer Helen MacInnes (married to Highet), philosopher Jacques Maritain, Bishop Austin Pardue, Jeffrey Potter, Jeanette Edwards Rattray, science and conservation writer Berton Roueché, Helen Stone, the theologian Paul Tillich, and the poet John Hall Wheelock.

1959

May 5. The Town Board rejects the County's Mental Health Association request to drop leaflets - loose, or, attached to balloons - from a plane.

The Board also discusses a claim that has found its way into several New York papers. Sopmebody has led the press to believe that East Hampton has the highest birth malformations in the State.

The charge is hard to understand. The number of annual Town newborns is small, and most of them emit their first cry at Southampton Hospital.

1960

January 1. The Suffolk County Charter is effective today. The office of County Supervisor - its first occupant was elected in November - replaces the County Coordinator.

(East Hampton Town Supervisor Richard T. Gilmartin was the only East End official to support the Charter. His peers had argued that the new government structure would tip the balance of power to the western towns, the tax rise would not benefit the East End, the County Executive's four-year term was too powerful, and that, while the office might be needed, it should be an appointed position made and overseen by the Board of Supervisors.

In 1958, Southampton Town Supervisor Stephen F. Meschutt told The Star, "If this charter comes to pass, three large towns will dictate the course of the entire county,"

May 26. The Star includes a special section on Montauk. State Park Commissioner Moses ends his article thus: "It is too bad that all of Montauk, excepting the village, was not made a State Park. Certainly we should have at least twice the acreage we have now."

1961

June 16. Where will all the garbage go, as East Hampton expands, new houses go up, and the population increases? A question so worrisome, it leads Town Board member Robert E. Vetault to remark, "The dump problem will come to haunt us." To help stave off this prediction, the Town Board hires a Syosset firm to survey disposal areas throughout the Town.

June 29. The newly-renovated First Presbyterian Church of East Hampton is dedicated in a morning service. Its two unequal towers and two front doors have been replaced by a single spire and a centered double door. The look is more reflective of the Village's New England heritage.

1962

November 6. New York State voters approve passage of Amendment Number Two. The ballot asks the question, "Shall the proposed amendments to article one of the constitution, repealing sections ten, thirteen, and fifteen, in relation to ownership of lands, escheats and Indian lands, ... be approved?"

Explaining the proposed Amendment, the State informs: "SUBJECT Eliminates obscure sections dealing with ownership of lands, escheat and Indian lands and other details made obsolete by passage of time or coverage under statutes..." (Section 15 of Article I of the State Constitution reads: "Certain grants of lands and of charter made by the King of Great Britain and the State; obligations and contracts not to be impaired.")

Voters unknowingly have given legitimacy to future State claims that grants and contracts, such as the Dongan Patent, no longer are valid. This raises Constitutional issues at the Federal level. The Amendment contravenes Article 1, Section 10, of the Federal Constitution which, in part, reads: "limitations of the powers of the several States. - 1. No State shall ... pass any Bill of Attainder, ex post facto Law, or Law *impairing the Obligation of Contracts*, or grant any Title of Nobility."

While the Amendment is part of the State Constitution, the State Legislature will remain in violation of the Federal Constitution. (Any overturn of the amendment would depend on the success of a grass roots effort to raise enough interest for a possible Court hearing.)

1963

April 5. For the third time, the Georgica Association defeats the Town and the County. In Riverhead Supreme Court, Justice Fred Munden rules that the Town cannot proceed with dune restoration on the Association's oceanfront property, and the County cannot raise the dune level and construct a drain from the ocean to Georgica Pond. Munden explains his decision: "I am convinced that the proposed intrusion by the county upon the plaintiff's land is not necessary for any protective purpose having relation to beach erosion."

1964

Autumn. Foundations for 200 one-family houses are laid in four areas of Montauk: Atlantic Ocean Front, Hither Woods, Long Island Sound Front, and Montauk Golf Course.

They are part of 31-year old Charles A. Piser's plan to make Montauk a haven for leisure living at budget prices. The houses are being constructed in assembly-line fashion, each segment of construction done at the same time. The fully-furnished houses will sell from $13,490 to $16,490.

With State plans to extend the highway to Montauk, and talk of a causewa,y, in the near future, linking Montauk with Connecticut, Piser has taken an option on 800 more building lots and is negotiating for others.

1965

May 16. Dial telephoning, for all but four-party service, becomes operational in East Hampton and Amagansett in the

first hour of Sunday. Those who find dialing difficult or tiresome, may request touch-tone dialing for an additional fee.
. This August, the State's Conservation Department releases its 53-page report on the Town's wetlands, both fresh and marine. The study, done at the request of both the Town and the Preservation Society of the East End (a new organization), carries the signatures of three separate department heads.

It is most critical of the Mosquito Control Commission's wanton draining of marshes, indiscriminate use of pesticides, and the Army Engineer Corps' dredging deep holes in Georgica Pond, and other waters, behind barrier beaches. It deplores the harm done to Hog Creek by carelessly planned dredging: "For the sake of a temporary channel, irreparable damage has been done to the stable shoreline."

Strict control is urged for any future development around Little Northwest Creek, "one of the least spoiled of any viewed on Long Island," and Northwest Creek "an interesting and unique estuary," whose marshy shoreline and bay bottoms need protection. "Vigorous control of sanitary facilities" is needed for Three Mile Harbor, already under stress.

Accabonac Creek is a "valuable estuarine wetland" and "an excellent fish and wildlife habitat" that should be protected. Its marsh is a "natural buffer zone especially important here since it prevents cesspools from leaching into these clean and productive wetlands."

Napeague Harbor is the "least aesthetically-pleasing part of" the Town; Montauk's Fresh Pond is "the nearest thing to a wilderness pond left on Long Island," and Fresh Pond, in Amagansett, is no longer fresh. Fort Pond "has escaped direct abuse," though "the surrounding lands are completely dominated by man;" and Big Reed Pond, whose impact by man is called "minimal," is a "fine habitat for migrating and breeding waterfowl as well as many other birds and mammals."

Hook Pond is "an excellent year-round feeding ground for waterfowl," and, though "man's modification of the landscape are noticeable everywhere...certain developments, such as the golf course, can actually benefit some species of wildlife."

Wainscott Pond receives high, high marks, and the notation that it probably is a stop-over for the largest population of ruddy ducks in the State.

1966

March 7. Milton Miller, President of the Baymen's Association, gives his annual report: In 1965, Northwest Creek, normally a large producer of shellfish, had none for commercial sale. The extensive mosquito control spraying of surrounding marshlands killed the seed scallops. He calls Georgica Pond "one of the few natural marine nurseries still free of pollution on the coast," and advises that it not be touched. Raw sewage inside the breakwater in Sag Harbor has killed $100,000 worth of scallops, and pollution has spoiled most of the shellfish in Lake Montauk.

May 23. Eighteen miles from DeNang in South Vietnam, Company B of the 1st Marine Division rapidly approaches enemy automatic-weapons fire. Hidden eyes watch the advancing tanks. At a given moment, a remote charge detonates a 500 lb. anti-tank mine. In an instant, Sergeant John Behan of Montauk loses both of his legs.

August 3. Supervisor Edward V. Ecker unveils the planned Bypass route envisioned by the County Department of Public Works. Reaching East Hampton over present roads, it would run past the north side of the airport, cross Route 114, Two Holes of Water Road, Old Northwest Road, and Stephen Hand's Path, just north of where it meets Cedar Street. From there, it would cross Hands Creek Road, Three Mile Harbor Road, Springs Fireplace Road to Abraham's Path, cross the Path before it meets Town Lane, continue and cross over Fresh Pond and Abraham's Landing Roads, before re-joining Montauk Highway. The Bypass is to have four lanes and a small divider.

December. Part I of the first Comprehensive Plan for the Town and the Village is published.

Prepared by Edwin S. Voorhis & Sons, Inc, consulting engineers and planners, and funded in part by the Village, Town, and State, and by a Federal Grant from the Department of Housing and Urban Development, the report addresses Existing Conditions in Part I and Target for Tomorrow, "1980 and Beyond," in Part II.

Part I cites commercial fishing and agriculture as two of the Town's leading year-round elements of the local economy, and notes that two of the main commercial fish firms employ between 25 and 70 people, year-round, and that underwater farming is a stable factor in the Town's economy.

While "the dominant agricultural products in East Hampton are potatoes, other vegetable crops and grain...the actual land devoted to farming has been on a steady decline since 1960 when, according to the U.S. Dept. of Agriculture, there were 41 commercial farms in operation, as opposed to 20 today."

On the other hand, the importance of the construction industry as the leading year-round employer is evidenced by the fact that, in 1960, it accounted for 10.58 percent of nonseasonal employment, compared with 9.6 percent for all of Suffolk County.

Part I summarizes the Town's summer economy as "rather unique in the Metropolitan Region, depending almost entirely on activities relating to seasonal residents, summer recreation, and tourism for support and that only a few months of the year...

"The major portion of the seasonal residences are used only during the summer months from May to September. While the inhabitants of seasonal units bring in tax and consumer dollars without creating large demands on public service on a year-round basis, it is equally true that many of the problems facing the public officials are a result of the impact of seasonal demands for services and facilities."

1967

. Part Il of the Comprehensive Plan is released in January. The Preface identifies the Town's "unique charm and character. Vast beach areas encircle the Town. Dunes, bluffs, wetlands, virgin woodlands, fresh water ponds, and other topographical features dot the landscape.

"The Village contains some of the most beautiful residential sections to be found on Long Island; a testimonial to residents who care a great deal about community development. There is a sense of simple dignity and quality about the community and so far, except in a few isolated instances, there has been success in preserving nature's gifts and controlling land development in general."

However, the consultants warn, the day is "fast approaching" when "'suburbia' will reach the Town." According to the Land Use Plan, the Town population, summer and year-round, should not exceed 63,7000.

1968

<u>April 26</u>. Mrs. Rattray's "Up and Down Main Street" goes on sale. The book is an informal historical tour of dwellings still standing on Main Street and some of its offshoots.

. "No Way to Treat a Lady," starring Rod Steiger, opens this summer. Its East Hampton connection is Mimi, Emily Cobb's tortoise-shell cat, who has a part in the movie. Mimi, who purrs in Springs when not otherwise engaged, is the mother of Gwen Verdon and Bob Fosse's cat. They live in Amagansett.

<u>November 10</u>. At 10:45 a.m., members of the Calvary Baptist Church in East Hampton march into their new church for its first service. It has been fourteen years since a Baptist Mission

in Town was organized, thirteen years since the Mission was recognized as an independent Baptist Church, and ten years since the church basement was completed and the first service was held inside.

The road towards this house of worship began in Southampton with the Rev. C. Ralph Spinner. He interpreted a dream message, "Go East," to mean that East Hampton was in need of a Baptist Church.

With permission from St. Luke's Church, Rev. Spinner has held worship services at St. Mathew's Episcopalian Chapel on Three Mile Harbor Road until this day arrived. The money needed to build the Baptist Church came from the community. The largest single donations were $10,000 and $20,000. No less important, however, were the unsolicited one, five and ten dollar contributions that shop, business, and restaurant employees gave the Rev. Spinner, when they happened to meet. In the words of Bertha and William Hopson, it is "truly a community project."

1969

May 7. Seventy students from East Hampton High School march from school to mass at Most Holy Trinity Church. Their presence is in protest to the American invasion of Cambodia and to the National Guard killing four Kent State students on the Ohio college campus. To and from church, the students carry placards that herald, "Thou Shalt Not Kill Anytime, Any way, Anywhere" and "In Times to Come if People Say We Were Civilized, The Lunacy of Our Government Will Attest to the Fact That We Were Not."

June 7. Robert David Cooper, the great-grandson of the last Queen of the Montauketts, is sworn in as a Town Police officer.

Cooper is the Town's first non-Caucasian member of the police force. Other than already knowing how to drive, Officer Cooper has not had any training for his new job.[27]

July 19. The Wainscott Sewing Society celebrates its 100th anniversary with an old-fashioned country supper in the Wainscott chapel. Baked ham, homemade baked beans, potato salad, and ginger bread with whipped cream are served. The original members met once a month at each other's houses, to sew for the poor. Boxes of clothes were sent to the Home for the Friendless, a New York City orphanage.

October 14/15. District One Board of Education holds a special meeting on the 14th, to hear high school seniors who oppose the Vietnam peace moratorium which is to be observed on the 15th in all East End schools. The students want to be excused from the symposium whose panel, they feel, is "loaded" in favor of the moratorium. Instead, they would like to hold an assembly on their position, next week.

The Board denies their request and suggests that the group lets itself be heard at the rally. On the 15th, one fifth of the high school students enter the assembly wearing black armbands. Both sides of the issue are heard without rancor in a dialogue that lasts considerably longer than scheduled. Seniors Joel Brill, Pat Flatteron, Phillip Markowitz, and David McDonough organized the peace moratorium.

1970

June 18. A little after 5 p.m. this Thursday, two policemen arrive at the Amagansett home of the artist, Robert Gwathmey, place him under arrest, and take him to police headquarters. There, he is charged under Section 136 of New York State's business law, with desecrating the American flag. The signed complaint was made by Donald Miller, of Springs, who had seen a flag flying from the Gwathmey house, with a peace symbol over the blue field. There are no stars on this banner, but, because it features red and white stripes and a blue field, it is seen as an American flag. Bail is set at $100, a Court appearance to follow.

The Town police had received other complaints since it was first put up outside the Gwathmey house Memorial Day weekend. It is identical to one of several standards that were shown recently on the Today show. This one was a house-warming gift from a friend of their architect son, Charles, who designed his parents' new home. It was bought at the Different Drummer in Manhattan.

July 10. Federal Judge Anthony Travia turns down Victor Rabinowitz's request to delay Gwathmey's pending court date, and to have a District Court panel of judges issue a ruling on whether Section 136 is valid in this case. Rabinowitz, a noted New York labor lawyer and East Hampton home owner, argues that if it is judged to be valid, it violates the constitutional right to freedom of speech. Gwathmey has been joined in the motion by the Amagansett artist, Bill Durham, who has made it a class action suit on behalf of others who might want to fly a "peace flag" of any design.[28]

July 11. Galvanized into action by a development proposal, a group of Montauk residents meet today to form "Concerned Citizens of Montauk."

At issue is a proposal that Eugene Haas made to the Town Board. Writing as a Montauk resident, Haas, who is the Zoning

Board of Appeals chairman, suggested that upwards of 1500 houses could be built in the Indian Field area (which both State and County recommend adding to Montauk Point State Park), and that a channel be dug from Lake Montauk to Block Island Sound. Opening the lake, he advises, would provide additional coveted shorefront property.[29]

September 20. At five a.m., Ernestine and Ibram Lassaw leave their house in Springs, pick up two friends, and drive the short distance up Fireplace Road to George Sid Miller's farm which fronts on Accabonac Creek. They become part of a large crowd that is gathering to watch *The Free Life* balloon and its passengers ascend at dawn, for a transatlantic flight. Already there are Alan Alda, (of Water Mill), Dick Cavett, (of Montauk), and, from Springs, Willem de Kooning, New Yorker cartoonist Sol Steinberg, and the writers Robert Alan Aurthur and Jean Stafford. Stafford's house is across the road.)

On the meadow with *The Free Life* is its volunteer land crew. Most of them are members of the Springs Fire Department. Dressed in red jumper suits, to distinguish them in the crowd, they have been on the field the last two days straight, working out last-minute details and corrections.

The past summer has been a learning experience for all of them. Their involvement began in late spring, after actress Pamela Brown and her stock broker husband, Rod Anderson, walked into the Barnes General Store, in Springs, and mentioned to its owners why they were in Springs.

They had been the ba.lloon's financial backers last autumn, when its first flight was scheduled. Bad weather conditions kept it from going up, and it was stored in Miller's barn for the winter. This time, Anderson will crew with the professional balloonist. The flight is scheduled for August. There is much preparation work to be done. No, he is not a balloonist.

Caught up in the excitement of Anderson's dream to be in the first balloon to cross the Atlantic, Dorothy and Clarence Barnes rallied the community around them. After work, and on week-ends, strangers became acquaintances became friends and family with the young New York couple and with each other, as the cadre of volunteers extended beyond Springs. Taking on different tasks, they helped to build the aluminum and fiber glass gondola to specifications, studied weather charts and ocean currents, learned the dynamics of ballooning, and the intricacies of weights and measures. The Barnes' brother-in-law, Gill Foster, has driven every week-end from Connecticut to oversee the technical aspects.

Lift-off is delayed. Winds are not right. A rip has been found in the lower outer envelope of the white and orange balloon. By noon, close to 1000 people have arrived with blankets, chairs, picnic baskets, cameras, the Sunday papers, romping family pets, and lagging children. Unseen in the pastoral tableau is the feeling that one is about to witness history, of a sort. This will be the ninth attempt, since 1836, to span the Atlantic in a balloon.

At 1:40 p.m., the winds have picked up and the "unimportant" rip is said to be mended. *The Free Life* is ready. Packed in the unsinkable gondola are electronic and navigational equipment, survival and foul weather gear and the Barnes' gifts of food, supplies, and a semi-automatic rifle. Gallon-size plastic jugs of water, tied to the netting around the gondola, are added ballast. The Stars and Stripes and the Union Jack fly from the point where the gondola and balloon are joined.

On board are Brown, Anderson, and the English balloonist Malcolm Brighton. Anderson opens a bottle of champagne and the three adventurers toast each other and salute the crowd. Brighton heaves several bags of sand from the gondola and instructs the ground crew to lift them up and carry them forward. The gondola raised, the crew runs with it across the field. Many in the crowd follow close behind, and the action is recorded on film, from the ground and the gondola.

Another order: "Everyone let go." The gondola waffles on its solo drift across the meadow. Down. Up. Down. Up. Some of the spectators continue to chase *The Free Life*. Laughing, crying, and cheering, they pursue the balloon with arms stretched upwards, as if they really expect to grab hold of, and return to earth, the *primum mobile* that brought them here today.

Brighton drops another sandbag. The gondola rises beyond reach. *The Free Life* assumes an affirmative course. The last sight of it from the meadow is of Brighton standing on the gondola's lip, Brown taking photographs, and Anderson waving his arms like a bird in flight.

September 21. A little after 7 p.m., a distress signal is picked up off Newfoundland: "Six hundred feet and descending. Signing off now to make the safest possible emergency landing on the water. Will try contact after landing."[30]

1971

May 7. Book Hampton opens in a former liquor store on Newtown Lane. It is the first shop in Town devoted to the sale of books, since the now-closed House of Books and Music opened on Main Street several years earlier. Its owners are Stein & Day editor, George Caldwell, who will be on hand, week-ends only, and Argentinean-born Jorge Castello, who will manage the store full-time. Castello, who was Program Director for American Marketing Association, wanted a reason to move out of Manhattan. Within two months, the idea of a book store turned into reality. Book Hampton will stock a full line of hard and soft cover books, current bestsellers, and classics.[31]

July 4. A "black liberation flag," with black, green and red horizontal stripes appears, for the first time, in an East Hampton Fourth of July parade.

September 19. One year after *The Free Life* rose into the sky above Springs, a memorial service for its crew is held outside Ashawagh Hall. A tree is planted and a plaque at its base is unveiled, Afterwards, Dorothy and Clarence Barnes host a buffet for the crew's relatives and volunteers.

October 22. Agents from the Suffolk County Board of Health and the Long Island office of the ASPCA arrive, uninvited, to inspect a private home on Apaquogue Road. It is the residence of Edith Bouvier Beale and her adult daughter, Edie.

Alerted by East Hampton's building inspector to existing conditions at "Grey Gardens," the County inspectors find the house (in the exclusive estate section) in an extreme condition. Animal feces and garbage litter the floors. Twelve sick cats hover about. Toilets do not work. Empty cans abound. The once-formal garden is a jungle of vines, and the site of an abandoned car.

1972

January 9. With New York attorney William Van Den Heuvel representing them, the Beales obtain a temporary Court order to halt further County Health Department proceedings. (The Department issued an order to the Beales on December 10 to vacate their house, or, be evicted.) Van Den Heuvel has been retained by his friend, Jacqueline Bouvier Onassis, who is niece and cousin to the Beale women.

In their complaint, the Beales charge that the County entered the house on a warrant issued to the ASPCA, which wanted to check on the cats. They also charge the County with invasion of privacy, claiming that its agents returned a second time, without any warrant to shield them.

January 31. In the sixth issue of Student Voice, the High School's underground newspaper, 12th grader Yolanda Smith writes: "...things couldn't get no worse for us blacks. We've had it. I've had it....we want to make the white students wake up to what's happening in this school, who we are, what we want, and to be treated as equal marked fairly...because there is prejudice in this school..."

May 20. "Howard Hughes moves to Montauk" heralds the East Hampton Summer Sun's front page. Underneath the eye-catching banner: "Multi-billionaire recluse believed residing in top two floors of Montauk's Six-Story office building." (For months, the media has speculated on the eccentric billionaire's whereabouts.) Before night falls, the news that Hughes has been "found" spreads across the country. Reporters from print and television start for East Hampton - Montauk, in particular.

May 21. The world starts to learn that Howard Hughes is not in Montauk, nor anywhere else on Long Island. The Summer Sun story is just that - a story. A fertile spin-off on the countless rumors about the eccentric man's whereabouts, written by the paper's founder and editor, Dan Rattiner.

June 10. Guild Hall's exhibit, "A Sense of Place" opens. The catalogue features quotations from the artists on how the place in which they live influences their work.

Balcomb Greene of Montauk: "The Sea influences everything I do, even if it's not a picture of the sea."

Julian Levi: "After twenty-five years of exposure (visual) to East Hampton, let me affirm that my painting has been intimately shaped by what I have seen and experienced.

"I haven't documented the scene as such... I have reached out for those symbols of the environment which seemed to match my picture-making and/or psychic needs ... channel markers, breakwaters, buoys, skies, the tides - for example."

John Little, whom Jackson Pollock had encouraged, years ago, to move from Washington D.C. : "'White Gestures' is the last work of a series of constructions which began in 1948. Materials used in this series were found on the beach in the vicinity of Ditch Plains and the Cove on toward Montauk Point...These works involved a definite sense of Place, the found object: where the ocean meets the land."

July 8. A newly-formed environmental group convenes a meeting in the atrium of Elizabeth and Tassos Fondaras's Further Lane residence. Most of those in attendance are summer home owners.

The main speaker is Dr. Ian Marceau, Director of Huntington Town's fledgling Department of Environmental Protection. The Department is developing an ecological inventory of Huntington and the Town's new zoning code will be based on its findings.

Marceau recommends that the just-incorporated Group for the Defense of the South Fork take a similar path: ""Start out by finding what the environment is...develop a natural resources inventory...which areas should be protected and how." Then, he adds, submit the information to the appropriate Village or Town government and call for a revised zoning code.

A Group founder, Harold Wit, advises the assembled that the Group is incorporated as a non-profit, tax-exempt agency. But, unlike others which are comprised of volunteers, this agency will have a knowledgeable full-time staff and the financial backing to pursue its goals. Marceau warns the meeting that when the Group submits its reports to a local government, it probably will need to initiate "class action suits" before a local government will take the Group and its report seriously.

Evan Frankel, who has extensive land holdings in both the Village and Town, says, "I see before me a very substantial group of citizens..." But, he warns, "You are third class citizens as far as the Village and Town think of you...Rise up in wrath ...tell them what you want." What they don't want, he adds, is "...a bunch of stupid, ignorant people ruining your entire environment."[32]

August 28. George Plimpton and his wife host a party at their Devon home. Their guests include numerous "names," from politics and publishing to summer's society and members of the Kennedy clan, etc.. Before the evening is over, Town police arrive, arrest and hand-cuff Mr. Plimpton, and remove him from his party. He is told that neighbors complained about the noise from the fireworks he was setting off from his front yard. Taken to Court, he is charged with not having a permit to shoot them.[33]

September. Art New publishes Harold Rosenberg's article, "Interview with Willem de Kooning." It reveals the artist's special afinity for the natural light and color found on the South Fork, and his wish to incorporate both in his paintings:

"...when I came here I made the color of sand - a big pot of paint that was the color of sand. As if I picked up sand and mixed it. And the grey-green grass, the beach grass, and the ocean was all kind of steely grey most of the time. When the light hits the ocean there is kind of a grey light on the water ... Indescribable tones, almost. I started working with them and insisted that they would give me the kind of light I wanted. One was lighting up the grass. That became that kind of green: one was lighting up the water. That became that kind of grey.

"Then I got a few more colors, because someone might be there, or a rowboat, or something happening. I did very well with that. I got into painting in the atmosphere I wanted to be in. It was like the reflection of light. I reflected upon the reflections of the water, like the fishermen do. They stand there fishing. They seldom catch any fish, but they like to be by themselves for an hour. And I do that almost every day."

September 8. Sidney Beckwith, director of Suffolk County's Health Department inspectional services, tells a packed hearing that "Grey Gardens" is now "in substantial conformity with the Suffolk County sanitary code." [34]

1973

June. Esquire magazine publishes Robert Alan Aurthur's "Hitting the Boiling Point, Freakwise, at East Hampton." The author touches upon a multitude of local subjects, groups, and individuals.

On The Springs and its people: "Real Bonackers speak with an accent that echoes early seventeenth-century English, and they've lived in this backwater of Gardiners Bay since the 1640s. They are people sparing of words and movement and one is certain they are not overjoyed at the influx of outsiders - artists, writers, and even balloonists."

On his house: "Though I've owned my house on Fireplace Road for seventeen years,. ..(it) is still known as the Old Parsons Place. And why not? The Parsons after all lived here and worked the land that runs down to Accabonac Harbor, or 'The Crick,' for nearly two hundred years."

On the editor of The Star: "Along with magnificent beaches, Gardiner's Island and the Long Island Railroad, Ev is one of our natural wonders...often enraging entrenched opinion, Ev has converted the Star to a bright, acerbic, award-winning journal which still serves local needs with an overlay of sharp, fresh writing."

Aurthur sees the Maidstone Club as "...a gothic fortress nestled in the dunes, at all times your super Wasp's nest, a sub-haven against those of the Jewish persuasion and itinerant Gypsies." Individually, he finds Maidstoners "gentle, jocular, and even broad-minded, but banded together they seem to have a way of taking over."

1974

January 2. When Judith Hope, the Town's first woman Supervisor, walks into her office, she finds it almost bare. In what only can be called a fit of pique, members of the losing administration in the November election removed all the files and put them in the basement.

June 29. Concerned Citizens of Montauk holds its first major fund raiser. The benefit barbecue on the grounds of Peter Beard's mill draws over 500 paying guests (way above the limit set) With an open bar, skewered pork loins, cauldrons of Montauk fish chowder, ears of corn for everyone, etc., they celebrate the opening of the County's new 900-acre park at Indian Fields. CCOM led the campaign for its acquisition.

July 1. A new bus service starts between the towns of East Hampton and Southampton. Hampton Jitney Inc. is running two "bike buses," passenger vans with trailer-mounted bicycle racks in tow between Amagansett and Southampton College.

September 12. In this week's issue of The Star, editor Everett Rattray's "Fifth Column" addresses Departure Days at summer's end: "...Rites of passage would be administered to summer residents staying on for the winter, with initiation fees to benefit the ARF. The ARF would be allowed to lock in its new pound any departing visitors caught leaving pets behind, and resident mutts would be invited to a public romp on the nearest deserted beach."

(Animal Rescue Fund does not yet have its own shelter. That is a dream for the future. At this time, the fledgling organization - it was incorporated in April - does not even have an office. The phone numbers listed in its classified "For Adoption" and "Found" ads belong to its three founders, Sony Schotland of Sag Harbor, Barbara Posener of Amagansett, and Dorothy Wahl of Southampton.

The animals whom ARF hopes to place in new homes are boarded at local animal hospitals, kennels and, on occasion, in private homes. This means that a prospective adopter (and the volunteer) may sometimes have to travel a considerable distance - "there and back" - to see what is available for adoption.)

1975

September 19. The Springs Historical Society holds its first meeting. SHS grew out of concern over proposed development on Old Stone Highway. Should it proceed, "Willow Hill," home of the late Ferris Talmage, would be lost. Part of the house predates the Revolution. SHS would like to buy it.

September 27/28. One of the films included in the New York Film Festival premieres on the 27th. "Grey Gardens," starring the forlorn house and its residents, has been filmed by the brothers Mayslie, Albert and David.

Newsday's issue of the 28th quotes Edie Beale's reaction: "I think they've done a gem."

Critics are less kind of the life that was lived, then, filmed there. The Beales are seen as "tormented" and "disabled," the house, as "crumbling."[34]

1976

February 25. New York State's Department of Environmental Conservation bans commercial fishing in the Hudson River for striped bass and other fish. The bass spawn in the river, into which two General Electric factories have been dumping polychlorinated biphenyl (PCB) into the fresh water system, since the 1940s. The industrial poison, which used to insulate transformers, is highly toxic to fish and a suspected carcinogen. Once the fish have absorbed it, it accumulates in the tissue.

The ban is of great concern to East End's commercial fishermen. Catching bass has been a major source of their annual income. Mature bass leave their spawning ground for the Atlantic Ocean. Some of them swim south, as far as Florida. Others head for the Maritimes, passing Long Island, *en route*. Last August, low levels of PCB were found in seventeen bass that were taken off Montauk. But, the small amount is not comfort enough for the haulseiners. They fear it is only a matter of time before the DEC imposes a ban on catching bass in local waters.[35]

Summer . This summer, Round Swamp Farm on Three Mile Harbor Road is entered on the National Registry as a Bi-Centennial Farm. It has been owned and operated by the Lester Family for over 200 years. The card table, from which the Lester sisters, Carolyn, Dianna, and Gail sold some farm produce is gone. In its place is a farmstand that features a wealth of produce, farm-grown and farm-made. The stand itself has served as backdrop for ads and the subject of articles.

September 8. The County Legislature adopts the County Farmland Acquisition Program.

The idea for having the County buy development rights to farms came four years ago from the Group for the South Fork. In mapping out all South Fork farmland, GFSF found that 50 per cent of it was owned by speculators.

Under the Acquisition program, a farmer can sell the County the development rights to his property, continue to work the farm and live on it. But, neither he, nor succeeding owners can develop it. The program is expected to save 15 percent of East Hampton's farmland.

. 1976 has not been good for catching bass. A thick mass of algae bloom, first seen in February, ran from Delaware to

Montauk. Haulseine crews used to earning $10/12,000 during the April-November bass season, took home less than $4000.

1977

April 24/26. While walking on Gardiner's Bay beach in Springs, 22-year old Emily Blumenstein stumbles upon four cow heads.

Called to the scene by her father, Town Board member Larry Cantwell thinks that the heads, minus their right ear, were severed the same way, for the same reason, in the last couple of days. Thinking that they might have drifted over from Plum Island, the site of government experiments that are so hush-hush, they breed the wildest versions of reality, Cantwelll phones there in the morning. An official tells him that the government only uses white-faced Herefords from Virginia and the slaughtered animals are incinerated.

Town Highway Superintendent and farmer, John Bistrian, identifies the washed-up heads as Holsteins. Perhaps they came from a Montan cattle ranch. For whom? Maybe they were tossed overboard at sea. When the tongue stamp reveals upstate marking, hi-jacking is considered. The mystery - and the imagination - continue.

Enter Jack Graves. The Star reporter phones the New York Times food editor and cookbook author, Craig Claiborne. His house overlooks the bay. Perhaps he can shed a proverbial light. He can. Claiborne and master chef Pierre Franey are doing a veal cookbook. Saturday last, they tried to prepare "tête de veau vinaigrette" and "mock turtle soup" with veal gelatin. Franey had spent an hour trying to skin the heads. Finally, in exasperation, he hurled them out the window.

1978

. The "floating zone" concept becomes effective this year. Under the ruling, a tract of land previously zoned for lesser density may be re-zoned to provide the site for a subsidized senior citizen resident complex.

1979

July 25. The Town Board holds a special meeting to hear why the Planning Board recommends less restrictive guide lines than those outlined by Town Planning Department head, Thomas Thorsen, in his 1976 "Motel Survey and Analysis."

Focus is on 106 undeveloped acres on Napeague, which is zoned for motels. Thorsen had recommended it be upzoned to residential. Among the Planning Board members' reasons for not accepting his recommendations are:

"East Hampton's greatest attraction is the ocean and here we have a nice stretch of beach for a resort industry..." (The speaker's father owns some of the 106 acres.)

"... quality motels would be no more detrimental than a lot of houses ... we're a lot safer working with motel owners than ... with private individuals." (Thorsen has recommended that 70 acres west of the Arrows Motel be upzoned to two acre lots.)

"The Board opposes more parks. We will rue the day when Napeague becomes another Jones Beach ..." (The State owns a considerable portion of Napeague).

1980

January 2. The Town Board, with a Democratic majority for the first time in fifty years, initiates an "interim development restraint." Under the moratorium, motels cannot be converted into cooperatives or into condominiums, while the process towards legislation to control such conversions takes place.

. The Long Island Regional Planning Board Population Study for this year determines that 49.48% of all East Hampton Town housing belongs to second home owners.

July 23. To the surprise of many, the Planning Board reverses last year's decision. Majority vote favors changing the Napeague strip to parks and conservation status. A dissenting member opined that park status would be as detrimental to the sandy isthmus as motels.

September 18. The Abstract painter James Brooks is honored in a ceremony held at the Rotunda at LaGuardia Airport. During the Depression of the 1930s, the government's Works Progress Administration (WPA) hired Brooks to paint a mural around the rotunda walls. Brooks named his work "Flight."

It remained there without consequence, until the early 1950s when the United States was locked in a Cold War with Russia. Some politicians used this "war" to their advantage. One of those people was Wisconsin Senator Joseph R. McCarthy.

A master at destroying lives through inuendo and complete fabrication, McCarthy bullied America into believing that under every rock, stone, and pebble, and behind every door, lurked American-born communists. With very little proof, people were branded "Communist," fireed from their jobs, and black-listed.

Caught up in the "Commie frenzy," an army general became convinced that the sickle, Russia's symbol, was a "message" painted on one of the rotunda walls. A couple of phone calls and the order went out from Washington to cover "Flight" with paint.

In the mid-1970s, Geoffrey Arend, whose office was in the building, learned about "Flight". He contacted Brooks, secured photographs of the mural and set up a display table in the rotunda. It called attention to the grievous error, and urged restoration of "Flight."

Over time, Arend raised enough interest and, through major contributors, Laurence Rockefeller and Reader's Digest founder DeWitt Wallace, enough money to pay for the mural's restoration.

What did that gen eral really see? The ellipse of a hole in the sky, above a man who, with caliper in hand, was looking up at it.

1981

July 1. The Zoning Board grants ARF permission to build a shelter in Wainscott. The Board reasons: "For many summer visitors - especially those with children - the picture of an idyllic summer is not complete without a lively puppy or kitten romping with the children and sharing their vacation hours. But puppies and kittens grow up and every summer has its September.

"For many of those hapless animals, the advent of fall becomes the time when July's pet turns into September's nuisance - too big and inconvenient to be accommodated in a City apartment. So, when September comes, many of these pets are simply abandoned in the East End communities, left to fend for themselves, to run in packs, or to meet death from starvation or at the side of a busy highway."

July 3. A rotund man steps out of a silver Cadillac on Three Mile Harbor Road and studies Harriet Henderson's water colors. They are clothes-pinned to a wire, stretched between two trees, at the foot of her driveway. Unbeknownst to him, the artist watches him from her house, on a rise in the woods. She prefers to let potential customers study her paintings without a feeling of pressure.

The fat man makes his pick. He grabs the two black portfolios propped against a tree, runs across the street, and jumps into a black limousine. With her mother's voice ringing in her ears, ("He's stealing my paintings,") 19-year old Ruth races down the hill, hurls herself onto the car's hood, grabs the windshield lip, and screams at the thief to stop.

In spite of her immediate presence in front of him, the thief pulls out on to Three Mile Harbor Road. While Mrs. Henderson runs behind the car, yelling "Stop that car," her daughter glowers through the windshield.

Sense returns to the art lover. He stops the car. Ruth slides off. He hands her the portfolios, and their owner asks : "Why did you do this?"

"Because they're beautiful," he answers, and leaves.

August 31/September 3. On the last day of August, Town Police Detective-Sergeant Richard Lia reports increased activity at a house which has been under periodic surveillance for the last three years. Five people have arrived and a large enclosed truck is in the driveway. A check of its New Jersey plates shows that it is registered to a major organized crime member. A round-the-clock watch is put on the Milina Drive house, which overlooks Gardiner's Bay. Federal and County undercover agents join Town police in the eight hour on/off shifts.

More people arrive. Nobody leaves except for trips to delis in town and in Southampton for huge quantities of food, and to Bridgehampton to have the van repaired. Wherever they go, the visitors are watched. Based on other movements, surveillance is put on the motel across the highway from the police station.

Three hours into Sept. 3, Lia and County Narcotics officer Jerry Tuthill hear a ship's motor in the bay. Sitting on the bluff, night scopes in hand, they spot two ships less than a mile from shore. A trawler and a cabin cruiser. For two hours, they watch while 289 bales are unloaded on to four motorized rubber rafts , and brought ashore. The two officers move to prone, but hidden, positions beside the steep path that leads from the beach to the house. The "off-loaders" pass within inches of them as they carry the bales to the truck. Afraid to make radio contact with headquarters, lest a police scanner is in the house, Lia races through the woods to Richard and Barbara Cooney's house, where he phones for reinforcements.

At 6 a.m., 50 agents descend on the summer rental and arrest its 18 occupants. A search of the truck reveals two tons of marijuana. A search of the house uncovers scanners, high-powered telescopes, a loaded .39 caliber revolver and two loaded nine-milimeter automatic pistols, nautical and aviation information, and close to $4000 in cash. Agents intercept the leader, on his way to the motel. There, they arrest "heavy-duty" organized crime figures who have been waiting for the signal to pay for goods delivered.

A little after 7 a.m., a Coast Guard vessel from the Montauk Station comes upon the 42-foot cruiser, "Unapplied Time," just north of Gardiner's Island. She and her crew of three are escorted to Montauk. About the same time, two Coast Guard

cutters bear down on the mother ship outside the Montauk breakwater. On board is 14-and-a-half tons of marijuana.[36]
December 18. The outgoing Town Board Democratic majority enacts "Local Law Number Four." It mandates "No local agency, as herein defined shall, by action of the Town Board, be established or abolished, nor shall the authority or function of any such agency be transferred to another local agency, or to the Town Board itself, unless said action shall be in the form of a local law adopted in the manner provided in Chapter 15 hereof." This is in response to Supervisor Mary Fallon's intent to abolish the Planning Department in 1982.

1982

January 15. The East Hampton High School auditorium is packed for the public hearing on the Republican Town Board majority's intent to abolish the Planning Department. Eighty persons have signed up to speak, and 2000 signatures are on a petition that calls for continuance of the Department. Several voices are heard before Frazer Dougherty rises to say:
"Let's give a vote of confidence to the Department. Everyone in favor, stand up." Almost the entire audience rises and applauds. Moved to tears, Supervisor Mary Fallon says: "...with this kind of reaction....We are keeping the department. Of course, Mr. Thorsen is part of the department."
February 19. Thirty-five days after Mrs. Fallon promised not to abolish the Planning Department, Town Board majority vote does just that. In what it call a "cost-efficient" move, the Board transfers Department duties to an outside consultant firm. Rochris & Associates will be paid $51,000 a year.
The Supervisor tells the assembled in Town Hall that she reversed her previous reversal because the full board was unable to reach a compromise, and adds, "I can live with my decision."
Others in the audience cannot. They verbalize:
"Absolutely treacherous."..."The Board's credibility is seriously damaged."..."An act of corrupt government." And, from a descendant of a founding settler, "For the first time in my life, I am ashamed to be a resident of the Town..."
March 24. The Citizens Planning Committee sues East Hampton Town. CPC contends that the Planning Department was abolished illegally (through resolution rather than through local law), and that "the new Town Board has violated numerous provisions of the law in its zeal to liquidate the Planning Department." In addition, the CPC calls the cost-cutting excuse as "at best, erroneous, and at worst, a fabrication."

March 29. The Town Board joins citizen concern over last month's Hither Woods purchase. Citing the property as the sole source aquifer, the Board passes a resolution to preserve Hither Woods. Its 1350 acres of forest, bluffs, and old trails includes land around Fresh Pond and land north of First and Second Houses, which are part of the State Park.

April 21. In Court, the Town attorney asks that the CPC suit be dismissed. The Town claims that "the petitioners have no standing to bring same," and argues that the "resolution concerning the Planning Department must be viewed as a reorganization of government, which petitioners have no standing to address."

The Town's brief states that "The abolition of the Planning Department in the respondent Town touched only the interstices of government. That means neither the individual petitioners, nor the petitioner committee, have standing to challenge the Town's action in this regard."

Following the Court hearing, CPC issues a press release: "It is outrageous that the Town Board majority has not only ignored the people of East Hampton, but now says that the people have no right to challenge the Board on legal grounds. The Town Board majority is evading the issue by claiming that the CPC is not a valid citizen's organization." The release advises that the CPC has signature support of over 3000 tax payers and voters, "with the numbers growing daily."

May 21. The Town Board holds a public hearing before voting to repeal "Local Law Number Four," which the out-going Democrat-controlled Board passed in December.

The Board majority calls the five-month old law both "cumbersome" and "confusing."

CPC chairman, Edward Gorman, tells the Board that "...its consistent trend is the people be damned."

Gus Ruhle reminds the Board that he has been an active Republican for forty years, but, "I'll be damned if I'll ever help a Republican in this Town again. You don't have to be a chicken to know an egg is rotten."

Amid cries of "shame" from the audience, the Board repeals the law along political lines.

. This evening, the Village Board names Larry Cantwell to be the Village Clerk, starting June 21. (The Councilman had advised the Board of his interest in the position, after learning that the present Clerk was retiring.)

. "East Hampton Heritage," a photographic record of the Town architecture, is published by W. W. Norton.

. (LVIS member Averill Dayton Geus had proposed the book idea at an LVIS meeting. She told the members that much information had been gathered when the historic district was being inventoried that she felt it would be a waste not to make it available to others. With grants from the Rock and Kaplan Foundations added to its own financial commitment, the LIVS sponsored the publication. Mrs. Geus, Chair of the LVIS Landmarks Committee, oversaw the project from conception to completion. Robert Hefner was project director. Robert A. M. Stern and Clay Lancaster wrote the text.)[37]

July 1. The Star reports that Planning costs are much higher than the Republicans' predicted figures.

. How soon we forget: In 1976, the Town published an historic map prepared by the Planning Department. One of its legends locates the site of old Indian graves on Fort Hill. Without a Planning Department to review new projects, the Town, through its consulting engineers, Greenman & Pedersen, has approved creation of half-acre house lots on Montauk. On Fort Hill. Over 188 graves.

December 20. The Town has a new Supervisor. Ronald Greenbaum, legislative aide to State Assemblyman John Behan, is the Republican choice to fill the seat vacated today by Mary Fallon. Four days earlier, Mrs. Fallon learned that a position had been found for her in County government. She is the new Deputy Commissioner of Consumer Affairs.

. At an evening meeting, Baymen Association members agree that a new group must be formed to save a prime source of their income from the ravages of proposed development of Barcelona Neck and the Grace Estate. Cathy Lester, who fishes Northwest Harbor nearly every day of the year, with her husband, Tom, and trap fisherman Stuart Vorpahl, Jr. are named to co-chair the new committee. Mrs. Lester has drafted a letter which the Association will mail, over her husband's signature, to 100 groups, politicians, and individuals, asking them for help of any kind.

The baymen are very concerned about the damage that building would bring to the area's historical and cultural sites, the ecological and environmental balance, and to future fishing, especially for scallops, in Northwest Harbor. Remnants of the Town's first port and earliest settlement at Northwest can be found on the Grace Estate.

Also still visible are 300-year-old trails which the early settlers cut through the woods to the first port. There, they harvested seaweed for insulation, and salt hay that was used to feed and bed the livestock, Whalers from Sagaponack and

Mecox traveled these same paths, finding it quicker for them to
reach the water than go to the harbor at North Sea..

Recalling the struggle of the ospreys and eagles to survive,
Lester writes, " I am asking you also to understand the plight of
the fishermen of this area who must overcome the strong
influence of the developers in order to win support of our cause
from the Town...A significant portion of New York's last
remaining untouched coastline will be destroyed unless
something is done immediately to stop or alter the development
plans for Barcelona Neck and the Grace Estate."

At present, the only protected areas are 94 acres of County-
owned wetlands and marsh that border Barcelona Neck's east
side, and 193.2 acres on its west side, which is owned by the
State's Department of Environmental Conservation.

1983

January 4. In his run for a seat on the Town Board, young
Tony Bullock focused his campaign on one issue: reinstatement
of the Planning Department. This morning, after being sworn in
at the Town Board's organizational meeting, he addresses the
issue.

Reading from a prepared statement, he says: "My campaign,
to a large degree, centered on this issue. I would not be
fulfilling my obligation to the people who voted for me if I did
not insist on hearing this issue at the first opportunity."

Councilman Hugh King exits the room to drink some water,
and the Supervisor departs for the bathroom. On his return, and
at Bullock's conclusion, Greenbaum suggests to Bullock that he
"see what the other guy has to propose before you grandstand
with something you know you'll never get off the ground."

January 12. The first meeting of the Baymen-sponsored group
takes place at the Group for the South Fork. In attendance are
individuals who happened to hear about the meeting, people to
whom the Group had mailed notices because of their expressed
interest in Northwest's future, as well as some recipients of the
December letter. The new group is named Northwest Alliance.

January 18. The Shoreham Opponents Coalition sponsors a
forum on the nuclear plant at East Hampton High School. Its
first speaker, Suffolk County Executive Peter Cohalan, decries
LILCO's fight "all the way" to submit to a design review and full
inspection before the plant goes on line. Then, aloud, he
wonders where the 200,000-plus residents around Shoreham
would go, in the event of a nuclear accident.

They won't go anywhere. Should a calamity occur, a plan on
paper calls for LILCO trucks to block main arteries, to prevent

evacuation from the East End. (Six weeks ago, the County revealed its "radiological emergency response plan." According to the $600,000 report, only residents within twenty miles of Shoreham would be evacuated. The County claimed it would be "more dangerous" to try escaping "to the west through the radioactive plume" than it would be for North and South Fork residents to stay at home.)[37]

February 8. The Town Board majority approves a local law to reinstate the Town Planning Department. The Democrat minority votes against it because it does not call for the Department head to come from a Civil Service list. Under Greenbaum's approved proposal, the position will be filled by a Commissioner appointed to a two-year contract. Bullock reiterates his January position: by-passing Civil Service "invites" a lawsuit from Civil Service.

June 2/3. East Hampton is well represented among the 3000 who walk two and a half miles to a Saturday rally on Shoreham's beach. On Sunday, many of Shoreham's opponents participate in a civil disobedience sit-in at the plant's gates. Only those who took mandatory training in non-violent action may climb the gates. 300 people are arrested. 138 of them are charged with trespassing. The rest are released.

July 9. One thousand guests converge on the grounds of food writer Craig Claiborne's waterfront house for an AIDS benefit. The party, sponsored by the East End Gay Organization includes an auction of works donated by international artists. Among them are South Fork residents Willem de Kooning, Elaine de Kooning, Roy Lichenstein, Esteban Vicente, Paul Davis, Robert Dash. The party raises $100,000 for the Gay Men's Health Crisis in NYC.

August 1. The Peconic Land Trust is incorporated. Founded in Southampton by John Halsey, a direct descendant of one of Southampton's original settlers, the non-profit agency is dedicated to the conservation of farmland and open space on both the South and North Forks.

August 8. Gov. Mario Cuomo signs into law the DEC-endorsed bill which raises the minimum size catch of bass from 16 inches to 24 inches. Declining bass stocks is the main thrust behind the bill. Effective November 7, the new size limit should allow the female of the species to spawn before being caught, and thus add to the bass population. The DEC has estimated that the new law will have less than a ten per cent effect on rod and reel fishing, while it will cut into 50 per cent of the haulseiners' catch.

September 4. The New York Times Sunday magazine features Paul Goldberger's "The Hamptons: The Strangling of a Resort." Commenting on the development that is blanketing the Hamptons, Goldberger writes that it "has triggered a battle with implications that reach far beyond Long Island's South Fork."

Noting that 145 applications for residential subdivisions or new commercial constructions had been filed in the last three and a half months, he calls the pace of building proposals "so rapid that The East Hampton Star, the local weekly, which has viewed the town's evolution with an intelligent skepticism for some years now, has not had a front page for months that did not feature a story about some new building project or zoning dispute."

"Farmland," he points out, "is not merely on the South Fork to give a quaint rural touch. Agriculture, along with fishing, has been the anchor of the region, and turning land over to development thus changes the area's very economic base."

October. Up to now, six subdivision applications have been filed with the Planning Board for development of Northwest. Their plans total close to 500 condominiums and single family houses in what New York art dealer and East Hampton resident and developer, Ben Heller, calls a "once-in-a-lifetime-opportunity." This *singular experience* also includes access to an 18-hole golf course, tennis courts, and riding horses.

Heller, who has initiated one lawsuit against the Town, with the promise of more, has told the Planning Board that he will end litigation and lower density if the Board approves his plans before year's end. He is well aware that the November election will bring an expected Democratic majority to the Town Board, followed by five-acre up zoning around Northwest Harbor. He told the Planning Board at its last meeting that his offer is "a creative way to avoid disaster...I shudder to think of the penalties to the community if it lost the suits. The entire bonding capacity of the Town would be absorbed."

November 3. The room at Southampton Town Hall is packed with East End fishermen and their supporters. They, and members of the State Department of Environmental Conservation, have come to a meeting organized by State Assemblyman John Behan. He hopes that the opposing sides to the State's new minimum size bass law will listen to each other's reasons.

One fisherman says, "You've taken away my income." Fifty per cent of it he says, came from catching bass.

Trap fisherman Stuart Vorphahl denounces the law as "the vilest form of social oppression...You're punishing the smallest group of people who catch the smallest amount of fish."

Another fisherman wishes aloud that East Enders could get the same consideration given Hudson River fishermen. Their minimum size catch is 14 inches. Here, in the Bay, the haulseiner says, they rarely catch stripers longer than 19 inches.

November 8. When the local Republican party turned its back on supporting the interim Supervisor in this year's election, it chose Councilman King to oppose Judith Hope, who first held the office in 1974. Left on his own, Greenbaum ran on the Conservative ticket. Today's election returns Hope to Town Hall with 55% of the votes. Greenbaum wins 24%; King 21%.

1984

January 3. Following the swearing-in ceremony before an overflow audience, the new Town Board Democratic majority rankles developers, worries landowners, and sends their attorneys into high gear with six proposed new laws:

• six-month moratoria on 25-+ acre subdivision approval, and on new motel site plans or building permits

• limit motel and cluster dwelling units to five per acre

• eliminate future motel use on Northwest Harbor, Three Mile Harbor, and the east side of Lake Montauk

• require a public hearing before a Town agency can be eliminated, or created

• drop a mandated fourth vote on proposed zone changes that permit 20 percent of those whom the change would affect, to sign a protest petition. (Present State law requires a fourth-fifths majority. But, a 1976 amendment to the State's Home Rule Law permits Towns, with exceptions, to pass local laws that amend or are contrary to present State statutes. If the simple majority law is passed and upheld in Appeals Court, it will set a precedent in the State).

Reflecting on the proposed moratoria, Supervisor Judith Hope says, "It seems that a Town that is 336 years old is entitled to a six-month respite while we get our act together, planning-wise."

With re-appointed Planning Department head Tom Thorsen supervising, there will be a major updating of the Comprehensive Plan of 1967/68.

January 9. A unanimous Town Board vote passes the six months moratoria and mandates a public hearing before a Town agency can be created or abolished. It splits along Party lines on the simple majority vote. The other two proposals are tabled.

February 17. LTV, the local public access television station, founded by Frazer Dougherty and others, broadcasts its first program, East End Magazine. The half hour show covers a Town Board meeting, ice boating on Sagaponack Pond, and a memorial service honoring the Rev. Martin Luther King.

August 1/14. The Town Planning Board adopts the revised Comprehensive Plan. It recommends five-acre zoning for Barcelona Neck, the Grace Estate, and Hither Hills; three-acre zoning for other areas; lower density of motel units per acre, and affordable housing.

On the 14th, Town Republican Committee Chair Edward V. Ecker announces GOP's general approval of the Democrat-initiated Plan. At a press conference, he says:

"Last November, the people who voted demanded action - a counter revolution, actually, - to stop the assault, to hold down hasty changes, to preserve what is, and to remember what used to be. A conservative revolution...that crossed party lines."

Credit for bringing the Plan to fruition goes to Planning Dept. Director Thorsen, fired in 1982 by the Republican administration, Planning Board Chair Debra Foster, who was not re-appointed to the Board during an earlier GOP Town Board :najority, and Planning Board attorney Fred Thiele, who resigned that position during the previous administration.

1985

February 2. The Atomic Safety and Licensing Board releases its findings on LILCO's proposed evacuation plans, in case of an accident at Shoreham. It calls the plans "fundamentally flawed." The 2775-page report cites the training program for emergency workers, communication and traffic management during the 1983 drill, etc.. (Because both State and County refused to take part in the simulated evacuation, LILCO personnel had to assume all roles.)[38]

May. Peter Matthiessen writes the Preface to "Men's Lives," his portrait of East Hampton baymen and their centuries' old fishing heritage. He describes their fellow townsmen as people who, "prospering on the bland resort community, have mainly lost a historical sense of the ocean character of the South Fork that attracted so many wealthy visitors in the first place. Few of the few who are even aware that a fishing community still exists enjoy the continuity with the past..."

June/August - In early June, huge masses of algae surface in the waters between the North and South Forks. Microscopic in size, the plant *Aureococcus anorexefferens* turns the waters brown, hides the sun from underwater growth, and ravages the rich marine ecosystem.

A helicopter flight over the waters on July 19 reveals that the algae bloom extends from Flanders Bay to Gardiner's Bay, where it is dispersed by waters from Long Island Sound and the Atlantic Ocean. Quick studies by County officials, marine biologists, baymen, etc., fail to provide a clear reason for the bloom's presence. Theories range from over-development of waterlands and attendant sewage effluence and residential waste water, to fertilizers and agricultural chemicals, to climatological conditions.

Whatever the reason, the promising scallop sets of spring are empty shells in August. Baymen, who count on the autumn scallop season to see them through the winter, will have to look elsewhere for work. (Traditionally, the East End scallop industry supplies 15 persent of the nation's scallop supply. In 1983, it realized $1,264,328. Last year alone, Northwest Harbor gave up 760,000 pounds of scallop meat.) [39]

August 20. This afternoon, ARF's Adoption Center opens in Wainscott. The Adoption Center design was contributed by architects Babette and Rick Suter, of Center Moriches. The design plans were overseen by a Building committee, chaired by Shirley Baty, which met once a week for many months before the final plans were drawn.

Separated from the rest of the building by a hall, the dog kennel has been built below grade and surrounded by a high berm to deflect noise upward, rather than carry through the woods to neighbors.

Six months before the Center opened, the Shelter Committee was formed to oversee its management. Led by Helena Curtis and made up of active ARF volunteers, this committee met every week to discuss and vote on myriad matters, from admissions policy and referral service (enabling some pets to be placed directly from one home to another) to supplies and food, to adoption hours and the text on adoption forms. It will continue to meet every Wednesday. From its members, will come the Adoption Desk volunteers, who will be on duty at least one afternoon a week.[40]

August 24. Concerned about talk of development along the wetlands of Accabonac Harbor, a group of Springs residents forms the Accabonac Protection Committee. Through the steering committee, comprised of APC's founders, APC will keep watch, inform the public, and lobby on behalf of one of the few remaining unspoiled ecosystems on Long Island.

"At present," co-founder Cile Downs explains, "the Town hasn't any laws to prevent development there. The attitude is that one cannot tell a person what he or she cannot do on private property."

In talking to Larry Penny, Downs says, "I learned that you can buy and build on wetlands if the town won't buy them. Whoever stops you from buying and building on them has to buy them. You cannot build where there is no potable water. So, the County's Health Dept. waits until deep winter, when the water table is at its highest, to find potable water, instead of in the summer, when more people are around and the water is brackish. The Harbor *is* in danger." So is its wildlife.

The Harbor is a bird watcher's paradise. More than 150 species have been sighted. Three of them - the Piping Plover, Osprey, and Least Tern - nest and breed around it. Four of the endangered plants species on New York State's Protected species list, grow around the Harbor: Swamp Azalea, Northern Bayberry, Marsh Pink, and Bushy Frostweed.[41]

.**November 15**. The Village Board of Trustees votes to delete Section 41-6 of the village code. It reads:

"Public bathing in any of the waters within the corporate bounds of the village, unless in a suitable bathing dress or covering, is hereby prohibited. No person shall walk or ride in any bathing suits, shorts, trunks or other apparel which does not cover properly the body and limbs from midway between the knees and hips to and including the shoulders."

1986

January 2. The Town buys the 516-acre Grace Estate from North Bay Associates, a consortium headed by general partner and negotiator, Ben Heller. Price for the wooded peninsula is $6.3 million, $500,000 of which is paid by The Nature Conservancy, for purchase of conservation easements.

(In 1981, Supervisor Fallon was unable to interest the Town Board in proposing purchase of the property for $3 milion, a price she believed was fair. Two years later, Heller told the Board his asking price was $16 million, a 400 percent mark up over his 1981 purchase price.)

February. Members of the Bay Emergency Action Coalition start to work on a marine sanctuary proposal. Its foundation is the draft of a 1979 State proposal, whose only East End support came from East Hamtpon. Citing home rule, the other towns rejected it on the grounds that it was too stringent on environmental restrictions.

The Coalition was formed last autumn when Dr. Jean Lane of Sag Harbor, Jeanne Marriner of Mattituck, Carol Morrison of Montauk, and others determined that civic action must address the polluted Bay system. In rewriting the proposal, they remove what Marriner calls "threatening" words.

July 14. The State DEC invokes an "indefinite" ban on bass fishing. Of concern are the very high levels of polychlorinated biphenyls (PCB) being found in the fish. Of secondary importance is the bass stock decline in polluted Cheasapeake Bay. The ban is expected to wreak havoc on the commmercial fishermen's livelihood, and to cost the charter fishing industry nearly a third of its annual income.

July 29/31. Tuesday evening, workmen disassemble MortimerB. Zuckerman's eight-foot wide satellite dish TV antenna from its mooring atop a dune. The publisher and his next door Drew Lane neighbors, France Anne and Frazer Dougherty, have been at odds over its presence since last September. The Doughertys say it is an impediment to their once-open view of the beach.

After Mrs. D.'s written pleas to Zuckerman failed and she learned that the Village lacks an appropriate ordinance to enforce its removal, she gathered signatures on a petition. Those who agreed that the dish was "inapropriate... distressing to those who value the serenity and beauty of this wonderful place," included Norman and Barbara Dello Joio, Anne Jackson, Eli Wallach, and Theodore Kheel.

The "mounting" feud made local and Manhattan papers, compelling Zuckerman to respond. He replied that enough trees had been planted, to hide the dish, in time; and, contrary to opinion, he does care about the beach. With no apparent relief in sight, Mrs. Dougherty then called on family friend, William King for help. On July 24, the noted sculptor positioned his response next to the dune on the Dougherty lawn.

"Quixote," an aluminum tube figure astride an aluminum tube Rozinante, faces his "opponent," the dish. In hand, he holds a 40-foot high lance. From it, one of two banners can flap (wind permitting). The 30-foot long orange sailcloth stands for weather foul, or, for peace. The 45-foot long red assault flag, made of aluminized nylon, represents attack or, resting in victory. Raising the assault banner netted the victory.

From Boston, a Zuckerman spokesman phoned in a statement to The Star and to Manhattan dailies: "Don Quixote has had so few victories over time that Mr. Zuckerman has decided to take down the satellite dish until the trees, which have already been planted, have grown large enough to substantially shield it from the beach."

August 15. Citing that "the identity of a people is founded on its past, and the Village...has many significant historic, architectural, and cultural resources which constitute its heritage,..." the Village Board adopts a landmarks law.

It will allow the Village Board "to protect...the landmarks and historic districts which represent distinctive elements of the Village's historic, architectural, and cultural heritage...enhance the Village's attractiveness to visitors and support stimulus to the economy thereby provided..."

(It has been twelve years since the LVIS wrote the Village Board, calling on legal ways to "encourage the preservation and renovation of existing buildings.")

August 22. Yellow tents grace the library lawn. This evening, the East Hampton Free Library holds its first fund raising gala. The $125 tickets admit their holders to a catered dinner and a silent auction. With federal revenue sharing funds at an end, the library no longer is "free."

August 25. In a July letter, asking various organizations to endorse a resolution that it proposes, the Bay Emergency Action Coalition pointed out "disturbing facts." Research has shown that "there is no governmental body, on any level, which is dedicated to protect the Bays; scientific information which would provide a basic understanding of the Bay's ecosystem is lacking; there is no comprehensive management plan for the Bay."

Today, BEAC holds a press conference at the office of the Group for the South Fork. Supporting its plan are representatives from 30 environmental, civic, baymen, and business organizations.

BEAC calls on public officials "to protect the environmental quality of Peconic and Gardiner's Bays," and suggests that a Task Force "develop a comprehensive management plan." With local, county, and state input, the Task Force would coordinate research and funding, inventory significant bay resources, identify potential pollutants and toxins in the waters, and establish a centralized scientific data base.

1987

May 21. The Montauk Lighthouse opens as a museum, under the sponsorship of the Montauk Historical Society. Automation of the beacon has made possible the transfer of tenancy.

September 14. "The Other Side of the Hamptons: Poverty Among Women" is the subject of an evening forum at

Southampton College. Speakers at the East End Organization
for Women event include women from East Hampton.

Lila Hoffman addresses the large discrepancy in lifestyles, in
East Hampton. She tells her audience of 24 women and one
man, "There are so many women and children suffering out
here ... in this particular community. It's so indecent."

October 19. The New York Stock Market plummets.

December 11. The first service is held in The Gates of the
Grove synagogue at the Jewish Center of the Hamptons.

When he designed the Sanctuary, architect Norman Jaffe
called on the traditions of eastern Europe, from where many of
the congregants' ancestors came, and on the region of its locale.
The gentle sloping roof is reminiscent of the Polish shetls. The
west elevation roofline is a series of staggered peaks, in the
shape of yod, the tenth letter of the Hebrew alphabet. The
shingled facade reflects the traditional style of houses found on
the East End. In all else, the building is singular, its interior a
spectacular blend of limestone, wood, and light.

1988

January 1. Starting today, fishermen who sell their catch in the
State must own a commercial fishing license.

July 29. Three years have passed since the *brown tide*
darkened Peconic Bay waters. At a conference on the bays
today, one speaker likens them to a 25-mile long "vast wet
desert, devoid of life." Another points out that even eels, which
can live in polluted waters, are "way down" in numbers.

Secretary of State Gail Shaffer says: "Nowhere is the pressure
on the shoreline more intense than right here....We are
nickeling and diming away our shoreline."

"Save Peconic Bays," BEAC's new name since it received tax
exempt status this year, determines that the Peconic Bays must
receive "national estuary designation," if they are to survive.
This would bring the waters under the Office of Marine
Protection of the U.S. Environmental Protection Agency, and
enable larger financial support for research and monitoring.

1989

May 17. In Manhattan, 47-year old refuse collector, William
Hawkins of East Hampton, is taken into Recovery at Mt. Sinai
Hospital. He is minus a kidney. A short time later, his right
kidney is implanted into Ronald Schellinger, also of East
Hampton. Three months ago, they barely knew each other. But,
on a February day, their wives met in Caldor's, and Rosemary
Hawkins heard that Schellinger had been hospitalized for

months, waiting for a kidney. When she mentioned it to her husband in the evening, Hawkins didn't hesitate before he said, "I'll give him one of mine."

. The effects of the 1987 stock market drop are evident this spring. Housing starts are down and many more "For Sale" signs contribute to the overall South Fork landscape.

August 14. With financial help from The Nature Conservancy, the State buys Barcelona Neck, a 341-acre wooded peninsula surrounded by a large saltmarsh complex. Payment for the State-condemned environmentally sensitive land is $15 million down. Court of Claims will determine the balance.[42]

Recipients of this money are Ben Heller, who paid about $6 million for it in 1981, and his lender. Mid-1988, the latter took steps to foreclose, just as Heller filed plans to subdivide the Neck into 49 lots. In November 1988, the State committed $1 million toward the purchase, if the Town could match the amount.

[The County offered to buy the Neck for $1 million in 1979. Mary Fallon, first as a Republican Town Board member, then as Supervisor, tried to interest the Board in approving the sale. But, regardless of its political majority, the Board did not want to see Barcelona Neck removed from the tax roles.

In 1967, Transcontinental Development Corp., then owner of the Neck and of 25 adjacent acres in Sag Harbor, suggested to the Sag Harbor Trustees that they propose "cluster zoning." If voters approved it, TDC wanted the Village to annex the Neck. With minimum size Village lots set at one quarter an acre, TDC could build 1300+ houses on Barcelona Neck. Appalled by the idea, the Trustees recommended instead minimum half-acre lots. In March 1968, Village voters agreed.

Barcelona Neck is a stop-over for the endangered black duck, and a habitat for least terns, ospreys, marsh hawks, rapin turtles, and other wildlife (possibly, including the rare southern leopard frog, which Larry Penny saw once).

Three hundred years ago, trails led to the salt hay and the town's first harbor, just as they did on the Grace Estate. Eighteen miles of them are walked today, claimed and protected by the Trustees in 1983, after Cathy Lester documented their public ownership.]

December 29. Deborah Ann Light donates 20 acres of Amagansett land to Peconic Land Trust.

Called Quail Hill Preserve, it is home to Quail Hill Farm, a seven-acre organic, biodynamic cooperative which is managed by the Trust.

1990

. The *brown tide* is back.

June 27. The Village Design Review Board informs Richard and Elizabeth Lear that they must restore the Italianate porch to their historic district house, even though it is of a later period.

During the boarding house era, small porches were added to some houses, to give paying guests room for outdoor seating. This porch had benches at each end. In removing the porch, architect Lear sought to highlight the entablature around the front door. When a Board member suggests raising the porch so that "we get our porch and you get your entablature," Lear replies, "...that would make it look worse than it did."

The Board gives Lear 18 months to restore the porch.[43]

November 1. The Retreat's 18-bed shelter opens somewhere in East Hampton. Its address is not given out, in order to protect visiting residents from further physical and emotional battering by an alleged loved one.

Founded in 1986, The Retreat itself came from a need first recognized by Town Police Chief Tom Scott, when he hired psychotherapist Mary Bromley to counsel rape victims. Bromley, who accompanied police officers when they responded to rape reports, discovered that many of the rape victims also were battered women.

After Mrs. Bromley spoke at a meeting of The East Hampton Rotary Club, at which Rotary member Rev. Fredrick Schulz acknowledged that he, too, has been counseling abused parishioners, and has been frustrated in being able to get them out of their abusive environment, a group of citizens organized a committee to found The Retreat and open an office.

A few months after Mrs. Bromley's talk, the Rotary Club pledged $13,000 in seed money towards a shelter. [44]

1991

July 25 After the Lears' experience, new historic districts are a "no-no" this year. At today's meeting of the Village Board of Trustees, Robert Hefner proposes expanding the village district with 262 more properties. It now contain a mere 67.

Lee Avenue resident Martin Fine proposes instead that the village forego any such idea. Saying that his Queen-Ann style house is "*my* house," he tells the Board, "I don't feel that you, or any other people who don't have a financial interest in it, should be telling me what color to paint it."

October 17. Stuart Vorpahl Jr. receives a summons in the mail. It cites him for fishing without a State license.

1992

March 11. In Town Justice Court, Stuart Vorpahl Jr., finishes cross-examining DEC officer Joseph Billotto, and returns to his seat. It is not unreasonable for an observer to think that the prosecuting District Attorney expects Vorpahl's case will self-destruct. Not only is he is defending himself, but, each time Cathy Cahill has asked the bayman if he objected to evidence that she wanted to admit, Vorpahl answered, "No."

Cahill tells Judge Edward W. Horne that she has no more witnesses. The fisherman waits until she has returned to her seat before he rises from his.

He holds a 25-page memorandum of Law, plus an extra page. That sheet lists the questions that he just got through asking Billotto, plus, in capital letters, two instructions: "WAIT TO SEE IF APPOINTED DISTRICT ATTORNEY RESTS. IF NOT, ASK THEM IF THEY REST THEIR CASE, THEN:"

Vorpahl waits. Cahill is silent. Vorpahl leaves his chair. The legs on which he now stands bear no resemblance to those that brought him into Court. His heart is racing. His head is throbbing. His mouth is dry. His hands are shaking.

"Does the State rest its case?" he asks the Court.

Cahill answers, "The State rests."

Reading from the top page, Vorpahl asks the Court to drop the action. He calls section 13-0335 of the State Environmental Conservation Law "unconstitutional," says that it "attempts to usurp the authority and exclusive jurisdiction of the" Town Trustees, as granted under the Nicolls and Dongan Patents, and asserts that the State does not have a Prima Facie Case. He also tells the Court that he is a poor man, without funds to hire an attorney.

Horne calls Vorpahl and Cahill to the bench. Vorpahl hands him his memorandum of 65 "Exhibits." Each one quotes passages from Town Records, both the Nicolls and Dongan Patents, history books, and Court records. The latter include nine cases between 1878 and 1991, in which the Patents were upheld. After Cahill browzes through the Memorandum, Vorpahl understands her to tell the Court that she does not see how the State would be able to respond to it. Horne does respond. Calling Vorpahl a marked man from now on, he advises him to get a fishing license.

Outside the Court room, a D.A. representative with little appreciation for history, brushes away a question with, "He'll never win. He's just quoting old history books."

April 4. Judge Horne renders his decision on the State's suit against Vorpahl: "Apparently at the granting of the Dongan

Patent, the Governor Generals(sic) of some of the colonies imposed a tax on the taking of a whale by the commercial fishermen. However, after the persistent lobbying of Samuel Mulford, a resident of East Hampton Town who was of the same mind as the defendant herein, King James II ordered the Governor Generals(sic) of the Provinces not to tax the taking of the so-called Royale Fish, whale, as it was in the interest of the crown to encourage the commercial fishery and the settlement of fishing villages in the colonies."

Horne concludes,: "The case is dismissed for failure to make out a Prima Facie case." While he has not won his case, Vorpahl has achieved a singular position in commercial fishing. Under the Double Jeopardy clause in the Constitution, he cannot be arrested again for fishing without a license.

July 28. For the past week, the Town has been plastered with posters put up by the Baymen's Association:

"WE FED THE PEOPLE WHO MADE AMERICA
        WATCH US BREAK THE LAW TO FEED THEIR INHERITANCE"

There they are on Amagansett's Indian Wells Beach, this fine Tuesday morning. More than 1000 people have come to watch. A very few will participate. Today's planned non-violent protest is against the State DEC'S continued ban on netting bass. While the State has eased some restrictions on catching the fish, it continues its stranglehold on haul seining, the main support of most of Amagansett's fishing families.

The advance publicity has drawn media representatives from here to Manhattan, a somber platoon of sun-glassed, brown-uniformed State Policemen and sun-glassed, green-uniformed DEC officers, three of the five Town Board members, a tribe of tie-and-suit-clad DEC men, the ever-dwindling colony of local fishermen, plus family members and supporters.

Voices speak out: "Five members of my family had their livelihood taken away from them" ...."We've got to fight this... you're talking about human rights"...."I used to work on an oyster boat in Oyster Bay and dig clams. These people are being economically strangled.".... "We all need to be patient and bring back this resource carefully and slowly."

The last voice belongs to a DEC spokesman. The one before it, to singer/composer Billy Joel, who has a house in Amagansett. It is difficult to comprehend the DEC position. According to its own estimates, the sporties caught 699,694 lbs. worth of striped bass, in 1991, while commercial fishermen took in 105,163 lbs.. In 1990, the "sporties" reeled in 434,177 lbs. against the commercial catch of 81,872 lbs..

While onlookers drink coffee from styrofoam cups and take photographs, the troopers stand apart in small clusters, and an eager soul distributes American flags.

Joel tells a reporter, "Another thing that hasn't been addressed is the consumer. Ninety percent of the bass goes to sports fishermen. Unless you own a boat, you can't get bass."

The time arrives. East Hampton Town Baymen's Association President Dan King and Don Eames climb into King's boat. Engine on, the red and white striped dory, with a blue field of stars on the bow (c. 1976) is launched into the water. As King heads it through the surf, Eames casts off the net, and cheers and whistles fill the salt air. (Seven years ago, the effects of the *brown tide* and increased DEC restrictions on bass fishing forced Eames to leave the waters for a land-based job.)

The launch truck with one end of the net tied to it, stays parked, while a second truck stretches the net some 400 feet down the beach. As the protest is played out, one officer starts his cam corder, while a trooper adjusts field glasses.

Nearly two hours later, winches on the two trucks haul in the net. A pair of labs cavorts around the splashing catch while the faithful crowd, not much smaller than earlier, closes in. In no particular order, Joel, Town Supervisor Bullock, Town Board member Cathy Lester, Town Natural Resources Director Larry Penny, Village Administrator Larry Cantwell, Town Planning Board Chair Pat Mansir, Baymen Association Secretary Arnold Leo and some twelve others take bass, as it is handed to them, and walk up the beach. For that, they and King and Eames each receive a DEC citation for being in possession "of undersized bass" or, for taking striped bass by other than angling.

September 2. The holders of the DEC summonses appear in Court. All plead not guilty. Trial date is November 25.

From behind a bank of microphones set up outside the Court, King tells reporters that the bass ban has cut his income in half. "I woke up with nothing to do. We had to leave the ocean and go to the bay. The pie in the bay had to be divided among more fishermen." The *brown tide* aftermath has left King and his crew "hanging by our finger nails." Emphasizing that baymen are not against *conservation*, he adds: "With bass stocks high and not being allowed to take our fair share ...this is discrimination."

Joel reads: from a prepared statement: "I am not anti-sportfishing.... I am for equitable allocation of a resource which all New Yorkers are entitled to." Then, responding to the spoilsport cries of a neophyte Lyndenhurst alliance, United Gamefish Anglers, he continues, "If people boycott my recordings because they are directed to...they are being manipulated by the same forces of censorship which have kept people from hearing both sides of this issue. I must question why these people don't want commercial fishermen to make a living,...and think that I and others who disagree... should be put in jail...."

Addressing his unsuccessful efforts over the last decade "to gain relief from the unholy cabal that controls the striped bass issue," Bullock says that the "political process is eliminating a way of life for our fishing families that has endured for hundreds of years."

March 12. Justice Ketcham renders his Decision on the Indian Wells Beach protesters. He dismisses all the charges. His reason? "Legal insufficiency of the accusatory instrument."

Arnold Leo and Larry Cantwell and others saw that the tickets were being written incorrectly. Yet, when they brought it to the attention of one officer, who was writing one of them incorrectly, he shrugged his shoulder and continue writing. How were they deficient? The number which is entered at the top of the ticket is supposed to correspond to the charge that is written out in at the bottom of the ticket. Nothing matched. Does that mean a conspiracy was afoot? (Who would admit to it?) The DEC denies it.[45]

September 9. Congressman George Hochbrueckner informs the East End that the Federal Environmental Protection Agency has entered Peconic Bay into its system as "an estuary of national significance."

One million dollars in federal funds will be allocated for the system, each of the next three years. How it will be spent will be decided by a group of federal, state, scientific, and citizen action committee members.

Hochbrueckner credits Billy Joel with helping to activate Federal interest. In 1991, Joel and then-County Executive Pat Halpin lobbied in Washington for the bill's passage. Because House speaker Tom Foley's daughter is an avid fan of the singer, Foley had a ten-minute chat with him. He was impressed enough by the entertainer's commitment to the issue, to move the languishing Peconic Bay study funding from the back burner of House priorities, to a front one.

(A question begs to be answered: If Foley's daughter had not been an ardent fan of the entertainer, would the bill still be simmering somewhere in Congress?

Whatever the excuse that may be offered as an answer, if it hadn't been for the four private citizens who, following the *brown tide* devatastation, founded the Bay Emergency Action

Coaltion and forged the route that led to today, there would
have been no reason for Billy Joel to be in the nation's capitol
on behalf of the Bay.)

Postscript

1993

September 1. With today's publication of The East Hampton
Independent, the Town has its second weekly newspaper. It will
be published on Wednesdays. The newspaper's *raison d'etre* is
addressed in its editorial: "Why The Independent? The birth of
a newspaper is not unlike the birth of a nation. It comes from
similar grumblings - in the belly of the people - to be heard, to
be represented, to be understood....We seek a middle ground by
which to negotiate our differences and celebrate our natural
resources - the land and the people."

November 29/December 3. For the past year, the Village
Design Review Board has compelled a consortium to rethink
its design proposals for the vacant Red Horse shopping
complex, that it bought. Calling the three buildings an
extension of Main Street, even though they are a mile distant
from that street, the Board wants a uniform look for the stores
that will reflect the Main Street ambiance.

Many changes later, the Red Horse partners received a
certificate of occupancy for their buildings. In summer 1993,
The Independent, Architrove, and Jerry & David's Red Horse
Market became the first three tenants. (Jerry and David are two
of the consortium's six members. When not behind the counter
of their market, they are New York business man and East
Hampton Village Zoning Board of Appeals member, David
Silver, and New York advertising legend Jerry Della Femina..)

In October 1993, pumpkins on bales of hay were placed on
the market's green. That display led the Village to issue the
market a summons, citing 18 violations.

Why the fuss over pumpkins that never turned into gold
coaches? The Village sign ordinance recognizes any outdoor
display as a "sign." Permits are required for such displays. This
"sign" does not have one. Neither does the Village Hardware,
nor The Golden Eagle, and Bermuda Bicycles, all of whom
have been displaying merchandise outdoors, without a permit -
and, *without* Village comment - for over 15 years each.

November 29. Moments after Justice Ketcham dismisses most
of the counts against Della Femina and Silver, he asks the Town
attorney, "What do you want to do now?"

"Have him arrested," Scott Allen answers.

Outside Court, Allen answers a question: "I understood that Della Femina was reluctant to appear in Court."

"This whole episode is like a bad Abbott and Costello movie," Della Femina comments when he hears about the warrant.

Dec. 3. Three days after turning themselves in the first time, only to be told that they couldn't be arrested that day because the officer in charge, who had the day off, hadn't done the paper work, the partners return to the scene of their "crime."

Followed by an entourage of TV and print reporters, they drive to Village police headquarters. There, because of the pumpkins on the market green, and the plants, cut flowers and the newspaper stand on the private sidewalk outside the market's entrance to the parking lot, the two men are handcuffed and taken in a squad car to Town Justice Court.

1994

May 29. Enez Whipple's "Guild Hall in East Hampton - an Adventure in the Arts" is published. In words and pictures, Guild Hall's Director Emeritus has covered the cultural center's first sixty years.

June 13. Justice Ketcham dismisses 23 of the 27 "pumpkin charges" against Silver and Della Femina.. In his 10-page Court Decision, Ketcham calls the Village sign ordinance too broad.

He finds that, while the market's outdoor displays qualify as *objects* that may bring attention, "...they fail to utilize letters, words or figures, and to maintain that their natural 'color' suffices..." would be "beyond reasonable interpretation and normal understanding."

Following the decision, Della Femina reiterates his contention that the episode has been one of "selective enforcement." He calls the Village suit against him "a disgrace," including "using the East Hampton Police, one of the best forces in the country, for the tedious dwelling on these charges."

Asked a question, he answers, "If I had a choice to do this all over again, I would have those pumpkins outside so fast. It gave me a chance to know a little bit more about myself. I also learned a lot about East Hampton. People here are decent. Good. Only a handful are trying to hang on to the power that they had. It is like the last days of the Soviet Union. The people who had the power can't understand why the populace doesn't want to go along with them, anymore.....Did you know that I received over 800 letters about this? That number is more than voted in the last Village election."

"Did he ever tell you what somebody on the DRB tried to do, the night before Della Femina's Restaurant was to open?" asks Della Femina's wife, TV journalist Judy Licht.[47]

June 25. Robert David Lion Gardiner is honored at The South Fork Natural History Society's annual dinner/dance. SoFo is recognizing Gardiner for "fostering the study of Gardiner's Island's social and natural history," by allowing scientists to continue documenting life on the island, when he is in residence. [48]

July 10. This evening, as they have done before, a number of year-round and part-time residents drive to Boys Harbor, the camp for underprivileged children that Anthony Duke founded in 1937, originally in Southampton. He was 17, at the time.

They pick up a group of six-to-nine year olds; then, traveling in a caravan of cars, return to their respective homes for a picnic supper and games. Two of the hosts are Nancy and Joe Scheerer. For the past 25 years, she has organized the picnic forays, asking different friends to welcome the younger children in July, the teenagers, in August

Mrs. Scheerer's father, Bishop Austin Pardue of Pittsburgh, helped generate community interest in Boys Harbor. The Pardues had a summer cottage in East Hampton. On occasion, he conducted Sunday service at St. Luke's Church. Duke had been bringing the inner-city campers, then small in number, to the church. Though they sat in the back, the congregation gave all indication of being less than enthusiastic with their presence.

A week after asking Duke how the community was reacting to Boys Harbor, and hearing that response was next to nil (save for derogatory signs that were nailed to the gates), Bishop Pardue announced from the pulpit, "I want to see everybody who is here, a week from today at Boys Harbor. It's going to have a fair. Come meet the children and the counselors, and have some fun."

Unmoved by the pronounced groans, Bishop Pardue offered a solution: "I can have the doors to the church shut, and let you out when I see all the hands of the people who will go."

He gave the order. The doors were shut. The hands went up.

"Ninety-five of those people showed up," Duke says this Sunday. "That is how Boys Harbor started to make friends with the Maidstone Club set, and with the community. That was the beginning of a very positive relationship between the Town and ourselves."[49]

ENDNOTES

1. The *Mayflower Compact* lasted ten years in the Plymouth colony. It served as the basis for the future government established there.

2. "Mr. Farrett's Island" is Shelter Island.

3. On page 23 of Judge Hedges' history of East Hampton an incorrect word is used in quoting East Hampton's Covenant. "...which we now possess." should read "...which we now profess."

4. New York Province remained under feudal control of the Lord or, Lady, of the manor of East Greenwich, in the County of Kent, until the Revolutionary War. Ownership of the manor descended to subsequent heirs of the last Lord or Lady, all of whom also succeeded to the English throne.

5. The "Charter of Lyberties & Privileges," on which the colonial government of New York Province was based, is the first covenant in the world in which the phrase "the people" appears. King Charles II rejected its authority because of that phrase, but, the New York Assembly already had adopted it.

6. Kidd was taken to London for trial. After being found guilty on five charges of being a pirate and one of murder, he was hanged. A piece of the cloth of gold which he gave Mrs. Gardiner is in the Long Island Collection of the East Hampton Library.

7. Take a walk through American history, with Samuel Mulford at your side. You won't find him in history books. But long before tea sank in Boston Harbor and the Bill of Rights and the Constitution were written, this man defied a colonial governor and the laws of a mother country, in the name of equal representation, fair taxation, and freedom to trade.

   Read his speeches to the Assembly and you might think he had drafted the Bill of Rights.

8. East Hampton's embargo against British goods preceded that which Continental Congress proposed.

9. The Academy name was changed to Clinton Academy after Gov. George Clinton came to East Hampton, to give a speech. He presented the school with the bell. It originally came from New York City.

   During the Revolutionary War, colonials removed the bells, rather than let them fall into British hands and be melted down for cannon balls. They were sent to Carlisle, Pa., where, if needed, the Americans would melt them down. However, enough ammunition was captured at the Battle of Saratoga to preclude that action. After the war, New York City asked for return of its bells.

10. When the Beecher children helped their father prepare his autobiography, he told them about their mother making the first rug in East Hampton: "There was not a store in town, and all our purchases were made in New York by a small schooner that ran once a week.

"There was not a carpet from end to end of town. All had sanded floors, some of them worn through...Uncle Lot gave me some money and I had an itch to spend it, bought a bale of cotton. She spun it and had it woven; then, she laid it down, sized it, and painted it in oils, with a border all around it, and bunches of roses and other flowers over the centre. She sent to New York for her colors, and ground and mixed them herself. The carpet was nailed down on the garrett floor and she used to go up there and paint."

The finished rug was placed in the front room. When Deacon Talmage came to visit he was afraid to walk on it. After staring at it for a while, he asked Rev. Beecher, "D'ye think you can have all that, <u>and heaven, too</u>?"

(Though altered, the Beecher house still stands at the corner of Main Street and Huntting Lane. It was bought in the spring of 1994 by the Village, to serve as its new Village Hall. The Village Police Dept. will have a sub-station there, mostly for use by the foot patrolmen. A small fireproof addition is being added to the historic house, to hold official records.)

11. After she became mistress of the nation's White House, Julia Gardiner Tyler brought several changes to Washington. She made dancing part of every social White House event. She initiated the custom of the White House band playing "Hail to the Chief," whenever the President made an appearance. She also helped secure the annexation of Texas, by lobbying for it ácross the country.

12. During the Civil War, it was not unusual at night, when fighting stopped, to hear Rebel and Union soldiers singing Payne's "Home Sweet Home" to each other.

13. The bell from the "John Milton" rests today on a table at the entrance to the Presbyterian Session House. It is mounted on a stand, enabling it to be rung. Among effects found were the ship's log and, in various jacket pockets, letters. One mother wrote her son, "No one knows my feelings but myself and God." Another, already a widow from a sea disaster, wrote to two sons, both on the "John Milton," about

their brother Daniel "going down to death in all his youthful beauty. With high hopes and lofty aims, thou hast gone out with the tide, leaving only a loving memory engraved on our hearts like ripples in the ocean, to show where thy bark of life has foundered."

The headstone for the "John Milton" crew reads, "This stone was erected by individual subscription from various places to mark the spot where with peculiar solemnity were deposited the mortal remains of the three mates and eighteen of the crew of the ship 'John Milton' of New Bedford." (Captain Harding's body was sent home.)

14. John Wallace arrived in East Hampton, in the spring of 1840. He came with a man servant and a Scottish brogue, but without a history that he was willing to share. Wallace lived at the local inn for the first five years. Then, having made new friends, he moved into the Main Street house of Dr. Abel Huntington and his daughter, Cornelia. He boarded with them until the last night of 1870 when, on his eightieth birthday, he died in his sleep.

From stories passed through generations, it appears that Wallace was a learned man, active in village affairs, revered by all who knew him, and of help to any one who sought his counsel. He was instrumental in the founding of St. Luke's Episcopal Church, for which he was a licensed lay reader.

Who was John Wallace?

According to information, said to have been uncovered long after his death, he was born John Wood in Edinburgh in 1785. After schooling, he achieved prominence as a lawyer, scholar, and civic leader, before rising to the esteemed office of Lord High Sheriff of Peebleshire.

(The office of High Sheriff usually was held by a wealthy land owner. After the Norman Conquest in 1066, it became the highest government position in each shire. The High Sheriff ran the shire and answered only to the Crown. When the High Sheriff's office was established in New York province - see *1655* entry - its holder answered to the Deputy-Governor.)

One story alludes to close relatives, an inheritance, and Wood/Wallace's warning that he would put the Atlantic Ocean between him and them, should they bring suit against him. The suit is said to have ended ten years later, in his favor, providing him with money that reached him each month through a banking agent in New York City.

Another story says that one night, the Lord High Advocate of Edinburgh asked a friend to warn John Wood that a grave charge had been made against him and he would be arrested in the morning.

Denying anything beyond a mere indiscretion - if even that - John Wood is said to have "died out of Scotland" that night.

John Wood/Wallace is buried in the South End Cemetery, near the cburch which contains a memorial window to him. A picture of John

Wood hangs in the library, in the corridor of stacks that lead to the Long Island Collection.

15. The bridge by amateurs eventually fell upon hard times, crumbled, and is no more.

16. Besides being used to insulate houses, seaweed was used as a fertilizer. It was common for farmers to drive to a beach and fill their carts with the marine plant. But, there came a time when some waterfront land owners objected to this. They viewed the beach as part of their property, and seaweed collectors as trespassers. To keep out the alleged interlopers, they threatened them, they built water fences, and they erected barricades of one kind and another. Thus was born the seed for what would become a lengthy and costly lawsuit.

Relying on the Dongan Patent wording, the Trustees saw the beach as *their* property, which they held for the Town. The *September 19, 1853* entry in the Trustees Journal shows that they resolved to defend any suit brought against someone for picking up seaweed.

A couple of cases ensued and, as promised, the Trustees took up the defendants' cause. But the suit that proved costly for both sides began in 1873. The defendant was Josiah Kirk, a farmer from Ireland, who had bought the old Mulford Farm in Northwest. It fronted on Shelter Island Sound.

The Trustees initiated an ejectment suit against Kirk after he emptied David Sherry's wagon of seaweed. They rested their case on the previous property owner's boundary line, which was said to have been at the cliff. The Trustees claimed that the Town owned the beach between that cliff and the high water mark. Kirk countered that, over time, the water had encroached upon the beach and had taken that Town property unto an during litigation was that those who settled Northwest in the 18th century nearly always referred to their land, if it ran to the water, as being bounded by the bay, the harbor, the water, etc. Reference never was made to it being bounded by Trustee or Town-owned beach/land.)

The suit came to Court in October 1874 but took seven years to conclude. Judge Gilbert ruled in Kirk's favor without even hearing the case. General Term of the Supreme Court upheld his decision, but the Town would not hear of that, and appealed. Appeals Court ruled that the case should have been put to a jury. It went to trial. The verdict came down on Kirk's side. Again the Town appealed. Appeals ruled for Kirk. But, by then he was dead, having spent his last months in an almshouse, broke from the costly suit.

The suit is said to have cost Kirk $40,000, and the Town a considerable amount in legal fees and judgment to pay. To help meet that obligation, the Town sold shore fronts of Hick's Island, Fresh Pond,

Cedar Beach, Point of Pines, and some of South Beach in Amagansett for $400.

17. In May 1889, the Trustees' suit against John Bowman was decided in favor of the Town. Bowman appealed. A second trial took place in October. The Town won. Bowman appealed again. The case was heard in General Court in May 1890 and one year later, the Court ruled for the Town. Bowman's deeds were voided and the land reverted to the Town. Two hundred dollars of the judgment rendered against Dominy was given to Bowman. The Court believed that he acted in good faith, when he bought the forged documents. All other deeds to underwater lands also were voided.

18. In his introduction to "Journal of the Trustees - 1897-1925," Henry D. Sleight wrote that executing the quit claims "worked wonders for Amagansett, Georgica, and Wainscott...it enabled descendants and heirs of original proprietors to sell ocean front and beach bank sites to city sojourners. These annual visitors to East Hampton, attracted by the many fine features of the locality....were enabled to buy and occupy lands and establish a summer colony along the ocean front."

According to what various Trustee Board members told Sleight, these quit claims did more towards the Town's growth and prosperity than anything else, including arrival of the railroad and that of good roads, after cars came into vogue.

Speaking of those dunes, on August 16, 1968, owners of oceanfront summer estates that cover the three-plus miles from Indian Wells Highway in Amagansett to the Maidstone Club, agreed to an idea that they had been mulling for some time. The 14 home owners who were in residence that day signed an agreement "to refrain from building any structures on the dunes south of a line which has been determined substantially in accordance with existing structures." The life of the agreement is 50 years. Among its signers, were Evan Frankel, Ben Heller, Henry Mann, William Hutton, John Kluge, and James Tyson.

19. The Ramblers still meet once a month, October through June. In the early years, its members would select a country to study. Committees would research different aspects of that country, each one giving a report during the year. According to Ginnie Schenck, while the format remains the same, meetings in the 1990s are lighter and more entertaining.

20. Art on the lawn still is a no-no in the Village's historic·district, and out of it. Seventy years after Brouwer failed, the noted East Hampton sculptor, William King, fared no better when he tried to interest the Village Trustees in a similar venture. King proposed that the green

across from the East Hampton Veterinary Group be a showcase for works of local sculptors.

He suggested that one piece of art be on display for six months and, if all went well, that it be replaced by another work, by another local artist. At all times, the Village Board would have final approval on what would be shown. In 1986, the idea was turned down again.

21. The artist Alfonso Ossorio bought the Herters' 55-acre estate from their second son, Christian A. Herter, in 1949. Mr. Ossorio covered the stucco with black paint, painted the window and door trims red and blue, and closed up some of the waterfront windows, to provide more wall space for his artwork. Because he lived year-round in East Hampton, Ossorio replaced the Herters' summer gardens with evergreen gardens. At his death in 1991, the property had become an arboretum with a 1000 varieties of rare evergreens. Since Ron Perleman, CEO of Revlon, bought the property from the Ossorio estate in 1993, the black, red, and blue paint has been stripped, and the house is being restored to its original look.

22. In 1936, fifteen year old Phineas Dickinson of Montauk revived cattle grazing on Montauk during the summer. He leased Indian Field from the Montauk Development Co. and charged six dollars a season (May 1 to November 1) per cow. Cattle from Southampton and Riverhead (and, according to his brother, Frank, "maybe a few from Patchogue") were trucked to a holding pen on Roy Lester's Pantigo Road farm. From there, on horseback, Dickinson and his brothers drove between 100 and 200 cows eastward. The seasonal grazing lasted until World War II.

23. Two days after the Germans landed in Amagansett and took the train to Manhattan, one of them decided to let the FBI in on their secret. Thirty-nine year old George Dasch, who had lived in the U.S. during part of the 1920s, confided his plans to fellow spy, Ernest Burger. Though surprised by the idea, the naturalized American, Burger, agreed to it.

While Dasch was preparing his astonishing move, the FBI was grilling Cullen. The agents didn't believe the young man. They thought that he could be part of a liquor smuggling operation, and was trying to cover up something that had gone wrong. The idea that spies might really be on American soil was hard to accept (especially in view of the line of radar towers that ran along the shore, from Montauk westwards.

Dasch called the FBI's Manhattan office, recounted his arrival, and said that he was going to Washington, where he wanted to speak with Hoover. The Washington agents were stunned when Dasch told them about the impending June 17 landing at Ponte Vedra, Fla. and that it was one of many to take place. If that was not news enough, any feelings of

American invincibility were quashed when Dasch pulled from his pocket a white handkerchief. On it, in invisible ink, were the names and addresses of a network of spies in full operation across the country.

Rationalizing that it would not do well for American morale (or, for himself) if it became known that the spies landed with such ease on American soil, the cunning FBI chief hid the truth, even from Congress. Hoover let the world-at-large believe that he and his men outsmarted the Germans.

After a military trial in Washington found the eight saboteurs guilty, six were electrocuted immediately, Dasch and Burger received stiff sentences, and the young Coast Guard sailor from Bayside, Queens spent the better part of the war as a good will ambassador for the U.S.. Cullen went from bond rally to parade to bond rally to interview, etc.. In 1948, President Truman pardoned the two Germans and they returned to Germany. Dasch later wrote about his experiences.

Vincent Grabowski, whose Coast Guard duties included beach patrol, told the author that before the spies landed, "patrolling" pretty much meant standing more than it did walking.

24. What would East Hampton Village look like today if the LVIS never had been founded? Walk and drive through the Village. Look at the elm trees that span Main Street (and the younger ones that will, in time). Look at elms everywhere within the Village - as the Village grew, the LVIS extended its concern beyond Main Street. That they are still here is due to the Tree Committee's concerted effort to save them when any elm is hit with disease. (The Committee also cares for other trees.)

Stroll across the green, enjoy the sight of the pond. The Greens Committee continues to pay for the green's upkeep and act as a watchdog over the pond. Have you noticed the trees and bushes and flowers and fencing at the railroad station, this year? Guess who cares for them.

In addition to these projects and to those mentioned in chapter four, the LVIS sponsors scholarships and book awards, decorates the Christmas tree at the sheep pound (across from the post office), and those along Main Street and Newtown Lane. It continues to work closely with the Village Board of Trustees, to see that nothing intrudes upon the Village's historic beauty. With high respect, the LVIS well could be called the "shadow government" of East Hampton Village.

25. Krasner was her husband's sole heir. When she died in 1984, her will established the Pollock/Krasner Foundation, to benefit needy artists. Krasner directed her executors to give her house and barn, and the land on which they stand, to the organization that would accept them, on her conditions. The buildings were to be converted "into a public museum and library...to accumulate and make available for study books, catalogs,

and other reference material relating to the work of artists who have lived on eastern Long Island."

Instead of being inundated with phone calls and letters of interest, Krasner's executors received very few. The gift came with strings. It had to be accepted within three years. No endowment would accompany the property and, save for six silk screen paintings by Pollock and the artists' considerable art book collection, the buildings would be bare.

Guild Hall and the East Hampton Historical Society submitted proposals. Both hinged on the Krasner estate including some funds with the gift, but Krasner's executors would not break the will. In the end, the Stony Brook Foundation, a non-profit affiliate of State University of New York at Stony Brook, accepted the gift.

Overlooking Accabonac Creek, the Pollock-Krasner House & Study Center, as it was named, is open by appointment only, from May to October. With Helen A. Harrison as its Director, scholars have access to the art library, including the personal collections of the artists, the oral history library, the art archives, and the visual facilities.

26. The Signa Gallery lasted four years. It closed because its three owners tired of spending more time on it than at work, in their own studios. Reminiscing about the gallery, Charlotte Park told the author, "The Signa Gallery was a wonderful thing for all of us." (She and her husband, the painter James Brooks, were part of the Abstract Expressionist movement,) "It was a place to show. It was well done. The whole movement brought excitement in the air, and it hasn't happened since.

"Everybody went to everybody else's studio and talked about each other's work. It was an exciting, sharing time. There was no jealousy, no problem then, because nobody sold. On the rare occasion when something did sell, you used to call up your artist friends at midnight, to share the news.

"Then people with money began to buy art as an investment. They would buy a work one year and put it up for auction the next year. While this didn't put large sums of money into the pocket of the individual artist, because he/she already had sold that particular work some time ago, news of the auction sales helped reputations, and some of the artists were able to raise their prices a little. But, not everyone fared as well. So, you stopped making those late night calls, in case your friend still hadn't sold. Those damn auction houses really screwed things up."

Asked about Guild Hall's reaction to the artists, Park said,

"In those days, the people who ran Guild Hall - its Trustees, not Enez Whipple, its Director - were really hostile towards us. I remember going to openings there and you could just feel the ice. Here were these ladies serving tea from silver tesapots, and here were these crude, crummy artists hanging around. But, they finally gave in. East Hampton has changed and now accepts them.

"It's true that, in the beginning, Abstract work was hard to take. It was completely different from anything that they ever had seen. There was nothing representational in it for them to recognize. What could they find in it? So, they weren't really at fault. We gave them a hard time!"

27. Robert Cooper explained his appointment as "The outgrowth of complaints and the protest march that followed the 1968 arrest of bank robbers. Village police, in search of the robbers are said to have thought nothing of stopping Black men and women on the street, at gun point, or, of going into one Black resident's house without a search warrant. Worse yet, when 15 protesters marched to County Deputy Sheriff Richard Webb's house on Floyd Street, he came outside and fired a gun into the air.

After a hearing in Town Justice Court on Dec. 17, 1968 acquitted Webb of "reckless endangerment and menacing," charges, the then-County Executive H. Lee Dennison commented, "The complainants received poor advice."

Cooper said, "There was no minority represented on the village or town police force. Men with whom I went to school recommended me. The late Sergeant Ronald Adams came to my house and talked to me about the force. Then, as if to reaffirm Adams' visit, the new police chief came to the IGA where I was working. He caught me as I was carrying packages to a customer's car. He said, 'We need you.' I told him I would have to talk to my wife about it. But, the crisis was at such a point that it became a civic and moral duty to say 'yes'."

Two days later, Cooper was measured for a uniform. The next day, it was ready. He was sworn in, given a gun and a car, and told to go out, then and there. "We want you visible on the street," he quoted Doyle telling him. Out he went, without a minute's worth of police training or any instructions on how to handle a gun. "I never had one in my hand, before that day."

His first crisis occurred within a couple of days. Cooper had to handle an accident on Napeague. "It was bad. The cars were wrecked and people were injured. My adrenaline was flowing, the wind was blowing, and my papers were flying all over. I didn't know how to write up an accident report. But, Charlie Disunno, whose Amagansett firm handled removing wrecks for the Town, knew. He told me to calm down and helped me write it up."

In the days that followed, fellow officers Paul Greenwood and Russ Sanders took Cooper aside, gave him advice, and told him how to handle situations that might occur. That was the extent of his official training.

28. Tried in East Hampton, the Gwathmey/Durham case was decided in their favor. The State Attorney General appealed, and the case went to the Supreme Court. The Supreme Court tossed out the State's appeal, declared illegal the Section on which it had been based, and overturned the statute. Rabinowitz, who has an E.H. home, and the Emergency Civil Liberties Union donated their services to the case.

Rosalie Gwathmey: "Victor was wonderful. He came up with all kinds of information. He cited Spiro Agnew (U.S. Vice President, under Richard Nixon) who wore a T-shirt with the American flag on it, and Raquel Welch, who had a bathing suit with a flag on her behind .... The mistake that many people made is that they thought that I had superimposed something over the stars in the blue field. I hadn't done that, at all. There weren't any stars on it. It never was a flag."

Bill Durham: "The East Hampton police were fantastic. They didn't want to arrest Bob, but they were forced to after Miller, who was a retired Navy man, filed his complaint. This was a very distasteful part of my life. But I'm glad we did it. We both received threatening calls and Bob's house had paint thrown on it. I was an active member of the Amagansett Fire Department, at the time. While most of the volunteer firemen didn't agree with my thinking, they kept my house from deliberately being set on fire."

29. Carol Morrison, one of CCOM's earliest members, told the author, "Our concern was to save Hither Woods and prevent overdevelopment along the shore. Hilda Lindley was the driving force behind the organization. She had been in New York during the winter and her house, not too far from the lighthouse, would have been swept up in the proposed development. When we first started, we wondered what else possibly could arise that would need our attention!"

30. Many people believe that Pamela Brown decided at the last minute to accompany her husband on the balloon flight. According to her closest friend, Genie Chipps Henderson of Springs, Malcolm Brighton gave the actress permission to join the crew, earlier in the summer. He told her that there was room, the added weight (she was very thin) would not be a burden, and having her aboard would be an asset. Another pair of hands. Another pair of eyes. Wrong conclusions were reached because Brown had not wanted her mother, who was ill in Brazil, to hear about her plans until just before lift-off. When she phoned Saturday night, her mother begged her not to go.

Weather conditions were relayed to the Andersons by Dr. Vincent Gardona of New York University. According to a friend of the balloonists, they did not learn of the storm north of them until an hour before they hit it. Yet, afterwards, when other meteorologists were shown weather maps of existing conditions that week-end, this same friend said that each one saw the storm on it, that it was predictable, well ahead of time.

31. Book Hampton "quenched a thirst" on the South Fork. "The two Georges" found themselves with customers willing to drive from Southampton, Sag Harbor, and Montauk, even in the heat of summer traffic, to buy books. In time, Caldwell gave up New York and opened Book Hampton South in Southampton. Not too long afterwards, Sag Harbor had its very own Book Hampton.

Book Hampton was the first shop in town to carry video rentals and the first to recognize that the South Fork had a growing Spanish-reading population. Since the E.H. store's 1994 move into two-story quarter, the partners have introduced occasional late Saturday afternoon readings by authors of their works.

32. In its first twenty-one years, the Group, now known as The Group for the South Fork, has had a significant influence on the South Fork landscape. Under the leadership of Nancy Goell, who succeeded Marceau as Director, then, of Nancy Nagle Kelley, the Group has kept in focus its purpose - to preserve the beauty and rural character of the area, and educate the public. To this end, it monitored government meetings; made suggestions to local, County, and State governments; took a local government Board to Court, when it found that proposed legislation threatened a sensitive area of the environment; and conducted environmental education workshops, in schools and for civic groups.

In 1975, the Group won its suit against East Hampton's Planning Board, which had given preliminary approval to development of "Gansett Dunes" over 44 acres of dunes, marshlands, cranberry bogs, and bluff. It led the 1979 fight to oppose rezoning part of Napeague for a series of motels, and sued the Planning Board for approving the site plan. And, it was instrumental in saving Barcelona Neck, the northern half of Hither Woods, and the Grace Estate, from development.

After the County Legislature's 1976 adoption of the Group's proposed idea of saving farmland, the County Purchase of Development Rights Program subsequently became a national model for farmland protection. The Group helped secure passage of the New York State Environmental Quality Bond Act in 1986, sponsored Save the Bay's 1986 press conference on the brown tide, which led to formation of the County's Brown Tide Task Force, and helped the Town launch its recycling program in 1987.

Since 1983, the Group has planted thousands of trees and shrubs in areas of the Town that need restoration, seeded local waters with shellfish, and erected osprey towers, woodduck boxes, and bluebird boxes. In 1991, the organization initiated the annual Great East End Clean-up, in which hundreds of volunteers removed and remove tons of garbage from dozens of sites on the South Fork. It had an important role in the concept and 1993 passage of the State's Pine Barrens Protection Act Bill, which includes a provision for East Hampton. In two years, the Town can join the Pine Barrens' Joint Policy and Planning Commission, which will enable it to take advantage of the Bill's guaranteed Environmental Protection Act. The Act is a dedicated funding source for land acquisition and other environmental purposes, at the State level.

33. George Plimpton gave up his Devon neighbors for more congenial surroundings. He moved to Sagaponack where he held several pyrotechnic galas, almost without incident. The exception was a tiny spark which dropped onto the shoulder of one man. He sued Plimpton for $11 million. The nuisance suit was settled out of Court, and pianist Cy Coleman, at whose Southampton home the man with the shoulder was staying, allegedly hasn't spoken to his former guest, since.

On the other hand, Plimpton has taken his love of fireworks to greater heights. Every summer, he and Fireworks by Grucci donate their time (in the case of the Gruccis, also their product) to an evening spectacular over Accabonac Harbor that benefits Boys Harbor. Plimpton (who always brings at least a couple of celebrity friends, to add an extra ounce of glamour or excitement to the evening) acts as the master of ceremonies. The evening gets off to an explosive start with a series of dedication shells, Plimpton announcing in whose memory or honor each one is shooting off into the night sky.

Fireworks guests can buy general admission tickets, which allow them to bring a picnic supper and spread themselves out on the Boys Harbor grounds. Or, they can buy the considerably more expensive tickets, relax on Luly and Tony Duke's front lawn and partake of a prepared picnic dinner.

34. The Beale house passed inspection. Today, their house, at the corner of West End Road is owned by former Washington Post editor, Ben Bradlee, and his wife, Sally Quinn.

Mrs. Beale was a sister of John Vernou Bouvier Jr., faher of Jacqueline Bouvier Onassis. Following her birth at Southampton Hospital in August 1929, Mrs. Onassis' parents brought her to the house they had rented in East Hampton, at the corner of Egypt and David Lanes. When that house fronted on Main Street in the 19th century, it was known as Rowdy Hall. It was a place where the young men - especially the artists - could stay. Ergo its "name."

Mrs. Onassis' paternal grandparents had a large house on Further Lane, in which she spent many summers, until her parents divorced. A "treat" for the chilldren was when their Aunt Edie Beale dropped in. She invariably would go to the piano and entertain the children with music and song.

In 1992, a County Housing inspector, who requested anonymity, said:

"The Beale incident never should have happened. The County came to realize that. It was an infringement on a person's rights to live as he or she may choose. Now, if a complaint is made, it must be made by the person who is being affected directly by the living conditions.

"In 1970, Part 21 of the State Sanitary code which was adopted by the newly-formed County Legislature, when it created Suffolk's Housing code regulations, allowed the Beale inspection. It became Article 14, several years later, when it was put into the County Sanitary code. It was repealed by the County Legislature in 1992."

35. In 1987, East Hampton Baymen joined other New York State commercial fishermen in a lawsuit against General Electric, charging loss of income due to the high levels of PCB found in bass. With the case scheduled to begin in State Supreme Court on August 19, 1993, GE decided to settle out of Court. Under the agreement reached on August 11, the corporation would endow a $7 million fund to benefit between 300 and 400 commercial fishermen.

36. As of 1994, the "drug bust" remains the largest marijuana seizure in Long Island history. Forty thousand pounds were seized, and, in spite of million dollar legal bills incurred on behalf of each defendant, all 33 of them were convicted and sentenced to from seven years to life."

"At the time," Lia said, much later, "I don't think we realized how big this operation was. It was nationally financed by organized crime."

37. Impetus for the research came in the mid '70s, with news that the State's Dept. of Transportation planned to widen Route 27, which becomes Main Street as it runs through each South Fork village

In its wake would go part of East Hampton's Village green and portions of historic properties. LVIS President June Kelly appointed a committee of three to go to Albany and try to stop DOT's plans. With help from Supervisor Hope, Albany listened. The New York State Historical Society then proposed that the LVIS inventory those houses and properties of historic and architectural value, which might be affected by a widened highway, interest the village in creating a historic district, and apply for admission onto the State's Register of Historic Landmarks. In 1988, the historic district was entered on the National Register.

38. Karl Grossman: "LILCO felt that East End people should stay home and take shelter in their basements. This would be alright if the houses were made of cement....The story of Shoreham, the tale of Shoreham is a story or tale of nuclear power of the late 20th century, to

the extreme. But it also is something that very much involves, from the beginnings to the ends, Long Island.

"Supported by scientists from the Brookhaven Laboratory, LILCO wanted to establish a base for many nuclear plants on Long Island. At one point, it was considering from seven to eleven such plants. The idea was that LILCO would become the nuclear wholesaler for the northeast, supplying localities where there is more residential build-up than presently found in Suffolk. Among the future plants would be three in Shoreham, four at Jamesport, one at Sagaponack. The federal Nuclear Regulatory Commission approved two plants for Jamesport; but, New York State, which set up a parallel system of licensing in the late 1970s, rejected any for Jamesport."

39. Shoreham never opened. And, it never will - at least not as a nuclear plant. On February 16, 1992, U.S. Energy Secretary James Watkins spent a few hours on Long Island. At a press conference, he remarked, "Shoreham's dead now." Then, assuming the position of an underinformed Cabinet member, he blamed its demise on "political hype" and "scientific illiteracy." Either he had no understanding of, or, no wish to acknowledge the combined massive efforts of the State, the County, and local groups that kept the plant from opening.

40 As of 1995, *true* cause of the lethal tide's origin remains unknown. Numerous hypotheses suggest a virus of undetermined origin, road run-off contaminants, and unusually dry summers that increased the bay system's salinity, lessened water circulation and multiplied the nutrients on which the organism fed.

One theory being evaluated under a federal grant at Stony Brook, suggests that iron may be *a* cause. (High concentrations of iron in the sediment of the East End, especially on its southern beaches, once led to its being mined magnetically.)

41. Without the Adoption Center's staff, Shelter Committee members might well be meeting all day, every day. Eleanor Burrows, who has managed the office since 1979, continues to be the regular lifeline between ARF and the public. The office handles Lost and Found reports; sets up spay/neuter appointments for ARFans and for pets whose owners need financial assistance; takes down information on animals waiting to be admitted; deals as patiently as possible with frustrated callers who have found an animal or a litter, and can't understand why ARF cannot receive it/them immediately; answers countless questions, and, with patience and concern, deals with the emotions of individuals whose pet has died or who are forced to relinquish ownership.

Led by Tami Smith, the kennel staff, whose senior members, Karine Deleski and Debbie Downs, have been at the Center since it opened, devotes itself to the well-being of each and every animal in the Adoption Center. They also are an invaluable asset to those Adoption Desk volunteers who know little about each dog and cat.

42. Among Accabonac Protection Committee's achievements, to date: lobbied for, and with Town help, succeeded in having the County's Planning Dept. do a complete environmental study of the Harbor; convinced the Town Board to purchase fragile wetlands lots, and, through a resolution, to oppose use of the hazardous insecticide, Abate, around Town waters.

43. The State and Ben Heller reached out of court settlement on the balance owed for Barcelona Neck. In 1990, the State agreed to pay $19.5 million more, plus interest. In all, a $40 million purchase, $39 million more than the County would have paid in 1979, had the Town Board not rejected the offer. One week before the State settled, the Town bought 33 acres adjoining the Neck. The price was $10,000 an acre.

Disgusted with East Hampton, Heller uprooted the rare trees and bushes in his East Hampton garden and replanted them on the grounds of his new Connecticut property.

44. In late 1990, the Village DRB told the Lears that they could forego restoring the porch, if they made a $5,000 "donation" to the Village. The money would be used for historic preservation education. This was seen as a form of "blackmail," and led the author stamp it that, in a letter to The Star. Another letter writer said that the questionable "donation" request did not set a good example for children.

The Lear battle made the papers around the globe. It also played a large role in 1991, when Village residents rejected Hefner's proposal that the historic district be enlarged.

45. Sherry Wolfe, who headed The Retreat's Board of Directors its first six years, explained that the shelter is not just for South Fork or East End victims of abuse. It is referred to by other agencies when no beds are available in their areas. Of the 54 beds available on Long Island for these victims, 18 are at The Retreat.

Complimenting the Town police, Mrs. Wolfe said, "It is important to recognize that the Town of East Hampton understands that sexual abuse ranges through all socio-economic levels. It is quite an extraordinary thing, that a Town government would recognize that. Even today, most of our country doesn't recognize it. If they perceive it, at all, governments think of it as occuring at the poverty level. Ever since the O.J. Simpson tragedy, I can't tell you how many times I have heard people here say, 'I never knew that people who had money were abused.'"

46. The sports fishermen's lobby remains unrelenting. Every year, new bills are introduced, whose sole aim is to strangle commercial fishing on and around Long Island. In 1993 alone, Gov. Cuomo vetoed three bills, one of which he called "needlessly harsh." Not only were the Trawler Bill's restrictions excessive, the bill had no bearing on reality. Its text did not reflect the agreement that had been worked out, over a two year period, between DEC, sports, and commercial fishing representatives.

Could the Trawler Bill be labeled fraudulent? When the question was put to him, State Assemblyman John Behan gave a hedging chuckle before he told the author, "Some people tried to say that everybody had agreed to this bill, but that was quickly dispelled. People who voted for it knew full well about the ten-part signed agreement that would put some of the onus on the recreational users - *if* their intent really was to help the fisheries around the inlets. It certainly was misguided."

This kind of dishonest behavior among elected officials only confirms that politics has no place in fisheries management. The Atlantic States Marine Fisheries Commission disseminates coastal fishery data to all the east coast states. Based on its broad guidelines, equitable regulations should be worked out between the State's DEC and sports and commerical fishermen. It might also behoove the three groups to review the Dureya-sponsored pact of 1952. Not many people know about it. (See **1952**.)

Asked for his opinion, on the issue, Dan King said, "As long as we have loose cannons, like the sports fisherman groups, they always will have a bill up against us. You can't trust them. There is no negotiating with their lobby, as it exists today. My message to all commercial fishermen is, 'Don't deal with them.' Their agenda is to get us out of business."

Paranoia?

"No," Arnold Leo said."They have a coherent, coast-wide plan to eliminate commercial salt-water fishing. If this were a question of pure conservation, we would go along with the regulations. But, it isn't. It is pure politics and a strong lobby. I think our 1992 protest is one of the reasons why we are still in existence."

47. Calling the lawsuit "selective enforcement," Della Femina said that one of the other outdoor display merchants was told that "they are after Della Femina."

"Fine. I'm here. I was not a political animal, but they politicized me. I'm not going to run for office. I am going to look around for others who might like to run. I've already begun to do that. I don't care if the person in office is my enemy, as long as he or she is fair, and treats everybody alike. You cannot push merchants around, the way we were singled out and treated, and think that we wouldn't respond. Those days are gone."

Emphasizing that he is not against the idea of a DRB, Della Femina told the author, " I'm glad that the LVIS initiated the idea of a Design Review Board and that it is taking care to see that the Village remains beautiful. I salute them. The concept of the Board is great. What is wrong is when a Board member - anybody, anywhere - uses his or her position on a Board for personal reasons."

"I was a witness to why this happened," his wife said. "When Jerry called their bluff, it became a power struggle. They just lay in wait for the next time."

Licht was referring to the either/or situation that threatened to keep the Village restaurant named Della Femina from opening on schedule, in 1992. Della Femina's attorney had received a memo from the VDRB attorney, concerning "Declaration - B.L.J. North Main Associates."

Under paragraph #4, the Board's attorney wrote, "I want to make it perfectly clear that the landscaped area, from the legal point of view, cannot be used in any fashion in connection with the restaurant. This means...no dining, no drinking, no seats, and no benches in that area."

The area referred to is the grass alley/walkway, which runs the length of the restaurant building's north-facing wall. It was created, via privet hedge and grass, at the Board's request because it wanted that wall to look more attractive. Restricting the area's useage, however, as a condition for getting the Certificate of Occupancy, is beyond the VDRB's purview. This fact was made abundantly clear at the last VDRB meeting that Della Femina attended.

"And I didn't raise the issue. The Board chair did. First, he told me that I couldn't have outdoor dining in the walkway. Then, when he admitted that the Board cannot grant outdoor dining permits, I asked him, 'If you cannot grant something, then how can you withhold it?" That settled, the Board voted unanimously to give me the CO. I went home happy. Then, the memo arrived.

"I was told that the Board's attorney said he was going on vacation in the morning and, if I didn't agree with the memo's conditions before then, I wouldn't get the C.O.. I made a phone call to the chair. I said, 'Now I don't want to open the restaurant. Instead, I want to take out an ad to explain why it didn't open.' I also said that a copy of the meeting's minutes- it is a matter of public record - and a copy of this memo would be part of that ad. They backed off, and I got the C.O.."

48. SoFo was founded in 1986 by Andrew Sabin, Jim Ash, Julie Held, Larry Penny, and other naturalists, who felt there was a void that needed to be filled between the work being done by The Nature Conservancy and that by the Group for the South Fork. It was for the general public and tourists to be able to experience a "hands on" understanding and appreciation of the extraordinary flora and fauna that is to be found on the South Fork.

In less than a decade, SoFo has made its imprint on the South Fork. Besides sponsoring annual "Open Space Management Workshops" and in-school environmental programs, and introducing a "Birding by Car" program for Senior Citizens and the Physically Challenged, it initiated the Bluebird Recovery Program after 1985's devastating fire in Hither Hills. Four pairs of bluebirds had been counted there, and two pairs had been seen in East Hampton. SoFo established bluebird trails and, with the help of volunteers, began monitoring them.

Almost extinct a decade ago, the local bluebird population has risen to 50 known pairs, raising between 250 to 300 young between them, each year. Impressed, the Upstate Bluebird Society changed its name, in 1993, to the New York State Bluebird Society.

49. Boys Harbor began in Southampton in 1937, when Anthony Duke was 17 years old. The owners of the Jessup's Neck property, where he established the camp, rented it to him for one dollar a year. Unable to return to Jessup's Neck after World War II, he rented two rooms in a Manhattan office building, in 1949. There, with the help of two social workers, he set up a counseling service for families, most of them one-parent households. By the mid-1950s, Boys Harbor owned a building, to which children came, after school, to do their homework and receive counseling, if they needed it.

In 1972, it leased a larger building on 104th Street. This one has 15 classrooms, a gymnasium, swimming pool, and a science lab. From 500 to 700 youngsters are there each day after school, immersed in homework, sports, drama, dance, physical education and other activities that are said to be lacking from most Manhattan public schools. Half of them usually stay on for six o'clock hot dinner.

"Out of the ranks of the Harbor," Duke said, "have come 35 lawyers, two PHD professors and people who ordinarily would not have had a crack at getting where they are today. Plus, a big bunch of kids who are now in their 30s/50s, who are not on welfare. We've come a long way since those first twelve campers at Jessup. We get involved in the lives of about 3500 kids a year."

Boys Harbor took another giant step forward in September 1993, when Harbor Academy, an accredited school for Kindergarten and First Grade, opened in Manhattan. Future plans call for it to go through grade six.

"Those students will constitute the central core of Harbor children," Duke said. "I've always felt that if you can get a core group of young children, starting at the age of five or six, and nurture them with kindness, discipline, expectations, and good examples, you can have a rippling effect that will extend to the rest of the Harbor children and beyond them, into their communities."

BIBLIOGRAPHY

Autobiography and Correspondence of Lyman Beecher, vol. 1, edited
  by Charles Beecher, Harper & Brothers, 1866
Collections for the Year 1809, N. Y. State Historical Society, 1811
Discovering Long Island, W.O. Stevens, Dodd Mead, 1939
East Hampton Heritage, Clay Lancaster, Robert A.M. Stern, Robert
  Hefner, Averill Geus, W.W. Norton, 1982
East Hampton History and Genealogy, Jeannette Edwards Rattray, 1953
East Hampton Town Records, all volumes
Fifty Years at the Maidstone, Jeannette Edwards Rattray, East
  Hampton, 1941
Historical and Descriptive Sketches of Suffolk County, Richard M.
  Bayles, 1874
History & Archaeology of Montauk Indians, volume 3 of the series
"Readings in Long Island Archaeology and Ethnohistory," edited by
  Gaynell Stone of the Suffolk County Archaeological Association,
  1977 (revised edition published 1995)
History of Long Island, Benjamin Thompson, E. French, 1839
History of Suffolk County, New York, W.W. Munsell, 1882
History of the Town of East Hampton, Henry P. Hedges, Sag
  Harbor, 1897
In Old New York, Charles B. Todd, Grafton Press, 1907
Journal of the Trustees of East Hampton, all volumes
Men's Lives, Peter Matthiessen, Random House, 1986
Pollock Painting photographic memoir by Hans Namuth, 1980
Revolutionary Incidents, Henry Onderdonck Jr., New York, 1846
Shore Front Rights in the State of New York, Stephen Mershon,
  Montclair, 1922
The American Revolution, Vol. I, by John Fiske, Houghton Mifflin
  & Co., 1891.
The Geology of Long Island, Myron L. Fuller, U.S. Dept. of Interior,
  Washington, D.C., 1914
The Gardiners of Gardiner's Island, compiled by Jonathan T. Gardiner
The Island, Robert Payne, Harcourt, 1958
The Land of Home Sweet Home, Marjorie Denton, Saville, 1940
The Long Island Railroad: A comprehensive History, Part VI,
  "The Golden Age," Vincent F. Seyfried, Garden City, 1975
The Money Supply of the American Colonies, Curtis P. Nettels,
  1964
The Refugees of 1776 from Long Island to Connecticut, Frederick
  Gregory Mather, Albany, 1913
The Second Fifty Years (1941-1991) by Averill Geus, Maidstone
  Club, East Hampton, 1991
The Shadow of John Wallace, L. Clarkson, 1878

They Came to Kill, Eugene Rachlis, Random House, 1961
Trustees Records of Montauk
Two Hundred and Fifty Years of East Hampton, Samuel Seabury, East Hampton, 1925
Up and Down Main Street, Jeannette Edwards Rattray, E.H. , 1968

COLONIAL RECORDS

American Archives, Vth Series. Compiled by A.A. Force
Documentary History of New York, vols. I, II, and III, arranged under direction of Hon. Christopher Morgan, Secretary of State, 1849
Documents Relative to the Colonial History of the State of New York, vol. II, edited by E.B. O'Callaghan, 1858
Documents Relative to the History of the State of New York, procured in Holland, England, and France, vol. III, compiled by John Romeyn Brodhead
Journals of the Provincial Congress, Provincial Convention, Committee of Safety, and Council of Safety, of the State of New York, 1775
Proceedings of the Provincial Congress

NEWSPAPERS, PERIODICALS, PAPERS

A Faithful Narrative of the Remarkable Revival of Religion in the congregation of East Hampton on Long Island, Part of the south Division of the Province of New York in October 1764, the Rev. Samuell Buell, 1765.
An Historical Sermon by the Rev. John A. Stokes
Architectural Record, January 1903
Bridgehampton News
Bulletin, Long Island Fishermen's Association, December, 1953
East Hampton Summer Sun, Dan's Papers, May 20, 1.972
Esquire, June 1973
Harper's Bazaar, August 1955
Harper's Weekly, September 10, 1898
Holiday, June 1947
Lippincott's Magazine, 1883
Island Forum (various issues of the monthly)
New York Herald Tribune
New York Times (daily issues; magazine, August 1983)
Sag Harbor Corrector
Sag Harbor Express
Scribner's Monthly, February 1879

Speech to the Assembly of New York by Samuel Mulford, 1714
The Bridgehampton Sun
The Brooklyn Eagle
The Century Magazine, February 1882; October, 1885
The East Hampton Independent
The East Hampton Star
The Signal, September 20, 1879
The Tarrytown Argus, 1892

BOOKLETS AND ART CATALOGUES

A Sense of Place, Guild Hall Museum, 1972
Amagansett, Carleton Kelsey, 1986
An East Hampton Childhood, Abigail Mulford (privately printed)
Art News, September 1972
Chronicles of the Town of East Hampton, David Gardiner (privately
    printed)
East Hampton Avant-Garde, A Salute to the Signa Gallery, Guild
    Hall Museum, 1990
Clear Water, 48-page "Guide to Reducing Water Pollution," Jeanne
    Marriner, Executive Director of Save the Peconic Bays, Inc.
East Hampton: The American Barbizon, Guild Hall Museum
En Plain Air. The Art colonies at East Hampton and Old Lyme,1880-
    1930, Florence Griswold Museum/Guild Hall Museum, 1989
H.M.S.Culloden, Marine Historical Association, Mystic, Conn.
Prints of Nature, Poetic Etchings of Mary Nimmo Moran, Thomas
    Gilcrease Institute of American History and Art, 1984
Springs: A Celebration, Springs Improvement Society, 1984

DIARIES AND PERSONAL JOURNALS

Juliet Hand • Fanny Huntting • James Madison Huntting
Rev. Samuel F. Johnson • Samuel Mulford
Adelia Parsons Sherrill • Stephen Sherrill

VIDEO

"Peconic Estuary: Natural Heritage in Jeopardy," half hour video filmed
under New York State grant by Gayle Marriner-Smith. Shows how
citizens came together to help save the bays. East Hampton residents
interviewed include Tony Bullock, Nancy Kelly, Cathy Lester, the late
Tom Lester, Larry Penny.

Index

A note from the author about the Index.
Personal names are missing. They were here, initially. But, I found it difficult to include some and not others. Who is to say that the more recognizable ones of today deserve to be listed over other names, with whom the present (1994) reading public may be less familiar?

Without prejudice, in alphabetical order, here is a sampling of personal names to be found within these pages:

Index